Epiphanies

A PRACTICAL GUIDE FOR YOUR JOURNEY TO
SELF-MASTERY AND SELF-EMPOWERMENT

Nikita D'Angelo

WOW Book Publishing™

Contents

PART 3
REMEMBERING THAT LIFE WAS SUPPOSED TO BE GOOD

Epiphany VI

Epiphany – *a moment of sudden and great revelation or realisation*

Self-mastery – *the ability to take control of one's life without being blown off course by feelings, urges, circumstances, etc. Self-mastery is that condition whereby your mind and body are your servants and not your masters*

Introduction & Preface

I am of the belief that everything in our life happens for a reason. I may not know what made you pick up this book, but I know it was not a random occurrence. Something within yourself drew you towards it. And you may not even know it yet–by following through on your impulse to read it–you are about to begin a whole new chapter in your life: a chapter of massive growth and transformation. If you have the ability to read these lines, then it would be right of me to assume that you are no longer a child. And as such, I hate to break it to you, but no one is coming to your aid. No one is coming to save you. No one is coming to solve your problems. No one is going to come into your life and make it better. As an adult, if you do not take responsibility for your own life–your thoughts; emotions; happiness; self-esteem; purpose; relationships–chances are nothing in your life is going to improve. Fortunately for you, you are already in possession of all the resources you need to solve your own problems, so nor do you need anyone else to come and save you. All of the principles and practices of self-mastery, coupled with the philosophy of self-empowerment are here to assist you in rediscovering what those resources are, and becoming your own hero. Of course, being a responsible adult can sometimes be a hell of a lot more stressful and difficult than being a child. Still, you wouldn't want to have it any other way. And as we continue to move through each chapter, the reasons for this will become clearer.

If you have picked up this book in hopes of discovering something new about yourself and the world that you live in, as well as what it takes to live a life that you truly love and deserve, then you've picked up the right book. We have an incredible journey ahead of us where you are going to learn everything you need on your quest to becoming all that you are capable of becoming. The primary goal of this book is that by the time you finish reading it, you become somebody who is at the complete cause of their life; not anymore at the effect. It is no mere speculation–but a fact–that most people live their lives purely at the effect of other people, and are at the complete mercy of their environment, biological drives, fears, opinions of others, influences, and social conditioning. As a result, most people's lives resemble a pawn being shuffled around a chessboard without any will of its own; a far cry from a player who is in control, and who makes all of the moves. Of course everyone *thinks* that they are living autonomously, but in reality, most people live out their entire lives vicariously through other people, without ever realising it. More often than not, rather than thinking for themselves, most people tend to adopt (typically unconsciously) someone else's idea of what it means to be human in this physical world of ours, and wind up paying too big a price for it as a result.

The reason why so many of us fall prey to an unfulfilled life of mediocrity is because we go above and beyond, and do everything in our power to avoid utilising our ability to think. Since we do not typically have answers to deep and profound questions that truly matter, such as: "Who are we? What are we doing here? What is life really all about? Where did we come from? What happens after we die?" and so on, we just hope that somebody would come along and tell us all about it. Why? So that we can worry about other–easier to comprehend, as well as to solve–things which do not induce a migraine when we think about them. Now what's the problem with that? Well, given the fact that thinking about the "unknown" is usually gut-wrenching and scary, the minutiae of everyday life is what gets our attention, instead of the things that actually matter.

Since a life of a human being is so utterly complex–is full of uncertainty and ambiguity–we make every possible effort to avoid taking responsibility for it out of fear of getting it "wrong," or making a mistake. And the way we accomplish that is by completely giving up our ability to think for ourselves, and allow other people to do our thinking for us. The problem with this approach is that we eventually arrive at a point where it becomes virtually impossible for us to come up with a single original thought, or creative idea of our own (which would actually benefit *us*), for our thoughts and perceptions have been completely hijacked. With that in mind, you might get a clue as to why there are so many miserable, unfulfilled, and ultimately sick people (be it physically, psychologically, emotionally or spiritually) in our world today. And that's because those to whom we give up our thinking do not necessarily have our best interest at heart. For the most part, their agenda is to influence the populace to want to buy from *them*; to work for *them*; to follow *their* rules; to listen to *them*; to go on *their* plan, and so forth.

Not knowing certain things while being kept in the dark with respect to how we should live our lives is frightening and uncomfortable, so much so that we'd rather be told what to do, how to think, and how to live, by somebody else who seems fairly promising in their ability to think for themselves. Unfortunately, those who are put in various positions of influence are usually corrupt politicians, uneducated media personalities, sleazy marketers and degenerate celebrities. Due to the fact that we do not have the willingness–and in most cases the time–to discover the truth about life for ourself we end up in a precarious position in which we become vulnerable to the whims of individuals for whom keeping us exactly where we're at (enslaved and uninformed) is in their best interest. Thanks to their uncanny ability to influence, they have no trouble convincing societies that the world is about to end any minute now, so there is no time to relax. That everyone is in a constant competition with each other. That happiness and self-esteem can only ever come from certain products, or ways of going about things. That we forever need something external to feel good about ourself. And so on and so forth.

Almost anywhere you look at any given time you're guaranteed to find an individual who is either unhappy, ill, scared, anxious, frustrated, lost and confused, insecure, exhausted, who feels powerless, inadequate, or insignificant. Why is that? Because most people are not living life on their terms and thinking for themselves: doing what *they* want; coming to their own conclusions; making rational choices. Instead, masses are in the grips of social conditioning, which, at every turn reminds them of who they ought to be; what they should believe in; what their personal wants and needs are supposed to be; what they are capable of; what they can and cannot think/say; as well as what is expected of them. In other words, the reason why most people lead mediocre, unfulfilled lives (which they secretly despise) is because they conform. The fact is when we choose to conform to other people's standards, beliefs, habits, principles and values, we invariably forfeit our own. And we do so purely for the sake of having safety and acceptance in the "herd." Which in the grand scheme of things is never worth the effort, because the herd has no idea what it's doing, or where it's going.

If, at present this sounds like an exaggerated, over-the-top depiction of the current state of consciousness in the world, I want you to take a moment to think about all of the different people you know, and honestly answer the following question: "How many of them do you actually admire?" In other words, how many people do you know in their late 40s, 50s, or even 60s and wish to be like them? At best, maybe a few. And that is because most people in the world are utterly lost and confused; they truly have no idea what they are doing and where they are going. Most people navigate through their entire life experience in a mental daze; merely doing what everyone else is doing. Naturally, after so many years of walking through life in such a fashion, what one is destined to become is not an inspirational, free-willed, and powerful human being, but an automaton. Something that is not much different from a purposeless, predictable, and easily controllable robot.

Now, by taking a good and honest look at yourself–the way you think and how you behave–is it possible that you might be on the same trajectory as the majority? Well, if you are not doing something different, if you are not following a different path, if you are not being proactive about your success and personal development, then you probably are. You are going to end up where they are. Because without any deliberate and conscious effort on our part, a mediocre life seems to be the default. Of course it is not all doom and gloom, because by choosing a different path–a path to self-mastery perhaps–you can begin to set yourself apart from the rest and start moulding yourself into an exceptional person who walks through the world with absolute ease; whom people look up to and admire; and who knows exactly where he/she is going in life, and what he/she wants to get out of it.

It is never too late to turn your life around, for every single person's life situation is subjective. That is, no circumstance or condition in your life is final, unless you convince yourself otherwise. Hence, if you ever find yourself stuck doing something which you do not want to do, or living the life which you no longer want to live, you actually have the power to pull yourself out of it, and catapult yourself into a completely different direction, which offers much greater rewards. It is solely up to you to decide what kind of a person you are going to become, and what kind of life you are going to lead. In every given moment you have that choice. You have at your disposal a set of incredible mental faculties with which you were born: faculties which can–and should–be utilised intentionally and strategically in getting exactly what it is you want out of life.

However, chances are great that those powerful, creative tools are lying dormant within you, which is exactly the reason why your life looks the way it does. And it isn't your fault either, since you cannot take responsibility for something that you don't even know is there. You see, those who are in various positions of power, primarily in industry and government–who assume major key positions, and who set the standard for what's considered a proper education–want to keep that knowledge a secret just to benefit themselves and their bloodline. In effect, sharing certain powerful truths with the masses is the last thing on their "to do list." For keeping the public ignorant by continuously dumbing them down through mainstream education, science, food, medicine, media, religion, and scarcity mindsets is essential in preserving the state of the world where the power is only–and always–in the hands of the few. Fortunately for us, however, "ordinary folk," the truth about life, our Universe, and the reason for our coming here, is not something that can be seized by some and then hidden away from the rest.

That "secret" knowledge–and therefore power–isn't kept somewhere in a vault which is guarded by an army. On the contrary, all of the knowledge–as well as power–resides deep inside each and every individual–every single person has direct access to it. The only possible way that this power can continue to go untapped and unexplored is if we continue to allow ourself to be distracted by all the things that don't actually matter, i.e. wasting our mental capital on managing other people's perceptions of ourself, or waiting for the next episode of our favourite TV series. Naturally, it follows that those who dare to challenge the status quo and boldly step outside of their social conditioning; those who are willing to question their limited perceptions of reality–which they have been programmed to adopt–move one step closer to setting themselves free from this mental prison (a state of ignorance). And may begin the process of re-establishing a conscious connection to their real, hypercreative, all-knowing, powerful self.

Since those in positions of power and authority are never going to share the knowledge which has the potential to eliminate all pain and suffering in our world, I feel obliged to share this knowledge with you in a way that I've come to understand it personally. But, before I do that, I need you to become familiar with the type of mindset which allows a person (from my personal experience) to hold on to that powerful, spiritual knowing, without ever losing it in the midst of all the chaos. I believe that since we are thrown into this "crazy" world of ours without some sort of a manual on what it means to be human, and are expected to overcome/circumvent all of the life's challenges with a flourish, then it stands to reason that we already are in possession of all the resources needed to make this life work for us...

My life's journey began in the land of Russia, in a place called Krasnoturinsk; a crappy little town with a population of approximately sixty thousand people, located up in the Ural mountains. What I remember the most is that it was absolutely freezing. That the majority of people living there were either depressed, angry, frustrated, or pissed off. There were many reasons for this, but I am not going to get into it here and now, for this introduction would have to be several hundred pages long. Suffice it to say, there wasn't much positivity in my hometown to focus on, especially around those times. (Mostly due to the recent fall of the Soviet Union, which caused all kinds of problems, particularly for the economy.)

It was February the 27th, 1992, when I joined the circus. I was born in the middle of nowhere, between a bunch of degenerates running amok, going crazy on each other (figuratively speaking). Nevertheless, as far back as I can remember I was always a happy kid. I've always had a deep sense of appreciation for the fact that life in the physical world was a possibility in the first place. I was always grateful for all the little things that are enormously valuable in our lives, and are extremely important. Such as the fact that we can see, speak, touch, hear, feel, and imagine. It is those things which came to us for free. But *because* they come to us for free, they are usually overlooked and are taken for granted by the majority. Personally, I chose to use those things as an excuse to feel good, and as a result I've never had issues with having a positive attitude towards life. For this reason, my mind would naturally interpret most situations–which other people perceived as negative, or bad–as either hilarious, or outright ridiculous. Consequently, even though I've been exposed to suffering, pain, and negativity, I was hardly ever affected by it.

From an early age I understood that life was absolutely priceless. That the experience of life will ultimately outweigh any kind of bullshit which we may encounter. The truth is, you intuitively knew this too, though you may have consciously forgotten it. In an attempt to refresh your memory I want you to think about the following. If I were to offer you ten million today to stop complaining for at least a decade and quit reacting to all of the negative outside forces, I am certain that you could pull it off with relative ease. But if I were to offer you ten billion with one condition that you don't get to wake up tomorrow morning, would you accept that deal? Probably not. Why? Because you know that being alive the next day is worth a lot more than that. In effect, tomorrow (no matter what it brings) is priceless! And so, knowing this to be true deep in your heart, why are you still not happy and are grateful by default? Why do you continue to allow negative comments and opinions of others to disturb your peace? Why do you permit one negative event to influence your psyche, which then affects other things in your wonderful life? Well, that is one of the mysteries, which, this book is here to address.

Understand that all of us were grateful to be alive for the first few years of life on this beautiful planet of ours. However, as we grew older, we began to get exposed to all sorts of bullshit. But no matter the amount or the degree of bullshit which we have had the privilege of going through, by the time we reach adolescence, most of us will have already lost touch with that sense of appreciation. One of the biggest reasons for this (among numerous others) is that we become conditioned by other humans–who've been here long before we had arrived–to believe that feeling good about ourselves for no apparent reason is abnormal, and that appreciation should only ever be expressed towards something new and fresh; never for what we already are/have.

As a result of this type of conditioning we begin to focus our mind in all kinds of petty and negative ways. And as we continue to do so, we eventually reach a point where we no longer feel happy, fulfilled, and at peace in our lives (usually by the time we become adults). A point where no matter what we do, we keep finding ourselves, again and again, bogged down by mental and emotional states such as: unworthiness; loneliness; fear; confusion; lack and limitation; dissatisfaction; anger; boredom; apathy, etc. In effect, the society in which we are raised (and this would apply to practically every country in the world) conditions us to believe–since the time we are children–that happiness does not come from the inside; that happiness must be absolutely contingent upon something external. And then, the same people who sell us on that idea begin to encourages us to look for that state of happiness in certain products; by aspiring to look a certain way; by following trends and adhering to certain ideologies (in places where it is forever fleeting).

I am certain that you've experienced this a bunch of times in your own life when you thought that a particular someone, or something was going to make you happy, but never did. For example, you know how good it makes you feel when you finally save up enough money to purchase a brand-new pair of shoes which you've always wanted to own. It actually does feel good for a little while, until that feeling eventually wears off. Or how about when you get your hair done by a professional who makes you feel like a new person? Sure, it definitely feels great for a while, until sooner or later that feeling about yourself wears off. Likewise, you know how amazing it feels to be having sex with a person whom you are seriously attracted to, but that good feeling too inevitably wears off. There are innumerable ways of experiencing positive emotions and, ultimately happiness. This is called "short-term happiness." It is forever fleeting; it is not sustainable. And if we permit external conditions to determine our degree of happiness in life, we doom ourselves. Because external conditions are not something that we can control, and are never permanent. What we have to be striving for instead is building an ecosystem of positive emotions; a system which we love; a system which we are in control of (that includes having a strong sense of purpose in life; hobbies; good friends; passions; goals; and empowering beliefs). Essentially, we have to ensure that our happiness does not come predominantly from the external world of material possessions, conditions, and circumstances, but from within ourself. So that regardless of what might be going on externally, our happiness, and sense of fulfilment in life does not get affected by any of it. And that is called "internal fulfilment," which *is* permanent.

For those of us who do not have an ecosystem of positive emotions set up–a system which continuously brings us joy–have no other choice but to look for external stimuli, or conditions in order to feel good. However, each time we do find something that *makes* us feel happy we never seem to realise that we are merely *experiencing* happiness; that we are not happy by default. The problem with this approach is that when those good feelings eventually wear off–because experiences are transitory; our world is constantly evolving, and things are always changing–we inevitably revert back to the default emotional states that we are accustomed to. As a result of our poor thinking habits we find ourselves in a loop, where we may have a certain experience, and feel happy about it, but before long we fall back to the emotional state in which we were prior to that experience. When this occurs, rather than questioning our ineffectual ways of trying to be happy, we instead look for something else to make us feel happy. And we stubbornly persevere in this manner–going around in circles–looking for happiness in all the wrong places. In effect, we become stuck in the never-ending pursuit of happiness.

Viktor Frankl, who was a Jewish psychiatrist and a Holocaust survivor once stated the following with regard to this: "*Happiness cannot be pursued; it must ensue. One must have a reason to be happy. Once the reason is found however, one becomes happy automatically. A human being is not one in pursuit of happiness, but rather in search of a reason to be happy.*" What he was essentially alluding to is the fact that if we are to experience genuine, long-lasting happiness in life, then we have to discover the reasons (which resonate with us on the deeper level) for our existence, as well as why it is we do what we do each and every day. If Viktor Frankl's reasons were so strong and ardent enough to fortify his mind to such a degree that even the unspeakable horrors of Nazi concentration camps were unable to affect the way he felt, then surely a few reasons of your own will get you through a break-up; a rejection; a loss of a particular item; a loss of a job; a missed opportunity; or somebody calling you a mean name. Seriously, the reasons for most people's unhappiness are laughable by comparison. What the majority of people call problems are not genuine problems at all. It is all a matter of perspective: something that we will be talking about in greater depth in the final chapter.

So the question becomes: what is it that gets your juices flowing? What is it that turns you on? What is it that motivates you to get out of bed in the morning? What is it that you are grateful for? That reason could be absolutely anything. It certainly does not have to be what other people consider happiness to be, since every person is fundamentally different when it comes to their personal preferences and most heartfelt desires. Personally, for me that reason is the simple fact that I get to experience life on this beautiful planet. Believe it or not, that's more than enough of a good reason for me to be happy, without disturbing my experience of life by asking someone/something to be different, or by needing any other thing that is outside of myself to be a certain way so that I can feel good. As a consequence, my happiness is relatively stable and consistent by default. Which is another way of saying that it isn't easy for the outside influences to put me into a negative frame of mind. Because my passion for living grounds me in a positive vibration, it prevents me (although to varying degrees of success) from losing my power by blaming someone/something else for how I feel. And by the end of this book you will know exactly what it takes to achieve similar results.

Now, before you make your first step towards a better future you have to accept a basic fact that emotions such as: happiness; love; excitement; passion, etc., are self-generating emotions–they come from within ourself (same principle applies to all other emotions). But from a lack of awareness of said fact, most people rely on the external world of conditions and circumstances to determine how they should feel. Most people allow their emotional states to be controlled by other people, material objects, circumstances, conditions and events, i.e. by forces outside of themselves. And only when they come in contact with something that they are in agreement with–something that they resonate with–will they give themselves *permission* to feel good. In effect, rather than living proactively (which means asserting their true thoughts, feelings, opinions, and beliefs, and unapologetically projecting them out into the world), most people are forever *reacting* to all manner of things that are outside of themselves, and allow all of *that* become the basis for how they feel.

In other words, the reason why people do not get to enjoy a life which they truly love and deserve is because they have become accustomed to living from the "outside in," rather than "inside out." If this sounds like something you do and you wish to get better results in the future, then you absolutely must get out of this paradigm as quickly as possible. Such a paradigm is based on insecurity, and therefore will continue to undermine your chances of success in most areas of your life. Furthermore, this reactive approach–which you probably have adopted–is especially advantageous for marketers when it comes to advertising and selling their products to *you*. That is, if you are not entirely certain as to what you think of yourself; if you do not know what you want; if you are insecure about where you stand physically, socially, ethnically, or financially, then you are more likely to develop a tendency to people-please, while completely disregarding your own desires, personal preferences, wants and needs. And that's where marketers want you to be.

The best-case scenario is you are going to fall victim to a dreadful need of wanting to fit in. As in, trying to live up to other people's standards and expectations in order to receive acceptance. This will translate into you constantly looking for that piece of self-esteem and sense of identity (which you so desperately need) in various products, positions, other people's opinions, or even drugs and alcohol. (Whereas the worst-case scenario is probably suicide.) Such a person can be likened to a bucket which has a hole right at the bottom of it. A situation where no matter how much of an effort you make to fill it up with water, water will continue to pour out. In effect, if you're coming at life from a reactive mindset, and looking for something external to fill the void, then the amount of stuff you get won't make any difference. None of the things "out there" in the external world can make you feel secure with yourself, for security is an inside job; it has to start with *you*.

The world outside yourself does not give a damn about your happiness; it just wants you to shut up and buy; to spectate; to conform; to consume. Their suggestions about what makes you happy are particularly biased, and are not at all in your favour. If you don't feel secure with yourself, if you are unhappy with your life, if you don't know what it is you want, and what to believe, and you decide to look to other people for guidance, you are f**ked. For by choosing to do so, you invariably become a perfect consumer who–by default–does not feel very good, and who is perpetually stuck in the pursuit of self-esteem (and ultimately good emotions). Your life begins to resemble a donkey who is convinced that it is only a matter of time until he reaches the carrot that is dangling in front of his face, while he's being taken for a ride.

Like a leaf in the wind you'll get dragged around in different directions by someone/something who's constantly implying or straight up telling you things such as: "*This* is what is cool. *This* is what you want. *This* is how you should think. *This* is what's popular. *This* product will make you happy. *This* is the hairstyle that is trending right now. *This* perfume will get you the girl. *This* is how you need to look. *This* is who you are. *This* is what's acceptable and what isn't. *This* is how someone of your age/height/status/racial background/whatever is supposed to act and behave like. *This* is what you value most." And so on and so forth. It is madness. However, the good news is that you can choose not to play that game. Because ultimately it is up to you–and only up to you–to decide how you are going to feel about anything.

No person, circumstance, condition, or thing has any real power or control over your mental and emotional states unless you *permit* them. And I am here to encourage you to stop giving your permission, and let it be the very first step towards reclaiming your personal power (the specifics of which we will discuss in the first part of the book). Starting today, how about *you* decide what makes you happy? How about *you* decide what it is you want and need? How about *you* decide what is trendy, what is funny, what is popular, what is beautiful, and so forth? Because if you can muster up the courage to make up your own mind, arrive at your own conclusions, and make certain decisions, without the input of others–and be ready to stand by them in the face of a challenge, or opposition–then people will become more receptive to your ideas, views, and opinions on things. This exceptionally powerful mental/emotional state of clarity, assuredness, confidence, calmness, and proactiveness will ultimately translate into your personal, social, and professional life, where you'll no longer be getting the short end of the stick, and become revered and respected among your peers. Now, I am aware that such a resolute mental state could easily be misinterpreted for arrogance, narcissism, or conceit. However, what we're actually going to be working towards is forming a better self-image; developing healthy self-respect; and becoming aware of the value proposition which you bring to the world.

Next, it is vitally important to accept the fact that nobody owes you anything, and have no aversions or resistance towards this–sometimes unpleasant–truth of life. What this means is that your success and happiness are ultimately your responsibility. Since every single person is naturally wired to be selfishly-oriented, means that no person will ever give a shit about you as much as you. Sure, people may "put you on," give you a head start, or provide you with a certain opportunity. But once the ball is in your court it is up to you to follow through and make it work. No one should ever be expected to share their own resources and take the time out of their life to ensure that you are winning and feeling good (unless they are being paid to do so). That is your responsibility.

For example, if your best friend happens to win a lottery, do not immediately assume that you are entitled to any of the winnings. Just because you are best friends, it does not necessarily follow that you are owed something. Obviously, such a good friend would naturally want to share with you, and he/she probably will. But, if you are *expecting* your friend to give you something–rather than just be happy for your friend–then you might poison, and then destroy your friendship with your poor attitude. Likewise, if a relative of yours happens to own a successful business, but never wants to hire you when you are looking for a job, and never gives you any money unless it is a loan, do not harbour any resentments against that person. You must accept that your family members do not inherently owe you something just because you are family. In order to get what it is you want there has to be a fair value exchange. So if you are not getting something you believe you are entitled to then maybe what you have been giving out lately just isn't enough. However, sometimes, even when you have done everything that is expected of you, people can still choose not to respond in like-kind. It is no secret that people have their own lives; their own problems; their own wants and needs. And to keep your sanity in your dealings with other people you need to be willing to give them freedom to be themselves without holding them responsible for how *you* feel. This can be easily achieved by adhering to the following principle. Whatever it is you decide to do, you have to do it for you; you must do your part and let the chips fall where they may. For instance, if you decide to give someone a smile or a compliment, do not *expect* one in return. If you decide to hold a door for someone, do not *expect* a thank-you. If you decide to offer a helping hand, do not *expect* them to do the same for you.

The uncomfortable truth of life is that even your mother doesn't have to be nice to you. She brought you into this world; she gave you "life." Everything that she does for you after the fact can be considered a nice, cushy bonus. Granted, it is her job and responsibility to take care of you until you become self-sufficient, that is true, absolutely. And it is your father's responsibility to ensure that you become self-sufficient as soon as humanly possible (usually between the ages of 16-18). After that, your parents don't owe you a thing. Thus, if it is not a guarantee that your own mother will be nice to you, you cannot expect other people–who are not even related to you–to give a shit about you. (Even though most people will, there are plenty in the world who will not, and who will only look after their interests.) Therefore, for the sake of your health–mental, emotional, or otherwise–you have got to become more self-sufficient. And what this means for you in a practical sense is this: whenever a person gives you something or decides to do something for you, you must perceive it as a blessing; not as an obligation on their part. Even if beforehand you have been helping and supporting that person so much that reciprocity should naturally be their next, reasonable response.

From a different person's perspective, you are not the centre of the universe; *they* are, and that's fine. Never hold other people responsible (ransom) for what you do, or how you feel. Whenever you decide to give, or do something for another, do it because you want to; not because you feel as though you *have to*. Otherwise, you might resent yourself as well as the other person for doing something which you didn't really want to do, and then find yourself expectantly waiting for them to reciprocate to no avail. Look, if a person chooses to reciprocate to your advances, opinions, feelings, or actions–great. But if a person chooses not to, it doesn't necessarily follow that they're a bad person; that something is wrong with you; or that they don't care about you. It might be that they're going through difficult times in their life and all they can think about is their problems. Maybe they don't have any mental capital left to even concentrate on what you are saying because their pet had recently died. Or maybe they are unable to effectively read social cues, and are therefore responding with inappropriate or incongruent gestures. The reasons are endless. So rather than feeling like a victim–feeling as though you are being mistreated or attacked–when someone doesn't meet your expectations, mentally take on the other person's perspective and genuinely try to understand where it is they are coming from. Realise that in most cases, however a person decides to behave or respond is a reflection of their own beliefs, character, and personal experience; it is about *them*. It is about how they feel at that particular moment in time. It is about their own interpretation of that particular interaction, or transaction. It doesn't say much–if anything at all–about you. But, if you are not in control of your emotions and someone proceeds to respond or act unfavourably towards you, then you are more likely to take it personally and become *reactive*. In turn, instantly getting pulled into their internal dialogue and emotional state, i.e. adopting their frame of mind. And if that person doesn't feel good, well now you don't either.

Consider this: there is an enormous difference between reacting and responding. When you react to someone (who does not have your best interest at heart) in any social interaction, you inevitably lose. Because when you are in a reactive state you enter the other person's view of how the world works. That is, you fall victim to their own perspectives, emotional states, and belief systems. In effect, if a person is feeling certain emotions which you wouldn't want to feel, or is projecting certain beliefs which you wouldn't want to believe–yet you become reactive to that person–you immediately lose yourself, along with all of your power and influence. For that person's beliefs about the world, about you, about your ideas, etc., have been imposed on you, and are now *affecting* you and your experience.

Understand that when you react to a person or situation, the person or situation is in control of you. But when you respond, you do not get sucked into opposing realities and ideas which you do not agree with. The way you do this is whenever there is a clash of ideas between two or more individuals, you must resist the urge to emotionally react, to justify your position, or to defend yourself and argue for what is right and wrong until you are blue in the face. Instead, you must mentally step back and *respond* from your own point of view, and your own emotional state. That way you get to keep your power and you stay in control. By the way, what is this power that I keep referring to? It is the power of your mind. Mind is such an incredible tool, it will readily assist you in having and becoming whatever it is that you want. However, if it is used incorrectly, if it is not kept under control, if it is idle, then it will just as readily annihilate all of the chances of success–in any endeavour–that you may still have. (We will continue to unravel the mysteries of the mind throughout the entire book.)

Back to the previous point. People will always have their own ways of looking at life. They will always have their own opinions, beliefs, biases, and ways of doing things; ways that are probably not in harmony with yours. To be that powerful, magnetic person–who walks through the world with unshakable poise–you must therefore be willing to accept the fact that there are no two people on the planet who are exactly alike. In order to hammer this point home I want you to conduct a following thought experiment. Imagine yourself walking down the street as you come across a homeless man sitting on the ground–begging. You might think that the right thing to do is to spare the homeless man some change, so that he can go and buy something to eat (because you are a nice person and you wish to help). Whereas another person (who also has a good heart and wishes to help) might see it as an utterly wrong thing to do. Maybe this person believes that giving the homeless man money will not do him any good (not in the long run anyway). Or maybe he knows that no matter how much money he gives, the bum will still be back in the same spot tomorrow anyhow–still hungry, still asking for change. So, rather than encouraging the bum's victim mentality and behaviour by catering to him, the right course of action is to give him nothing and completely ignore him. Just to make the point that what the bum is doing is ineffective. Now, if enough people were to treat the homeless man the same way, then his survival mechanism (DNA) would sooner or later realise that relying on other people for survival is not a very good strategy. As a result, his survival instinct would not allow him to starve to death; it would eventually prompt him to regain his consciousness (to whatever degree possible), pull himself together, and find a job (or devise a better strategy to survive).

In light of the fact that you–as an individual–have different beliefs, different ways of thinking, different ways of looking at life, and all that goes on in it, you might become upset or angry with this person by assuming that he is mean and insensitive for ignoring the homeless man. But is he? You must understand that there isn't a single person alive who is exactly like you, who thinks like you, and who sees things the same way you do. Every single person on this planet is unique, due to various factors such as: genes; upbringing; environment; cultural conditioning; religious beliefs; preferences; biases; personal experiences, and a myriad of other influences. And as such, whenever another person does certain things differently than you–who thinks differently, behaves differently, or expresses different beliefs–it does not make them a bad person. It does not follow that other people are wrong, or dumb just because you have different ways of doing things, and think that you are right. We live in the world where not everyone is going to think the way you do, and not everyone is going to behave the way you do. It does not innately make other people wrong, or inferior if they happen to disagree with what you believe to be "right," or noble. If we are talking about what is right and wrong in the given scenario–then, if we wanted to–we could also argue that actually you are the one who is wrong here. Because when you are choosing to give money to the homeless–in your version of reality you think that you are helping and doing the right thing–however, what if what you are doing instead is validating and further encouraging their hopeless, powerless, and victim-like mentality by *rewarding* their behaviour?

You may think that you are doing something good and honourable, but in actuality you are enabling them to stay the same; to stay passive and inactive, while not having to think for themself. You are demonstrating to them that laying in the gutter, and wallowing in self-pity is a viable strategy, since other people always seem to come and rescue them. As a direct consequence of your actions you are inadvertently further advancing the poverty, apathy, and self-defeat epidemic. (Look, I am not suggesting that you think twice before helping people, or giving money to the homeless. You can do whatever you want. But what I *am* saying is that if somebody else happens to conduct him/herself differently than what you'd expect, do not hold it against them. Realise that every single person has their own philosophy of life and conceptions–which make sense to them–of how the world works.) You have no actual way of knowing why do people behave as they do. And as such, the only responsibility you ever have–when dealing with others–is to put it out; to lay it on the table; to give it away; to say thank you, or sorry; to offer your help; to state your opinion; to do your part; to ask that person out on a date. Whatever. Anything that happens after the fact is not in your control, and in most instances isn't your burden to carry. All what you are responsible for–and always in complete control of–is the energy and intentions that you put out into the world, be they in the form of a thought, feeling, or deed. Trying to control anything else outside of that is a waste of potent energy and a perfect recipe for a raging headache.

Becoming a person who is energetically and emotionally grounded, collected, unreactive, self-sufficient, and self-reliant are the major key factors in achieving self-mastery. The degree to which you are able to master yourself is intrinsically linked to the degree of happiness and fulfilment you will enjoy in your life. So what do I mean by self-mastery anyway? Simply put, self-mastery is about developing a higher degree of self-control, entitlement, and self-reliance. It means being at the cause of your emotions; rather than at the effect. It means to have the ability to motivate, guide, and empower yourself through the proper use of your intellect, hence the term: self-empowerment. Self-mastery demands that you carry out a thorough audit of the many different aspects of your personality and begin to tweak your physical, mental, and emotional dials in order to take back control of your thoughts, emotions, actions, and ultimately your destiny. The degree to which one is able to master oneself is going to determine the type–and quality–of relationships one is going to have and enjoy. As well as how good and effective one will be as a business partner; a parent; a lover; a friend; a leader; a teacher; a speaker; a role model; an influencer. Generally speaking, the greater one's understanding–and the greater one's control–of oneself, the greater success, satisfaction, and happiness one is going to experience in life in return.

Personally, I understood full well what the advantages of a positively-oriented mindset and unconditional happiness–which are essential components to the whole self-mastery equation–were, for as long as I remember. I was raised primarily by women–caring, compassionate, and loving women–who rarely offered anything but encouragement, unconditional love, and reassurance. Growing up in such environment–that was conducive for the development of a healthy mind–gave me freedom to develop my own thought patterns without the interference of other people's suggestions about what I should believe in. Not to say that I was spoiled; far from it. But rather, I was never pressured to think and behave like the other kids my age. I was never expected to follow other people's rules, and take everything seriously. I was never forced to believe certain things, or speak, dress, and act a certain way in order to please others. I was never asked or pushed to reach anyone's expectations but my own. In effect, I was blessed with an opportunity to experience life in any which way I chose, and learn things about life, myself, other people, and the world without being judged (though still being guided in the right direction) when I did something wrong. Naturally, I ended up developing a strong belief in myself, where regardless of what may happen on the outside–with respect to mistakes and failures–I would still, and always be "enough" and okay on the inside.

This does not mean, however, that I always felt great, and was happy a hundred percent of the time, of course not. Frankly, I don't believe that it is possible, or even natural to be happy all of the time. I believe that we absolutely should experience and indulge ourselves in a wide range of different emotions. As long as we do not dwell on some of the less positive ones for too long (because that's when it becomes a problem). Taking into consideration the environment which I came from, it is no surprise that I have had my fair share of negative experiences. I've seen messed up things, and I've been through trauma-inducing incidents. But I've still managed to come out relatively stable–both psychologically and emotionally–on the other side of it all. The reason for this is that I never ruminated on the negatives. I never identified with negativity. I never focused on it long enough that it would degrade my life experience. Rather, I interpreted all forms of negativity as some kind of a "glitch in the system"–an anomaly–something not even real.

From a young age it was evident to me that our world was full of awful conditions and ideas that were unproductive–that did not serve me. I knew that just because something bad, or unpleasant was happening around me (or anywhere else in the world), it did not necessarily follow that I *should* be experiencing it too. As I observed various things–no matter how *rational* they may have seemed to others–I'd think to myself: "You know what? It doesn't matter. I'm going to feel good anyway." But never in a defensive or reactive manner. Rather, I was able to respond this way from a place of lightheartedness and understanding. If I were to attempt to put my thought process into proper words, it would be described as something along the following lines: "I hear/see what you are saying/doing, yet somehow I can tell that your interpretation of reality is inaccurate. Therefore, I choose not to believe, or indulge in your inappropriate response to it."

Everyone can to do this; everyone has the ability to create their own stories about what various events mean as they observe them. There are no exceptions. The truth is, however, rather than thinking positively–entertaining thoughts of a good nature–majority of us tend to focus on the wrong side of things. People are typically paying more attention to all of the things that are going wrong in the world: the injustices; the wars; the crime rate; the global warming; the terrorists; the violence; the homelessness; the politics; the racism; the virus. Whatever. And as they continue to do so, they begin to loosen the connection to their personal power, for they inevitably begin to construct beliefs–about themselves, about the world, about life, and about other people–that are unconducive to living happy, fulfilling, and productive lives.

Fortunately we have the power to improve the quality of our life simply by improving the quality of our thoughts. Given the fact that a belief is just a thought which had been thought of repeatedly, means that if we consciously choose to repeatedly entertain a better thought, our belief about that particular subject is going to improve. Stated differently, if we are to have any hope of enjoying a more rewarding lifestyle in the future, then we must be willing to consciously visit and reexamine some of the limiting beliefs that are holding us back from going after whatever it is that we *really* want. The most important step that you can take towards becoming a genuinely happy and internally fulfilled individual is to cease paying attention to everything that is going wrong in your life, and stop being a nitpicker; a fault-finder; a quitter; and a complainer. Instead, become more optimistic and solution-oriented by learning to be grateful for all of the things that you already have.

At this point you might be wondering: "Happiness? Who the hell cares? I have got bigger problems to worry about. My rent is due and I don't have money to pay it. I'm in debt. My partner is nagging and dragging me down. There is a mountain of more important things that need to be done before I can relax and even think about my happiness." If you are in the grips of such convictions you have to realise that happiness is not a destination. Happiness is not something that can be attained or derived from a particular thing or person; status or living condition; circumstance or event. In truth, happiness is a *baseline*. Happiness is a state of being, which intelligent actions and ideas flow from. The kind of ideas and actions that are in alignment with our most heartfelt desires. Happiness is the foundation from which we approach life and do everything else that we do on a daily basis. In effect, happiness is not a place at which we can arrive by getting/completing/achieving_____. (Fill in the blank.) Happiness comes from the inside. Happiness is a state of being which can be honed and nurtured. (We'll discuss happiness more extensively in the third part of the book.)

Once you learn and internalise the principles outlined in this book you will seldom, if ever, buy something that you don't actually need; find yourself doing things that you don't really want to be doing; second-guess yourself, or question your ability; look to other people for directions of where to go in life; or regret some of the things that you have done, and decisions that you have made. The basic formula for never getting things wrong and living your life in the way that you have intended it to live–before you even came into this world–is always the same. Which is: get in the right state and then create your plan of action; get in the right state and then ask your boss for a promotion; get in the right state and then have a conversation with your significant other; get in the right state and then go to the store; get in the right state and then discipline your children. In other words, if you are to ensure that your actions produce nothing but positive and constructive results, you need to follow a simple formula of: getting happy and then…; getting happy and then…

You see, pure presence, happiness, confidence in our ability, and sense of invincibility is our natural state to be in. However, what invariably happens as we grow older is we lose touch with this powerful state by getting conditioned away from it. As a result, anything that we then do from any internal, emotional place that is not aligned with that state, our actions become *off*. The choice of words becomes *off*. How we interpret a particular situation becomes *off*. The decisions we make become *off*. We try to tell a joke, and nobody laughs. We go to strike up a conversation, it becomes awkward. We try to sell a product or service, and nobody buys. What I've observed in my personal life is that whenever I catch myself feeling negative, pessimistic, or angry, then even things on the outside begin to conspire against me, and also become *off*. For example, I'd be walking and suddenly trip, or I'd get hit by something, or my jacket would get caught in a door handle and pull me back vigorously, or I'd hurt myself in some ridiculous way, or I'd drop something that I was trying especially hard not to. I see this happening in people's lives all of the time. And the verdict from my observations is that when we aren't feeling good, nothing good happens as a result. In effect, no intelligent action, constructive solution, or positive outcome can ever come from a negative state of mind. A mind that is positively-oriented is truly a powerful one.

What I would like you to take away from this book is a shift in your approach to life; a shift in your consciousness; a shift in your awareness; and to adopt a philosophy of self-empowerment. That way you give yourself a better chance at creating and enjoying the life that you want and deserve. Albeit you will never become a master, or a "finished product" so to speak, where you can finally stop and relax in terms of your progress. Improving your life and becoming the best version of yourself is not a destination; it is a lifelong *journey*; it's an ongoing process. Never make the mistake of thinking that you have "arrived," regardless of how knowledgeable you think you are, and no matter how much you have already achieved and accomplished. There is no destination on your journey to self-mastery, since there will always be something else for you to learn, or to improve upon. To lead a happy, meaningful and successful life therefore you need to become a lifelong learner. You must fall in love with the idea of studying and constantly learning. You must never stop developing your knowledge base with respect to all of the things that interest you. Because the truth is, the moment you stop learning, is the moment you stop growing. When you stop growing and stretching yourself beyond your current results (comfort zone), what you are inadvertently doing is suppressing the life force inside of yourself which forever wants to grow, create, expand, and express more of itself through you.

The moment you cease stretching yourself mentally, emotionally, physically, spiritually, or in any other meaningful way, is the moment discomfort, dissatisfaction, frustration, and unhappiness begin to rear their ugly heads. Why? Because one of the basic truths of nature is that life is always moving; it is always in motion. Nothing in our Universe stays the way it is for very long. Nothing actually stays the same; things are always changing–even if ever so slightly. If you don't cooperate and move along with it, then you will lag behind. In other words, if you're not proactively moving in one direction (supposedly towards growth and self-actualisation), then naturally–and by default–you're moving in the opposite direction (degeneration). If you think that you are staying the same when you stagnate, procrastinate, and do the same things every single day–without improving yourself, or your life situation in any meaningful way–then think again. Because you might be moving into trouble without even knowing it. Realise that the spiritual side of your personality is *constantly* stretching and reaching out for something more. But when you choose not to cooperate and put up resistance to your growth (because you've become comfortable with where you're presently at), this "tug of war" so to speak between the comfortable, physical part of you, and the ever-expanding, spiritual part of you manifests in all kinds of negative emotions and states, such as: fear; anxiety; frustration; anger; apathy; boredom; helplessness; depression, and so on and so forth. (More on this in chapter 3.)

As we are about to dive into the book I want you to keep in mind that I'm not going to be giving you some kind of a quick fix, or a magic pill that will instantly transform your life. Such a pill doesn't exist. You actually have to take your progress into your own hands and do all of the work necessary, since nobody else can *think* for you, and nobody else can *feel* for you. Though what I *can* do is lay down a path for you to follow; a path which has been proven to work for myself and many others. I will take you by the hand and "baby step" you from where you are to where you want to be. Though you are still the one who needs to move your feet. In effect, nobody can drag you to your own success; you can only be guided to it. In case you are convinced that perhaps these ideas will not work for you. That it only works for some and not for others. Or that you have to be particularly intelligent in order to learn and understand these concepts, then you must get rid of these convictions at once–they are not true. Confucius, a Chinese philosopher once said: "*By nature, human beings are similar, but by practise, we get wide apart.*" Meaning, your appearance, your voice, your language, your sex, your skin colour, your place of origin, or your talents–physical/tangible aspects of you; things that are on the surface–are secondary, and have zero power, or control over the quality of your life experience. The fact is, you already have all that you need to become the best version of yourself, within yourself. You only need to learn how to connect with it and bring it out. Which is precisely what you are here to learn.

The ideas and principles shared in this book will work for anyone, no matter the gender, age (within reason), place of birth, racial background, living condition, financial situation, occupation, and so on. It doesn't even matter what had previously happened in your life which resulted in you arriving to where you are now at. You may have been losing, struggling, and failing miserably up until this very moment. However, none of it has any real power, or influence to determine whether you succeed or not starting today. Because every moment is a new moment. In every given moment you have the power to choose in which direction you want your life to go. All that you need in order to begin your journey, and start building a life that you have always imagined, is an open mind and willingness to learn.

It took me a hell of a lot of painstaking study to finally understand why we humans do what we do, and why we don't do some of those things that we want to do. Practically none of these ideas are mine–I did not originate them. I'm just a connector of dots between what we do and how we think, as well as what we get in our lives as the result of what we think and do. Even though I've been (unconsciously) living by a number of these principles naturally for a long time, still, I was never able to put them into proper words and explain to other people how certain things actually worked. That being the case, throughout my adolescence I'd sometimes think that I was weird, or that something was wrong with me, because I could never explain myself (my attitude and perspective) to other people. The fact that I couldn't just be "normal" like everybody else, and agree with the way things were, made me stand out like a sore thumb and garner unwanted attention.

Sometimes people would say: "Why are you smiling? This (apparently) disastrous event just took place and you are snickering, what is wrong with you?" or "So what if that person is rich? He is obviously special; he is a genius. Riches are not for us ordinary people. Stop trying to be something you are not and just be normal!" Since I could not explain myself I sometimes felt that maybe they were right; maybe something actually *was* wrong with me. I was completely alone; nobody else around me interpreted life the same way I did. But I couldn't just turn it off. I couldn't stop being me. I always knew that there was something incredible about us humans; something that most of us were not aware of. For that reason, I never stopped thinking, observing, studying, researching, and really trying to understand who we are, why we are here, and what the hell is going on. It was difficult for me to even socialise a lot of the time. While people were conversing with me–instead of paying attention to what is being said–I'd be stuck in my head thinking about all of the different things which I wanted to know the answers to.

Fortunately, at a certain point I began asking the right questions, and in time, stumbled upon the right resources. After many years of studying and searching for the truth I've managed to find a number of highly successful, happy, healthy, wealthy, intelligent, and amazing individuals–who had accomplished great things in their lives–and I instantly resonated with them. One by one I began to study their private lives and their material. With each new idea and revelation I was becoming more conscious and more aware as to why I thought and felt in ways that *I* did, and why other people thought and felt the way *they* did. Since then, I knew that I wasn't alone. I knew that I wasn't weird. I knew that these ideas (which I will be sharing with you here) were sound, and that it was the right way to go about life after all. In effect, while I wasn't sure of myself and many times have doubted my perspectives and beliefs, all of those great thinkers–on the other hand–were unapologetically embodying them, completely owning them, and leading fantastic lives as a result.

This book is not about leading you to believe what I believe and become rigid and inflexible in your approach to life. Life, as we know it in this world is complex, and therefore will certainly demand that you exercise your own ability to think in order to make it work for you. Those who succeed in living joyful and fulfilling lives are in non-resistance to this fact, and are extremely pliable and adaptable to whatever life chooses to hurl at them. Your life experience will inevitably have its good times and bad times; its ups and downs; its highs and lows. And if you are not flexible enough and unable to adapt, you will end up getting destroyed. That said, what we are going to be working towards throughout our journey is allowing "life" to be what it's supposed to be–unpredictable, uncertain, full of surprises and ambiguity–all the while being fully present, spiritually grounded, unreactive, resilient, controlled, and emotionally/mentally stable individuals in the midst of it all.

Every single epiphany that I've had on my journey to self-mastery was a *"Eureka!"* moment, accompanied by a rush of energy zooming through my whole being. They were those *"Aha!"* moments, which–if I had to verbalise them–would say something to the effect of: "You get it now." But only "getting it" is half the battle. And that's precisely why I think of this process as a *journey*. Do not think for a second that your journey is going to be difficult; it won't. Because you don't actually have to learn and master *everything* that is presented in this book. Gaining an understanding of just one principle (emotionally, as well as intellectually) will skyrocket your life into a different dimension. All of the key elements which I've learnt and have discovered over the course of a decade–key elements that'll help you drastically improve the quality of your life, as well as to stay in control of that life–all blend into each other. You can think of this book as a beautiful jigsaw puzzle, in which every epiphany represents an individual piece. It is imperative, therefore, that you resolve to reading the entire book before assuming what this picture–which I'm about to share with you–actually looks like. In effect, this book was written deliberately in a particular manner where each new chapter builds upon the previous one, in such a way that if you relate them to one another you'll have the biggest chance of seeing the entire picture without any distortions.

To mentally prepare you for what is coming I want you to proceed with an open mind, and embrace the idea of making a change. In other words, if your present life philosophy is not working out for you as well as it should, then you have nothing to lose by disregarding everything you already know and becoming receptive to a new, totally different approach (even if only for the duration of reading this book). It goes without saying that if you wish to enjoy a happy, fulfilling life, then you have to quit giving away your ability to think to others and being a sheep–doing what everyone else is doing, and thinking what everyone else is thinking. Sure, you can go with the safety of the herd, but the herd is going around in circles. It may feel secure and comfortable but it's a terrible place to be in. Your life is *your* movie, so be the star in it, and the director of it. Take life into your own hands and create an epic story to tell for generations to come. Realise that behind every achievement, breakthrough, and innovation there are individuals who stood out from the crowd, thought differently, openly expressed their ideals, and fully believed in their vision, regardless of what everyone else thought of them.

Finally, I'm not going to bombard you and bore you to death with too many statistics, surveys, testimonials, stories, case studies, and so on and so forth–in other words–with evidence and proof. The evidence and proof are all around you. And any person perspicacious enough will have no trouble acknowledging them. Therefore, I am simply going to feed you raw, uncensored, straight-up awareness of who you really are, what you are really like, and what the purpose of you being here is. It has been a great pleasure putting this book together for you. I've absolutely loved and enjoyed every second of it, and I'm certain that you will enjoy it too. Understand that the positive changes you desperately wish to see in this world begin with you as an individual. Once you have mastered yourself, you can then begin to master your world. I know that you will get great value out of this book only if you use it. Take the time to really think about what you are reading. Relate these ideas to your own experiences, to other people's experiences, and reflect on them. Skimming through this book and forgetting about it will not do you any good, unless you practice the ideas contained within it and put them to good use. That being said, if you are ready to learn what it takes to claim the wonderful life which has been waiting for you all along, then settle yourself in a comfortable position and let us dive into it…

"The first and greatest victory is to conquer yourself; to be conquered by yourself is of all things the most shameful and vile." – Plato

"Socrates demonstrated long ago that the truly free individual is free only to the extent of his own self-mastery. While those who will not govern themselves are condemned to find masters to govern over them." – Steven Pressfield

PART 1

UNDERSTANDING YOUR CREATIVE NATURE AND PLACE
IN THE WORLD

Epiphany I

The Meaning

"The meaning of life is whatever you ascribe it to be. Being alive is the meaning."
– Joseph Campbell

To clarify a few things before we get into this chapter I'd like to note that I am not a religious person. Even though I believe in a universal power that is greater than our physical selves–power which governs our world, our Universe, and everything else in it–I do not believe that it is a person (like us)–sitting somewhere on a cloud–who is responsible for this power. Moreover, I'm not at all interested in bashing anyone's beliefs or religious views. I sincerely respect each person's personal beliefs as far as what this power–called God–means to them. If your beliefs provide you with comfort and quality of life that you truly love and enjoy, then you don't have to take anything what I am about to share with you in this chapter at face value. You are more than welcome to reject all the following ideas entirely if your relationship to–and understanding of–God is undeniable. Nevertheless, I would be doing a great disservice to all of those people for whom religious ideas simply don't work, by keeping everything that I know about this great power, and our relationship to it all to myself. That said, to kick things off I have to ask you…

Have you ever asked yourself questions such as: "Who am I? What am I doing here? What is the meaning of life? Where did I come from? What happens after I die?" (And other similar questions.) At some point you probably have, and so have I. At a young age–somewhere around fourteen years old–I began to really question my existence. I would often ask myself: "Where did I come from? What am I supposed to do here? What will happen after I die? What happens after all of this is over?" Since I had no idea, I was extremely scared of death–I truly did not like the idea of dying. Many sleepless nights ensued as I desperately tried to figure it all out prior to dozing off. Typically I'd keep myself up for hours–terrified–unable to find a comforting thought. Considering that I absolutely loved being alive right here and right now, in *this* body, in *this* day and age, in *this* place, and with *these* people, it used to really bother me and make me feel depressed knowing that one day it is all going to end. Many nights before drifting into sleep I used to sob uncontrollably because my thought process–at the time–was that after I was done on planet Earth, all that would be left for me to experience is eternal darkness. Essentially, the reason why I was afraid of death is because my undeveloped mind weren't able to imagine death being anything other than eternal darkness where there were no sensations; no emotions; no laughter; no seeing; no talking; no friends; nothing!

Naturally, this made me wonder: "What is the point of all of this then? What does it all mean? Is what I'm doing here even worth anything? Life is so beautiful, why does it have to end so horribly?" Yet, even though that is the way I sometimes thought, I still did not believe that we simply happened to come to life (by random chance) for a brief period of time, only to go right back to "nothingness" when the experience is over. There was something inside of myself which would not allow me to accept and continue to entertain thoughts of such nature. As I became progressively frustrated with my crippling fear of the unknown, I've made the decision to study, and educate myself ruthlessly for many years which followed. Remarkably, it didn't take me long to have my epiphany. At the age of twenty-one it dawned on me clearly and made perfect sense. And so today, I'm no longer troubled by disturbing thoughts such as "nothingness" or "darkness." At this point in my journey I welcome death just as much as I welcome life. The inevitable nature of death no longer prevents me from experiencing my life fully. Ever since I became aware of the fact that cycles of life and death were necessary for the continuation of life, those sleepless nights have disappeared. I'm now completely at peace with the fact that my current experience of life will one day come to an end. And I am no longer saddened by the fact that my conscious awareness will one day be taken out of my current physical body and drift somewhere else. For today I understand that I'm an eternal being who's destined to have many more such experiences; that "death" as we know it is just an illusion.

RELIGION

The biggest resource for answers to complicated questions such as: "What is the meaning of life?" is theology, which I have explored for a very long time. Unfortunately, religion did not work out for me, for many different reasons. One of which is that there were dozens of religions out there, and every single one of them claimed to be the right one, while all the others were wrong, and whose followers were going to burn in hell. (Try to explain that to your loving God.) I just couldn't accept that. My understanding is that the reason why any person may wholeheartedly believe in any particular religion–even when there are no sound arguments to support their beliefs–is only because that person happens to be born at a particular time, in a particular place–by mere chance–where that particular religion is being practiced and propagated... think about this.

Richard Dawkins, an author of "The God Delusion" once pointed this out when he said: "*Let's assume that you are a Christian. Being a Christian, you know what it is like not to believe in another religion because you are not a Muslim, and you are not a Hindu. Now, why aren't you a Hindu? Well, because you haven't been brought up in India. If you were brought up in Denmark at the time of the Vikings you would be believing in Thor. If you were brought up in classical Greece you would be believing in Zeus.*" That statement made me realise that trying to understand the true nature of God by attempting to get acquainted with a certain group of "chosen" people who reside in this physical world, who have the *right* book containing the *right* set of principles, rules, names, and among whom God himself dwells, is a hopeless pursuit.

Considering that practically ever since the beginning of time there were all kinds of civilisations that have practiced one form of religion or another in their lifetime, then there must have been *something* right with all of them. So rather than arguing for who was right and wrong, I began to search for that universal *something*. But instead of analysing different rules, names, and images of gods–when looking at and comparing different religions–I had to dig much deeper and look for an underlying premise, or belief which major religions had in common. And I found it. In fact, it wasn't difficult.

Even though every religion has its differences, it is evident that they all agree on one fact. Which is that we are non-physical beings; that we have a soul; and that there certainly *is* a power which animates, penetrates, and motivates the Universe–power called God. Now, with these statements I completely resonate, but it still wasn't clear to me as to why God was typically depicted in human form. Because if we are non-physical beings–souls if you will–then why would God himself be someone like us? As in, manifested in a lesser (physical) form. In other words, if our physical bodies are lesser forms of manifestation–a microcosm of something much bigger than our physical selves–then why would God have physical characteristics? Because if he actually did, wouldn't that make his powers limited? And if God had limitations just like physical beings do, then how could he ever possess the ability to be omnipresent and omniscient? Obviously he wouldn't.

I am fully aware that it may appear as though I was proactively arguing against religious ideas on my quest to find truth, but that would be wrong. What it was is that whenever I'd earnestly try to entertain religious concepts and ideas, my natural impulse was to reject them. Yet that impulse was not coming from my own ideas, opinions, biases, or beliefs, because I hadn't had any (relative to the subject of God). I was exceptionally open-minded, and I still am. Rather, that uneasy feeling was coming to surface of its own accord. If I had to put what I was feeling into words, I'd say that it felt as though if I did try to adopt a certain religion with certain beliefs, and began to abide by them, then I would actually become less than what I already was.

In essence, I felt much happier, freer, and more empowered without a religion. Because religions have countless restrictions, limitations, and rules for people to follow if they wished to be considered good people, and to live a life that is worthy of God's praise and approval. But I was already living a good life. I was already a good, honest, joyful, and loving individual. I was happy by default. Why then would I need to continually praise, revere, and obey someone to be considered good and worthy, when I was already good and worthy? It just didn't make any sense. Unfortunately, since most people in the world do not feel this way about themselves as a result of negative social and cultural conditioning, what they end up doing is turning to religion to tell them how good and worthy they are. But the problem is that religion usually makes matters worse as it builds upon that conditioning, rather than dissolving it.

Consider the following: a religion that's being practiced the most in the West is Christianity. Christianity states that we have to accept Jesus Christ as our Lord and Saviour so that he can forgive our sins and allow us entry into heaven. (Yes, we are all just a bunch of sinners; really horrible people. And if we don't repent, the eternity is going to be rather bleak.) On the other hand, a religion that's being practiced the most in the East is Buddhism. Buddhism states that we must achieve enlightenment through their teachings and practices in order to stop our karmic cycles of death and rebirth. Once again, assuming that something is inherently wrong. That the cycle of birth and death is not something which was purposefully put in place for the continuation of life, and for the expansion of the Universe, but rather an unfortunate tragedy that needs to be stopped.

So you see, it seems as though it really doesn't matter on which side of the globe you are born, because as soon as you get here there will always be those who are quick to point out what is wrong with you. Granted, many religious ideas are actually spot on; they resonate with me deeply, and get me thinking in powerful ways. Ideas such as that we were created in God's image. That we should treat others as we ourselves would like to be treated. To live in the present moment, rather than the past or future. That abundance is our birthright. That whatever we ask for we shall receive. That we should be compassionate and forgiving towards ourselves and others. That before we pass judgement onto others we should look at ourself and be concerned with our own faults and misconduct. And so on and so forth.

However, most other ideas just don't sit well with me. For example, the concept of heaven–at least in Christianity–is one of eternal life which takes place somewhere in the clouds after we die. There, we will be surrounded by our friends and family (some of whom we may not even get along with) forever, and ever. What an insufferable fate. All pettiness aside though, let us imagine for a moment that we are now in heaven. Don't we need to eat to keep our bodies functioning properly? Do they have bathrooms there, or behind a bush will suffice? Or is there no need to nourish ourselves in heaven in the first place? And if that is the case, then all of the plants and trees are there for decoration purposes? Likewise, are we allowed to wear clothes of our own choice, or do we have to wear white robes for whatever arbitrary reason? And if so, then what if we don't like the robe? Do we just suck it up and deal with it? And what about our appearance? Is it the same as when we were alive? And if so, then why do we have to appear in the same form for all of eternity in which we appeared in the physical world once? Personally, I'm aware that my physical appearance is not me; it is not who *I am*. I understand that my body is just an instrument; a vehicle which allows me to fully experience the reality of a physical world–nothing more. With this reasoning in mind, why would I have to bring this instrument (or even the appearance of one) into another dimension for all of the eternity where it would serve no purpose?

How about kids or infants? What happens to those who are unfortunate enough to leave this world as a baby? Are they destined to be stuck in heaven for all of the eternity as an infant? All the while the only form of communication they are familiar with is "crying." Or what about those who have a physical disability which leaves them immobilised? Do they immediately get healed and regrow amputated limbs once they enter into heaven, or do they have wheelchairs there? On numerous occasions I have asked religious people the following question: "What will happen if you die as an old person, are you just going to be ancient and derelict forever? That would be awful." And this is the common answer which I was able to elicit from them: "Not at all, in heaven everyone will be twenty-five years of age. Everyone will look their best." Seriously, who comes up with this stuff?

I completely empathise with anyone unfortunate enough to lose somebody close to them; somebody they love. I understand that religion can provide people with comfort and hope, even if we are unsure as to how exactly it all works. However, even though the idea of heaven provides comfort and some relief, it is nevertheless a very sad concept. It does not allow us to celebrate life. Instead, it makes us feel powerless. It produces feelings of separation and longing for eternal happiness and peace. It perpetuates the idea that our world is bad, unfair, full of pain and suffering, and that we will all soon be liberated from it. It makes us feel as though life is fragile, and that we are insignificant mortals who are at the complete mercy of it. Of course, none of this even comes close to the truth, as you shall see in the upcoming pages.

Now look, if it states in the book of Genesis that "Man" was created in God's image and likeness, maybe what it really means is that God had endowed you and every other human being on the planet with his own powers and abilities. So that we could take care of our own personal worlds, rather than forever begging somebody else to come along and solve our problems. In other words, when theology mentions the "image" of God, maybe it isn't referring to surface layer characteristics of a physical human being (an older gentleman with a white beard, with two arms and two legs). But rather, it is referring to intellectual or spiritual characteristics of a creative being; a powerful, creative force–a *creator*.

"Don't expect God to do for you what God can only do with and through you."

One would think that if God created the entire Universe, which is continuously expanding wouldn't he have bigger things to worry about than this tiny little rock that we know as planet Earth? While watching over every single soul and pandering to them, correcting them, making sure that everyone is on the right track. (Paradoxically, we *are* being guided and supported, but not in a way that most people think.) Do you seriously believe that what we do here in our lifetime ultimately matters all that much? Before you know it you'll be gone, and everything you own will belong to somebody else, while you reincarnate into–not unlikely–a different world in a different galaxy. In effect, the Universe is so vast (and, in fact infinite) that our planet can be likened to a little anthill, where you will find ants running around, going about their "ant" business. It just isn't all that impressive, or important. Because as you lift up your head and see everything else that our beautiful planet has to offer–besides the little anthill–you instantly forget about it and quickly move on to explore something else–something more interesting.

Undoubtedly someone will protest: "Well, God does care about us and everything that we do, no matter how small we may be. Because we are part of him, he is part of us, and he loves us." And I would reply: "Of course, but God loves you so much so that he accepts you completely. He loves you *unconditionally*. Which means that he is not intimately involved in how you are experiencing life. He allows you to make your own decisions, arrive at your own conclusions, and play the role of a god in your own personal universe. Even if you find yourself stuck in an unbearable situation, God *allows* you to experience it fully." Why? Because God is not able to meddle in your experience; God granted you the ability to decide what it is you are going to create for yourself. And if you create suffering, even if you do so unconsciously, or as a result of ignorance, then so it will be. God gave you absolute freedom of thought, as well as the tools necessary–ready at your disposal–to experience life in any which way that *you* choose. (Now that's *real* love!) This is extremely important to understand, because you may be getting nowhere by searching and asking for divine guidance from above, not realising that the reason why you can't seem to get an answer is because the guidance is within you.

Turning to the Holy Bible when looking to discover certain truths about ourselves, life, and God is certainly a wise decision–a step in the right direction. However, we have to proceed with a critical mind without interpreting everything that we read literally, otherwise we are going to find ourselves in a pickle. The Bible is full of ridiculous rules with respect to what God wants us to do and how God wants us to live. Personally, while studying the Bible, in many instances it felt as though I was being given orders by someone who was not at all wise, powerful, and self-sufficient. But rather by someone who was childish and insecure (given the fact that if we chose to not love and accept him, then he would make certain that we burn in hell); who exhibited a lot of petty human emotions, judgements, and limitations.

For instance, when I've learnt that God had finished his creations on the sixth day and took the seventh day off to rest, I had to pause and think about that for a minute. Because why would God need to rest for? It didn't make sense since *action* and *effort* are forces that are only viable in a dimension that is governed by time and space, i.e. a physical plane of existence. Which naturally follows that God doesn't need to rest, because he is not operating in a realm of matter, where energy could get depleted through exertion. It is only we, humans (and other lifeforms) who need to rest, because we live in physical bodies that have limits–that must be frequently recharged. Applications of such limitations to something that is limitless and infinitely powerful–God–can only be expected from a human. Which leads me to the following point.

Knowing all of this, if we then dare to challenge the status quo and ask the question: "Where did the Bible actually come from? Who wrote it?" The answer is a bunch of humans of course (or prophets). Humans who have certainly had their own unique emotions, judgements, beliefs, limitations, biases, agendas, perspectives, etc. And besides, the Bible was written thousands of years ago, and it was not originally written in the English language either (or, in my case–Russian). Which follows that by the time you and I have laid our hands on it, it was already translated and edited by thousands of people, a thousand times beforehand. Once I realised this, it became difficult for me to continue to rely 100 percent on the Bible to provide me with adequate answers as to who I was, and what I was supposed to be doing with my life. It would be just as foolish as walking up to a stranger on the street and asking them: "What do you think?" In other words, God did not write the Bible; it was a human job. It doesn't even matter whether God had actually spoken to the people who wrote it (or had shown them some things), because they still had their own minds, their own agendas, and their own ways of interpreting events. In effect, whatever the source of that wisdom was, it still invariably had to go through a filter–which is the human mind–before it was ever documented. And perhaps this is not the discussion that we should be having in the first place. Because maybe what those "prophets" have been hearing and seeing all along wasn't even God. They could have very well been tripping balls while under the influence of DMT (the burnish bush) for all we know.

All in all, Bible is still very much on point regarding many truths of life, and so I am not discrediting it. However, what often happens is that people tend to misinterpret what is being said in the scriptures. The reason for this is that when we try to understand things which we cannot see–non-physical things; things of a spiritual nature–we can only understand them to the extent to which our physical, limited awareness will allow. Although once we develop a higher level of awareness and begin to understand the *true* nature of God, we will realise, first of all, that there is no such thing as sin. Which means that it really doesn't matter how we choose to live our lives on planet Earth. We will not be punished for our mistakes and misbehaviour when we leave. Why? Because every time a person engages in negative, deceitful, violent, or harmful behaviour, that person is not acting from their natural place of alignment with–and connection to–who they really are. Any of it can only ever come from a place of ignorance, or unconsciousness. In effect, evil is a human condition; God and Satan have absolutely nothing to do with it.

The fact that the world was not ready for that level of understanding at the time when religions were becoming more prolific, is precisely the reason why theologians had to exercise caution when conveying such truths to others. Thereby, isn't it plausible that propagation of the existence of Satan, as well as the promise of eternal torture in hell for those who were not complying with God's wishes is nothing more than a fabricated, perfectly terrifying concept which incentivises people to conform and live their lives in a certain way, rather than it being an absolute and an unquestionable fact of life?

I am convinced that that's exactly what it is. Just a well-intentioned, life-preserving scare tactic. And if your argument is something to the effect of: "So what if religion has its rules and limitations, even if they are fabricated? People shouldn't be allowed to know that what they do here is not punishable by God. That every individual–no matter what they've done–will immediately re-emerge back into the non-physical, loving, pure-positive dimension which they originated from without any judgments or hick-ups. People must be told what's righteous and what's not. Otherwise they'll run around and cause trouble–assuming that God doesn't mind when they act out of ignorance. People need guidance because if left up to them, only God knows what might happen. There are a lot of stupid people in the world. Without a concept of sin and eternal hell how else will they know that ill-will, pain and suffering are not welcomed, even though they have absolute freedom to create exactly that? Knowing that they are completely free to do whatever they please leaves them without any incentive to refrain from acting and behaving in ignorant ways. Something certainly needs to be done in order to keep their unconscious behaviour in check and the promise of eternal hell accomplishes exactly that."

Well that's quite a compelling argument, and it does a good job of keeping people's unconsciousness at bay to a respectable extent. But what about all of those people who do not believe in, or practice any religion at all? Who do not regularly pray or attend the church? Yet are living wonderful, loving, and virtuous lives that are absolutely worth modelling. How do they obtain their guidance? How do they manage to live in ways that are "pleasing to God," and are in absolute accordance with that which most religions teach their followers, without ever being instructed on any of it? Well, the reason they are able to this is, is because God is everywhere and in everything. God communicates with every single person all day, every day, no matter the nationality, gender, or age. It doesn't even matter whether a person is blind or deaf; whether they are disabled or paralysed; whether they speak a particular language; whether they're located in one continent or the other; or whether they believe in one thing or another. It is a colossal mistake to assume that one can only find God in a certain building (church, synagogue, or mosque), because God is much closer to us than we realise.

You must understand that God had endowed you, me, and every other human being alive with something that we call emotions. Our emotional system is actually a guidance system which indicates in real-time, moment-by-moment, whether we are expressing the true nature of God and doing God's work, or not, in the form of emotions. By paying attention to how we feel we get to conclude that if we are feeling a negative emotion of any kind–as we think, say, or do anything–it is God's way of directly *indicating* to us that we are going in the opposite direction. In other words, presence of any negative emotion simply means that we are not expressing our true, loving, powerful, and godly nature, at least for the time being. And even though we are being looked after and reminded of our ignorance through emotional signals, God does not have the authority–or more specifically, the desire–to assert himself and stop us in our act of ignorance. Because in the physical realm, we are the ones who are in complete control. Which means that it is up to us to correct course if we so desire. In effect, we are all eternally loved, guided, supported, and advised, but we are not puppets on a string who are being manipulated, dissuaded, or controlled–for whom God has a particular plan in mind.

The more you become aware of your true nature, the more you realise that hell and Satan are simply man-made concepts. Even Jesus never talked about Satan, or hell in a literal sense (unfortunately after the editing process it appears to be the case). He only talked about the *unconsciousness* of human beings, or the egoic mind, which most people tend to develop. Jesus' whole message can be summarised in one of his statements: "*Father, forgive them for they know not what they do.*" What he essentially meant is that human beings themselves are capable of all kinds of atrocities; we never did need Satan for that. He meant that we should never be angry and impatient with our fellow humans for their acts of ignorance and unconscious behaviour, because they don't even know that what they are doing is wrong. For the most part, Jesus talked about our own suffering, our own misuses of the mind, and our own unconsciousness. Yet many are convinced that Satan is the problem. Whereas others go so far as to believe that Satan is the prince of our world. That we were put on this earth for some sort of a test to see who will fall prey to, get seduced by, or succumb to his influence. And once who do, won't be worthy of God's love and approval. But the way I see it is that Satan–prince of this world as they would have you–is not a person, or a god. Rather, it is a synonym for greed, power, ego gratification, fame, desire to dominate, jealousy, envy, hatred, fear, and so forth, which people who live unconsciously–with no awareness of who they are, and what they are really like–tend to fall prey to. And as a consequence, are not able to receive all the good that God is offering to them all day, every day (and that is ultimately what hell is).

We humans tend to observe certain things and call them evil, horrible, and vile. Since we are at a loss for answers as to why or how something like "this" could ever happen, we explain it away by pointing the finger at Satan. Some even argue: "Well, if there is a loving, all-powerful God who guides us and wishes for everyone nothing but longevity, good health, and well-being, yet all kinds of tragedies and disastrous events are still taking place all over the world, then there must be something else that has the power to manipulate events and influence how people think and behave, wouldn't you think? It only makes sense that there exists a malevolent force of some kind which wants to see us suffer." But the truth is, humans do this to themselves. All of the pain and suffering stems directly from our ignorance and misuses of the mind. (More on this later.) It is not the Devil, although it sure as hell can feel like it sometimes. There is no source of evil in our Universe; it is a big fat lie. There is only a powerful stream of love and well-being. Whereas something that we call evil comes from resistance to–or disconnection from–that powerful stream. Evil is merely an absence of well-being; it is not a source in itself which has life, consciousness, and ability to assert itself uninvitedly into anyone's experience and proceed to wreak havoc. Satan, Devil, Iblis, and whoever else, are nothing but figments of "Man's" imagination. These concepts have been fabricated by certain individuals who merely wanted to exercise control over other people–to make them afraid and get them to conform.

Esther Hicks, who is a wonderful human being, an inspirational speaker and author of "Ask and it is Given," which I highly recommend that you read, had put religion and our connection to that which we call God into a proper perspective when she said: "*Being connected to this power, or to who you really are is an individual thing, but religion hinders this truth usually more than it helps it. Because most religions are more interested in what you can do for them as a body than they are in helping you to find your own connection, and helping you to become individually empowered. There is always an underlying premise in most religions that is hurting you, and even though they do not really say it out loud (it is not obvious) it is still very much rampant in their implications. What they are really saying is that individually you're weak, but in numbers you're more powerful. And it speaks in absolute contradiction to what you knew before you came forth into your physical life experience. Because you knew that every individual who connects to the goodness of who they are, have all of the power of the Universe at their fingertips."*

What I took this to mean is that it was never about forming clans, joining cults, following daily rituals, going to church gatherings and praying on our knees five times a day. But rather, it was always–and only–about rediscovering our relationship to this great power that we call God, and then re-establishing a conscious connection to it. But when we try to accomplish this by getting involved in a particular religion, we shoot ourself in the foot. For religion doesn't want us to become self-sufficient and self-empowered. Religion doesn't want us to know that we are *that* which we call God. The ideas of self-mastery, self-efficacy, and self-empowerment have been purposefully edited out of the scriptures. Because true self-sufficiency and independence were considered a threat to religious authorities. And understandably so. If we knew who we really were, and what we were capable of, then we would no longer feel the need to get involved in any religion.

She continued: *"What most people call God is very different from their image of God. As humans have discovered that God had created them, they then began to recreate God in their own image. The reason for this is because when a human being forms a perspective of something like God, and then tries to make everything fit into that perspective (to make it relatable), there is bound to be tremendous distortion in that process. Because you cannot understand God from your limited, physical, human perspective. As humans, you were comfortable with seeing God as someone who was like you, but who was much bigger and much more superior, who had all of the answers, and who was an overall exaggerated version of you. Sometimes it is unsettling to feel and to believe that you are that what you call God, because you see yourselves as bags of flesh, blood, and bones. (Who are we to be on the same level as God? We think to ourselves.) And so, in the process of making that exaggerated image of God humans have subverted their own image of 'self.' In other words, by making this distinction between Man and God, Man has humbled himself and made himself into an inferior mortal who's separated from this exaggerated entity which he calls God."*

What Abraham is essentially saying is that God is not a human-like entity who is bigger, better, and smarter; who lives in one place or another; and who has nothing in common with us pesky little humans. Rather, God is Divine Consciousness, and every form of life is part of that consciousness (we all have direct access to it). This means that you *are* what you call God; you *are* the creator of worlds; you *do* have all the answers; you *are* powerful; and you *are* eternal. You must embrace that idea and begin to ride that wave.

In order to have an honest, harmonious, and powerful relationship with God you must close the gap between yourself and God. And how do you do that? You do it by becoming consciously–as well as emotionally–*aligned* with that which you call God. You don't necessarily become aligned with God by intellectually knowing certain things. The only way to know whether or not you are aligned with God is by the way you *feel*. When you feel love, you are God. When you feel happy, joyful, ecstatic, peaceful, purposeful, apprecia-tive, kind, loving–and other high-vibrational states of a similar nature–you are God. You are not a sinful mortal who must repent and pay for his or her ancestors' "sins." God never judges you, or anyone else, because God is not a human being who is full of petty human emotions. God does not have the capacity to think a negative thought, or even experience time in a way that we humans do. For if he did, the eternal nature of all things would not be a possibility. Understand that this power loves you unconditionally, because it is *this* power which lives in everyone and in everything. And it is this power which expresses itself through all-that-is. All things considered, you did not come here to prove yourself; you came here to rediscover yourself.

ENERGY

"You are the creator of your own personal Universe." – Abraham Hicks

"You have the energy that creates worlds at your fingertips."
– Abraham Hicks

If we are going to find out more about ourselves and this power which ani-mates, penetrates and fills the interspaces of the Universe, there are only two main sources of reference which we could reliably turn to: theology and sci-ence. If we were to ask a theologian: "Who is God? What is this power that you call God?" The theologian would tell us something to the effect of: "God just is. He can neither be created, nor destroyed. He always was, and he al-ways will be. He is the cause and effect of himself. He is all-knowing and all-powerful. He is one hundred percent evenly present in all places at all times. And he forever expresses himself in form, through form, then out of form." Let's say that for whatever reason we aren't willing to believe, or accept that.

So we turn around and we ask a scientist instead: "What is it that makes all of this possible? What is it that animates every living and inanimate thing? What is this thing called energy? Describe energy to us." And a scientist will say something to the effect of: "Energy just is. Energy can neither be created, nor destroyed. It always was and always will be. It is all-powerful. It is impartial (it doesn't care whether we use that energy to brighten up a beautiful home or create an atomic bomb). It is one hundred percent evenly present in all places at all times. And it is forever moving into form, through form, then out of form."

Now, it seems that we are talking about the same thing here, only using different names while describing it, yet the activity is precisely the same. So how would I explain this? As far as I'm concerned religion has been around for thousands of years, which leads me to believe that it probably originated from a time when we lived in tribes. Back then people didn't know what energy was, there was no way that they could even consider it. Given the fact that something like electricity–which is similar to this great power in many respects–wasn't around. Moreover, the tribal leaders were usually men, and because they were physically stronger than the opposite sex, wiser and more resourceful, they convinced themselves that if there is a God, then he must be a male. Consequently, making themselves inferior to this power which they would then fear and worship. However, we are no longer limited in our understanding of how things may actually work. Today, we all know what energy is. We may not know exactly how it works, but we know that it exists.

Consider this: everything in our Universe is made up of energy. You are energy; your thoughts are energy; your body is energy–your physical body is in a continuous state of vibration; it is always moving. Everything else that you see and come into contact with is energy. Everything is in a continuous state of movement; nothing rests. Your physical body, as well as other material objects may appear to be still and solid, but they are really not. They only *appear* to be so to our physical senses. If you were to put your body under a certain type of microscope you would invariably see a mass of energy vibrating. And this would apply to every other physical, material object.

To help you grasp the significance of what we are talking about here, it may be useful to look at it in the following way. First of all–on a larger scale–we have the entire Universe. Then, if we begin to magnify and take a closer look we will find our galaxy. Then we will find our planet. Then we will find individuals. And then–if we keep going further still–inside of our bodies we will find organs. Then cells. Then molecules. Then atoms, and then *energy*. In effect, energy is where everything starts. Your body even has an energy field that radiates and vibrates. And although you will never be able to see it with a naked eye, if you keep perfectly still and pay close attention you'll certainly feel it. You may think that I am referring to your pulse, because that is all you're able to feel in the beginning. However, if you continue to practise being still without engaging any of your sensory factors you'll realise that your whole body is actually vibrating in-between your pulse.

When I understood what makes us human and how the Universe essentially works, the mystery of death had been completely resolved for me. Today I have zero ounce of fear of death. My reasoning is that if energy cannot be destroyed–it can only move into different form, or state of vibration–then death as we know it is just an illusion. If energy cannot be destroyed–and all that we are is a mass of energy–then that postulates only one theory: theory of *life*. Which ultimately means that there is no death.

As we raise our consciousness and begin to understand what we are really like, we inevitably realise that our physical and spiritual sides are actually connected. They are one; not two, separate, mutually exclusive things. If we take the idea which every electrician will attest to, that electricity can only work from a higher to a lower potential, as well as the fact that energy always returns to its source of origination, and then relate this understanding to our experience in the physical body, it will become evident that the reason why we're able to experience life in a physical format (a lower dimension) is because it is an extension of a higher, spiritual dimension, which is the driving force behind it. This essentially means that when any person experiences "death," what actually happens is that the person's consciousness leaves the body–that is vibrating on a physical level–and immediately transitions back into a dimension which that consciousness originated from.

"Fear comes from uncertainty; we can eliminate the fear within us when we know ourselves better." – Bruce Lee

Bob Proctor, who was a fantastic teacher, a world-class public speaker, and author of "You Were Born Rich" gave a perfect explanation of this energetic connection–of all things–in one of his seminars. He picked up a glass of water and he said: *"We call this glass because of the speed that it's vibrating at, but it is actually energy. We call the substance inside of the glass water, but it is actually energy too. Everything is energy, only vibrating at different speeds. While the energy is in the vibratory state that it's in–in the glass–we call it water. We call it water because it is vibrating on a physical level. If we would add heat to that energy (that we call water) we wouldn't call it water any longer. It would still be the same ener-gy, but it would be moving faster–at a higher speed or rate of vibration. And then we would call that same energy steam or vapor. We would call it steam or vapor because now it is not in a physical vibration, it has moved into an astro-vibration. But, if we continue to add heat to that energy, we wouldn't call it steam or vapor any longer, now we'd call it air, ether or gas. And we would call it that because it is no longer in the astro-vibration, it has now moved into an etheric vibration. But it is still the ex-act same energy, only vibrating on a different frequency."* He further added: *"The only difference between one thing and another is in density, or in amplitude of vibra-tion. All electromagnetic waves have their own rate of frequency–which means the number of changes in direction per second. The electric wave spectrum is in a scale of vibration, and is divided into regions. And one must remember that these regions are not actual divisions, but arbitrary spaces that cover frequencies, which manifest in our senses in different ways. Each region blends into both–the one above and the one below–like the colors of a rainbow."*

A frequency is a level, or rate of vibration, and every frequency is con-nected to the one above and the one below. There is no line of demarcation where one ends and the other starts–they are all joined together, like the col-ours of the rainbow. And so the reason why we are unable to see air with our physical sensory factor "sight" is because air is vibrating on a different fre-quency–relative to our sensory factor "sight." The only way that we are able to see air is with our inner eye of *understanding*. (Although we cannot physi-cally see it, our understanding tells us it's there.) The same principle applies to a human personality. That is, the physical side of ourself that we can see, and the spiritual side that we cannot see, both exist, and both are just as real. They are both expressions of the same thing (same energy; same life force). They are just different sides of the same coin.

All things considered, there is absolutely no good reason to fear death, because there is no death. Sure, our bodies will die (cease to function), but the essence of us will forever live on, because we are eternal beings who can never cease to exist. In the Bhagavad Gita (a profound scripture of a Hindu origin) it says: *"Immortality is the birthright of every human being. When a person becomes conscious of this fact of life, when he develops an awareness of who he truly is, then to that person death is no more traumatic than taking off an old coat."* Per-sonally, the way I view death at this point in my life is as follows: You know when you are dreaming your dream feels completely real to you. No matter how ridiculous your dream may be, you still feel as though it is happening for real. In other words, since the vividness of your dream is so utterly convincing, you are completely bought-in to that dream. But when you wake up you begin to realise that it was just a dream; that it wasn't real. And no matter how good or terrible the dream might have been, you gradually begin to forget about it and just go on to do whatever it is you usually do. When you come back around, you simply tell yourself: "Of course it was a dream! How could I have fallen for that?! Of course my life is here and now, not where I (my conscious awareness) just came from."

Well, I believe that when we "die" and immediately transition back to where we came from, we will all feel the same way about the lives which we have lived in our physical world. In effect, life *is* a dream. It is just a brief moment in time, and there will be many more. There is nothing serious–that ultimately matters all that much–going on here. And as we make our transition back into the non-physical, we will not be missing our lives, our friends and relatives. Because we'll inherently know that they are also having their dream. That soon they will wake up from it and share a (not a literal, but energetic) laugh with us about how serious we thought it all was. That being said, if your dream was horrible–if people lied to you in your dream, if they hurt you, mistreated you, or maybe even killed you–after you wake up from that nightmare, are you mad? Are you sad? Do you feel guilty? Are you angry? Do you feel any resentments? Probably not, because you know it wasn't real. It didn't affect who you essentially are in any meaningful way. So what you do instead is breathe a sigh of relief and then laugh, or cry out of joy.

"What men call death is but a journey to a new city in another dimension of life."
– Joseph Murphy

To wrap up a previous thread and explain why different religions have different rules and images of their Gods, we must understand that in order for a person to be able to work with an idea, or concept, that person has to have a clear image in their mind to work with–an image that is *relatable*; an image that makes sense. You see, human beings think in *pictures*, and without a picture to work with we become confused. For this very practical reason, if religions began to explain to their followers that God was energy-like, that God doesn't speak, that God doesn't have a name, a face, or place in which he resides, then people would get confused, and as a result, would not be able to understand the concept. As a consequence, there are now hundreds of religions out there that differ from one another in some way. And that's because we have thousands of different cultures in the world, as well as hundreds of ethnic groups, and every one of them needs to have an image that is relatable to *them*. So, in order to eliminate confusion what happened was that different religions had to say to their followers: "Your God looks like you. Your God lives where you live. Your God speaks the language you speak."

With that in mind, it is utterly pointless to try and argue for which religion is the right one, because they are all right. They are all essentially pointing to the same truth–that we are spiritual beings who live in physical bodies, and that one day we will become one with our God. Sure, they may use different names, conjure up different images, create different rules, and relay different stories. Though ultimately they're all spouting the same truth. So it really doesn't matter which religion we decide to look into, because the truth can be found in all of them. As Bob Proctor once said: "*The truth is something like the center of a town. It really doesn't matter which side you approach it from because when you get there, you are still in the same place.*"

Whenever I find myself in a conversation with someone discussing the subject of God, it becomes evident rather quickly that even though I'm not a religious person, I still believe in God. While unable to process such a seemingly self-contradicting stance on the matter, people typically ask: "But how do you think about God? If you do not have a religion then who's your God? How would you describe your God?" And the answer to those questions is always something to the effect of: "I interpret God as a conscious light. As a pure-positive, creative energy that is all-knowing, that is aware of itself, and that is superintelligent. God is everywhere, and in everything. God is an unconditionally loving consciousness that is forever seeking to express itself in as many different ways as possible, in order to become *more* than what it already is, for the sole purpose of expansion and fuller expression."

By actively avoiding religion as a foundation, or standard against which my understanding of God has to be measured, I do not make the mistake of assigning any rules, conditions and limitations to God. In my version of reality, this great power truly has no limits. This power that I choose to call God is Source-Energy, God-Force, Spirit, or Infinite Intelligence. There are literally hundreds of different names that we can use when referring to this power. However, it truly doesn't matter what we call it, because we're still referring to the same thing. The reason why I happen to resonate with those names in particular is because–unlike the traditional label "God"–those labels haven't been violated or wildly misinterpreted, at least for the time being.

The bottom line is, most people in the world are operating from a false premise that one can only find–and have any real chance at developing a relationship with–God through some kind of religion. They are convinced that the church and the pastor are the gateways to that relationship. However, no one *has* to believe in anything in order to benefit from all that God has to offer. Nobody needs to adhere to certain rules and follow certain practices, or attend rituals in order to have a harmonious relationship with the "creator." Truly, God is not interested in what you believe or don't believe; what you do or don't do; what you eat or don't eat. That which is God is only ever interested in you being the powerful creator of your own experience that you specifically came here to be.

SOURCE-ENERGY

"You are a spiritual being, a living consciousness, living in a physical body for the sole purpose of creation and expression." – Abraham Hicks

"You are an extension of Source-Energy having a human experience." – Abraham Hicks

Most people think that we are mortal, physical beings who are having some kind of a spiritual experience. But in order to begin reclaiming your creative power you have to acknowledge the fact that we are eternal, spiritual beings who are having a brief human experience. Notice even how we refer to ourselves as human beings; not physical objects. We are living *beings*; not things. The clues to our nature, and what we're really like are right under our noses. Yet most of us remain ignorant our entire lives–we go to our graves without ever realising who we really are. Of course a great place to start is by internalising the fact that we are beings; that we are living consciousness; that we are life itself; and that we are eternal. We are not our conditions and circumstances. We are not our thoughts and feelings. We are not our bank accounts, status, achievements, and material possessions. We are not our sex, nationality, or skin colour. We are not our name, and certainly not our body.

Everything that we see is an expression of this great power, and it is *this* power that we are all working with. This power which created the Universe and everything else in it; this power which keeps our planet spinning in its orbit in perfect proximity to other planets; this power which keeps beating our heart, circulating blood through our veins, and is operating all of our internal bodily functions, it is *this* power which is continuously flowing to and through us, and it never stops flowing. Sometimes (virtually all of the time) we just have our "blinders" on, so we don't even get to see, or recognise our intimate relationship to this great power.

But we can begin to pull down these blinders simply by detaching from all of the noise and hustle of our everyday life from time to time, and asking ourself the question: "Who am I?" Whenever you do this and really ponder that question, you are bound to realise that your body is something that you have. That your name, your brain, your limbs, your conditioning, your feelings, your thoughts and beliefs are not *you*; they are merely things you *have*. And when it comes to "you" who is it that we are referring to? Who are *you*? If you are not your name, brain, thoughts, sex, or body, then obviously you are something bigger than all of those things; something intangible that *possesses* those things. In effect, all of those surface layer aspects define us as individuals. However, deep down at our core we are all essentially the same and, in fact connected, because we all come from the same source.

Since we are unable to experience another person's point of awareness it gives off an illusion that people (as well as animals and other lifeforms) are separated from each other. But the truth is everything is an expression of the same consciousness. The only difference is in levels of expression–or in other words–levels of consciousness. For example, a cow has more life force than a caterpillar because its nervous system is significantly more complex. A hawk has more life force than a chicken. A human has more life force than a monkey. Yet it is the exact same life force which animates all of them. The difference is that the beasts of our planet are in what is called a *simple* state of consciousness. They do not possess an intellect; they do not have the ability to think, or rationalise. They cannot become aware of themselves, because animals don't have the conscious part of the mind which would allow them the capability to perceive the environment around them, as well as within them subjectively. In effect, unlike humans, animals operate primarily by instinct. For instance, when a domestic cat gets hungry, she knows that she's hungry, but she doesn't know that she knows it. That is why each time you are trying to put food into your cat's bowl, rather than waiting for you to finish, she instead impatiently tries to push her face into it. Why? Because the cat doesn't know that she's supposed to wait, and that she's not going to starve to death one minute from now. All that she can do is follow her instinct, and her instinct is telling her: "You are hungry. Find food, now!"

Although animals are extremely aware of their surroundings–their outside world–which makes it possible to train them to behave in certain ways, still they are unable to consciously and mentally go inside of themselves and look at their inner world, and think: "Who am I? Why am I doing this? Why do I feel like this?" You'll never see a dog salivating and then becoming self-conscious about it: "Oh no, I am dribbling again. I am such a mess. What is wrong with me?" as it tucks its tail between its legs and walks off in shame. Likewise, since an animal does not have the ability to rationally *think* about its behaviour is exactly the reason why animals are inherently dangerous.

What is different about human beings, on the other hand, is that we are in what is called a *self-conscious* state. We are completely aware of our objective, as well as subjective worlds. Unlike animals, we have been gifted with an intellect. Therefore, we have the creative ability to operate with our higher, mental faculties. Precisely for this reason, whenever you get hungry, you know that you are hungry, and you also know that you know. And although your instinct is telling you: "You are very hungry, just get the food into you now!" through the use of your intellect you are able to stop yourself from pushing your face into the food while it is being prepared, and wait. In effect, because you have direct access to the conscious part of your mind, you therefore have the ability to override your instinct by rationally thinking and coming to a conclusion that you are not going to starve to death five minutes from now. Obviously we humans are far more complex and more consciously aware than our animal friends. Though be that as it may, still we're all expressions of the same life force, which could be described as *consciousness*.

This difference in conscious awareness between animals and humans is also the reason why you can be your true, silly, totally weird self around an animal, but significantly less so around your fellow humans. The presence of an animal or a human baby does not intimidate you in the slightest, because their state of consciousness is pure and non-judgemental. (An animal doesn't have an intellect, which would grant it an ability to compare, assess, analyse, rationalise, and ultimately judge. Whereas a baby's intellect has not yet been developed, therefore, it too cannot judge.) Because you know that babies and animals are unable to look at themself and their outside world subjectively–meaning that they cannot judge and laugh at you when you say or do something dumb–that is the reason why you simply don't care and you feel completely at ease acting a fool around them.

"The only thing about a man that is a man… is his mind. Everything else you can find in a pig, or a horse." – Archibald MacLeish

By observing the animal kingdom it becomes evident that animals feel completely at home in their environment–they blend in; they know exactly what to do and how to behave. Whereas humans are completely disoriented, because we have the ability to create our *own* environment. We humans have been gifted with an intellect. We have at our disposal higher, creative, mental faculties, which are: imagination; reason; memory; intuition; perception; and will. And the way we use our intellect determines our emotional state. While the emotional state that we are in determines how we behave. Which naturally follows that if we are in control of our emotions then we are in control of our behaviour, and therefore in control of our lives. (More clarification on this later.) We truly are creative beings in charge of our own world, simply by virtue of the fact that we're free to think and feel whatever it is that we choose. Through the use of our mental faculties we get to choose whatever it is we wish to become. For instance, you might know a person who embodies characteristics of a compliant and obedient sheep who readily follows orders and blindly conforms to other people's standards and rules, who is afraid of conflict, and who tiptoes through life without making too much noise. And you might also know a person who embodies characteristics of a lone wolf, who lives life on the edge, who follows his/her own standards, who feels totally free, and who does whatever the hell he/she wants. And it all depends on how one chooses to use his/her intellect.

When it comes to misuse of our creative abilities, Abraham Hicks had told us–on numerous occasions–the following: "*Before you came into this physical body and into this physical life experience you all said, 'I will be a deliberate creator of my own experience, and I will enjoy my creations.' And the Source-Energy part of you said, 'We will offer you this energy which creates worlds whenever you are flowing it productively.'*" And that perfectly explains why we are such inept creators. Because when we feel sad, when we yearn for something, when we feel doubtful, insecure, unhappy, ungrateful, afraid, ashamed, guilty, or angry–when we feel a negative emotion of any kind–we are not in our place of power; we are not plugged into the stream of our Source. And although Source is always flowing to and through us, it cannot help or be of any real value to us in such instances, because we are vibrating and dwelling on lower frequencies where Source never goes. The frequency of Source is high! Vibrations of empowerment, ecstasy, love, happiness, joy, appreciation, gratitude, confidence, contentment, peace–and the like–are the kind of vibrations that are guaranteed to connect us to this creative power. The fact is, all humans are born with an inherent understanding of these principles, but what typically happens is we get punished out of this powerful emotional stance. We become conditioned to think that feeling amazing by default–and for no apparent reason–is not normal. And that in this harsh, chaotic, and unforgiving world of ours we have to struggle, suffer, and work hard to earn it.

However, if you look at a baby, babies are born in a brilliant vibration. They are totally alive; they feel invincible; they believe they can do anything. Babies are completely open, and are ready to learn. They are ready for us to teach them how powerful they really are, and encourage their creativity. But the trouble is that a baby's intellect does not develop right away. That's why a baby is at the complete mercy of her environment for a number of years to come. Which is a real shame because even if a child feels that some of the information about herself and her world is wrong or counterproductive–that it absolutely contradicts her godly nature–she nonetheless *has* to accept that information and eventually start to believe it. On average, for the first six years of life kids do not have significant enough access to mental faculties which would allow them to think critically; to rationalise; or to discard information and reject ideas that do not serve them. For this reason, children are extremely impressionable; any idea can be planted into their minds–be they positive or negative. Sadly, I have yet to meet a person whose parents taught them to believe that they could be, do, and have anything they set their mind to; that they are the creator of their own experience; that they have infinite potential; that they are eternal beings; and that perfect health and abundance–in all areas of life–is their birthright.

So what does typically gets planted into a child's mind, when the mind of a child does not have the ability to defend itself yet? Everything that was planted into the minds of her parents, and her parents' parents. Not to mean that anything is wrong with that *per se*, for if parents do decide to plant some good, positive seeds of encouragement, unconditional love, creativity, and a healthy dose of curiosity, then that is all well and good. Yet it is very painful for me to watch majority of parents interact with their kids. I always seem to hear things along the following lines: "You can't go up there! Get down! No! Don't touch that! Put it down! Be quiet! Shut up! Sit down! Listen to me! Do what I tell you!" And all of this dense, controlling energy is being directed at little kids. Not knowing that their child's undeveloped mind interprets those words as: "Okay, it seems that my parents only love me when I do exactly as they say. I have to be more careful now. I must forget about my uniqueness and creativity before it gets me into trouble, and just try to fit in. I better stop trying to be different and be more like everyone else–that feels safe. Because when I see negative reactions coming from my parents, I feel like they don't love me. And if my parents stop loving me, that means they could abandon me. If they choose to abandon me, I will not survive, because I'm not able to take care of myself just yet."

The Meaning

Since a child's level of awareness is extremely limited and their faculties are undeveloped, children have no other choice but to comply, and conform to their parents' limitations of the mind, which they have inherited from the previous generation. Consequently–though, for the most part without meaning to–most parents end up raising standard children (relative to their truly unbounded potential). Of course, most parents are well-meaning. Their approach to raising children comes from a natural place of trying to keep them out of harm's way in this sometimes "brutally unforgiving world." However, more often than not it backfires. Overprotective parents tend to think that in order to raise happy, mentally healthy, successful, and confident children, they must never be exposed to any stressful situations, so that they don't become traumatised, or scarred for the rest of their life. But there simply has to be a balance between keeping them safe and secure, while also helping them develop mental/emotional strength. For depriving a child of any challenges, negative emotions, and even physical pain–while showering them with love and reassurance–breeds an unrealistic view in the child's mind as to how the world *actually* works. You know that a child's life will undoubtedly be filled with all kinds of mistakes, losses, failures, heartaches, break-ups, rejections, unmet expectations, pains, and upsets. As a grown adult, you know full well that that is inevitable. And if you are trying to shield (keep away) your child from all of that–giving the false impression that none of it is even a possibility–then when those experiences eventually do occur, the now-grown adult will be ill-prepared, and will have no clue as to how to deal with it.

Therefore, a much better way of raising your child to be healthy–both in mind and spirit–is to give your child freedom to explore. Which will invariably put your child at risk of getting hurt. But when your child actually does come face-to-face with a particular situation, or problem that is causing them mental, emotional, or physical distress, all you have to do is teach your child that the challenge, or problem at hand is temporary; that it will be resolved; that the physical hurts and negative emotions are never permanent, and are not necessarily bad. In other words, rather than following your initial, motherly instinct and immediately running to your child's rescue–wrapping your angel wings around them and alleviating the pain–teach them to be more resilient instead. Teach them how to bounce back and recover from emotional or mental distress, so that they will grow into kind of people who can handle pressure, criticism, failure, loss, defeat, and whatever else life decides to hurl at them. That way your children will have the biggest chance at creating the type of lives that mentally sharp and emotionally secure adults tend to enjoy.

Chances are you can relate to having your creativity, as well as freedom of expression completely sucked out of you by the time you've reached your late teens. And if that is the case, do not be alarmed. For you are not a helpless child anymore. You do not have to allow your past to dictate the quality of your life experience today. Through the proper use of your mental faculties (which, typically by the age of twenty-one are fully developed) you can heal your past traumas, form new beliefs, build a new, powerful self-image, and create a brand-new identity. But in order to reclaim your creative power you must accept a simple–yet powerful–truth that you came into this physical life experience from Source-Energy. And that Source-Energy part of you is still flowing through you while you are having your experience. But what is the significance of this? It means that the power, or intelligence which created our Universe–along with every other minute and intricate detail, which makes everything work in perfect order–is at your service. You have direct access to this intelligence, and you have the ability–through the use of your intellect–to direct this energy towards the manifestation of anything you seriously want in your life. Be it the state of your physical body, an empowering self-image, a successful business, or a harmonious relationship.

Yes, you are limited (to an extent) in terms of what you can do with this creative power on planet Earth (in Abraham Hicks' words: "*You are not able to scrape enough dirt to mold together a planet and launch it into orbit*"). But, even though it may seem as if you exist primarily on a physical plane; you are not your physical body. Your physical body is just an instrument. And as a matter of fact, it is a perfect instrument for Source-Energy, God-Force, Spirit, or Infinite Intelligence to express itself through. In effect, what you really are is a powerful creator who is eternal; not a weak mortal who is at the mercy of life's conditions and circumstances. (I feel that I must clarify something important in case some of you are becoming confused. When I mention Source-Energy, God-Force, Spirit, or Infinite Intelligence throughout this book, I am talking about the same power–we can even call it God. I'm only using different names where I see they fit best just for the convenience of it. I put forth a great effort in avoiding the label "God" because there are too many limiting connotations and misrepresentations that are associated with it at this point.)

In spite of the fact that your ability to manifest in the physical format is limited by time and space, you are still more than capable of accomplishing unfathomable feats which nobody else thought were possible. With the right frame of mind–unwavering faith and determination–you can't fail. Nobody in the world really knows what you are capable of accomplishing, or becoming. Since you have infinite potential locked up within you, it is impossible to measure infinity and put a ceiling on it. This creative life force–that is always flowing to and through you–forever wants you to grow; it wants you to share your gifts; it wants you to develop new talents and abilities; it wants you to set new and higher goals. And when you get there (when you achieve this or that), it wants you to go further still; it wants you to become all that you are capable of becoming. In fact, you can't avoid your own growth, it is inevitable. The mere act of living life causes you to want to be, do, and have more than what already is. Because every time you reach a goal, or arrive at a new destination, you access a new (and different) vantage-point (to borrow Abraham Hicks' verbiage), from which new desires are immediately born.

You can think of this process in the following way: Imagine walking into a tall building and looking out of the ground floor window, from which the view is rather uninspiring. All that you are able to see is that which your current position allows you to see. So then a natural desire to see more gets born within you, and you decide to move up to the 10th floor. When you arrive at the 10th floor you realise that there is much more to see than you had previously thought. And that inspires you to move up even higher, maybe to the 30th floor. And when you arrive at the 30th floor you realise how much more there is to explore, and that thought yet again inspires you to move up even higher, maybe all the way up to the roof. When you get to the roof you are aghast at the sight of all the possibilities which lie across the landscape, and that inspires you to want to see even more. In effect, as you are moving up the floors, each new level invariably expands your horizons and inspires a new vision or goal within you. However, this metaphorical building which you are navigating in your current physical life experience does not have a roof. Which means that there will *always* be something else for you to "see."

You have to quit holding yourself back from the natural unfoldment of your desires. You have to stop resisting your evolution and sabotaging your development with self-doubt and unbelief. When you resist growth in any area of your life you become complacent and comfortable with where you're at. Which is ultimately where uneasiness, discomfort, dissatisfaction, and all kinds of negative emotions come from. It is effectively God's way of saying to you: "You better pick yourself up and get something done: achieve something, or become someone. Otherwise, if everyone decides to do what you're doing, then all of this will soon come to an end." Never-ending desire of all species–even single-celled organisms–is the driving force behind life and it is the reason why our Universe continues to expand, and therefore exist.

In a certain way of looking at it, what happens when you become complacent is you develop an internal tug of war between your higher, spiritual self–that part of you which forever wants to grow, produce, expand, and express itself–and your lower, physical self, which only cares about your survival: your DNA. You have to understand that when you are in a situation where you have easy access to shelter, food and water, your DNA is happy. If you are comfortable with where you're at, your DNA doesn't want you to make changes, it doesn't want you to take risks, and it doesn't give a damn about you being happy. As long as you are alive, as long as you have food and a comfortable home, then from the point of view of your DNA you are all good–you are winning! Even if you are alone in the immediate environment–especially now that we have access to Internet porn at a click of a button–your DNA still thinks that you're sexually active; that you are reproducing. All your DNA cares about is that you survive and reproduce. It doesn't care about your happiness, evolution, aspirations, hopes and dreams. So for the sake of your happiness, as well as mental/emotional health, you have to let go of the need for safety and begin thinking *beyond* your survival.

The problem is that our modern world is structured in such a way as to incentivise masses to fit in; to conform; to be like everyone else; to not stand out and make waves; to not think outside the box and blindly accept the status quo. This is the main reason why so many people in the world–who conform to society's standards–become totally unhappy with their lives. That is because it is not in our nature to fit in; it is not in our nature to be like everybody else. Every single person is unique. Each person has different thoughts, beliefs, perspectives, views, tastes, etc. To conform and follow the herd may be the most logical thing to do in the animal world, but never for human beings because all of us live in our own unique little worlds inside of ourselves. Even though we share one and the same world which we live in physically, it still doesn't change the fact that our inner worlds are never alike.

By recognising this simple truth it becomes a no-brainer as to why there are so many individuals who are unhappy and frustrated with their lives today. They constantly have problems with their health and find themselves in toxic relationships, they hate their jobs, they are completely enslaved by other people's opinions–their approval and disapproval–and they are completely lost with respect to what they are supposed to be doing with their lives. In effect, rather than living their lives as individuals and creating unique identities for themselves, most people simply cave in to the pressure of taking on the identity of whatever the group/class/culture they are surrounded by.

Because we get socially conditioned to do what everybody else is doing from an early age, we never even get the chance to discover our true selves, as well as what it is that *we* want. We merely imitate and copy what our parents are doing, what our neighbours are doing, and what our friends are doing. And we do this by instinct in order to preserve social stability and familiarity. But why? Because it seems scary trying to accomplish something that hasn't been done before. It seems scary leaving the herd behind and venturing out on our own. It seems scary going against social norms and expressing ourselves freely for fear of being ostracised. It seems scary grabbing life by the horns and going after the things we really want for fear that we might fail. It seems scary trying to take on a leading role and assume full responsibility for our lives out of fear of going down the "wrong" path.

However, we simply must develop courage and push beyond our comfort zone, because if we don't, then we are destined to continue to get what we have always been getting, which is not much. This tendency to fit in has a very strong influence on humans; it is engrained in our DNA. We are so afraid to be exiled from the group that we'll go above and beyond to avoid criticism, ridicule, and scrutiny. Granted, our ancestors who lived in tribes absolutely had to follow strict rules and adapt to social norms of the band. Because if they got themselves kicked out, then that meant certain death, as they would not have been able to survive all by themselves in the wild. That survival mechanism is still very much active within each and every human being alive today (for a good reason too). That's why we get the same traumatic thoughts, feelings of fear, and images of our reputation (and our lives) getting completely destroyed when others don't accept us. For example, you can feel this mechanism at work when you're sitting in a quiet classroom full of students, and the teacher asks you to stand up to answer a question, while every head in the room turns and stares at you. In that very moment you are probably experiencing the exact same emotions as if somebody just pointed a loaded gun at your head. The reason for this is that your DNA thinks that by not giving the correct answer, or by being perceived by your peer group in a negative way, then you will get kicked out from the tribe and die alone a miserable death.

If we are ever to become deliberate creators of our own reality who lead happy, meaningful lives, we absolutely have to get over this fear because we literally don't live in tribes anymore. Today this mechanism is close to obsolete. That is, we no longer need protection from a pack of wolves that are circling our tent. We no longer need to worry about whether or not we will eat tonight. We no longer need social alliances that include people with different skills. For in today's world, we can hire somebody else to do our bidding. In other words, we will not die if people don't accept us, laugh at us, reject us, or think we are complete and utter idiots. Our tribe is no longer made up of a few hundred people. Today, our tribe consists of billions of people, most of whom are approachable, helpful, and civilised.

It is a given that when you are being your authentic self, and are confidently going after all the things you want–without the slightest need for other people's approval–there will always be those who dislike you, ignore you, and avoid you. But so what? You are not going to die, or wind up alone. The truth of the matter is by being yourself and sticking to your guns, even in the face of strong opposition, you are bound to alienate a lot of people, but invariably attract those who get you, who are on the same wavelength as you, and who love you for who you are. Conversely, if you're constantly trying to adapt to other people–always going along with whatever it is that they think and want–then you'll find millions who like you with minimal effort. However, chances are great that none of those people will be madly in love with you, and be ready to fight for you and everything you stand for.

Nowadays people are so afraid to be alone that they turn themselves into social chameleons who openly agree and go along with certain ideas (that even contradict their own personal values) while they interact with one particular person, but then turn around–and without hesitation–immediately go along with a completely opposing set of ideas while they interact with a different person. People in the world today seem to have no problem abandoning their own beliefs and values for the sake of being liked by someone who they themselves might not even like. And I am not trying to belittle anybody here, because we've all been there at one point or another. For whatever reason, humans tend to develop egos that like to derive their sense of self from other people. Our job, however, as fully developed and self-aware adults is to recognise whether or not we are in the grips of our egos. And if we find that to be the case, then we have to commit to leaving those egos behind. Because egos–by their very nature–do not accept themself as they are, and for that reason they are ineffective, fragile, unstable, and ultimately weak.

So rather than feeding our ego (a mental construct that is impossible to please), how about we become friends with our "real self"–our higher-self–instead? Our higher-self is powerful, confident, loving, and stable. It knows our inherent value, and it does not deviate from that knowing regardless of what is going on externally. Even if we are alone and are hated by everyone we know, even if we are deprived of the entire world's love and approval, it still doesn't affect the way that we feel about ourself. For unlike the ego, our higher-self is self-sustaining; it gives love and approval from itself to itself.

Steven Pressfield, the author of a phenomenal book called "The War of Art" (which I highly recommend) stated the following with regard to this issue: *"The human being isn't wired to function as an individual. We are wired tribally; to act as part of the group. Our psyches are programmed by millions of years of hunter-gatherer evolution. We all know what the clan is; we know how to fit into the band and the tribe. What we don't know is how to be alone. We don't know how to be free individuals."* In my personal opinion the mark of a self-empowered individual who knows what it means to be free, is one who can be completely comfortable with himself, all by himself, and be alone without actually feeling lonely. It is one who no longer needs anybody to validate his self-worth and approve of his character. And it is one who can entertain himself without the company of others, or any external stimulation, because he has learnt to generate good emotions from within himself. Ultimately, accepting yourself and becoming comfortable in your own body, as well as learning not to care about what other people think of you–to a point that it stifles your freedom of expression–is going to be the biggest step you take towards unleashing the creative genius that lies within.

YOUR CREATIVE POWER

"The only limits we have are the ones we impose on ourselves." – Bob Proctor

Let us now take a closer look at this creative power and see how we can better utilise it to help us accomplish whatever it is that we're after. If you have heard the story of Thomas Edison's light bulb invention, then you know that it took Edison thousands of tries to perfect the incandescent light. But, does that mean that Edison failed thousands of times before his idea came to fruition? Well, the way that he chose to interpret the whole situation was that he merely ruled out thousands of ways which didn't work. What a powerful reframe of a seemingly hopeless situation that is. If he had stopped on his 100th attempt, accepted defeat and told himself: "Well, I've honestly tried, I guess it just doesn't work," then today, we would most likely still be using candles as the only viable source of light. Truly, thousands of failed attempts is more than enough to discourage most people from continuing to pursue whatever it is that they are trying to accomplish. Fortunately, Edison never considered failure as an option, which resulted in him drawing solutions, ideas, and images directly from the source which has all of the answers. Now, in so far as trying to understand how we too can create things in our life, we first have to determine whether Edison had managed to create something out of nothing, or did he merely become *aware* of something that was already here?

"Believe and your belief will create the fact." – William James

"If you can believe, all things are possible to him who believes." – Mark 9:2

In the vibrational (spiritual) reality everything already exists, and everything is already done. With respect to the light bulb invention, all of the resources, materials, and ways of getting it done have always been here. Edison simply happened to be that person who became aware of how to put it all together. In other words, Edison did not conjure up something which didn't previously exist, and thus introduced a new idea (manifestation) into the Universe. A fully functioning light bulb have always existed, albeit only as a "potential" or "possibility." It was only waiting for someone to become aware of how to turn it into its fully manifested form. Think of it in the following way: everything that we could possibly imagine already exists in a vibrational form in a non-physical dimension of infinite possibility. And humans (creative beings) have the creative ability–with the power of "thought"–to reveal more of the "stuff" which this infinite possibility has in store. In effect, whatever it is that you want to be, do, and have is already here–albeit in an energetic form–it is just waiting for you to align with that energy and bring it into reality.

"The creation waits in eager expectation for the sons of God to be revealed."
– Romans 8:19

Source-Energy is all-knowing; it knows what we want, what we require, and what we are looking for, even without our need to utter a word. So if there is something in particular that we are trying to achieve, Source will guide us to the answers which we are looking for, in such a way that we'll be able to see them, and grasp them. However, only when we are tuned in to the right frequency long enough are we able to receive the various impulses that are being offered to us. Source is unable to reveal anything when we are dwelling on lower frequencies–where Source never goes. Source is inherently focused on the solution, and if we are focusing on the problem–and we are under the influence of that vibration–then we are operating on a frequency where none of the answers can ever be found. In order to get whatever it is we want, we have to get on the same frequency as "that" which we are looking for is on, and begin to offer all of our thoughts, feelings, and actions as we move towards it from that vibrational standpoint. Doing so ensures that Source will continue to lead us in the right direction by offering to us thoughts and impulses to go *there*, to say *this*, to do *that*, to avoid *this*, until what it is we want manifests in the physical reality in the quickest time frame possible. Now, in no way am I suggesting that things will begin to magically fall out of the sky right onto your lap, or spontaneously appear before your eyes. Rather, what might happen is you will get a hunch, or idea so strong that you cannot help but act on it immediately. Or a particular picture might flash on the screen of your mind, that'll remind you of something, or make you feel a certain way, and prompt you to take a certain action. You may see something in a dream (which feels totally different from all of the other random, ordinary dreams), and when you wake up from it you'll know exactly what you have to do. Or maybe a new person will show up in your life who has absolutely nothing to do with your desire, but who will introduce you to someone who does.

Nobody really knows in which way the Universe is trying to guide and delight you all day, every day, and it is not your job to try and figure it out either. Your only work is to have faith (faith that is based on understanding) and continue to expect that whatever it is you are looking for will eventually show up in your life, and it will. However, if for whatever reason you fall off your higher frequency (by giving in to self-doubt; by not seeing any immediate change or progress, and giving up; by not trusting the process; by getting distracted and sidetracked, etc.), then you will not be able to see the answers which you are seeking, at least for the time being. But not because the power had stopped working, or had abandoned you. (This power is always working. You will never shut down the workings of this power. The process of "revealing" never stops.) It's just that the vibration of a problem/question and a solution/answer are two different vibrations. And what comes to you is always determined by which vibration is active within you the most. So if what you want isn't coming you just have to examine where your focus predominantly lies. In that, are you expecting it to happen, or are you thinking about all of the reasons why it won't happen?

When you find yourself dwelling on lower frequencies–by entertaining negative thoughts; by worrying and doubting; by ranting and raving about how life is unfair, and how real the struggle is–you unwittingly put yourself into a "holding pattern" (to lend Abraham Hicks' terminology) where there is no divine guidance, and no magic. Why? Because the vibration of Source, and the vibration which you are currently in, are no longer in resonance–not in harmony–and therefore completely oblivious to one another. It would be as if somebody behind you were trying to get your attention by screaming at you, all the while you had your earphones in on full blast. So what you must do is take off your metaphorical earphones (adjust/shift your vibration), and allow yourself to hear (receive) what is being offered (revealed) to you.

An example of someone who were willing to listen and continue to "receive" until their desire came to fruition were the Wright brothers. Long before Orville and Wilbur Wright began working on the project, building a flying machine was something that humans all over the world have been trying to accomplish for centuries. However, despite the many efforts made by top professionals, scientists, and engineers, it was no easy task. Of course, as we have already determined, the way to do anything is already here. And so the Wright brothers simply happened to be the ones who managed to put all of the pieces together back in 1903. All the while everybody else around them thought that they were crazy; that such a feat was not possible for them, because they were mere bicycle mechanics–what the hell did they know about aviation and aerodynamics? Evidently, Wright brothers were not dissuaded by what other people thought about what they were doing. The difference in attitude was that the Wright brothers were inspired by their vision while the sceptics were paralysed by the precedent. In effect, most people will not believe anything until it is complete; until they can see it in its fully manifested form. Whereas the geniuses of our world begin with a clear vision/image in their mind, and then backwards engineer until that vision becomes a reality.

Average people are so encumbered by their limitations of the mind that they don't even bother to look for solutions and possibilities, and as a result they never find them. The Wright brothers, however, were brave enough to expand their mind beyond what already was, and began working with their creative faculty of imagination–where they could actually see themselves flying. Consequently, Source began offering them impulses and all kinds of solutions for the realisation of that vision. Sure, they did fail a bunch of times, but they never stopped believing in their vision, and therefore persisted. The road to their eventual success involved a ton of trial and error. But, like Edison, they knew that failure was simply part of the process. In the end, they did accomplish a first successful flight in a self-propelled aircraft–a heavier-than-air machine–which stayed in the air for twelve seconds, and in subsequent runs for almost a minute. What a great result! And building upon that success, today we have planes that fly hundreds of miles per hour, for many hours on end across the globe. Granted, there was more to it than pure imagination, still, it does go to prove that whenever a person is inspired by a vision–rather than thinking within the parameters of what already is–that person gains access to all of the resources necessary to take that vision and turn it from a mere concept into a concrete fact.

It truly doesn't matter if what you wish to achieve hasn't been done before, and it doesn't matter if other people don't believe in your vision either. If you can imagine it, and if you yourself can believe in it, then you will get it done. By watching and studying those who have used their creative faculties for all sorts of achievements in their life (things that were previously considered impossible) can encourage all of us to quit deriving our sense of what is possible by looking at history–letting it dictate what can and cannot be done. It can help us recognise that we are all working with the exact same power, and with equal amount. It is only a matter of how far we're willing to take it. And that, in effect, the so-called geniuses of our world have/had no more of this power than you and I, and realise that we too can make history.

"This great power is in no way limited by the precedent, or by what has gone on before." – Bob Proctor

A perfect example of somebody willing to make history was Karl Benz. Karl Benz invented the first self-propelled vehicle (an automobile) in 1885. Again, the fact that there were no horseless carriages at the time, everybody around Benz thought that he was out of his mind for trying to invent something that would drive by itself. You can only imagine the amount of pressure and ridicule that he was subjected to while working on his vision. It must have been extremely discouraging and mentally exhausting, so much so that I am willing to bet that many in Benz's position would have caved in to the pressure and folded their hands. It has been reported that in an attempt to remove at least some of the pressure and ridicule Karl Benz would take his creation out for a test-drive late at night, when everybody else were fast asleep. And understandably so. For Benz was trying to accomplish something that was considered a pipe dream–pure fantasy. However, through the proper use of his mental, creative faculties his fantasy eventually did become a fact. Karl Benz absolutely believed that it was possible–he kept his faith. He utilised his creative faculty (the will) to concentrate on the higher objective (his vision); rather than becoming immobilised by concentrating on a lower concern (people's opinions). And in the end, his idea (fantasy) did become a reality. This particular achievement once again proved to us–mere mortals–that the Universe will reward anyone for their unwavering faith and perseverance.

Another great example is a British athlete, Roger Bannister who had accomplished a feat which people have been trying to complete for thousands of years: to run a mile in under 4 minutes. Such a feat seemed so utterly unattainable that the "experts" had to conclude that it was impossible; that the human anatomy wasn't built for it; that it could never be done. However, in 1954, Roger Bannister came along and he did run a mile in under 4 minutes. But how could this be? Everyone knew for a fact that it was impossible, how the hell did he do it? Well, it seems that Roger Bannister did not put his faith in the experts, and instead completely and utterly believed in himself. It has been reported that in preparation for the event he regularly envisioned himself accomplishing the feat in his mind. So much so, that he became absolutely certain he was going to do it.

Through the use of imagination Roger Bannister convinced himself, as well as his body that the feat was possible for him. Even without any real evidence, or actual proof that he was going to succeed, he ran a mile in under 4 minutes. Now, a peculiar thing about this particular breakthrough is the fact that within a short period of time (a few weeks) other athletes began to run a 4-minute mile, and even a few high-school students. How come? Did everyone suddenly acquire more strength and physical prowess? Or did the laws of physics and gravity suddenly change? I don't think so. What happened is that a new standard was set. Roger Bannister's success became the proof that other people needed for their own success. Not realising that they didn't actually need the proof. Because like Roger Bannister, what they really needed was imagination and belief. But, being the humans that we are, we first have to see something–which has never been done before–be completed by somebody else before we can believe it to be possible. And because we start to believe, often times we too end up accomplishing that very same feat.

Essentially, the key takeaway from all of the above examples is that everything you want to be, do, and have is already here. You can seriously have anything you want, but only if you dare to believe in your fantasy, and trust that the Universe will help you turn it into a fact. Understand that if you are able to imagine a particular "something" in your mind's eye, it follows that the Universe has the wherewithal to deliver it to you. You simply wouldn't be able to form an image, or idea of something that couldn't be done. Another way of saying this is that if you can see something in your mind, then you can be sure that you can hold it in your hands. Do not be afraid to be the first who sets the standard. When you get that sinking feeling that you cannot do something, realise that it is only a reflection of your old conditioning; not of your potential. If you can form an idea in your mind, and if you can imagine what it would be like to have it, then that's a clear indication that it is possible for you. And in order to receive that which you have envisioned, all what you must do is begin to move towards it with unwavering faith that you can have it, and take appropriate action with an expectant attitude.

"We are only limited by weakness of attention and poverty of imagination."
– Neville Goddard

"Whatever the mind of man can conceive and believe, it can achieve."
– Napoleon Hill

If nothing is created or destroyed, and if everything is already done–it is only waiting to be revealed–then what else are we not aware of? What else is out there in the ether, ready to be picked up by somebody willing to dream and imagine? I think it is a good question to ask ourselves from time to time. And to put this question into practical use in your day-to-day life, begin by asking yourself: "What is a better way to utilise my free time? What is a better way to improve the quality of my relationships? What is a better way to do what I do professionally? What is a better way to serve others? What is a better way to raise my children?" Whatever problems, or issues that you are currently facing, you can begin to ask Source for solutions in the form of intentions. In other words, do not try to communicate to Source-Energy with your words (though you can if you wish, as long as your intentions are congruent to what you are saying), because Source is not hearing your words; it only responds to how you *feel*. When you are wanting to implement certain changes in your life, or are attempting to accomplish something that you really want, your words are not at all necessary. You just need to acknowledge what it is you want, really think about how you would like things to be, and then begin to offer all of your thoughts, feelings and actions as if it is already yours. The fundamental keys to creation is you have to believe, and expect.

By assuming an expectant attitude–knowing for certain that it is only a matter of time until you find whatever it is you are seeking–you trigger the powerful Law of Attraction (which we will cover extensively in the 4th chapter) to work on your behalf. You begin to magnetise all of the people, situations, resources, circumstances, conditions and events into your life that will be responsible for producing the desired results you seek. It is so liberating to know that every single one of us has infinite potential, regardless of how dumb we've been taught to believe we are. We are all working with the exact same power, there are no exceptions. All of the power there is, ever was, or ever will be is simultaneously present in all places, at all times. It is available to you, me, and everyone else right now, and in every other moment. A human being is a perfect channel for the expression of this power. It is only a matter of tuning ourselves into the frequency of that power and working in harmony with it. No person has any more of this power than you, or anyone else. This power is 100 percent evenly present in all places, at all times. Nowhere does it state that it is present 20 percent in China, 50 percent in Britain, or 30 percent in a woman, and 70 percent in a man. No, it is 100 percent evenly present in all places at all times!

So get happy. Get excited. Become at peace with the way things are. Get in touch with your higher-self and start looking at your world through the eyes of Source. Nothing is ever wrong with you, or this world that you live in–that is the way Source sees me, you, our planet, and everything that goes on in it. This Intelligence did not make any rejects; it did not make any mistakes. Quit distracting yourself by all of the "wrongness" and "badness" going on in the world, and start creating. Yes, obviously our world is far from perfect, there is more than enough to be pissed off about, and that's perfect! There will always be challenges and struggles in your life and mine, which is absolutely fine. We must accept it for what it is and come to a place of non-resistance to this fact of life.

There is a great question that perfectly illustrates this point, which goes as follows: "Why do dogs risk getting dirt, bugs, and all kinds of crap flying into their eyes as they stick their heads out of car windows?" The answer is because having all this crap flying into their eyes is a small price to pay for the exhilaration of that ride. And that is exactly how we felt about life when we decided to come forth into this physical life experience. This is your life, and this is where it all happens. All sorts of crazy shit is going to happen in your life–that is a given–but it's all right. Because the experience of life itself ultimately outweighs all the pains, discomforts, and inconveniences (no matter how trivial or severe) that you may have to experience along the way.

Stuart Wilde, who was a brilliant spiritual teacher and author shines a light on this principle of non-resistance to "what-is" in his book (audiobook version) "Miracles." He pointed out the following: "*If we take a look into all of the peace movements, poverty movements, employment movements, protests against wars and drugs, it is easy to see that people are yearning and rushing for things, and what they are really saying is that the world is not okay.*" It goes without saying that most people resist the natural evolution of life, they have a difficult time accepting life for what it is at any particular moment in time, and they just want everything to be perfect right now! (On which frequency do you think they are operating when doing that?) If you convince yourself that the world is not okay, and you are devoting most of your focus and attention on all of the things that are going wrong, then you are not helping it to get better. For when you are focused in that way, you are not part of the solution. Because you are practicing–and thus–perpetuating the energy that *is* the problem.

Stuart further added: "*For you to have a transcendent lifestyle of true power where everything flows to you naturally, you have to see this world as already beautiful.*" In effect, if you want to see positive, long-term changes in the world, you will never make that change by forcing it (pushing and protesting). You can only achieve a long-lasting change from the place of power (understanding, influencing, and leading by example). He continued: "*A powerful person sees the world as already beautiful because he understands that inside the mayhem, inside the struggle, there are all sorts of growth experiences going on. Inside the difficulty, the famine, the wars, there is 'Man' struggling through his inadequacies to discover himself! And if God wanted to change the world I don't think that it would be a problem to infuse the minds of men full of pure, loving, positive, peaceful energy, along with a great sense of sharing and a profound sense of oneness so that every living person could have enough abundance. Yet God cannot infringe upon us for he allows everyone to come up gradually and understand these perceptions naturally.*"

If everything were already perfect, our evolution would suffer–it would be boring. Think about this. If everything was already perfect; if we already had everything that we ever needed; if there was nothing left for us to want and to create; nothing left to strive for and to desire, how utterly dull, uninteresting, and ho-hum of an existence would that be? You must be willing to see the world as divinely perfect the way that it is now. No one and no thing ever dies or gets destroyed; everything is only in the state of *becoming*. Everything that happens, happens for a reason–it has a greater purpose–even if your belief system, or sense perceptions tell you otherwise. The change will certainly happen; the change will come. The better days are on the horizon. We don't need to force it, and we don't need to rush for it frantically. Heaven on Earth is absolutely achievable, but it will take time. And that is really a good thing. We truly wouldn't want everything to be perfect now. Yes, there were times when we had to fight for our lives, scramble for limited resources and try to survive. However, we have evolved beyond that a long time ago, now it is perfect time for everyone to thrive!

We are sophisticated biological machines, full of creative potential, capable of incredible feats, but we are outdated machines. For we are still running around with the same ol psychological/biological programming which had been installed by our predecessors hundreds of thousands of years ago. The world is changing fast, make no mistake about that. These days we have to sprint to keep up; otherwise we will get left behind. We have to catch up and begin updating the software in our brain by developing an understanding of who we *really* are; not who our parents and social conditioning told us we are. It is about time we begin to raise our consciousness, and at long last come into our own personal power.

Stuart Wilde's philosophy asks that we think of God as consciousness, rather than a personality, because we are all part of that consciousness. If we continue to think of God as someone or something outside of ourselves, then what we are really saying is: "I do not control my life, some entity above me is controlling my life," and that's not a very powerful position for us to be in. When it comes to becoming aligned with this great power, Stuart Wilde had further advised: "*You need to internalise this God figure–this pure light of expansive energy–inside yourself. And once you do, you will no longer have to go by your religious practices, rules and limitations that are holding you back. The God-Force is impartial, it doesn't have emotions the way it portrays in the Bible–with God being pleased over here and angry over there. This God-Force which permeates all things is consciousness which has your evolution at heart, and it loves you because you are it and it is you. However, it is not intimately involved in how you are experiencing life (it doesn't mind whether you are happy or unhappy, because all experiences are valuable). And if you are able to pull out of this emotional (and judgemental) relationship with God, then you win back your power.*"

Source-Energy loves you so much that it accepts you for everything that you are, and all that you have become (that's what unconditional love truly is). Because you see, if Source-Energy were emotionally involved in your life then that would not have been complete acceptance would it? It would have been conditional. But the truth of the matter is that Source does not have any opinions or judgements about you whatsoever. I understand that at first this may seem as if Source doesn't care about your experience, or your evolution, but that would be wrong. What it actually means is that Source loves you so much that it allows you to take the time to become whatever it is you want. Source had given you complete freedom to experience the ups and downs of growth and evolution for yourself. And for that reason, Source could never decide anything for you. It granted you the ability to make decisions, along with all of the tools necessary to ensure that your decisions are sound.

Source is eternally walking your path with you; guiding you and supporting you. But you will always have the final word as to where you want to go, what you want to do, and what you want to become. Therefore, there is absolutely no need for you to suspect that you are being controlled by a higher entity like a puppet on a string, or that there is a grandiose plan–out there somewhere in the sky–already laid out for you, which you need to discover and then fulfil. So forget about trying to figure out what your destiny is. Let go of the need to try to find out what your spiritual quest is. You came here strictly for the experience, whatever that may mean for you. Everything that truly matters is naturally taken care of. Which means that there is nothing which you absolutely have to do, other than to live your life fully. There is no right or wrong when it comes to your personal life experience. Because every experience (positive or negative) contributes to your evolution, and to the expansion of the Universe. (More on this in the next chapter.)

Before we move on to the next epiphany, I would like you to accept the fact that something as wonderful as heaven is already here. And that something as horrible and insufferable as hell is also already here. The lowest frequency, the highest frequency and everything in-between is already here; all of it is available to us in every given moment. Good and bad–both of these worlds are readily available to us on the moment-by-moment basis. The only question we have to ask ourself is: "Which world are we choosing to experience?" Or more specifically: "Which frequency are we tuning ourself into?" To demonstrate how our own perception, and choices in attitude affects our state of being; our state of vibration–that determines which end of the spectrum we're setting ourself up to experience–I want you to imagine two people observing a beautiful fireworks show through the hotel window. Person (A) is enjoying the show, he is taking it all in, and he feels good about it. Person (B) however is also trying to enjoy the show, yet he cannot help but keep thinking about the smudge on the window which is in his field of view. And now this person is angry at the fact that he is unable to see the show properly through a nice, clean window–and he feels bad.

Now, let us examine what actually happened here. Both of these people are standing in the exact same place–next to each other–looking through the same window. However, all that person (A) sees is the beautiful show, even though the smudge is right there in his field of view, he doesn't even see it; his brain doesn't register the smudge; it completely ignores it. He is looking at the situation through the eyes of Source, which says: "I will not allow anything that's out of my control to dictate and potentially ruin how I'm feeling about these amazing fireworks." Whereas person (B) chooses to focus on the smudge; all what he sees is the smudge. He is looking at this situation from the perspective of his ego, which says: "I should always get what I want no matter what, because the world revolves exclusively around me. Why is this always happening to me?! I knew that we should've checked in to a different room!" And on and on those kinds of thoughts proliferate and dominate his mind to a point where the fireworks don't even matter anymore. All that this person really wants to do now is whine and complain.

Ergo, one person holds the truth that the show is actually quite impressive, meanwhile the other person holds the truth that it sucks. In this situation, which person do you think is right? What is the actual truth here? Well, the truth is, both of these people are right, in their own mind. Both of them are stating the truth–their truth. So what is the point? The point is that whatever you get to experience in your life is determined by where you choose to direct your focus. It is all about how you think. It is about your perspective. It is about your level of awareness. That is what's going to dictate your emotional state, as well as the degree of control of it you'll have. It is never about what's happening on the outside; you do create your own reality–your own heaven or hell so to speak. Your external reality only becomes what you unconsciously (and also consciously) project into it. Why else do you think that people who reside in the same town can live very different lives; walk down the same road and have different experiences; or observe the same event but see entirely different things? Because every person's perspective is unique. In effect, if what you're experiencing is something that you aren't able to enjoy, then by improving the quality of your thoughts, you will invariably improve the quality of your life experience as a result.

In conclusion: the answer to the question of the meaning of life (without it sounding cliché) is whatever you make of it. There is nothing in particular which you came here to accomplish–in terms of a test, a mission, or a quest. You didn't come here to suffer in hopes of achieving spiritual enlightenment in order to transcend the physical realm of existence and graduate to higher dimensions. Nothing of the sort is going on. You already are spiritually perfect; you already are whole and worthy. You chose to come here as an extension of the God-Force simply to create and to express yourself more fully in a physical format, purely for the joy of it, and for the fun of it. Your life experience can be likened to playing an instrument, or dancing–the point of it is expression. It isn't about hitting the last note, or move, for the sake of getting it over with–for the sake of getting it done. For the experience of life *is* the journey. The living of life *is* the meaning. It is that simple, albeit not easy.

In order to make life easier you just have to pay close attention and take in the lessons which life wants you to learn–before you can honestly begin to enjoy it–such as letting go of attachments. You must never base your sense of identity and self-worth on the material things that you have. For the material possessions are here today, and are gone by tomorrow. If your whole sense of self is derived from something external, then when that very thing inevitably makes its departure, what will be left of you? And so, in order to spare yourself the unnecessary hurt, you must accept that life is about moving forward; life is about change. You must come to terms with the fact that nothing stays the same for too long. And if you continue to cling on to something without allowing it to leave, or change, then you will be unapologetically punished for your ignorance. (More on this in the last chapter.)

Source wants you to be abundant. Source wants you to live in harmony with the ebbs and flows of life. Source wants you to grow and explore new possibilities. Source wants you to become all that you are capable of becoming. Due to this natural desire for continual growth, when you get stuck in a scarcity mindset–where you are clinging on to something for grim death–life is designed in such a way that it will continue to rip your attachments away from you (enough times) until you finally realise that it doesn't matter. Until you realise that it doesn't change or affect who you essentially are. Until you accept that when the things that you love get swept away by the currents of change, life should go on perfectly fine without them. So, rather than yearning, craving, and wanting something back–feeling sad about something that you've lost–instead, become more appreciative and grateful for the fact that it was in your life to begin with. Simply acknowledge all of the positive aspects regarding that person, object or condition which you've experienced in your life, and let it go. Because wanting things to stay the same–not wanting them to change, and resisting that change–is a lower form of consciousness which breeds endless pain and suffering.

Likewise, you have to learn to stop identifying with your thoughts that are generated from your false sense of self–or in other words–your ego. You have to realise that the reason why your life sucks is not because you are incompetent, or because you are not worthy of a good life, but because you are in the grips of your ego. That realisation should prompt you to put forth an effort to stop identifying with your thoughts, and perceiving reality through your self-image–the lens of your ego–and instead becoming more present to the moment. Once you get into the habit of being more present you will realise that most of the problems you think you have are actually not real problems, but mere mental projections of the egoic mind. Becoming more present to the moment will help you understand that you're not your petty, negative thoughts, that are sabotaging your happiness and ruining your life. Eckhart Tolle, a brilliant spiritual teacher says that what we are is a "witnessing consciousness" or conscious awareness behind our thoughts–we are the observers of our thoughts–but we are not our thoughts. And when you train yourself to disidentify from your mental chatter and start living from your heart, you become totally new and improved version of yourself for whom victimhood, defeat, and self-attack is no longer part of the experience.

Before we move on to the next epiphany what I would like you to take away from this chapter the most is the awareness of the fact that what you really are is pure consciousness–when you are not in a physical body–that is free of any resistance, judgements, and prejudice. A consciousness that is totally alive; completely fulfilled; full of love, potential, and creativity; has everything that it will ever need; is infinitely present; is eternal; and is complete. And while you are alive in the physical world, your main responsibility is to align with that consciousness, and direct its creative power into all that you do and come into contact with. When you begin to identify with that level of consciousness while you are alive in your physical body, then amazing, unimaginable, almost miracle-like situations and events will begin to take place all around you as you move through your life experience. And as you come to a realisation of just how pleasant and effortless your life can be–when you think and act under the influence of Source–you will no longer be willing to settle for anything less than that and the world becomes yours for the taking.

"One who is connected to Source is more powerful than millions who are not."
– Abraham Hicks

Purpose

"The meaning of life is to find your gift. The purpose of life is to give it away."
– Pablo Picasso

"Life is never made unbearable by circumstances, but only by a lack of meaning and purpose." – Viktor Frankl

It goes without saying that there are millions of people in the world who are having a terrible time trying to understand what it means to live life on purpose, so much so, that in the end they never end up doing anything productive. While some are completely unaware as to how to go about finding their purpose, others do not have a full understanding as to *why* they even should strive to live life on purpose. What you may already know about the idea of purpose is that having a sense of purpose gives your life meaning. That purpose provides you with a sense of direction in life. And that it allows you to strive towards something meaningful; something larger than yourself. And that would be correct. Having a strong sense of purpose in life is one of the major key elements on our journey to self-mastery, and shortly you will understand why it is important.

I have found that there are two pitfalls which people generally fall into when they set out to build meaningful and fulfilling lives. On one end of the spectrum there are those who are "living their purpose," but are not healthy, fulfilled, or happy. And whenever I see this, I always think to myself: "Really? How could you not be happy? You have all of the resources in the world, and all the freedom you want. Why do you continue to work yourself to exhaustion while putting your happiness on hold–never enjoying the results of your labour? You are forever stressed out, you are always tense, you are not laughing, you are under constant pressure, your health is deteriorating, and you are not at all enjoying the process." And what I've come to understand is that the reason why we do this to ourselves is because we believe that goals are to *get*. We believe that achieving goals is about getting them done, and checking them off our "list" without any consideration for joy along the way. When we set out to go after some of the things we want in life, we naturally start out feeling passionate and thrilled about what we are doing. However, somewhere down the road–as the terrain inevitably becomes a little rough– we forget that we were supposed to enjoy what we're doing, and it becomes more or less a burden which saps our energy. But, it doesn't have to be that way. We just have to remind ourself that we set goals in order to grow. That we actually want the emotions; the ups and downs; the highs and lows, that we get to experience along the way. Because that is what makes the end re-sult (whatever it is we are trying to accomplish) so good and meaningful.

For instance, imagine yourself planning a trip around the world, where you get to stop at various places and experience many of the beautiful land-scapes and vistas that our planet has to offer. But, instead of actually taking the trip, you say to yourself: "You know what, that sounds like a lot of work. Going on this trip means that I will have to do this thing and the other; go there and wait here; buy a ticket here and get a stamp there. Besides, my fi-nal destination is back at the house anyway, so why go if I'm already here?" But you don't ever say that do you? Because it is not about the destination. It is not about a few minor annoyances that you may have to experience along the way. You are fully aware that it's about the journey itself and the experi-ence that you get out of it. However, when it comes to our goals, we tend to think that it's somehow different.

Or imagine playing a video game in which you have to move through a number of different levels, where each new level becomes increasingly more difficult. As you manage to reach the last level and beat the final boss–finally finishing the game–it obviously feels good for a minute, and you feel a sense of accomplishment. But what follows immediately after is a sense of: "Well, it's done now. Now what?" And if you ask yourself: "What was the point? What did I enjoy the most?" and really think about that, you will realise that the point was to go through each and every level; to complete each challenge which prepared you for the next. And as you overcame each obstacle, that is when you felt the most engaged and energised. And by the end of it, the joy, and the excitement you felt–along with a real sense of accomplishment–was accentuated when you finally reached the end and have received the reward. But what would happen if you were to punch in a cheat code, right from the beginning which would allow you to immediately arrive at the last level and get your reward, watch the final cutscene, and finish the game without having to go through any of the challenges? In that case, you would have completed the game, sure, but it wouldn't mean anything. Yes, you would have accomplished something, and had the opportunity to experience the end result. However, there would be no context or references to back it up. In other words, there would be nothing there which would indicate that you are now a better person, or a better player in this particular example.

Likewise, you never go to the cinema to watch the ending of a particular movie and just get it over with; you go for the whole experience. For example, if you are watching "The Matrix" from the very beginning, and you get to watch Neo kicking ass at the very end of the movie–deflecting bullets, destroying the agents, and flying off into the sky–you feel good! Your mind is blown! The fact that you've experienced the ups and downs; the twists and turns; the near-misses; the heartaches and betrayals, all of the built-up emotions ended up exploding into a climactic "end result," which actually meant something. Now, imagine if you didn't watch the whole movie, but you only saw the ending, where Neo kicks ass and flies away, you'd probably think: "Meh… that was pretty cool. Can I have my money back?" In effect, the reason why the ending has any real impact, or meaning, is because of the journey it takes to get there. Relating this back to your purpose in life, surely you didn't have to sacrifice your happiness, feelings of joy, excitement, and overall well-being to be doing whatever it is you've decided to do. You just have to accept that the uncertainties, the lows, the losses, and the plateaus are part of the process. And overcoming them is what constitutes growth.

But on the other end of the spectrum there are people who have no idea what their purpose should be in the first place. And the best example of this type of person was myself. When I first began studying the subject (the importance of cultivating a strong sense of purpose) I didn't have a clue where to start. I didn't know what my purpose in life was. In fact, not only did I not know, I was downright confused. Because what I've learnt about the idea of purpose (and how to properly set goals) from various different sources was two completely different and opposing theories:

> (A): You came into this world for a particular quest or mission. You already have all that it takes within you to fulfil your life's purpose, because you were born with certain inner talents and abilities. You just have to discover what those abilities are, and nurture them. Then you have to dedicate your entire life to expressing your inner talents and abilities via particular vocation, if you are to evolve and live a happy, fulfilling, meaningful life. Or put differently–fulfil your life's purpose.

(B): You didn't come here with a predetermined goal in mind; you just have to try a number of different things first. You need to explore the variety of your physical world, test out different paths, and eventually pick something that excites you the most. It has to be something that you really love to do; something that you are passionate about; something that motivates you to move out of bed every morning. And once you have picked whatever it is that you are going to do, you then have to commit to it 100 percent, put all of your eggs in that basket, do not deviate from it, and burn the boats. (Meaning that you cannot quit, or change your mind and do something else instead.) You have to dedicate your entire life to it and commit to getting better at it every single day–if you wish to fulfil your true life's purpose.

At face value, both of these ideas directly contradict each other, yet both contain elements of truth in them. The fact that I was not ready for that level of discernment explains why my late teens were such a confusing time for me. I did not have the foggiest idea as to what I was supposed to be doing with my life, primarily because I did not know what I valued the most. I was passionate about a lot of different things. And to make matters worse, and even more confusing, while I was studying the subject of purpose over the course of many years, I was developing passion for a number of other things. Soon enough, it became extremely frustrating, so much so, that for years, I simply froze in a suspended animation, and did not make any major moves in any direction for fearing of making a wrong decision.

Of course I knew that I simply had to make a decision and choose a direction, but it wasn't easy because I wanted to do it all! I didn't want to miss out on anything. What was holding me back was the conviction that I had to be very careful with my choices, because maybe I was passionate about all of those things, but as life goes on, I might not be as passionate about them any longer. I thought that if I did pick something which turned out to be a wrong choice for me I would be screwed. Because I would have to be stuck with it for the rest of my life. My predicament could be likened to a person getting a tattoo, and then realising later that it was a dumb idea. In the heat of the moment we always seem to think that getting a particular tattoo is the best decision we've ever made in our lives, until reality strikes and we look back at it in regret, and cringe, telling ourselves: "What the hell was I thinking?!" Bearing this in mind I was extremely cautious when deciding what it is that I was going to do. It was very difficult for me to make up my mind and finally decide which path I was going to throw myself on. I thought that if I chose a particular path, but for whatever reason end up failing at it, or no longer enjoying it, then what am I to do?

Fortunately, in time I've come to realise that my purpose didn't have to be this one particular thing, that would sabotage my happiness if I were to turn my back on it later down the road, while all of the time, energy, and effort invested in it would be wasted. Yet the truth is, one's purpose in life is nothing like a tattoo; rather, it's more like the following. Your purpose in life could be absolutely anything, though it still has to be something that you are passionate, or excited about. It has to be something that you're willing to do for free. Because the growth, the joy, the excitement, and the vigour that you get out of it is priceless. There is practically nothing else in the world which could remotely make you feel the way you do when you engage in it. In other words, it has to be something which you absolutely love to do; something which makes you feel totally alive, and energised. It is all that you ever think about. And you can't wait to wake up in the morning so that you can engage in it all over again.

However, most likely (although not always) a time will come when you reach the pinnacle of your purpose and master it completely. And when you begin to feel that way, it's a clear indication that it is time for you to set new goals. Let us understand this right away: if your purpose doesn't stretch you as a person anymore; if you are not learning anything new anymore; if you know exactly how to do it; if it is no longer a challenge; if you feel that you have outgrown it; if you do not see any more room for improvement; if you have lived your purpose to the best of your ability, and held nothing back–you have left it all on the field so to speak–then in that case you get to choose a different path–a path which you are also passionate about–and make *that* your new purpose. You do not have to keep doing something that you have outgrown, and doggedly keep at it because you think you have gone beyond the point of no return. Realise that if your present path doesn't fulfil you any longer, or is no longer in alignment with your values, you are absolutely free to choose a different path, and blaze a new trail. You don't have to stick with something which is no longer working out for you. And the time which you have spent on it is never wasted either, because you always learn something valuable from the experience. Even if you are not aware of that "something" that "something" still makes you a better person than you were before it. So never be afraid to let go of something that no longer stretches you, or fulfills you, or excites you and brings you joy, just because it's comfortable and you know exactly how to do it.

Purpose

In the previous chapter we've learnt that we get to decide what this life means to us, and that there is nothing which we absolutely *have to* do–we are free to do whatever we please. In effect, there is no right or wrong when it comes to choosing our purpose in life. If you feel that your purpose is to be a stay-at-home mother; to look after your family and raise your children, that is a legitimate purpose. If you feel that your purpose in life is to take it easy; to chill with your friends and smoke weed all day long; to go through your life and just observe things as they unfold–if you are a person who can truly find happiness in that without bullshitting yourself–then that is a legitimate purpose. Success means different things to different people. As long as you are doing something deliberately; as long as you have made the *decision* that you are going to do something, or to become someone by your own choice, and go after it by your own choice, then you are considered a successful person who lives life on purpose.

"A successful person is the one who says: 'I am going to do this, and I am going to become this,' then begins to work toward that goal. That person is considered a success." – Earl Nightingale

If you feel that your purpose in life is to build massive businesses and empires to try and accumulate as much money as humanly possible, while brutally crushing the competition along the way, then that is a legitimate purpose. If your purpose in life is to work at Starbucks and serve delicious coffee all day long–because you resonate with the company's values–then that is a legitimate purpose. It doesn't matter how big or small your purpose may be, as long as it is something that excites you and gives your life meaning. But you have to do something, there is no other way around it. Every person *must* have a purpose in life, no matter what it is. Because life without any direction, or meaning can be likened to a life of a zombie, i.e. walking around unconsciously and aimlessly until the day you die.

Yes, being the wise human that you are, you can rationalise all day long and tell yourself that you *are* living. But if you truly have nothing to aim for; if you don't have some kind of an end goal in mind which you are earnestly working towards–walking around in a state of indifference and apathy–then none of your interactions in life will have any real substance, or significance. With respect to your spiritual growth and contribution to the world, your interactions with everyday life will be more or less pointless, and meaningless. In order to counter this terrible fate, and ensure that we are not living a passive life–caused by the lack of understanding pertaining to what it means to have a strong sense of purpose–I'd now like to answer some of those questions that people typically have, such as: "What is my purpose in life? How do I find my purpose? What does it take to fulfil my purpose? And why is it so difficult to stay on my path and stick to my purpose?"

But before we get into this, understand the following. When it comes to our purpose in life, both sides of our personality–physical and spiritual–play important roles. Therefore, we have to address both sides if we truly wish to grasp the whole picture, since both sides are interconnected, and directly affect each other. If we do not understand the role of either one, then what we get is a recipe for a frustrated and unfulfilled life that so many of us are unwittingly cooking. For now though, all you need to know is that one side of our personality is focused on–and solely interested in–our personal growth. Whereas the other side of our personality is focused on–and solely interested in–adding as much value as possible to others; contributing positively to the world. However, both sides–even though they differ in their modus operandi–complement each other, and therefore should certainly be understood.

"Every man must have a purpose; every man must have a goal."

PURPOSE & CONTRIBUTION (OUTER PURPOSE)

"He who has a why to live for can bear almost any how." – Friedrich Nietzsche

You don't have to look too far to find individuals who get easily offended by other people's comments, opinions, and behaviour. Individuals who get easily crushed amidst all the chaos and uncertainty that is going on in the world. Individuals who get wiped out after losing their jobs in which they had been working hard and honestly for years. Individuals who become depressed for months–and even years–after their long-term partner decides to leave. Individuals who become discouraged, and completely give up trying when they set out to achieve something but fail. It is evident that without a strong sense of purpose in life people get easily distracted from their highest good. They tend to complain; indulge in negative self-talk; judge others; harbour anger, hatred, jealousy, and resentments within them; they hardly ever feel at ease with themselves; and they enjoy watching other people fail, because it makes them feel better about their own failures, inadequacies, and shortcomings.

Living in such a poor emotional state for prolonged periods of time inevitably results in a formation of a profound sense of injustice, and "learned helplessness." Those who are unfortunate enough to find themselves in such a downward spiral, never seem to achieve/accomplish anything fruitful. This for the most part happens as a result of not having a sense of purpose, and it can happen to anyone. Some of the people you love and care about the most are probably stuck in such a spiral. Of course this doesn't mean that they are bad people. Most people are generally nice, friendly, and caring people, who simply happen to be stuck in a loop–a mental haze, which is not pleasant for any person to be in, and is not particularly easy to get out of. Now, since you aspire to surround yourself with positive, like-minded people on your journey to self-improvement, you may be tempted to completely cut them out of your life, for they have become too toxic to be around. However, distancing yourself completely from some of your relatives and close friends (whose influence had become too detrimental) only causes unnecessary friction. A better way therefore of going about improving your circle of influence (friends), is to continue to appreciate the people who already are in your life, and still be willing to spend time with them, only less frequently. And when you do make plans to see them, just make sure that the visit is brief.

The major reason why those of us who lack a strong sense of purpose in life tend to indulge in negativity, is because lack of clarity in our values and direction in life naturally affects our sense of personal boundaries. For when we lack a clear sense of direction in life and someone is being rude–someone is trying to push us around; someone is being nasty towards us; someone is yelling at us and trying to convince us of how bad of a person we really are– we're more than likely to take on their negative energy, and become upset or angry as a result. Because when we do not have a strong sense of purpose in life, we in turn do not have a boundary against anything that isn't helping us to move towards that which is important to us. We do not have a boundary against influences that aren't serving us.

If you are to get anywhere in life, you must have a strong sense of purpose. Which is another way of saying that you must have a very good reason for wanting to accomplish whatever it is you want to get done in life–if you are to ensure your success. For if your life's purpose is ill-defined and lukewarm, then it will have that "sort of, kind of, wouldn't it be nice" type of energy behind it. And it is highly unlikely that it will withstand the currents of other energies that are much more potent (since they are more certain), that are coming at you all day, every day (most of which are negatively charged). In effect, if you do not have a good enough reason for wanting to accomplish something–something which is of paramount importance to you–then sooner or later you're going to give in to negative self-talk, thoughts, feelings, behaviour, and ultimately low-consciousness. For instance, let us say that you are overweight, but you wish to become more fit. If you do not have a good enough reason for wanting to lose the excess weight, then eventually you are going to cave in to the temptation of wanting to eat greasy, unhealthy food–food which titillates your senses, and feels good–even though you know that your actions are not moving you any closer to your goal–and in fact–they are further pushing it away.

The question is, why would we ever do that, knowing full well that we shouldn't? Well, because there is no reason for us *not* to do it! (Read that sentence again, really feel it, and let it sink in.) You see, you have to have a bigger reason, a clearer vision, a stronger purpose which will *automatically* make you do the right thing. You must get to a point where you no longer have to deplete your willpower in order to "act right." A point where you no longer have to force yourself to stop responding, thinking, or behaving in a manner which pushes your goals further away. Put differently, you have to reach a point where you no longer have to consciously think about what you should or shouldn't do. And you can achieve this by creating a vision for yourself so compelling and rewarding that it overpowers the temporary pleasure, or the false sense of satisfaction which you get by engaging in an unhealthy dietary practices. By complaining and derping around. By adopting the role of a victim. By slouching on your couch all day long–watching television, or playing video games. Or by trying to convince others of how much your life sucks, and how hard it actually is, so that you can feel justified for staying in your comfort zone, and not take any action towards improving your life situation as other people–who also do not have a purpose in life–nod in agreement.

When you have a strong sense of purpose (a clear direction) in life, you intuitively know what the right thing to do is, in any given situation, and in every moment. I personally love the way Owen Cook–social dynamics coach and a phenomenal public speaker–presents the idea of purpose and personal boundaries, and how the two connect: "*As your sense of purpose increases so do your boundaries in life. Because if you want to accomplish whatever it is you want to get done in your life, you have to be very careful about what influences you allow around yourself: what type of people you surround yourself with; what kind of energy you surround yourself with; and more importantly, your own behaviour.*" What Owen is essentially alluding to here is that it is actually not very difficult to avoid negativity. We can easily choose to ignore undermining comments; we can choose not to accept other people's opinion of us; we can draw a boundary when someone is crossing the line. However, if we are eating unhealthy foods; indulging in sloppy thinking; engaging in unfocused behaviour; procrastinating; gossiping; becoming angry/upset as a result of something that somebody said, in that case we're failing to put down a boundary on *ourself*, from the lack of a sense of purpose.

Owen elaborates on this idea with a following analogy: "*We know that on planet Earth gravity is caused by mass. When we have mass we get gravity, and the gravity sucks in the ozone layer around the planet which then protects it. As a human being, it would be helpful for you to think of yourself as a planet when it comes to your purpose. When you have a strong sense of purpose, i.e. you know where you are going in life and you know what needs to be done, then that vision, direction, or mission becomes the mass which creates its gravity. That critical mass then begins to pull in the armour of 'personal boundaries' around your purpose which then protects it, i.e. not allowing you to complain; to slack off; and ultimately get thrown off your path and purpose.*" In today's world–as a productive and proactive individual you wish to be–it is absolutely essential that you have this "armour." Realise that, actually, there aren't many beliefs which you have–as well as emotions that you feel; thoughts that you have; conclusions that you come to–that are of your own conscious choice. For an individual who hasn't yet mastered his own emotions–who doesn't know what he really wants, and where he is going in life–is virtually like a sponge. For this reason, if we were to take a person who is generally positive and put him/her into a negative environment, before long, that person would become negative themself. Of course, that is not always the case, but it is common that the environment does take its toll on people–be it psychologically, emotionally, or otherwise. Now, I know exactly how detrimental our environment can become to our growth, success, and happiness in life when we do not have a strong sense of purpose...

Generally speaking I am a positive, optimistic, and collected individual; I don't sweat the small stuff. But having to work in various places–typically factories–what I have generally observed is that those types of environments were very negative, and petty in nature. Just as surely as I would make other people laugh, and make them feel good about themselves from time to time, I just as readily found myself feeling petty and negative a lot of the time also (because at the time, I did not have a strong sense of purpose). Working various 9-to-5 jobs made me realise that I didn't have as much influence (particularly in those environments) as I would have preferred. Keep in mind that I was mostly surrounded by people who were working in those environments for 10, 20, 30 and even 60 years. These individuals were completely defeated by life; they had no hope, plans, or vision. The warehouse, the assembly line, and the forklift truck *were* their life. Now, what do you suppose happens to a man/woman who has been carrying out the same menial tasks, day in and day out, for decades. What kind of person do you think does that way of living produces? Well, not exactly a joyful, hopeful, or inspirational one. These individuals were not at all interested in hearing about my plans, what I had going for me, and how they could also be doing the same. They were not receptive to new ideas, or better ways of thinking. They were never happy for–and supporting of–their friends and family who had courage to start a business, and actually succeeded. All they really knew how to do was gossip all day long; complain; discuss other people's problems; and get drunk on the weekend while watching football. There wasn't any room for any discussion about how to get off the hamster wheel and build better lives for ourselves.

Any honest attempt made by myself to initiate a constructive conversation, leaning in a positive direction would get shut down by statements such as: "You need to stop dreaming mate, you will never make it. Rich people are evil, they won't let you win. If you want to be rich, you need to learn how to scam other people and f**k them over. We are sweating our asses off around here, doing honest work, and we get paid for it in peanuts. The government keeps taxing us on everything. By the time we pay our bills we have nothing left to give to ourselves. The government won't make it easy for you. No one gives a shit about you; no one is going to assist you. If you want to get anywhere in life you need to have rich parents, or contacts. You need to have a business degree, and at least ten years of study at a prestige university under your belt before you can even think about earning more money. Just forget about it, stop wasting your time. Shut up and get back to work."

As they began elaborating further and explain how all those statements were true (they felt passionate about them and completely believed in them), And what is interesting is that I also began to feel as if they were true. And I too became pessimistic and negative at times, albeit only when I was around those people, and in those environments. However, after my shift was over, and I found myself away from them, I'd no longer feel those disempowering emotions, and I'd no longer think those negative thoughts. So you see, even though I was a positive, ambitious individual, and even though I knew that "their way" was not a proper way of thinking, I was still consumed by their negative vibration. This used to happen to me when I was in my early twenties, since I did not have a strong sense of purpose in life. Nowadays, in my thirties, it is virtually impossible for anybody, or anything to make me think something negative–let alone *believe* it.

Purpose

Personal experience had taught me that even though we exert influence on our environment; our environment also exerts its influence on us. It is so essential that we understand this. Because when our environment feels a lot more certain, and more passionate about *its* perspective and values, than we do about our own, then we are doomed to forever live at the effect of others. In order to ensure that we do not get pulled in wherever the wind decides to blow, we must have a strong sense of purpose in life–a critical mass of sorts–that will act as a shield against all of the crap that is coming at us. And it begins with developing a laser-sharp focus; following certain disciplines; cultivating personal boundaries; and determining our own unique intentions in life. Once our mindset is in the right place, then it really won't matter what might be happening externally. Because the beliefs that we uphold; codes of conduct that we adhere to; and goals that we set, will be adequately protected, and thus will not be influenced (at least negatively) by anything external.

Having a strong sense of purpose in life prevents you from becoming a leaf in the wind. It prevents you from not being sure as to what you should believe in. It prevents you from searching for happiness, validation, approval, and love outside of yourself. It prevents you from looking for somebody else to follow; to tell you what to do, and how to think. It prevents you from constantly looking at what other people are thinking and doing, while trying to blend in to please them. It also prevents you from breaking down, giving up, and losing all hope when things don't go your way. In effect, your purpose in life is the "armour" which protects your psychological and emotional health. It is what allows you to walk through the world with absolute ease while deflecting all manner of bullshit which life decides to throw at you.

For instance, if you are unfortunate enough to lose your house; if your partner decides to leave you; if you become bankrupt; if you get fired from your job; if you fail your studies; if your family hates you, and doesn't want anything to do with you–whatever–you don't allow yourself to get negatively affected by it. Because your purpose is more important, and much bigger than all of those things combined. In other words, your purpose is what fulfils you and sustains you; not your house; not your job; not the other person; not other people's love and approval; not your family; and not your partner. Typically, a person who makes someone (another human) their sole purpose in life, who then finds him/herself in a situation where there is lack of support coming from that someone, he/she has nowhere else to turn to for reassurance and inspiration. As a result, his/her spirit gets crushed, and he/she becomes enraged, depressed, or even suicidal.

Whereas an individual who has a strong sense of purpose in life (a purpose that is not an unpredictable human being) would not have the *luxury* to wallow in self-pity; to beg for people's love and approval; or plead for things to be different. A man of purpose gives love and validation to himself–from himself. A man of purpose does not need these things from other people, because his purpose is what fulfils him and inspires him. He understands that humans are fickle, and that it was never their job to adapt to him, and make sure that he feels good. He understands that his life's purpose, and the way that he feels about his purpose, are the only constants. As a consequence, his emotional cup is so full that it overflows with love, happiness, and joy. Unlike the bucket with a hole in it–whose happiness is dependent solely upon something external–the cup is self-sustaining. It pours all that is good in him out into the world, affecting everything he comes into contact with in a powerful, loving, positive way. We could say that his cup runneth over.

"Where there is no vision, the people perish." – Proverbs 29:18

As you set about exploring what it is that you would like to do with your life do not get frustrated with yourself if you are having a difficult time finding your purpose, or if you don't know what it is that you are good at yet. Everyone is good at something, it is only a matter of discovering what that *something* might be. Rest assured, as long as you are trying different things, then you are doing it right. And it is not possible to make a wrong decision either. So do not get stuck in an analysis paralysis like I did for many years.

Don't overthink this, because you can always rethink your choice. If, for example you pick a certain path and decide to go for it, but later realise that actually it is not something that you would like to be doing after all–because it is draining you of energy and doesn't bring you joy–then simply get rid of it and pick a different path. But here is an important paradox: once you find a certain path–a path that seems promising–you still have to burn the bridges behind you and commit to it 100 percent, at least in the beginning stages. Because if you do not commit to something 100 percent, then by not giving it your all may make you feel as though what you are doing is not for you. Or maybe it was. But you will never know because you didn't fully dive in. You simply took a few modest steps towards it, and at the first sight of a setback, unpleasant experience, or failure, you backed out and didn't follow through. In other words, when we set out on any particular path, the terrain is usually quite bumpy in the beginning stages, and it takes some time to adjust. But if we are unable/unwilling to get past this rather boring–and a lot of the time–

difficult stage, then we'll never know whether the path was the right one or not. If we are to successfully get over this potential initial hurdle, then rather than waiting for things to get easier, or more exciting–waiting for passion to arise–we instead have to proactively psych ourselves into whatever it is we are doing and generate that passion from within ourself.

"Do the thing, and you will get the energy to do the thing."
– Ralph Waldo Emerson

Generating passion from within ourselves requires a lot less effort when we know that what we have decided to do in our life will produce some kind of value. So we have to take some time to take inventory and imagine what our life would look like if we were to become very good at whatever it is that we had decided to do. And once our brain realises that we would get great value, or some kind of benefit–be it a sense of accomplishment; personal development; money; love; attention; recognition; satisfaction; or approval–by becoming extremely good at it, it rewires the reward circuit in our brain which makes us feel good about doing it, even when the path becomes bumpy and unpleasant. What this means is that if you happen to feel bored, uninspired, or not good about doing something, yet you push yourself and blast through it anyway (because you know that there is a worthwhile reward at the end), your brain realises that what you are doing is important to you. And what it does is it activates the reward system in your brain which associates positive emotions with whatever it is you are doing; it makes you feel as though you are doing the right thing, and that by doing it you are going to win.

Your brain is a stubborn, extremely complex piece of equipment, but it is on your side. Its primary function is to keep you alive. By acknowledging that the primary goal of your brain is to keep you safe, you can begin to use it to your advantage, and help it to help you. You see, when your brain realises that it cannot stop you from doing something, it has to harmonise with whatever it is that you're doing, and start helping you along the way. When it comes to setting major goals in life, and going after those things you want–travelling unfamiliar territories–your brain does not want you to take risks. And so, like a stubborn horse, it simply won't move. Your job is to convince your brain that it doesn't have a choice but to follow you and, through physical action coax your brain to be nice. When you take physical action despite the resistance your brain is offering you, you flip the script, in the sense that instead of being flooded with fear and anxiety, you're now being offered solutions, right impulses, and a heightened level of awareness and focus.

For instance, because your brain wants to keep you alive, at first, it will flood you with fear and anxiety as you stand at the bottom of a rocky mountain looking up, in order to dissuade you from climbing it. But, if you push through that initial resistance and fear that your brain is flooding you with, and begin climbing the mountain anyway, then your brain will immediately switch sides and start helping you climb all the way up. Why? Because your brain knows full well that if it continues to flood you with fear and anxiety in the middle of your climb, it may throw you off and make you fall to your death. The fact that your brain cannot stop you from taking physical action, it would have to get rid of fear and anxiety, and resort to helping you focus on the next sturdy rock which you can grab on to, and the next, and the next. Once you kick-start this kind of momentum when going after the things you want–by focusing on all of the good that will come to you as a result of what you are doing; instead of being consumed by fear and resistance–there is no way that you can fail. Pushing through fear and resistance enough times will inevitably bring you to a point where you very much enjoy doing whatever it is you are doing. A point where your brain, mind, spirit, and whole of the Universe are supporting you and helping you every step along the way. This becomes an upward spiral of success. Because as you get better at something you become more successful at it. As you become more successful at what it is you do, you begin to enjoy it even more (because of the many rewards that you're reaping). And since you are enjoying it more, you are operating from a highly creative state, which guarantees to bring you more success.

Now, while it is true that you absolutely can be, do, and have anything that you desire, because you are a powerful creator of your own experience–you're absolutely capable of doing anything which another person is capable of doing, since nobody is cut from a different cloth. Keep in mind that different people *do* have different innate talents, traits and abilities, which come to them naturally, and it would be foolish not to acknowledge and utilise them. The best move that you, myself, or anyone else can make is to identify some of those unfair advantages and unique strengths that we have, which we can then improve upon and utilise to the maximum of our ability. For example, take Shaquille O'Neal who was considered one of the greatest players in the NBA. Being 7'1" and weighing almost 330 pounds, he becomes a great candidate to play professional basketball. However, imagine Shaquille growing up with intentions of becoming a dancer, or an actor instead. Chances are he would have never done as well in those professions as he did in professional basketball. Or imagine if Mike Tyson (who was a perfect fit for professional boxing–with his stocky physical build, incredible power, agility, speed, and menacing look) ignored the fact that he has a frontal lisp, and strived to becoming a rapper, or a comedian instead. Certainly that would have been the wrong choice for him–an utter waste of a great talent.

Analysing your own strengths and weaknesses is enormously valuable when it comes to figuring out your purpose in life. Because doing something that you naturally excel at is more easily enjoyable and, therefore requires a lot less effort and mental gymnastics to become successful at. Of course, it is not at all necessary to stick to something which you have an aptitude for, because you are capable of developing any new talent and ability, and beat incredible odds. But there is something to be said about looking inward–to see whether you already have something within yourself that'll give you an unfair advantage over the rest–if you are having difficulty finding your calling looking outward. If you're having difficulty finding what it is that you truly love to do–here is a pro tip. Picture yourself living the life that you have always imagined. Where you are exceedingly wealthy and happy. Where you have travelled most of the world, and have practically seen it all. Where everyone loves you and thinks that you are swell (which eliminates the need for validation and approval of others). Where you have your dream car collection, your dream home, your dream partner, and a ton of good friends who love and support you. Where your entire family is joyful and healthy. Where you are in a fantastic physical/mental/emotional shape. Where there is absolutely nothing which you have to do anymore. Where you no longer have to work a single day in your life if you chose not to, for your current fortune is more than enough to last you a lifetime. Now, once you have this mental movie playing in your mind's eye–mixed with strong emotions–ask yourself: "What is it that I would like to do in order to pass the time for the rest of my life, even if I were to never be compensated for it?" And your honest answer to that question may just lead you in the right direction.

Above all else, you always have to be striving towards becoming a person of greater value–being creative and contributing positively to the world. Every person has something useful to offer to the world, because every individual lives a unique life experience which other people can learn and benefit from. Don't keep it all to yourself out of fear of failure or ridicule, but focus on those people who would greatly benefit from what you have to share. Don't let other people suffer from not knowing or using that which you have to offer, out of fear of criticism. Share your unique gifts, talents, and positive energy with other people freely. Quit thinking that people are judging you, laughing at you, and waiting for your downfall. Instead, instil a strong belief in yourself that the whole world is rooting for you, and is impatiently waiting for your unique products, services, and expertise. Get out of the little box that society is forever trying to keep you in and let everybody know that you exist. Become a somebody and let the world know that you are here damn it!

Rather than aimlessly floating through life like a useless turd–just cruising by and going through the motions–sit yourself down and start seriously thinking about what you want, and why you want it. Begin setting goals that stretch you physically, mentally, emotionally, and intellectually. Assume full responsibility for the quality of your life, and stop giving away your power to other people–expecting them to lead you in the right direction, and make you happy, because they won't. Nobody has the power to make you happy but you; nobody knows what you *really* want, except you. And if you yourself don't even know what it is you want, then you are destined to forever be doing what other people want, until it demoralises your spirit and completely eats away at your soul. Don't take the importance of having a strong sense of purpose in life lightly. Because if you are not being proactive about your success and happiness, then a passive life of quiet desperation is what awaits you. Why? Because mediocrity is the default. It will latch onto anyone who falls back into unconsciousness. In order to avoid this dreadful fate you have to be mentally/emotionally stable, grounded in your energy, and totally engaged with life. I understand that life can sometimes be harsh and unforgiving, so much so that it can slap you right back into unconsciousness. But it is utterly pointless wishing for your life to get easier, because life will always be what it is–unpredictable, and full of unpleasant surprises. Instead, strive towards cultivating core confidence; developing new skills; becoming mentally/emotionally resilient; having a fluid personality, and being more flexible in your approach to anything. That way, the possibilities in life truly become endless for you. Yes, it may feel that staying on top of your game takes a lot of effort. However, when you have a strong sense of purpose in life you are going to want to cultivate all the aforementioned qualities and perspectives naturally. And when you do, you will be ready to gracefully and effortlessly Aikido those proverbial "slaps" away from you when they come.

"To get what you really want in life, you need a clear goal that has purpose and meaning behind it. Once this is in place, you can focus your energy on the goal and become obsessive about it. When you learn how to focus your energy, amazing things happen." – Tony Robbins

PURPOSE & YOU (INNER PURPOSE)

"Your life's purpose is to be the deliberate creator that you've come here to be."
– Abraham Hicks

Here is a kicker for you: your ultimate life's purpose is not so much about what you do and what you achieve; rather, your purpose in life is about who you *are*; it is about who you become; it is about how you feel. In other words, your purpose is the creation and evolution of *you*. You didn't come here specifically to create things, although you most certainly will. You didn't come here to form relationships, although you certainly will. You didn't come here to build businesses, create movements, and assist others in getting what they want, although you probably will. Rather, you came here to explore the contrast of your physical environment for the evolution and expansion of *you*.

You see, while you're going about your business; moving through your life experience, making certain decision with respect to what you want, and then offering your creative energy accordingly, the external results turn out to be all kinds of different things that are secondary (out here in the physical world), but the underlying result is the continual growth and expansion of you. Esther Hicks ever so eloquently explained what our purpose in life really is while channeling Abraham in one of her workshops: *"From wherever you stand you are always reaching for something more, and when you allow yourself to align with that 'more,' then the new vantage-point allows you to go further still. So, it is not a purpose, but it is a steady stream of purposes as far as you can allow yourself to go. It's a steady and never-ending unfolding of new desires, new accomplishments, and new alignments."*

Think of it in following terms: as you go about your daily life you come into contact with all kinds of things: be they people, situations, conditions, or events. And when you see something that you would like to be, do, or have, you experience something that we call desire, and your higher-self instantly becomes it. In effect, the exposure to life automatically causes you to ask for something more, while the higher-self version of you (which is the real you) instantly becomes all that you have asked for. Thus, there is absolutely nothing which you have to do, other than to live your life. Because everything is naturally taken care of. But the real purpose of your life, or the reason why your consciousness needs to be focused in a physical body in a physical dimension in the first place, is because your higher-self is incapable of asking, and therefore causing expansion. In other words, the fact that Source-Energy dwells in a dimension where there can be no thought of lack, shortage, or resistance (because it is already whole and complete), it has to focus a part of its consciousness into a lower dimension where thought can be continuously taken beyond that which it has been, i.e. giving birth to endless desire which causes endless expansion. And that's what constitutes infinity, or eternity.

This is why life on planet Earth (and other planets in other galaxies too) is so vitally important. Because there will always be something more to ask for, since there can never be enough of what we don't want. In other words, when we see injustice–we desire more fairness; when we see lack and limitation–we desire more abundance and opportunity; when we see struggle–we desire more happiness; when we see sickness–we desire more health; when we see conflict–we desire more love and peace; when we see control and restriction–we desire more freedom. Conversely, if we jump high–we cannot help but want to jump higher; if we run fast–we cannot help but want to run faster; if we make a million–we cannot help but want to make ten million; if we create one piece of art–we cannot help but want to create even more. In effect, the environment in which we live, endless desire is pretty much guaranteed. And each time that we desire something our higher-self instantly becomes it, spiritually and vibrationally. While the only responsibility we have is to catch up with those desires–or our expansion–and become one with it.

However, when we are doubting ourselves, when we are focusing upon the lack of what it is we want and acknowledging the absence of it, when we are thinking about how nice it would be to have it (reinforcing a false premise that we don't already have it), when we don't know how to get what it is we want, and where to even start, or when we don't feel deserving of it, then our emotions will shift, and our vibration will shift. And that shift in the opposite direction to what we desire–and what we have become–will manifest as a negative emotion within; be it discomfort; disappointment; discouragement; anger, whatever. And when we are feeling a negative emotion of any kind, that is a direct signal from our higher-self, indicating to us that we are moving away from what we desire. That's what negative emotion ultimately is. Our purpose–our only work–therefore, as spiritual beings who are having a human experience is to remain on course–up to speed–with our own desire in order to joyfully experience our expansion. (We will discuss in greater detail as to how exactly this is done in the next chapter.)

Take my desire to write this book as an example. When I came up with the idea to write a book about the various ideas which we're discussing here I felt ecstatic, I felt great, I couldn't wait to get started. When I began to write the very first chapter I didn't feel any negative emotion or resistance about it whatsoever, and I continued to put it all together without any complications. But then–completely unprovoked–I began to get inundated with doubt and I began thinking to myself: "What am I doing? Who am I to write a book? I'm not a writer. Why am I even doing this? Nobody will want to listen to what I have to say anyway. There are plenty of professionals out there who know a hell of a lot more than I do, so why would people bother listening to me?"

In the wake of such thoughts I completely stopped writing for a while, and I stopped thinking about what I was going to write next. But then something strange happened–I became unhappy. I began to feel deflated and de-motivated, and I couldn't figure out how it could have happened to me, and why? Because I absolutely loved my life and the general direction in which it was headed, so why did I feel so lethargic and apathetic? Fortunately, it did not take long to realise that the reason why I haven't been feeling like myself is because I was holding myself back from something which I had set in mo-tion–the desire to write a book. As I looked back at the draft, along the notes which I've gathered over the past decade of study, I remembered how much I wanted to share that knowledge with others, in hopes that it might help at least a handful of people improve their lives. After that reminder to myself, I silently vowed: "Okay, regardless of the doubts, fears, and uncertainties that I'm experiencing, I am going to go ahead and continue to write anyway until I finish the book." And then, something interesting happened. I began to feel good again. I immediately came back to my old self again. And that's when I knew for a fact that finishing the book was something which I had to do–at that point in my life–because I had already asked for it. And I have decided that if I were to feel those negative emotions again–if I were to feel as though I didn't want to do it anymore–that I would just go ahead and do it anyway; that I would persevere and blast through the resistance. Sure enough, every time that resistance surfaced, and I blasted through it, I haven't stopped feel-ing good about writing and sharing these ideas since. In the end, I have con-cluded that it would make no difference if no one would agree to publish the book, or if nobody would understand it. For the emotions and the expansion which I was getting out of it were necessary for my own growth and happi-ness. It felt as though I was writing the book for myself; for my own good.

To break this down and relate it to what we're discussing here, what ac-tually happened was the following. A desire to share with others everything I've learnt on my journey to self-mastery–contribute positively to the world–was born within myself. Feeling excited about the thought of such an undertaking, an idea to write a book came into my mind rather quickly. While under such a strong impulse to act, I wasted no time in getting started, and began to put it together. (A desire to do something more was born within myself. My higher-self instantly became that "more," and I began the process of catching up with it.) But, after some time, I became encumbered by negative thoughts–primarily fear and self-doubt–which forced me to stop writing and resume my usual routine–which was in place prior to my new desire. However, the routine–which had previously brought me joy–no longer felt satisfying; it felt like I was missing something. (While my higher-self was still sitting there writing the book, I was moseying around somewhere else without this all-important part of myself, which were calling me to come back to it.) Soon enough, I realised that the reason why I didn't feel happy with what I was doing anymore is because I was being called to do something else which I had already set in motion (to write the book). As soon as I redirected all of my focus and attention back onto writing the book again, it felt as though I had picked up a part of myself that was left behind–sitting at my desk–and we quickly joined forces again. In due course, joy and satisfaction ensued. (I managed to get back on the frequency which my desire was on, by releasing all of the negative thoughts of not being good enough. And as a result, I became–once again–vibrationally/emotionally aligned with my desire.)

You see, all that is required in order to reliably determine whether you are living your life on purpose or not is to ask yourself a question: "Am I joyful? Am I happy?" If you are, then you are living your life on purpose, or at the very least, moving in the right direction, so keep at it. But if you are not, then you must go a step further and ask yourself: "What is it that I'm avoiding?" In other words, what is it that you feel you must do, but for whatever reason are not doing? What is it that you are putting off, that is gnawing at you and slowly eating you up? When you identify exactly what it is that you *should* be doing, then for the sake of your happiness and well-being you need to develop courage to blast through your doubts and fears, and boldly go after it. Granted, by the time we become adults, it becomes impossible to reliably identify everything that we've asked for. And so, the way of going about it, is rather than trying to pinpoint specific things which we think we need to do (because that will only drive us crazy), we just have to make joy our primary focus in life and allow ourselves to be guided by our emotions–it is the language of God. That way, we practically ensure that we'll continue to fulfil everything we've ever asked for, and have become.

If you are still unsure as to how your desire relates to you feeling a particular emotion, I want you to think about this in the following way: Imagine you and your soul are walking side by side through your life together. One day, late at night, you come across a big pile of gold (something that you really want) sitting on top of the hill, and you point at it and say to your soul: "Wow! I would love to have that!" (a desire being born), and your soul says: "Very well then" and instantly teleports itself to it (becoming one with your desire). But while standing at the bottom of the hill, looking up, you begin to worry and doubt yourself because the climb looks dangerous–since you cannot see the route to your desire clearly; it is too dark. However, your soul–who is really just another version of you which exists in a higher dimension–knows the way up, and it has all of the answers. And even though this version of yourself cannot communicate with you with words or gestures, it can communicate with you clearly in the form of emotions (a foolproof form of guidance). Through the constant use of positive as well as negative emotions your soul is able to guide you to your desire, and correct you when you are wandering off your path. So what your soul begins to do is call you towards your desire by projecting onto you a positive emotion when you are on the right track, and a negative emotion when you are moving in the opposite direction of it. And it continues to do so until you finally experience the desire.

When you understand this emotional/vibrational relationship you have with your higher-self, you allow yourself to be guided by your feelings, until you eventually get to experience your desire. But when you do not, you give birth to a new desire and proceed to anxiously look at the unpredictable and uncomfortable path ahead of yourself, and you turn around–you walk away. All the while your soul stands there, along with your desire, ceaselessly calling you towards it, hoping that, eventually, your emotions will get the better of you and at long last help you find your way to it. But, the further that you move away from your desire, and the longer you delay taking steps towards it, the worse you will feel. In effect, when you feel a negative emotion of any kind recognise it as a warning–a signal–which indicates that your higher-self had expanded into something more, while your current choice of thoughts is not allowing you to join your higher-self in that new perspective. And that is ultimately what negative emotion is.

To summarise: you don't need to put forth a lot of effort to try and discover, or realise your life's purpose, at least on a spiritual level. Your higher-self has it all figured out; it is handled. Because as you are moving through your life experience, and you happen to find something that you want, your higher-self instantly becomes it. Likewise, when you find something that you do not want, your higher-self in turn recognises what it is you would prefer–something that you *do* want–and becomes it also. As such, the ever-evolving aspect of who you *really* are cannot be stopped. Your only purpose therefore is to continue to catch up with your own evolution in order to experience as much of it–and to whatever degree possible–while you are alive, for no other reason than that it feels good. Which is, in effect, a longer way of saying that the purpose of your life is joy. Growth and expansion is not your purpose, or mission in life; that is inevitable. It's going to happen regardless of what you do. Your purpose, or calling in life is always just one thing: *alignment with the Source-Energy part of yourself.* This evolved–and improved–version of you is what you want to be reaching for, and that is what you are ultimately being called to. You are forever being called to the fullness of what your life experience had caused you to become. Your higher-self is forever guiding you to become one with this new and improved version of yourself, and who created this expanded–higher-self–version of you? You did. In effect, you are being called to yourself, by yourself, and your emotions are always letting you know–in real time–where you stand in relationship to your own expansion.

Ultimately, your purpose is to be a joyful creator of yourself. You don't need to look for any particular path to execute this purpose because the spiritual path which you are on, is always "on." You'll never be able to get yourself off this path for as long as you live, because your life and everything that happens within it *is* the path for the creation and evolution of you. On an intuitive level you already know how this works. You know that this life experience will indefinitely continue to cause you to desire something simply because there is never enough of the things you *don't want.* And every time you ask/desire/prefer to be/do/have something more the larger part of you becomes that "more." (You can sometimes feel this happening if you're perceptive enough.) And what you also need to understand, is that when you have your death experience and leave your physical body, you'll instantly become everything that your life experience had caused you to become. How come? Because when you have your death experience, and leave the physical body behind, you instantly let all the resistance, along with all the baggage–which you have picked up along the trail of life–go. Baggage–in a form of negative thoughts; beliefs; perspectives; environmental pressures; social conditioning; health of your body, and so forth–that was weighing you down and preventing you from experiencing your expansion.

To help you grasp this idea more readily, I will borrow Abraham Hicks' clever analogy and ask of you to imagine yourself as a cork floating freely on the surface of water, when your conscious awareness isn't bound to a physical body, encased in the physical world. And when you come forth into this physical life experience, predictably, along the way, you begin to pick up all kinds of ideas that are not helping you float freely, and instead are holding you down under the water. However, when you "die" (I quote because there is no death) and leave your physical body, you will instantly bob right back to the surface of water, because there is no more resistance, or anything else that can hold you down (primarily your own negative thoughts). Your purpose then–you could say–is to enable your cork to float freely while you are alive in your physical body. Why would you wait until you have your death experience to–at long last–become all that you have evolved into? When you can let go of the resistance (things that are keeping the cork under the water) and join the perspective of your higher-self now (bob back up to the surface).

The reason why we get to experience our expansion fully, and in an instant, at the time of our death, is because the physical part of ourselves is no longer there–no longer in the way of our well-being. It no longer contradicts the Source-Energy part of ourself through worry and doubt; by being afraid; by feeling insecure; by second-guessing ourself, and being unsure as to what to believe; by feeling exhausted as a result of non-stop work; by feeling nauseous as a result of the drunken antics of the previous night; by feeling mentally weak and confused as a result of consuming too much junk, processed food; by throwing ourselves into a rage because we are stuck in traffic; or by stressing ourselves out because our boss had already warned us that if we're late again, we are f**king fired! I think you get the point. There is literally an infinite number of ways in which we tend to keep our cork under the water. But there is only one answer–or solution–to all of it: achieving alignment, by whatever means necessary, with our higher-self.

Before we continue on to the next chapter why don't you try to come into alignment with your higher-self right now? Set aside five minutes of your time to sit down in complete silence, and begin to look for any excuse in the world to feel good–tuning yourself into a higher frequency. Close your eyes, relax your body, focus on your breath, and start to imagine. Do not get frustrated with yourself if your mind is running rampant, and you can't seem to concentrate. What you can do, is rather than going along with every random thought that is flooding your mind, instead, use your breath as an anchor to stay present (by redirecting your focus back to it when your mind begins to wander). Just stay calm, breathe slow, and think about what it is you really want to be, do, and have in your life. Imagine yourself having it, being it, or doing it, and feel as though it is already yours (do not try to think about *how* you are going to get it). The operative word here is *feel*. And once you get the glimpse of the emotions that you feel by experiencing what you want in your mind's eye, practise feeling this way as often as possible when you come out of this relaxed state, and resume your interactions with your everyday life. If you take your time to do this for at least thirty days, I can guarantee you that it will be only a matter of time until it becomes a reality. Not just in your imagination, or out there vibrationally in space. But also in a physical world for your eyes to see, and for your hands to touch.

"We are here in this world for a divine purpose: to know imagination."
– Neville Goddard

Emotions

"The quality of your life is a reflection of the quality of your emotions."

In this chapter we are going to answer the question as to what exactly your emotions have to do with creation. The short answer is *everything*. In essence, your emotions exist for the purpose of helping you to come into alignment with who you've become in the process of living your life. In no way is this a complicated idea. You only have to acknowledge that there exists a higher-self version of you–which you've been helping to evolve, ever since the day you were born–and that evolved version of yourself is forever calling you to become one with it. And when you allow yourself to follow the call–you feel positive emotions, but when you don't–you feel negative emotions.

Once you understand this simple truth you will know with absolute certainty that the reason why you would ever feel a negative emotion (such as fear; anger; frustration, etc.) is because you have a strong desire about something which had summoned a lot more energy than your current thoughts are allowing to flow through (at that particular moment in time), and it feels bad. Likewise, when you feel a positive emotion of any kind (such as happiness; joy; satisfaction, etc.), it is a clear indication that you have a strong desire about something towards which you have zero resistance; thereby your energy is flowing freely in the direction of it, which feels good.

It is extremely liberating to know that you–just like everyone else–have access to this form of divine guidance. So you don't ever have to explain anyone else's behaviour, try to correct them and get them to agree with you, or blame circumstances, conditions and events. Because the emotions that you feel are always–and only–ever about the difference in energies between you and your higher-self; it has nothing to do with anyone, or anything else other *than* yourself. Of course, being the humans that we are we tend to believe that the reason why we feel bad is because we have observed something unpleasant, or have come into contact with someone intolerable. But if we are ever to achieve mastery of our own emotions we have to accept the fact that the reason why we feel bad is because we have a different opinion about that someone/something–may it be a particular person, circumstance, condition, or event–than our higher-self does, and as a result, negative emotion ensues. In effect, we do it to ourselves.

However, not many people are willing, or ready to accept this truth, for a panoply of different reasons, a host of which are obvious. But if you are to live your life as a powerful, resourceful, and deliberate creator of your own experience (whom you absolutely intended to be, even before you were born into this world), then you have to commit, and be willing to look at different things (that may seem unpleasant, or downright awful) from the perspective of Source, before your knee-jerk reactions and conditioned ways of responding kick into gear. Indeed, it will take time to reprogram your current conditioning, and adopt new–more powerful–beliefs. It will be challenging in the beginning stages, no doubt about it. However, in the end, the difficulties that you'll have to go through will be disproportionately outweighed by the state of mind and emotional equilibrium that you will eventually achieve.

When you regain control of your emotions you will begin to experience life in a completely different way, where everything will begin working out perfectly for you. The main reason being is that when you catch yourself becoming consumed by a negative emotion, you will no longer feel the need to condemn yourself, other people, events, conditions, or circumstances for the way you feel (further amplifying and prolonging your negative state as a result). Instead, you will know exactly what is causing you to feel the way you do, and you will know exactly what needs to be done in order to bring yourself back to a higher–a more positive–state of vibration, and thus continue to receive all of the good that Source is offering to you all day, every day.

"You are an ever-expanding being, and your emotions will guide you in keeping up with your expansion." – Abraham Hicks

EMOTIONAL GUIDANCE SYSTEM

"Negative emotion means, you've become something that you are not letting yourself be. The better you feel, the more you are in alignment with what you have become; the worst you feel, the more you are in resistance of it." – Abraham Hicks

In order to grasp the importance, and also the purpose of your emotions we have to begin with a basic premise that, while you are moving through your life experience–mentally sifting and sorting through the contrast of your environment–inevitably something shows up; something that you'd like to be, do, or have. And when this occurs, immediately, figuratively speaking, you launch a "rocket of desire" into the Universe (sometimes without you even knowing it consciously). And in order to keep up with your desire, and with what your life experience had caused you to ask for–and become–you have to *ride* that rocket of desire, by becoming a vibrational/emotional match to it. Here is a much better way of putting it. The process of keeping up with your desires, personal preferences, and that amended, ever-expanding version of yourself is a 3-step process (Abraham Hicks' concept):

- Step 1: *Ask*. The first step is easy since you are launching rockets of desire all day, every day; you cannot help but do that. You are constantly in the process of asking simply by virtue of the fact that you're alive on this physical planet. The contrast of your life experience naturally causes you to ask; it is inevitable. In effect, life does the step 1 for you; you don't have to do much of anything in order to accomplish step 1.

- Step 2: *Source Answers*. The second step is also none of your concern. Since you have launched that imaginary rocket of desire into the Universe, the higher-self part of you instantly becomes it. Meanwhile the universal Laws begin attracting all of the necessary parts to that new version. In effect, there now exists an improved version of that which is you–your higher-self–and the universal Laws have already brought, and are still bringing all of the cooperative components to that vibrational version of you. But in order to merge, and become one with that improved and evolved version of you, it is just a matter of becoming a cooperative component to it yourself, i.e. harmonising with it; becoming a vibrational match to it. In other words, that improved version of you is already living everything that you've ever asked for. The only question is: "Are you now a vibrational match to that evolved version of yourself?" Which leads us to the next, final step…

- Step 3: *Allow (receive)*. In order to experience your full expansion and become the beneficiary of all that you've ever asked for, you must allow yourself to receive it. You must figure out somehow, someway to become a vibrational match to that higher-self version of you. This is the only work which you have to do. And the purpose of this chapter is to help you understand exactly how you may do that. (As an aside, even after a decade of faithfully studying this material I still do not believe that I can do it justice in the few pages that follow. Thus, I highly recommend that you go straight to the source of this information, and check out Esther Hicks' material at www.abraham-hicks.com. Esther is such a beautiful, articulate soul, that even just by watching, and listening to a few of her recordings, the confusion you may be experiencing will be replaced by absolute clarity. Moreover, if you want to get the full experience I highly recommend that you attend one of Esther's workshops, or cruises, where you'll have the opportunity to ask your personal question and have it answered in real-time.)

Anyway, let's look at exactly how you might go about accomplishing step 3. For instance, if you've been asking for more money (I'm going to use the example of money, because most of us can relate to it), you can't be complaining about not having enough money, while at the same time be a vibrational match to having more money. Yes you have completed step 1, and you did it again and again; you have asked and asked, while the Universe had already lined everything up for you. All of the ideas, people, and circumstances have already been orchestrated on your behalf. You have no way of knowing how much has been done in lining up the circumstances and events that will produce the manifestation that you seek (in this example–more money). But the truth is you don't need to. You don't need to know when, or where your desire is coming from. Your only work is to find a way to become a vibrational match to your desire, and in order for you to do that you have to believe that your desire is already yours; that it is already here; that it is already done, even before you can see it. By feeling as though you already have it (because you do–you just can't spend it yet), you allow it to flow into your experience naturally; rather than blocking your desire through constant practice of contradictory thoughts, which invariably put you into a contradictory vibration. (You have to understand that certain thoughts you think stir up certain emotions within you which results in you moving into a certain vibrational state. And by observing–paying close attention–to the emotional/vibrational state that you are in, you get to determine exactly what is in the process of coming to you: is it your desire, or is it more uncertainty and lack?)

In order to make certain that what is coming to you is your desire, you have to trust in workings of the Universe; you have to believe that your wish had already been fulfilled, and is already on its way to you. You have to release all thoughts that contradict your desire and direct all of your focus and energy upon the good that you about to receive. The reason why most people never get to experience what they desire, is because they've been trained by other–very practical, logical, and realistic–humans that in order to believe something they first need to see it. When what they actually need to do is believe it so that they can finally see it. Otherwise, they will continue to regurgitate the same old reality and past results, over and over again, as they look at the current state of their bank account–acknowledge how empty it is–and then offer a strong vibration about it, which is most likely to be lack and deficiency. In effect, most people do not live their lives as deliberate creators of their own experience because they are forever stuck in step 1. From the lack of understanding, people are always asking, but never receiving. What people typically do after they have done step 1 is rather than moving to the final step, they continue to give their focus and attention to the very thing which caused them to ask in the first place. Not realising that by observing what-is can only bring them more of what-is. So when they see that no change is taking place, and no progress is being made, that makes them feel worse, which brings them back around to step 1, causing them to ask all over again.

This 3-step creative process requires that you practice the frequency of your desire before it can flow into your experience. In other words, if you've been asking for more money, then you have to get off the frequency which caused you to ask, and get on the frequency of your request. Because everything that comes into your experience is a perfect vibrational match to how you feel; not what you are wishing, or hoping for. In effect, you can wish to have more money all day long. But, if you do not feel good when you think about money, then you continue to practice a vibration that's preventing you from receiving what you've asked for. Therefore, the negative emotions that you sometimes feel are not your enemy; they are your friend. They are not there to tell you that you are an ungrateful son-of-a-bitch; that something is wrong with you; or that you do not deserve what you are asking for. Rather, they are indicating to you that, right now you are not allowing yourself to be all that you've asked for. Whenever you feel a negative emotion about something, the only reason why it feels bad to you is because you have expanded into something "more"–with regard to that particular subject–and now your choice of thoughts is not letting you go in the direction of your own expansion. Essentially, a negative emotion is only an indicator of this gap between where you are, and what you know, and where your higher-self is, and what it knows about the same subject.

Think about this, if your life did not cause you to give birth to new desires, and therefore did not cause you to move in the direction of something, then you would never feel any negative emotion about anything. For example, imagine if a random person were to call you and say: "Hello, you don't know me, I just wanted to call you and let you know that you'll never hear from me ever again." You would have absolutely no reason to feel any negative emotion about that particular interaction, because there is no desire involved. As a result, there would be no negative emotion of lack, or a sense of loss. You'd probably reply to them: "Okay, that'll be fine with me, good-bye forever." But imagine if your own mother, or your best friend had called you and told you this, that would be a whole different story wouldn't it? Because there *is* desire involved (not least to see them, and to speak with them).

Remember: you are an eternal being who is forever in the process of becoming more, and when you hold yourself back from catching up with your own "becoming more," your emotions will alert you by sending you a negative signal–telling you that you are moving in the opposite direction. When you don't understand the true purpose of your negative emotions, then you are not going to like them–you will try to resist them and wrestle them to the ground. But when you understand that the negative emotion is trying to tell you something very important, then you acknowledge the immense value of all your emotions, and you stop resisting them. When it comes to keeping up with your desires, without exception, you have to work on closing this emotional gap between where you now are and where you are going, or between what you now have and what you want to achieve, by feeling as though it is already done. You genuinely have to feel, and believe that it's already yours, even if at the present time you can't seem to find any evidence of it.

"You cannot have a happy ending to an unhappy journey." – Abraham Hicks

Your negative emotions are truly your friend; they exist primarily to let you to know when it is time for you to adjust your mental dials, and correct your vibration. Your emotional system can be likened to a dashboard in your vehicle, which shows you clearly when something is amiss. For example, when a maintenance light comes on–flashing in bright red–in your vehicle–clearly indicating that something is out of place–you never ignore it, and keep driving. No, what you do is you fix it, because you know full well what the consequences will be if you don't. The same principle applies to your emotions. If you don't pay close attention to how you feel, and continue to ignore your emotions, then sooner or later you will run yourself into a ditch. Essentially, your emotions are not causing anything, but rather, they're indicating something. Your emotional system is your guidance system which reports to you in real-time where you're at relative to everything that you want. That's why you have to make peace with the negative emotions that you feel from time to time as you move about your life. For negative emotion means that you're sane; it means that your emotional system is working properly, and in your favour. As counterintuitive as it may sound–we *need* negative emotions.

Think about it, what do you suppose makes a psychopath so unpredictable and violently dangerous? It is when the limbic system (part of the brain which is responsible for recognising one's own and other people's emotions) becomes damaged in some way, and is no longer functioning properly, that the afflicted person loses the ability to feel empathy, or sympathy for himself and others. Which means that he'll have no compassion for his victim's own fear and pain, because he doesn't even know what it is. The fact that a psychopath is incapable of feeling fear, means that he has zero impulse control. Thus, inflicting physical pain onto others doesn't feel wrong, while pleading and screaming doesn't even register. Obviously this does not mean that every individual with the same (or similar) brain disorder is a menace to society. However, I think you understand just how important it is to have a negative emotion–a safeguard–such as fear, which makes people think twice before doing something rash. A healthy person is unable to harm another–and feel nothing; let alone feel good about it. When we do end up hurting someone when the situation calls for it, even then, we never feel great about ourselves after the fact do we? For it is against our godly nature to intentionally harm another and cause them pain and suffering.

Your emotions are completely on your side, even the negative ones, and when you feel them it doesn't mean that something is wrong with you *per se*. It just means that you are choosing to entertain thoughts that are not in harmony with what you are really like, and what you really want. We can relate this to a GPS system in your vehicle as a perfect analogy. When the voice of your GPS tells you to take the next left turn–but you get distracted and miss the turning by accident–the voice never tells you: "What the hell are you doing? What's wrong with you? You're going the wrong way! You've done this so many times now, and I'm not going to help you anymore because you are hopeless." Is that what actually happens? I think not. The GPS can only ever tell you: "Make a U-turn when possible," and it will continue to repeat itself like a broken record until you finally make the damn U-turn. But the system is not mad at you. There is nothing wrong with you. Nobody is at fault here; all is well. You have all the time in the world to get on the right track, since nobody is sticking a gun to your head, demanding that you stop being such a sloppy driver. And that is precisely the manner in which Source is guiding you all day long–you have all the time in the world to correct course.

The reason why I feel the need to mention this is because I see so many people beat the crap out of themselves for feeling some of the emotions that they feel from time to time. And I would like to get you to a place where you make friends with your emotions. Rather than becoming consumed by some of those negative emotions that you sometimes feel and allow them to muddy the waters. What you can do instead before those vibrations gather more momentum, is first take a step back and acknowledge them: "I feel nervous. Probably because I'm making too big of a deal out of this." "I feel fear. That's interesting." "Why do I feel so awful? Did I really mean what I just said?" Then, simply observe your emotions from an outside perspective–detached–and begin to adjust your mental/emotional dials–that is all. Do not create a story in your mind about how you are a bad person; how you are a victim; how you don't deserve to be happy; how you are being punished by God; or how terrible and unfair your life actually is. In other words, you have to stop *identifying* with your thoughts and emotions. You have to quit assuming that your thoughts and emotions are who *you are*, especially when those thoughts and emotions are of a negative nature. Your thoughts and emotions are not you; what you are is an observer of those thoughts and emotions.

You have absolute control of your life experience, since you possess the God-given ability to choose which thoughts you are going to think, that will in turn evoke emotions which you *do* want to feel. Never spend your time thinking about how you are a victim of your circumstances, conditions, and other people's behaviour towards you. Because the only thing which you can ever attract into your experience is similar to that which you are energetically sending out. And if you're moping around–feeling sorry for yourself–then what do you suppose you are attracting more of when you do that? Exactly, more victimhood. And that, I can assure you is not going to yield you many (if any at all) opportunities in life. If you honestly wish to have a more productive, joyous, and fun-filled experience of life, then you absolutely have to commit yourself to studying and practicing the very ideas which we are discussing here. Do not bury your head in the sand when it comes to regaining control of your emotions just because it is difficult at times. Ignorance is not bliss; it is a joyless pit of confusion and despondency.

A major step which all of us can take with respect to understanding our emotions better is to realise that the reason why we feel negative emotions is because we are observing something–be it another person, situation, circumstance, or event–through the wrong lens. That lens is ignorance; lack of understanding. We are simply not aware that when we give our focus and attention to something unpleasant, and maybe even try to fix it, we inevitably feel worse because the higher-self part of ourself is looking at that particular thing also, but from a higher level of awareness and understanding–a higher perspective. In effect, while we're all the way down at the bottom along with that particular situation–bickering; wrestling with it; trying to win the argument–our higher-self is forever holding a higher perspective, and is only ever focused on the solution. Our higher-self will never go down to where we are in order to fetch us and lift us up; it just holds a higher perspective and waits for us to join it in that perspective. But when we choose not to (whether consciously or unconsciously), a negative emotion is then introduced.

In other words, the reason why you sometimes feel "bad" is because the larger part of you is continually offering solutions in a form of positive, non-resistant thoughts; whereas you are sometimes offering fear; frustration; anger; confusion, etc., in a form of negative thoughts. Hence, what you are feeling is the lack of inner harmony–caused by the clash of perspectives between the two parts of yourself–which manifests as a negative emotion within you. Understand that the higher-self part of you is vastly intelligent. It knows full well that whatever you give your energy to, that very thing begins to grow–it picks up momentum and becomes more prominent. Therefore, your higher-self will never join you in your negative perspectives–your fear; your anger; your bickering; and your resistance–because it knows that that will only make the situation worse. Your higher-self can only ever give its energy, focus, and attention to the solution; to the answer; and to a better way.

That said, if you wish to eliminate negative emotions from your life to an immense degree, then you have to practise joining the perspective of your higher-self more often, until it becomes second nature. You must learn how to close the vibrational gap between you and your higher-self. This work can be accomplished in a number of different ways: studying and developing a greater awareness; practicing meditation and becoming more present to the moment; changing your beliefs and perspectives; surrounding yourself with positive people; eating the right food and keeping your body free from junk; forming new positive habits; and all in all, becoming a more happy, healthy, optimistic person. This inner work which you have to do might seem laborious, but you wouldn't want to have it any other way. That is, you wouldn't want your higher-self to follow you everywhere *you* go, for you don't have a clue. Sometimes you don't even know where you are going, or what the hell you are doing.

If your higher-self were to follow you everywhere you go–rather than to keep a steady focus on a higher frequency (a better-feeling thought)–then you would never feel any discrepancy between the way you feel and whatever it is you're doing in your everyday life. Why? Because the *whole* of your being would be on the same page; in agreement; and on the same frequency as you. This would mean that if you chose to engage in a destructive behaviour, your higher-self would have to trust that all of the harmful and unproductive behaviour you're engaging in is actually something positive. In that type of dynamic, your life would most certainly turn out to be a disaster. For without your guidance system, constantly working for you and instantly letting you know when you are veering off your course–away from your highest good–it wouldn't take long until you'd find yourself in absolute ruin.

Though the good news is your higher-self can never abandon you. Your higher-self *has* to have your best interest at heart, because your higher-self is an integral part of you; it *is* you. So, you do not ever have to worry about being left alone to figure things out for yourself. However, having direct access to all of this wisdom, and divine form of guidance, comes at a cost of having to "deal" with negative emotions from time to time. The fact that your higher-self will always be there means that negative emotion will always be there too–whenever it's due. But do not hide, or run away from your emotions. Do not condemn your emotions, ignore them, and pretend as though things are going well when they clearly aren't. You have to acknowledge your negative emotions and listen to them, because they're telling you something valuable. If you resort to ignoring your negative emotions or use drugs to numb yourself from them, then you'll continue to miss out on every opportunity to better yourself, or your life situation as a result of a false belief that the negative emotion is wrong, and undesirable.

Now, catching up with your higher-self and joining it in a different perspective doesn't mean that you need to be forcing yourself to like something that you don't actually like, in hopes of *making* yourself feel good. That's not the message here. Rather, your work is to see whatever it is you are observing for what it is–neither good nor bad–without creating a narrative or a story about it in your mind, while at the same time being ready to take the necessary steps towards improving it, if you have the resources–or desire–to do so. However, when you are observing something unpleasant; something that you do not care for; something that is not affecting you; or something which you cannot do anything about, then do not give it any more of your energy than you need to. That will usually be enough to prevent it from coming into your own experience, or ballooning into a bigger issue. Granted, sometimes that "unpleasant something" can be another human who is in your personal space–who might be out to make you feel as bad as they do. For that reason, sometimes you simply have to go against your higher-self and use the physical, action-oriented side of your personality in order to get rid of them.

For example, as a man, imagine that you and your partner are going out to have a nice evening together, when you happen to come across a random drunk on the street, who decides to spout an obnoxious comment directed at your partner. Ultimately the right thing to do in the given situation (from the perspective of your higher-self) for everyone involved is to continue to walk as though nothing had happened. This is where the reality of the situation is unpleasant, but you're looking at it through the eyes of your higher-self–the lens of understanding. You understand that this person might be jealous of what you have. Maybe he had a rough upbringing, and acting belligerent is all that he knows. Maybe he is experiencing excruciating mental, emotional, or physical pain. Maybe he is mentally ill, or depressed. Or maybe someone he loved dearly had recently passed away, and he doesn't know how to deal with his emotions. Whatever the case may be, it isn't your job to try and figure it out; it isn't your problem; and is none of your business. There could be a number of different reasons as to why he is acting that way, but one thing is for certain: he's not connected to his higher-self. Consequently, he is acting out of ignorance, or unconsciousness. But since you are observing the whole situation from a higher perspective you don't feel the urge to attack; you actually feel sorry for him. Instead, you wisely choose not to engage with this person, and you keep walking. You silently wish him all the best, because after all, he is a fellow human being who happens to be stuck in some kind of a mental/emotional rut. That way, you get to keep your power and your experience does not become distorted by somebody else's negative vibration.

However, sometimes it doesn't pan out that way does it? Because negative energy wants to spread, and infect everything else around it. It will do whatever it takes to not be ignored. So let us suppose that the drunk begins to follow you while spouting obnoxious comments; trying to provoke a reaction out of you, and maybe even groping something he shouldn't. Well, in that case, I don't think you are going to care about how high your higher-self is, because you are still going to punch him in the face. But at the risk of him falling over and sustaining a fatal injury which may cost you your liberty for the next decade, and possibly for the rest of your life. Obviously that would be the wrong course of action for everybody involved. But considering the stage of evolution that we're at as human beings, situations where we *have to* go against our higher-self still often occur. I am also guilty of going against myself from time to time–taking certain actions and doing certain things that I didn't feel like doing. Sometimes, it is not possible to avoid getting sucked into unconsciousness of other people through understanding alone. In some instances diplomacy is simply not enough. Sometimes force and physical action is required, and unfortunately that's just the way things are today.

There are millions of people in the world who are still ignorant regarding the truths of life, with whom we share the same world. So it is not a big deal if you happen to bump into–and react to–one of them at some point in your life. The fact that there are so many of them means that it is bound to happen. However, by raising your own vibration you are drastically increasing your chances at never having to deal with any such person. Because the Law of Attraction (which we will get to in the following chapter) will never put someone who you are not in vibrational resonance with in your vicinity. Though it isn't practical or even possible to always be in a positive vibration. And so, if you do happen to bump into somebody who is asking for trouble, don't make the mistake of dwelling on those lower frequencies for long. Just do what you have to do, get out of there, and forgive them. And forgiveness come from the understanding that the actual culprits are not people; it is ignorance, which breeds unconsciousness and brings out the worst in them.

Remember when I said that the positive changes you wish to see in this world begin with you? That is what I meant by it. Because if you don't take the necessary steps towards a better change (adopting a higher perspective), then who will? The intoxicated asshole? I don't think so. As you take the initiative and begin to educate yourself, your family, and friends; your friends will in turn educate their family and friends. And as more and more people become accustomed to living in this new and improved way, the new generations that are coming forth will be less inclined to grow up ignorant. As you can probably figure, if that is the direction in which we are headed, the "obnoxious asshole" personality will eventually become extinct. Can you imagine a world where every single person is actually comfortable with themself, fun to be around, understanding, loving, honest, and decent? I can only imagine the heights which we'll be able to reach in such a cohesive, cooperative society. We would accomplish so much more and, before we know it, literally create heaven on earth. For we would no longer be getting any benefit, or false sense of satisfaction whatsoever from engaging and indulging in lower energies which do nothing but destroy and retard our evolution.

Of course, nobody knows when that time will come, but it is up to us as individuals to kick-start the momentum of that shift in consciousness, and to uplift each other. Rather than wasting our creative energy on trying to make somebody else's life a misery, why don't we start creating and offering solutions instead? We are forever facing ecological problems, spiritual problems, social problems, political problems, mental problems, and a myriad of other personal battles that we are all struggling with. Such as: finances; education; relationships; addictions; depression; health issues; self-esteem issues; abandonment issues, etc., the list is endless. Which is to say that there will always be problems for us to solve in one form or another. But why don't we finally reach a point where we have better quality of problems to solve? We'll never get anywhere until we stop constantly manufacturing new problems that, in effect reincarnate and perpetuate the old ones.

At any rate, now that we know what our emotions are–and are not–let's explore in more depth how we can better utilise our emotions to help us create, acquire, achieve, and become whatever it is we want in our lives.

EMOTIONS ARE MANIFESTATIONS

"Be happy with what-is while being eager for what's coming next."
– Abraham Hicks

Immediately after we're born we begin to get inundated with all kinds of information pertaining to what it means to be a human in this physical world. However, more often than not the information–or education–that we receive comes from those who either don't want us to know the whole truth, or those who don't know very much about successful living. As a result, we become conditioned to live our lives exclusively on a physical level–to navigate our world solely with our physical senses. To understand the world that we live in only by what we see, hear, smell, taste, and touch. To measure our level of success, and degree of happiness in life by the material/tangible things that we have–things which we have *manifested*. And those manifested things justify the way that we feel. For instance, if someone were to ask you: "Why are you so happy?" or "What are your reasons for feeling good?" It would only be appropriate for you to point your finger at certain physical manifestations in your life, and tell them: "This is why!" It makes sense, right? I believe that it does, and I don't have anything against that. I understand full well that we came into this physical, time-space reality so that we can enjoy the beauty of our material, physical world. There isn't anything wrong with acknowledging and appreciating the physical, tangible, material things which we have. Though, be that as it may, it is nonetheless in our best interest to begin viewing our emotions as legitimate forms of manifestation also, and here is the reason why...

"There isn't anything that you want for any other reason than that you think you will feel better in the 'having' of it." – Abraham Hicks

The actual reason for why we want to be, do, or have anything in our life is because we believe we will be happier when we get it. In other words, what we really want is not the thing itself; rather, it is the emotions that the thing in question will give us access to. That is what we're ultimately striving for–be it money; inanimate objects; a lover; a certain status; a career, or whatever else it may be. In effect, the reason why we want anything, is because of the way it makes us feel. Now, in order to achieve a respectable degree of mastery of our emotions, we have to come to terms with the fact that we possess the power to feel any emotion at will, long before any one thing (with which we associate a particular emotion) makes its way into our experience. Unfortunately, because of our limited awareness and lack of understanding the external stimuli, conditions, objects, events, circumstances, people, etc., seem to be the only medium through which we are able to experience positive emotions, and why is that? Because that's the way our grandparents did it; that's the way our parents are doing it; and it's also the way all of our friends do it. Essentially, we have merely been trained by other humans to operate in this way. We've been conditioned to give all of our focus and attention purely to the physical. All the while completely overlooking the creative, spiritual part of our nature. And since Spirit is where everything starts, you now may get a clue as to why we are forever having a difficult time trying to manifest anything worthwhile.

In one of her workshops, Abraham Hicks told us the following with regard to manifestation: *"Human beings tend to look at manifestations all wrong. Because what people usually mean by manifestation is that there is the idea of them owning a brand-new car, and then there is a physical car in their garage, and the car in their garage is the manifestation. Or, there is the idea of them being in love, and then there is a physical person in their bed, and person in their bed is the manifestation. For most people, manifestation is a moment which they are perceiving through their physical senses: they can see it; hear it; smell it; taste it; and touch it. That is what most people mean by manifestation. But, when you begin to include emotions into the idea of manifestation–when you begin to think in terms of emotional mani-*

festation–then you are on the right track. Because the emotion is what you are ulti-
mately striving for; the emotion is what you are really wanting."

Essentially, none of us want money for the sake of having paper in our wallets, so that we can give it to somebody else in order to get something in return–purely for the sake of having it. (A robotic relationship with money.) What we really want are the emotions that the idea of having lots of money makes us *feel*. So if your desire is one of having more money, then you have to make this distinction and start reaching for emotions that the idea of having lots of money elicits from you. You have to match your state of vibration to that of financial freedom; security; well-being; and abundance, by asking yourself: "What does being financially secure feel like? How does a person who is financially free think, talk, dress, act, and behave like?" Then through the use of your willpower you can begin to think, feel, dress, and act like that person would, regardless of your current conditions and circumstances that might stand in contradiction to your idea. (Nobody is preventing you from doing this. Nothing can hinder, or impede your creativity but your own limitations of the mind.) This, in turn becomes your highest chance at attracting to yourself–and rendezvousing with–all of the good that the vibrations of financial freedom and abundance have to offer.

Abraham Hicks teaches us that what trips most people up is the lack of awareness of the fact that every subject is actually two subjects: that which is wanted on one end of it, and the absence of it on the other. While the vibration that's active within a person the most–relative to any one particular subject–indicates exactly which part of it is in the process of becoming. For example, if you have negative beliefs about money; if you feel as though there is never enough to go around; if you believe in scarcity, lack and limitation, then you are setting yourself up to experience more of lack and limitation in your life as the result. On the other hand, if you believe in abundance, and if you feel that all is well, then you will continue to experience prosperity and abundance in all areas of your life, regardless of how many times you lose your fortune, and be forced to start all over again. And so, if you have limiting beliefs about money, then it really doesn't matter how much you visualise, meditate, and pray to have more of it. For you'll never attract something into your experience that, deep down you don't truly believe, or expect.

You have to understand that whichever emotion (positive or negative) you feel the strongest when you think about any one subject–whichever end of the double-edged sword so to speak that you are focused upon the most (are you focused upon having the money, or are you focused upon the lack of it?)–whichever vibration is active within you the most, that is what you're ultimately going to get. If you're wondering why that is so, then you have to remember that energy is continuously moving into form. And your thoughts about money is a form of energy that's in the process of coalescing with other similar energies, until that thought-energy becomes a full-blown manifestation. So then, by paying attention to the vibration that is active within you the most–how you truly *feel* when you think about money–you get to determine whether you are moving towards acquiring more money, or towards having more of the same.

"Be happy in anticipation of what's coming." – Abraham Hicks

In order to put your emotions into a proper perspective you have to understand that the reason why you want anything in your life is because you believe you will feel better when you have it. Meaning that the manifestation you seek is the emotion; not the "thing" in question. Now, if you are waiting for something to come into your experience *before* you can feel good about it, it will not come. Because the Universe is responding to your thoughts about it now (your current state of vibration); not how you are going to feel about it later. Consider that thinking thoughts of having something while feeling good about it, and thinking thoughts of not having something while feeling bad or impatient about it, are poles apart. Precisely for this reason, you must find a way to feel good about your desire *now*, if you are to ensure its arrival. This can be achieved by trusting that the Universe is responding to your request and begin to revel in the "vibrational unfolding" of your desire (Abraham Hicks' terminology). In other words, if you wish to experience your desire then you need to fall in love with the *idea*; rather than the physical manifestation of it. For whatever reason, our Universe is structured in such a way that it wants us to enjoy the journey and the process of bringing our ideas into our physical reality; not the end result. So whether we like it or not, that is simply the price we have to pay in order to experience what we desire. And I don't know about you, but risking to appear foolish in the eyes of others, or be considered impractical, irrational, or silly, in the process of receiving everything that I've been asking for, is a price that I'm willing to pay.

Having said that, once you give birth to a new desire, begin to enjoy the lover, the house, or the money, in the privacy of your mind, while it is in the process of becoming. Assume that your creation is already complete, and is already making its way to you. Get out of your own way and quit paying attention to the absence of it–offering a vibration of how desperately you want it; thereby further emphasising that you do not already have it–and begin to enjoy the unfolding of your desire. The Universe doesn't give you what you want and what you are waiting or wishing for; it can only ever give you that which matches your current state of being, i.e. what you're presently projecting outward. The Universe is forever responding to your current vibrational state (your vibrational offering) which is a by-product of your emotions, and your emotions are a by-product of your thoughts. Therefore, if you wish that the Universe would bring into your life something greater than what you already have, you just have to improve the quality of your thoughts relative to that particular something, and allow the rest to take care of itself.

Abraham Hicks calls this "the art of deliberate creation." Which means creating our reality deliberately; rather than unconsciously, and by default. What most people do, is they will think of something that they want, and offer a vibration that is in harmony with their request. But then, they will look at their external reality for any evidence of it–where there is none–then offer a completely different vibration, which prevents them from getting it. If you wish to live a life that you have imagined for yourself then you have to practise being a deliberate creator, by trusting in the power of your thought more than you trust in what you see in your immediate environment. However, it is highly advisable that you practise being a deliberate creator by yourself at first, at least in the beginning stages of learning this material. Since this is not common knowledge practically anywhere in the world most people are likely to think that you're batshit crazy if you tell them what you're learning and trying to accomplish. **Trying** to explain to others the things you are learning and discovering about yourself in a book such as this, will only impede your progress, especially when you yourself haven't yet internalised these truths. For this reason, I suggest that you keep this knowledge to yourself and practice these ideas in solitude without telling anyone about it. I suggest that you begin to get creative by yourself at first, and that you begin with something minor–something that is believable to you. That is, do not try telling yourself how you are going to become a billionaire next year when you are still working a regular job, and have virtually no business experience. Or how you are going to become a professional athlete in the next ten months when you haven't even been to the gym once. A little practicality at a start wouldn't hurt.

That said though, do not allow my limitations to become yours. You are more than capable of achieving/becoming whatever it is you desire in quantum leaps; rather than in small, well-thought-out steps. Our Universe cannot distinguish between big or small; difficult or easy. Because everything just *is*.

Therefore, it isn't so much that it takes a lot of time, patience, and hard work to manifest something huge and worthwhile, compared to something small and easy. Your belief in what is possible is always going to be the biggest determining factor when it comes to the level of difficulty, and the time it will take to actualise your goals. Moreover, whenever you think about what you want, you have to be precise/definite in your mental imagery. The Universe will not respond as promptly and efficiently as you'd like to a wishy-washy, sort of, kind of, not sure, foggy, misty, and nebulous concept, that you yourself can't even comprehend and put into proper words.

In order to ensure that your vision becomes a full-blown manifestation in the quickest time frame possible, you need to crystallise your vision, and get emotionally involved with it, by asking yourself: "What does my vision look like? What does it feel like? What are the surroundings? What does it smell like? Are there any people around? If so, what are they doing? What are they wearing?" and so forth. The more vivid, the more specific, and the clearer your mental image becomes, the quicker the Universe can respond to it. Once you have formed a crystal-clear image of what it is you want, you then need to accept that it is already yours; that it is already done; and that it is already making its way to you. When you endeavour to do this, you will naturally feel good about your desire; thereby putting yourself in the exact vibration which you have to be in, in order to attract it into your experience. As you continue to go about your life with complete and utter knowing that all is well insofar as your desire is concerned, without even worrying about whether it is going to come, or when it is going to come, then you will begin to get inundated with all kinds of thoughts, impulses, ideas, people, circumstances and events that will move you closer to the realisation of it.

When you can refrain from uprooting your desire prematurely and impeding the creative process by thinking that it doesn't work; that it is taking too long; that you do not deserve it; or that you are doing something wrong, then it becomes only a matter of time until you can spend it, drive it, or sleep with it. This is how the process of creation really works. This is how you create your own reality and get everything that you desire. The truth is, you are always creating your reality, you just aren't conscious of the fact that you are. And that is the reason why sometimes you get exactly what you are trying to avoid (by thinking about it, and thus feeding it your energy). Though by the end of this book, I hope that this will no longer be the case for you.

Let us continue to build upon the idea that one of your goals in life is to become financially secure, so that you don't have to worry about the subject of money any longer, so that you can be more free, and take advantage of a lot more opportunities. It is true that you do not have to have money in order to attract money, but you cannot feel poor and attract money. The key is you have to improve the way you feel about money, before things can begin to change. You can do this in several ways. One of which is by giving less of your focus and attention to the way things presently are (for in this moment, you are still poor), and instead begin to tell stories which lean more in the direction of how you would like things to be. If you conduct yourself in such a manner, then it won't take long until your point of focus will shift; your vibration will shift; your point of attraction will shift, and what comes back to you as a result of your vibrational shift will be quite different than what you are used to.

Another great way is through appreciation. If you begin to actively look for things to appreciate (such as the fact that you woke up this morning, or that you have eyes which enable you to read these lines), and hold yourself in that vibration consistently enough, then you will begin to see all kinds of opportunities around you. You will begin to detect all the different ways in which the Universe is trying to assist you in getting what you want. A state of appreciation is one of the highest vibrations there is (refer to the image on page 322). Such a high vibrational state will make you feel abundant and excited about the money, even if the digits in your bank account imply otherwise. And when you feel that way, you become a vibrational match to all the money that you have been asking for. In turn, allowing yourself to receive it more quickly since there isn't any more contradictory energy within you.

The more you practice the vibration of appreciation, then the more likely you are to rendezvous with someone who will lead you towards the money. Or you will get an idea out of the thin air, so strong, that you cannot help but act on that idea. Or a chain of events will unfold right where you stand, that will guide you directly towards the money. You never really know how the Universe is going to give you what it is you want, but the state of appreciation exponentially improves your chances at acknowledging and identifying the necessary step which you need to take to get there. And the beautiful thing about appreciation is that it doesn't matter what the object of your appreciation is; all that matters is the vibration itself. Meaning that, if a particular subject makes you feel appreciative (petting your cat; watching your kids play; or knowing that you do not have to worry about where your next meal is going to come from), then continue to focus on that subject until you find yourself in a state of appreciation. Then, if you begin to revel in that positive state, your vibration will positively influence other subjects that are also important to you, and they'll also begin to improve. The state of appreciation can be achieved by anyone, for there will always be something in our lives to appreciate. No matter how terrible our current conditions and circumstances may seem, there is no denying that the typical life experience for an average person today is way easier, a lot more comfortable, and more luxurious, than it was for kings and queens just a few hundred years ago.

One of the reasons why most of us do not get to experience the things that we desire, is because we are forever offering our vibration–the way that we feel–based upon what we are observing. The problem with that is, when what we are observing feels good, then more good things are coming to us. But when what we are observing feels bad, then more bad things are coming to us. And if you haven't noticed, the world that we live in is mostly focused on poverty; lack; limitation; control; famine; fear; war, and the like. No wonder why the "bad" is usually what's coming to us. But of course people have all kinds of rationalisations for this. They call it bad luck, accident, fate, destiny, karma, misfortune, or God who's choosing when it is time to bless them and when it is time to punish them. When in truth, the reason why anything would ever come into our experience, is because our state of vibration is in resonance with it. If we only take the time to pause and pay very close attention, we will see that the correlation between how we feel and what happens as a result of how we feel is always a perfect vibrational match; it is always accurate. It doesn't even matter whether it is someone/something else which makes us think and feel a certain way, or if we ourselves decide to think and feel a certain way–by our own conscious/unconscious choice. Because either way–and in any case–we are still feeling what we are feeling, and what flows into our experience still matches what we are feeling.

We have to understand that it is not about God, karma, fate, destiny, or what have you; it is always about our point of attraction, which is based on what we've got going on vibrationally; it is based on what we are habitually thinking about. Unfortunately, mind is not something that we're encouraged to exercise direct control over. On the contrary, we are conditioned to leave our minds open and take on board whatever comes our way–whatever other people are saying, thinking, and doing. As a result, most of us are not aware that *we* are in control of what we think, and how we feel; not the insensitive comment; not the other person; not the opinion; not the traffic; not the bank account, nor anything else outside of ourself. For example, when I am stuck in traffic, and I really need to get somewhere, but there is nothing that I can do about the traffic–all what I can do is wait and move forward as fast as the traffic jam allows me to–I'm not going to be honking my horn and screaming in rage because I have to be somewhere important. Instead, I'm going to re-frame the situation in my favour, and say to myself the following: "All right, the Universe knows where I have to be, and what needs to be done, so being stuck here is probably a good thing. Maybe, if there wasn't a traffic jam right now then someone was going to crash into me and possibly kill me–if I were to keep moving at the usual speed." Now, whether this is objectively true or not is unimportant; what is important is how that thought makes me feel.

Once I understood that the way I feel is going to determine the kind of experiences I will attract, I've made the decision to condition my mind to be-lieve that I am always in the right place, at the right time. Granted, I am far from perfect with this. Being the human that I still am, sometimes I lose my cool, and protest against certain experiences. However, the fact that I rarely condemn the present moment and all that goes on in it, the Universe has no other choice but to continue to place me exactly where I need to be. It is then my job to find the rightness of why I'm experiencing what I'm experiencing. Even when a certain experience seems negative, or unpleasant, it is up to me to find what's right about it. Infinite Intelligence knows exactly where I need to be, and when. So who the hell am I to claim that something is wrong with where I'm at, just because my current choice of thoughts about that situation is not up to speed with that broader perspective–that wisdom?

"Energy flows where attention goes." – Tony Robbins

In our Universe there is no such thing as exclusion; there is only inclusion. There is no such thing as a "no." Because by saying no to something, we are still giving it our attention. And attention given to anything is interpreted by the Universe as a big fat *yes*, which then gets incorporated into our vibration. That is, if we are pushing against something that we don't want–something that we wish would go away, or become less intense–by the virtue of the fact that we are giving it our energy, it has no other choice but to grow and actu-ally become "more." In other words, we cannot fight fire with fire; war only breeds more war; protests against racism; drugs; crime; terrorism, etc., only bring more of it, as it feeds off of our energy. Mother Teresa knew this prin-ciple all too well, she said: "*I was once asked why I don't participate in anti-war demonstrations. I said that I will never do that. But as soon as you have a pro-peace rally, I'll be there.*"

The same principle applies to prayer. People are usually praying for the things that they don't want, or wish to avoid, but then they experience exactly that. Because they are unaware of the fact that Source-Energy is responding to how they *feel*, not to what it is they say, they assume that God is probably busy. But what's actually going on is that because they are emphasising the "unwanted," is the exact reason why they continue to experience more of "unwanted." When this happens, a person will typically conclude: "God has forsaken me," or "God is not listening." Yet the truth is, if people are praying and asking for solutions to their problems–merely *hoping* that things will get better–while secretly harbouring vibrations of hopelessness and powerlessness, and *expecting* the worst–not knowing whether God will answer the prayer–then that uncertain energy can only bring more of uncertainty.

That's why it's so vitally important that you internalise this God figure–this great power–inside of yourself, so that next time you pray it becomes an affirmation to yourself; rather than a request to someone outside of yourself. Develop a sense of authority over yourself; become your own counsellor and a confidant. Be nicer to yourself and don't become a victim of your own negative self-talk. Realise that Source-Energy only ever expresses itself through you as love, joy, harmony, and peace; Source has nothing to do whatsoever with your own–or anyone else's–suffering. Source has nothing to do with all of the injustices; the bad and the evil in the world. It is people's resistance, or opposition to that flow of unconditional love and well-being which produces those conditions. It is their own negative and destructive thinking which brings about all of those things that we deem wicked, sinful, and unholy. It's a wasted effort when you try and blame God for your own–or anyone else's–suffering, because God has nothing to do with it. All that God is offering you all day, every day is love, care, guidance, and strength. If you are experiencing anything other than that, then all it really means is that you are pinching yourself off (by practicing negative thoughts; by suppressing negative emotions of anger; hatred; guilt; jealousy; fear; sadness, and the like; by harbouring resentments; or by blaming and condemning) from that powerful stream of well-being. In effect, you do it to yourself.

Knowing that every thought–especially one which is mixed with strong emotion–has tremendous attraction power, incentivises you to only focus on the positive side of everything, and stay poised and unreactive amidst other people's unconsciousness. Because if you are hating, condemning, or blaming something/someone (even if your hatred is justified) you're still embodying those negative emotions yourself. You might think that it doesn't affect you because you're directing that hatred towards someone else, but the Universe nevertheless picks up on what you are projecting outward, and sends more of it right back to you. That being said though, there is nothing necessarily wrong with having to experience negative emotions from time to time. You just have to remind yourself not to dwell on them for very long, because by doing so, you're increasing your chances of collapsing into unconsciousness. And the best defense against unconsciousness is continuous, conscious awareness of your vibrational states. So that if you happen to catch yourself in a negative vibration, then rather than becoming consumed by that energy, you instead give yourself an opportunity to correct course, before it picks up momentum and becomes an *actual* problem. In the following chapter we will be looking at what unseen forces are at play in your life and mine, which are responsible for the type of experiences that we get to have. And when these forces are properly understood, we can begin to work in harmony with them and begin to improve the quality of our life experience as a result. But before we get into that, here is a quick summary of the role of your emotions:

- Before we can begin to grasp what our emotions are and why we have them, we have to first heed Abraham Hicks' statement: "*As you came forth into this physical life experience, the 'wholeness' of who you are didn't come. Part of the consciousness that is 'you' came forth and is focused here in your physical body. But, the larger part of the consciousness that is 'you' remains non-physically focused in a stable, loving, and non-resistant place.*"

- Your emotional system is your guidance system which (with pinpoint accuracy) helps you to determine where you stand vibrationally in relationship to everything that you want. Consider this: as you go about your daily life, your exposure to the contrast of your experience inevitably inspires you to say: "I would love to have that," or "I would love to become that," and your higher-self instantly becomes the vibrational equivalent of it, and then patiently waits for you to catch up with it. Why? Because once you come across something that influences you to experience a desire, you cannot "un-come" across it, and pretend as if there is nothing better out there for you than what you already have. You cannot go back once you discover something better for yourself, since a new desire had already been born, and the larger part of you had already become it. There is no regression in our ever-expanding Universe; only continued growth and expansion. For instance, if you have ever driven in a Ferrari but had to go back to driving your Toyota, then you know that the above statement is true. Although you can pretend, and lie to yourself that regression is a normal, natural thing, while you put up with the heap of crap that you might still be driving, but if you can be honest with yourself, then deep down you never truly like it, at least not anymore. That is because a desire to drive something a lot better had been born and your higher-self had already gone there. But, when you are not up to speed with your own desire, that's when you feel a negative emotion. And the negative emotion is trying to show you that the larger part of you is already enjoying everything that you've ever asked for, while you're still moseying around.

- The reason why you would ever feel a negative emotion about something is because you have a different (less constructive) opinion about it than that positive, loving, and understanding Source-Energy part of yourself has. This is the reason why you inherently know when something doesn't feel right. Because the larger part of you is walking your path with you; it eternally stands in contradiction to the negative perspectives which you hold. Think about it, if the higher-self part of you were not there for you–guiding you, and letting you know what you had always known, even before you came forth into this physical life experience (that well-being abounds; that there is only health; vitality; love; joy; and abundance; that there is no death; that we're eternal beings, and other truths of a similar nature)–then you wouldn't feel icky indulging in negativity. In effect, negative emotions wouldn't feel bad to you. For, if deep down–instinctively–you never knew what happiness, love, or joy was, then grief; guilt; shame; hatred; depression, etc., all of those negative emotions and vibrational states would feel completely natural to you. Because you wouldn't know any better. But the fact is, you *do* know better (maybe not consciously). You do know that high vibrations of joy, love, happiness, and peace are what makes up your spiritual DNA; you *are* love; you *are* happiness; you *are* free; you are all of those good and powerful things. Maybe you have forgotten this. Maybe it is something that you never think about. But the larger part of you will never forget; it will always know, and it'll never cease to hold on to these truths steadily, and indefinitely. Thus, you have to become friends with your negative emotions; they're not your enemy. They're simply reminding you that right now, in this moment, you are not up to speed with who you *really* are; that you are forgetting something extremely freeing–something that you inherently know.

- There isn't anything that we want for any other reason than that we believe we will feel better when we have it. However, from a lack of understanding, most people will try to convince you that if you wish to be happy, then you need to go out and get whatever it is you want, and only after you get it, you can experience it, and have an appropriate emotional response to it–presumably joy, or happiness. But this is completely backwards. Because if you are unable to feel happy about what you want while it's in the process of coming to you then the type of energy you are projecting out into the Universe is counterproductive. In order to allow yourself to receive whatever it is you are asking for, you have to harmonise with your request, and begin to feel happy about it *now*, regardless of your current conditions and circumstances. You have to ask yourself: "How would I think, how would I feel, how would I speak, and how would I behave if I already had it?" And then begin to think, feel and act that way regardless of what's happening in your external reality. If you are able to do this (and anyone can), inevitably you will begin to attract all of the things requisite for the actualisation of your request as a natural consequence of the universal Laws (primarily the Law of Attraction) responding in accordance with your vibrational offering.

- Everything starts in a form of vibration, and that vibration becomes a full manifestation only when it gathers enough momentum to expand into something more. Relating this to your ability to create your own reality means that everything starts in your mind, or more specifically, it starts with your thoughts–you create your own reality by the virtue of the thoughts that you think. However, only the thoughts which you entertain habitually and regularly–thoughts which you are emotionally involved with–is what creates your reality. So, it does not mean that if you think about something today it will show up in your experience tomorrow. First, the thought has to be practiced long enough before it may begin to attract all of the necessary components for its manifestation. You see, there is a buffer of time before we can have whatever it is we're thinking about, and that's actually a good thing. The fact that our thoughts do not instantly materialise truly serves us. I don't know about you, but I wouldn't want to live in a world where I would have to deal with an alien creature of some sort if I were to randomly think about one. (How dangerously absurd would that be?!)

- Some individuals who learn about the workings of the powerful Law of Attraction (which we will cover extensively in the next chapter) for the very first time mistakenly convince themselves that they can pretend to feel good and still get whatever it is they are wanting. Or they try to force themselves to enjoy the process of creation, while secretly resenting the fact that nothing had happened yet. If this is something to which you can relate, then for your own benefit you have to understand that you will never be able to "cheat the system" by faking happiness. You may get away with deceiving a few people here and there, but the Universe knows when you are bluffing. You will never be able to trick the Universe into giving you something that you are not emotionally (vibrationally) ready for. You truly have to tend to your emotions and care about how you feel. You genuinely have to feel good in the process of going after all of those things that you say you want in life. Because the Universe is not responding to how you will feel in the future; it can only respond to how you feel now, i.e. the vibration that you are offering in this very moment.

- To shore up your vibrational offering do not try to figure out how you are going to get whatever it is that you are after–leave the "how" to a power wiser than yourself. Once you decide on the "what," and the "why," Universe will make sure to deliver the "how." You see, whenever you ask yourself questions to which you don't have the answers you lose your connection to the perspective of Source. Because the vibration of a question and that of an answer are two completely different vibrations. If you are going to ask questions then make it a habit to ask only those that lead you further in the direction of your desire; rather than away from it. For example, asking the question: "Why do I want it?" will set up a vibration within you which will allow the momentum of your desire to go further; whereas: "How will I get it?" or "Where will it come from?" will slow down the process, and possibly jeopardise the progress that you've already made. The reason for this is that you always know the answer to your "why" but you don't necessarily have the answer as to "how." Hence, the "why" is more likely to move you in the right direction and keep you on the frequency that the answers which you are looking for are on; whereas the "how" will almost always slow down the momentum which you have already established. When you are asking something which you do not have the answer to, you introduce resistance to the "creative process" equation.

All in all, you need to reach a point where you are no longer willing to listen to other people complaining and criticising one another. A point where you derive no satisfaction from somebody else's failure because you yourself haven't been winning for a while. A point where you no longer feel the need to win an argument just to see somebody else be wrong. A point where feeling good is what matters to you the most. A point where you are only willing to look for solutions; rather than whining about the problems. However, do not make the mistake of assuming that, since what truly matters is that you feel good, that you can just go off and meditate in a cave, or stare at a tree for the rest of your life–that if you make yourself feel good–Universe will take care of everything. That you can just sit there, do nothing, and wait until the Law of Attraction drops everything you deserve right onto your lap. Sorry to tell you, but that's not how this works. And that's not what life is about. You did not come here for the sole purpose of feeling positive emotions all day long, while completely ignoring life as it unfolds around you.

A life worth living is one in which you are willing to fully engage with your world physically, spiritually, and intellectually. That means constantly setting new goals, and overcoming various challenges. Learning new things about yourself, and destroying your limitations–be they physical, mental, or otherwise. Meditating regularly, and becoming more grounded in your own energy. Gathering as many experiences as possible, and seeing how much of your infinite potential you could actualise in your current lifetime. Creating useful products and services–offering as much value to the world as humanly possible. And most importantly, never getting bogged down in specifics: labeling yourself as being one extreme (a physical human being who is only ever interested in material, tangible, physical stuff), or the other (an enlightened, spiritual being who doesn't need anything but fresh air, and a peace of mind). To get the most out of life you have to work towards achieving a perfect balance between these two extremes, and learn how to maintain a seamless equilibrium by means of exercising and enjoying all aspects of your personality. That's the way I'd encourage you to live. For that is who you really are (a living consciousness that is complete), and that is what you came here to do (to enjoy the beautiful nature of the physical world, and be inspired by the contrast of life to create and give birth to as many new desires as humanly possible, for no other reason than that your nature is to create).

"Begin to see yourself as a soul with a body, rather than a body with a soul."
– Dr. Wayne Dyer

Laws of the Universe

"The natural laws of this universe are so precise, that we don't have any difficulty building a spaceship, sending people to the moon, and we can time the landing with a precision of a fraction of a second." – Dr. Wernher von Braun

"You can act in accordance with these laws, or you can disregard them, but you can in no way alter them." – Wallace D. Wattles

In this chapter we're going to get acquainted with a number of powerful and immutable Laws which govern our Universe, our world, and everything else in it. Though because these Laws–or principles–are extremely broad with respect to understanding and application, I intend to confine their methods of operation specifically to your personal success and happiness in life. What you must know about these Laws first and foremost is that they are inflexible; that they are always working; and that they could neither be broken, nor changed. One of the natural laws which governs our physical world–that we are all very familiar with–is the law of gravity. Everybody knows that if you jump out of a window–it doesn't matter whether you are a good or bad person; it doesn't matter who you are, how old you are, or where you are from–you will always go down and never float up. Even if you're not aware of the law of gravity, and you don't understand how it works, the result will be exactly the same regardless. Well, the same principle applies to all of the other Laws of nature. Meaning that, it truly doesn't matter who you are, what you have, or what you know about them, because they are always working, and in the exact same manner for every individual. That being said, it is going to be in your best interest to devote some of your time here to learn about these Laws and gain a much deeper understanding as to exactly how the Universe in which you live actually works.

These universal Laws refer to the unwavering and unchanging principles which govern every aspect of our Universe, and are the means by which the planet Earth–as well as the entire Universe–continue to exist, thrive, and expand. Those who understand these Laws and work in harmony with them are able to create lives that they truly enjoy. Whereas those who are ignorant of them continue to believe that various events, conditions and circumstances which they find themselves in are random series of events, or occurrences, over which they have zero conscious, deliberate control. However, once you become aware of these universal principles, you will realise that everything happens by design; that every effect in your personal life has its cause; and that, in every case–whether you are willing to admit that to yourself or not–you are responsible for that cause.

"The mind, once stretched by a new idea, never returns to its original dimensions."
– Ralph Waldo Emerson

LAW OF DIVINE ONENESS

"A person experiences life as something separated from the rest–a kind of optical delusion of consciousness. Our task must be to free ourselves from this self-imposed prison, and through compassion, to find the reality of oneness." – Albert Einstein

The Law of Divine Oneness decrees that we're all connected, and that we're all one. We're connected to everyone and everything in our Universe–we are all part of the same creative consciousness. This means that everything we say, think, and do, affects everyone else just like a ripple effect. The fact that we are connected suggests that the way we treat others is the way we treat ourselves, hence the adage: *"Love thy neighbour as thyself."* The Law of Devine Oneness reveals the fact that we do not exist and live in isolation. Everything that we say, think, and do has a direct impact on those who come within our sphere of influence. Likewise, everything projected by those whom we come into contact with, directly affects how we think, feel, and act. Just being cognisant of these truths will ensure that in the future you'll be more careful not only with respect to how you choose to express yourself outwardly, but also how well you filter inwardly, as in how selective and consciously aware you are with respect to which ideas you allow to enter into your subconscious.

Knowing about this Law incentivises us to send love, appreciation, and gratitude out into the world, as well as to everyone else in it. Because by doing so, it ensures that our own lives will be filled with love, happiness, and abundance in return. Granted, this is no easy task. It can sometimes be difficult to love, and appreciate our neighbour for who and what he is, especially when he keeps beating his wife. Of course, when we see injustice we absolutely should step in and offer help, but by condemning the other person we inadvertently condemn ourself. In order to avoid making this mistake we have to recognise the truth that people would never be doing some of the disgusting things they do, if they only knew that what they were doing was wrong. Rather than condemning them and expressing anger or hatred towards them in hopes of forcing a positive change upon them, we need to become more understanding and compassionate, and instead lead them in the right direction through the power of our influence.

We have to understand that each time a person expresses negative energy, acts in harmful ways, or indulges in destructive behaviour, what they are actually doing is expressing ignorance. In effect, people are not usually conscious of what they are doing, and just because somebody else wound up creating a horrible reality for themselves, it doesn't mean that we should also have to live that reality, by virtue of the fact that we share one and the same world. Just because somebody else has chosen to produce a reality for themselves that is miserable–full of pain and suffering–it does not mean that we have to give it our focus and attention and get involved in it. Something that can help us avoid becoming affected by all of the destructive ways in which other people choose to live their lives, is an observation of the fact that people are inherently good. In other words, we have to accept that every single person who is considered to be "bad" was once innocent–a creative spiritual being who was pure, loving, full of potential, and excited to experience life. Essentially, nobody is born a villain; no one is born with intentions of wreaking havoc on the world, and to despise their life. Their conditioning, and the tyrants they become takes place only *after* they're born. We don't know what those people have been through. We don't know what they've been subjected to. We don't know what had been planted into their fragile, impressionable minds when they were little babies. Who are we to judge them?

Think about this, if nobody ever teaches you and explains who you really are, what your mental faculties are, how to properly use them, and what you are supposed to be doing with your life, then there is a great chance that you will begin to misuse your mind because you don't know any better. This can manifest in a number of different ways. You may come across something unpleasant in your life, or observe something on the television–and because of your lack of understanding–you may get upset and become negatively influenced by it. Likewise, somebody close to you might just treat you poorly–physically beat you, and plant various negative ideas into your subconscious mind–in an effort to convince you that you are unimportant, and that you'll never amount to anything of value. And since you are unaware of the truth that everyone creates their own reality, you may get emotionally involved in what you are seeing, hearing, and ultimately experiencing. As a result, you will interpret their negative ideas as ultimate reality–the ultimate truth. Subsequently, you'll naturally begin to develop beliefs which support this dark reality, for example: "The world is against me; the world is a horrible place." "I hate people; they are all liars and cheaters." "You should never be honest and kind in this world, or you will get hurt." "The way to get ahead in life is to step over other people." "You can't trust anyone." "All rich/black (or any other background or race) people are evil, and I have to punish them."

At the end of the day, ignorance is what causes people to adopt all sorts of beliefs that separate them and push them further away from other people; beliefs that speak in absolute contradiction to our true nature. Yet, when we begin to understand that what those people are doing is expressing their ignorance we become more compassionate towards them. And instead of forcing them to change we simply demonstrate to them what's right through the clarity of our own example. Obviously there are instances where it is virtually impossible to love and appreciate certain people who are in our presence, because their energy is so negative that it almost overwhelms us. Sometimes it can be difficult to keep calm, and try to keep our focus on all of the good qualities in certain people whom we interact with, especially when they are having a "pain-body attack" (Eckhart Tolle's terminology), while screaming in our ear. Trying to love and appreciate all humans can be a daunting task. Some individuals are so enthralled in their negative, low-vibrational reality that even when we are trying to be nice, they nonetheless believe that we are out to get them. Truly, it is not a pleasant experience to be around a negative person when we ourselves feel good. So, if you happen to come across a difficult person, what I suggest you do is just leave them alone, and love them from a distance. That way, you get to keep your power, your peace of mind, and your sanity, without getting sucked into their negative world.

"All forms of life are simply variations of a single theme. We are all in fact one being doing the same thing in as many different ways as possible." – Alan Watts

I have previously mentioned that science and religion both agree on one particular notion, even though they use different names to describe it. Theology tells us that God is the cause and effect of himself; that he can neither be created, nor destroyed; and that God is evenly present in all places at all times–theology tells us that we are spiritual beings. Science, on the other hand tells us that energy is the cause and effect of itself; that it can neither be created, nor destroyed; and that it is evenly present in all places at all times–science tells us that we are energy. Now, if everything in the entire Universe is comprised of energy, while God is just another word for energy, then it is safe to assume that everything is comprised of God. From this perspective it follows that we are all connected to everyone and everything at a quantum level.

You can never truly be alone, because you and everybody else are connected to and, are in unison with Source, the Infinite Intelligence, the living consciousness. The major hindrance to understanding something as deep as this truth lies in the fact that our eyes deceive us. It is impossible to overlook the fact that we all live in separate bodies. That we have different names; different perspectives; different thoughts and ideas; different appearances; different voices; different skin colour; that we speak different languages. From our physical perspective, it is only natural to conclude that people are different; that they are not like us–they are strangers with whom we do not have a thing in common. However, one who has developed a higher level of awareness, he or she understands–without a shadow of a doubt–that we are all expressions of the same creative consciousness. That person knows with absolute certainty that we all came from the same Source; that we are all connected to each other; and that we are all essentially the same.

LAW OF VIBRATION

"If you want to find the secrets of the Universe, think in terms of energy, frequency and vibration." – Nicola Tesla

The Law of Vibration is the primary Law in our Universe, since vibration is the starting point of everything. The Law of Vibration decrees that nothing rests; everything moves; everything vibrates. Everything in our Universe is made up of energy, that is vibrating at different speeds. Sound is vibration; smell is vibration; taste is vibration; colour is vibration. All that we see, hear, smell, taste, and touch is also vibration. What we are doing as human beings is we are simply translating these vibrations through our physical senses into things which we can perceive. However, because we get trained by other humans to navigate our world purely with our physical senses ever since the day we are born, it does not take long until we become so good at it, that we don't even realise that that is exactly what we are doing. Invariably we reach a point where it becomes almost impossible for us to even consider the possibility that when we look at any particular solid object, what we are looking at is actually energy that is vibrating at a very high speed. The very fact that energy is imperceptible to the naked eye, naturally, any object that we might look at, or interact with simply *appears* to be solid and stationary, when it really isn't.

Albert Einstein revealed in his greatest equation $E=mc^2$ that matter has an inherent amount of energy to it; that mass can be converted to pure energy; and that energy can be used to create massive objects which didn't previously exist. It represents the idea that matter is nothing more than stored energy; every physical object in the Universe works as a container for stored energy. Think about a hydrogen bomb as an extreme example. This bomb is a physical object which contains an enormous amount of stored energy, and that energy can be released–on a ridiculously huge scale–upon a violent impact. Interestingly enough, the amount of energy that is stored inside an average-sized human being is more than enough to explode thirty such bombs. This gives us a rough idea as to how resourceful and powerful of a container we actually are. And so, the next time you're about to tell someone how you don't have enough energy to do something, you should think again, because you may just want to rephrase that. (It is not that you don't have enough energy, but that you do not have the desire, or incentive to release that energy.)

Everything has its own vibrational frequency: a book; a pencil; a car; a stone; a tree; a piece of garment; and even our thoughts and feelings. For example, a rock may appear to be stationary when we interact with it through our physical senses. However within the solid rock there are millions of subatomic particles that are full of energy–moving at a certain speed, or vibrating on a certain frequency–which makes up that rock for what it is. In effect, that rock is actually moving; it is vibrating. Literally, everything in our Universe is vibration; it is vibration first and foremost. Sometimes it is challenging for us to accept that, since our sensory factors are so good at interpreting vibration, that when we look at an apple we see a green, round-shaped fruit, that is relatively firm and sweet, so we conclude: "That's a real, solid apple." However, once we develop understanding, we'll know that an apple is nothing more than a container for a certain amount of energy, that is vibrating at a certain speed, or frequency, which makes the apple appear as it does to our physical senses.

Finally, with regard to vibration, I want you to consider the following. Energy moves in waves, and those waves come in various ranges of amplitudes, intensities, frequencies, and speeds, which give them unique qualities and behaviours. Energy waves travel through mediums, or fields such as air;

water; and even awareness. Think about all the different mobile phone frequencies that are accessible to us at any given moment in time. There are billions of people in the world today who own mobile devices, and every person's device has its own unique frequency. When we dial another person's phone number what we are actually doing is tuning our own mobile phone's frequency to the frequency of theirs, so that we can establish a clear and direct channel of communication with that particular person. Or how about all the different TV, as well as radio channel frequencies that are whizzing over our heads all day long? Just because we cannot physically see these energy waves it does not mean that they aren't there. Case in point, an aerial, or satellite dish in your home that is connected to a television set will allow you to tune into those frequencies—or as we more commonly call them—channels. So even though you might be unaware of all the different frequencies that are present with you in the room, if you switch on your television and tune into the frequency of a particular station, you will be able to see/hear what is being broadcasted on that station. Now, the question is, when you switch to a particular channel, do you make it travel hundreds of miles to come into the room where you are sat, or do you simply gain access to something that was there the whole time? The answer is of course the latter. And if you decide to change the channel, you'll immediately get a completely different broadcast, and even though you might be sitting in the exact same spot when you make the switch, the frequencies which you are tuning into (the channels that you are surfing) do not overlap and stack upon one another.

You might be wondering: "What does this have to do with anything?" The significance of this lies in the fact that the same principle applies to our thoughts. Thought waves are one of the highest forms of vibration, and are extremely potent in nature. Thought-energy has tremendous attraction power, and it will quickly attract other energies that are in resonance, or in harmony with it. The fact that there is an infinite number of frequencies that we can tap into, as well as the fact that nothing in the Universe gets created or destroyed, means that all of the things which we want to be, do, and have in our life are already here. Poverty or prosperity; fear or courage; sickness or health; depression or happiness, whatever. We do not have to force anything to come into our experience, because everything is already here. If you don't particularly enjoy what you are currently experiencing, all you have to do is change your mental dial, and tune into something that you would prefer. In effect, if you only dare to think good thoughts related to freedom, happiness, love, abundance, good health, and so on, even in the midst of a reality that hardly warrants that level of positivity, then that reality will eventually dissolve and turn completely and utterly into something else. (It isn't much different from watching a drama movie with a depressing storyline, that makes you feel bad, but then realising that you would like to feel better and switching to a wholesome family adventure which has a happy ending.)

By becoming familiar with the Law of Vibration you can see how important it is to engage in activities that make you feel good. To think positive thoughts. To listen to music which makes you want to dance and sing your heart out. Or to watch movies which uplift your spirit and make you laugh. To never complain about things which you don't have, and start being grateful for all the things which you do have. The point is you have to keep yourself in a high vibrational state as often, and for as long as possible, to ensure that what you predominantly resonate with is that which is good and pleasant. The highest possible vibrations which anyone could emit would be those of love; happiness; joy; appreciation; and positive expectation. So if you make a commitment to emit such vibrations in your everyday life as frequently as possible, then you will inevitably begin to attract a wonderful life filled with purpose, prosperity, good health, and happiness as a result.

"The Universe doesn't hear what you are saying; it only feels the vibration of what you are offering." – Abraham Hicks

"Everything is energy and that's all there is to it. Match the frequency of the reality you want, and you cannot help but to get that reality. It can be no other way. This is not a philosophy, this is physics." – Albert Einstein

LAW OF CORRESPONDENCE

"I think, therefore I am." – Rene Descartes

The Law of Correspondence decrees that our outer world of conditions and circumstances is a direct reflection of our inner world of thought. It implies that our reality is a mirror; a reflection of what is going on inside of ourself. Which is to say that if we deem our external reality in a negative way, then it so corresponds that we feel worse inside. In effect, if our life is not moving in a positive direction, then blaming/condemning other people, circumstances, conditions and events is exactly what is keeping us where we do not want to be. If we want to see positive changes take place in our life, then we have to be willing to point the finger at ourself; to look inside ourself and realise that we–and we alone–are the ones responsible for where we're at, and for every-thing we have. The external world of conditions and circumstances is not the cause of our discontent, it is the effect. The external world can only ever mir-ror back to us what we are mentally/emotionally projecting into it.

In order to live a life that we want we have to accept that nothing in our outside world can change for the better, unless we first make corresponding changes on the inside. Since "thought" is where everything starts means that before we can enjoy a better quality of life, we first have to improve our ha-bitual ways of thinking. Trying to determine exactly how much our thinking is skewed, as well as how far we must go, may be done by observing the life situation which we currently find ourselves in, and that will reveal to us the quality of our past thoughts. Our dominant thoughts in the past have actual-ly shaped all of the conditions and circumstances that we presently find our-selves in; everything that exists in our life today is unequivocal evidence of our past thinking habits. Fundamentally, your present life is a microcosm of thought waves which you have sent out in the past, that perpetuated the ac-tions you've taken, and those actions led to the manifestation of your current results–in all areas of your life. Now, if that is true (which it is), then the im-provements which you are seeking, do not lie in your electing a much nicer government, or your employer giving you a raise. But in making few, simple (although not necessarily easy) tweaks in your perspective.

"When you change the way you look at things, the things you look at change."
– Dr. Wayne Dyer

It is understandable why we would rather blame someone or something else for how we feel, and for what we are getting in life, than to admit our igno-rance, and incompetence. However, if you are going to live a joyful and ful-filling life as a powerful, deliberate creator of your own experience, then you have to be willing to take full responsibility for your thoughts, feelings, and actions. You have to regain control of your life by taking an honest look at yourself, and conducting a thorough audit of your thinking patterns in order to pinpoint exactly why you are today where your life has brought you. Set aside some time to ask yourself: "What are my thoughts, feelings and actions towards my social life? What are my thoughts, feelings and actions towards my financial life? What are my thoughts, feelings and actions towards me as a person? What are my thoughts, feelings and actions towards people?" And so on. Self-reflect, and really think about your attitude, your behaviour, and your habitual ways of responding to various experiences that come into your life. If you are willing to do this, you will uncover precisely what your deep-rooted beliefs are which make you act the way you act. And once you identify which beliefs are serving you, and which do not, you may then begin to correct course in the private of your own mind, without going about your life hoping, and sometimes demanding–but in every case to no avail–that everyone else improves their thinking, so that *your* life can change for the better.

"If you think that other people are the cause of your problems you are going to have to send the rest of the world to the psychiatrist for you to get better."
– Dr. Wayne Dyer

Thoughts are a potent form of energy, and energy that's held on the inside is forever seeking expression on the outside. Whenever we generate a thought in our conscious mind and get emotionally involved with that thought, that thought-energy has to express itself on the outside, and so it'll begin to move the physical body into appropriate action (as within, so without). That energy can manifest itself in a number of ways: our posture; body language; tone of voice; the choice of words; health effects; and overall attitude. If the energy which is being summoned is of a negative nature, then the physical body will be compelled to express it in negative ways. When we're wrapped up in a negative vibration, we just can't help but to adopt a poor, contracting, and disempowering posture, e.g. head down; slouched shoulders; avoidance of any eye contact; dragging our feet, and so on. Conversely, when we are in a positive vibration, we naturally assume a carefree and loose body language, e.g. standing straight and upright; head up high; shoulders back; a welcoming smile; looking people in the eyes; walking with purpose, and so on. Our state of vibration also affects the range of expressions we have access to. But more importantly, it affects our attitude–something that should certainly be kept in check. Because it is our attitude that's going to determine our success in the areas of personal/social relationships, creativity, and finance.

Our attitude is comprised of conditioned ways of thinking, feeling, and acting in certain situations, or around particular people. Attitudes cannot be faked, because our attitudes are continuously being telegraphed through our behaviour. Every person can accurately determine another person's inner attitude through their subtle interaction with them, and then communicate accordingly. Essentially, your attitude is always reflected back to you through the way other people interact with you and treat you in return. So, if you are having difficulty analysing what might be going on inside yourself, then all you need to do is take notice of how most other people are treating you, and you will have your answer. But, if you continue to try to fix other people (believing that they're the cause of your problems), then no positive change will ever take place. For example, I personally know an individual who–no matter who she interacts with–always ends up fighting, either verbally, or physically. Almost every time we happen to chat, she always tells me how everyone she meets is a total asshole, and is forever trying to get a rise out of her. Even though I explained to her–on numerous occasions–that it is her own attitude which is causing her problems, she is still doggedly convinced that it's other people who make her angry. As a result, while she is pointing her finger at others–venting her rage–she's completely oblivious to the fact that her eyes are full of judgement; her voice is obnoxious, and rapport-breaking; her expressions and gestures are repellent, and offensive. In effect, she still doesn't realise–even in presence of such clear evidence–that she does this to herself.

How about health? What you must be aware of is that our thoughts and feelings are often reflected back to us through corresponding health effects. If negative thoughts pervade our mind, then we will manifest stress, anxiety, and physical ailments as a result. The fact that energy is always moving into form means that even if we are trying to suppress it, it will still move somewhere. For example, if we have been engaging in a negative idea, which had produced feelings of stress on the inside, then even if we now try to ignore it, that stress would still have to express itself as a tense neck and head muscles on the outside. Our thoughts truly play a significant role in keeping our physical apparatus in a healthy, functional, and harmonious state. If we are chronically thinking negative/destructive thoughts, and becoming emotionally involved with them, then in some cases, those thoughts might even kill. Make no mistake about this, your mind is an extremely powerful tool, and if it is used incorrectly (especially for prolonged periods of time) it'll inevitably lead to a disastrous outcome. The expression: "Worrying oneself to death" is actually truer than one would like to think…

I have heard of an incident which took place in 1988 numerous time by now, from different sources, about a railway employee who had accidentally locked himself inside of a refrigerator boxcar whilst performing several final checks on some of the railroad cars before leaving the site. When Nick realised that the rest of the crew had already left the site, he began to panic. Apparently he had been screaming and banging inside of the car for some time, trying to get someone's attention, but nobody heard him. Given his expertise he concluded that he'd ultimately freeze to death if he were unable to quickly make his escape. With one failed attempt after another to save his own life he finally resigned to his tragic fate. The reason we know this to be the case, is because he used a knife to etch sentences inside of the car, describing his thoughts as he moved closer to death. The writings on the floor said the following: "I am becoming colder." "Still colder, nothing to do but wait." "I am slowly freezing to death, I can hardly write." "These may be my last words." And sadly they were. But the strange thing about this story is that when the crew members arrived back at the site the following morning, slid open the car door, and found Nick laying there–dead–they were shocked, because the refrigeration unit in the car was inoperative. After the investigation, the verdict was that the temperature inside the car indicated 55 degrees Fahrenheit, and it never dropped below 50 throughout the night. In effect, Nick had become the victim of his own negative thinking. This man had used his ability to reason (one of the intellectual faculties) incorrectly. He permitted–what he thought were–his circumstances to control his thinking (vibration). In effect, he presumed that it was the end, when there was no need for that presumption. But the mere fact that he *believed* he was going to freeze to death, he inadvertently put himself into a vibration which was in harmony with that belief, ultimately resulting in hyperthermia as the autopsy later revealed.

Obviously this is an extreme example of an individual who had become emotionally involved with a wrong idea, but it is a true story. It incentivises us to think twice before we permit the outside world (other people; circumstances; conditions; events) to control our thinking. For the sake of our well-being we need to learn to live our life from the inside-out. To focus on solutions, and only see the upside of things (until proven otherwise). To see ourselves in perfect health. To have faith that everything will turn out to be all right. And to *expect* good health and fortune. Do not underestimate the power of your thoughts, especially when facing a serious health issue. For feeling positive or optimistic about the condition–as opposed to pessimistic or honorary–will be the main determining factor between recovery or not.

Lastly, when it comes to personal relationships all you need to know is that if you are a positive, easy-going, and good-humoured individual on the inside, then you will invariably have strong, open, and honest relationships on the outside. Period. In other words, if you are a decent, honest human being, and you have good intentions, then you won't have to put a lot of effort into finding people who are on the same wavelength. That being said, if you are having a difficult time socialising and making friends, then maybe there is some inner work that needs to be done before your social life can improve. Understand that the people who you interact with are always picking up on your thought-vibration, and are reflecting back to you exactly what you are giving to them. Therefore, if your social life is not where you would like it to be, then you might want to do some introspection to see whether you are being a downer, or a value-leech. Where instead of feeling good about yourself and offering value, you feel bad about yourself, and are trying to take value, which drives people away. Of course it isn't always about you, you could be the nicest person in the world, yet still get treated like dirt in return. Now, if you can recognise that in your personal relationships that is indeed the case, then maybe the people that you are associating with are not the type of people you should be around. But ultimately, you shouldn't have to bribe, guilt-trip, pander to, and be overly nice to someone to make them want to be your friend. The Law of Correspondence implies that, as long as you are treating others as you yourself would like to be treated, then your own circle of positive, honest, and like-minded friends will form itself naturally.

LAW OF ATTRACTION

"Everything that's around you right now in your life (including the things you're complaining about), you've attracted." – Joe Vitale

The Law of Attraction is the most powerful Law in the Universe. The Law of Attraction is the manager of all vibrations; an orchestrator of all conditions, circumstances, and events. The Law of Attraction states: "The essence of that which is like unto itself, is drawn." In basic terms this means that like-energy always attracts like-energy, and what this means for you in a practical sense is that, if you allow a particular experience to negatively affect how you feel, then Law of Attraction will not be able to surround you with positive things which would make you feel better. The Law of Attraction reveals that different thoughts vibrate at different speeds, and thoughts can only attract other thoughts that are of a similar nature, and are on the same frequency. Thus, if you're thinking negative thoughts, then you'll attract negative outcomes into your life; conversely, if you're thinking positive thoughts, then you'll attract positive outcomes into your life. This is not a secret, or ability which is strictly reserved for special few; every human being operates in this way whether he knows it or not. It has been proclaimed by great thinkers, leaders, philosophers, and teachers alike throughout the history of mankind that we literally become what we think about the most; that our inner world of thought is continually shaping our outer reality of conditions and circumstances.

The most important thing to understand is that, in our attraction-based

Universe there is no such thing as exclusion; there is only inclusion. The Law of Attraction only knows one word–which is *yes*. There is no such thing as a "no," or pushing against something unwanted, because by virtue of giving our attention to it, it gets invited into our experience. In other words, when we give our attention to something unwanted; something that we don't wish to experience, and would rather avoid, what we are actually saying is: "Yes! Come to me this thing I do not want." With that in mind, you may get a clue as to why most people never live the type of lives that they want to live. And that's because most people are unaware of the existence of this Law and how it works. Universal Laws do not care whether you acknowledge them or not; they are always working. You may not know how the law of gravity works, but if you throw yourself out of a window–you will still hit the ground. Similarly, those who don't understand the Law of Attraction do create their own reality, they only do it by default. That is, they do it in response to what they are observing, and are in reaction to. They are offering their thoughts–which in time become their new experiences, or perpetuate their current experiences–from a place of observing what already *is*.

For instance, if you are trying to attract more money into your experience, yet nothing seems to be changing/improving, the reason for this might be the fact that you are paying too much attention to what-is. You might be looking at the current state of your bank account where the "what-isness" of your current reality reminds you that, indeed you do not have enough money. So what happens is you emit a vibration out into the Universe which says: "I still do not have enough money," while the Law of Attraction brings into your experience more of "not enough money." Likewise, if you are sick, and you are trying to get better, but you listen to your doctor who tells you and shows you how sick you actually are–the what-isness of your current reality–what naturally happens is you focus on sickness. And the Law of Attraction cannot bring you the cure. Now, when you find yourself in such a pickle, all you must remember is that the current state of your bank account, or your diagnosis merely proves that you *have been* in a certain vibration which brought you to that point. But it does not mean that you have to continue to stay in that vibration, and perpetuate that reality. You are better off looking at your bank account, or your diagnosis and telling yourself: "That was yesterday," and then, through the power of your thought create a new "today."

Every single person has the God-given ability to redirect their thoughts, and originate new ideas. Each person has the God-given ability to put themself into a brand-new vibration–at any given moment in time–which the Law of Attraction always–and only–responds to in the present time. The Law of Attraction can only ever respond to your now-vibration; to thoughts which you are thinking now; not yesterday, or tomorrow. Therefore, do not spend any more time than you have to on figuring out what, who, when, how, or why? Simply acknowledge what it is you want, and give your undivided attention to *that*! To be more effective when going after the things you want in life you have to tell yourself: "I want *this* and I'm going after it!" Avoid saying things that contradict your own desire, such as: "I want this, *but* I don't know how. I want this, *but* I'm too old/young. I want this, *but* I don't have enough money. I want this, *but* I don't know where it will come from. I want this, *but*_____. (Fill in the blank.) Because every "but" instantly contradicts your desire. Just as quickly as you launch a rocket of desire–instead of riding it out–you just as quickly jump off of it before it can start gathering momentum, or put differently, gaining power–and to be even more specific–attraction power. I advise that next time you think about something that you want, you get rid of the "but," and start to feel as if you already have it. Do not try to figure out *how* you are going to get it, because the "how" will only slow down the momentum. You do not need to know how you will get what you want. You only need to know *what* you want, and *why* you want it; you only need to know *where* you want to be, and *why* you want to be there.

"Keep your focus on how you want to feel and let the Universe fill in the details."
– Abraham Hicks

Since the Law of Attraction responds to your dominant thoughts–your most cherished beliefs–it is highly recommended that you ask yourself: "Do I hate poverty more than I love prosperity? Do I hate misery more than I love happiness? Do I hate chaos and confusion more than I love order and stability?" Because you see, the thing that you love is yours, and the thing that you hate is yours as well. Whichever vibration that you resonate with the most–be it love or hate–when you think about any one particular subject, you increase the possibility of it gathering momentum and eventually becoming yours. So pick what you choose to believe wisely. The Universe doesn't know if what you believe is serving you or not. It simply registers what you're offering vibrationally, and the Law of Attraction proceeds to bring you more of it.

Likewise, make sure that everything you say comes from a place of confidence and power; rather than from yearning and uncertainty. For example, when you say things such as: "I wish that I were happier," or "I wish that I could overcome this problem that I'm having," the Universe says: "Yes, you do wish to be happy. Yes, you do wish to find answers to your problems." And that is the end of it–you *wishing*–because the Law of Attraction brings you more of "wishing," so keep wishing. What you should be saying instead is: "I'm so happy and grateful for the life that I'm living, there is nothing that I cannot be, do, or have. If there is a problem, I know that I will handle it. I truly have everything that I want." And the Universe will say: "Yes, you do live a happy life, and you do have everything you want. You do have everything under control–all *is* well," and the Law of Attraction will start bringing you more of *that*. Even if what you are saying is not necessarily true, even if you feel uncomfortable affirming these statements out loud, even if you feel like a fraud for saying such things, I can guarantee you that if you continue to repeat a lie to yourself, over and over again, then in approximately twenty-one days you will begin to believe it. This is not an easy thing to do however because your brain will protest: "What are you taking about? Quit bullshitting yourself! Get back to reality and take a look around. You are such a mess and a complete liar." And that's precisely why you need to develop patience, and a sense of authority over your mind in order to overcome that little voice in your head which wants proof, not promises. To do this, you just have to believe in the power of your thought and creative imagination more than you believe in the objectivity of your logic. And take action despite the fact that your brain wants you to think you are being irrational/unrealistic.

Make no mistake about it, your brain will try to fight you with logic and demand solid proof; it will insist that you explain how anything that you are saying could possibly be true. But, you must not be deterred. You must keep telling yourself that you are going to succeed in getting/becoming whatever it is that you want. You have to imagine it; you have to feel it to be true; and you have to practice the vibration of it daily. In time, it'll begin to feel completely normal to you, and soon enough, it'll become your reality. You know why? Because *you* are the creator of your life experience. Not your brain; not your conditioning; not your past experiences; not other people; not circumstances, conditions, or events. *You* create your own reality, because you have the God-given ability to originate new ideas at will. You have the God-given ability to think any thought you choose, anywhere, at any time–and as a result–place yourself into a whole new vibration. It really doesn't matter what happened in your life ten years ago, one year ago, or even an hour ago. Every moment is a new moment; every moment is a new opportunity for a better thought; a better feeling; a better result; a better life! Knowing that Law of Attraction can only respond to the vibration that you are offering *now*–not ten years, or ten minutes ago–leads to an awareness of the fact that your past experiences have absolutely zero power to influence your life experience today (unless you allow them to). How amazingly liberating is that?!

"Imagination is everything, it is the preview of life's coming attractions."
– Albert Einstein

"That which I give thought to I begin to attract. That which I give thought to with emotion I attract more quickly." – Abraham Hicks

My introduction to the Law of Attraction was through "The Secret," a movie I had watched several times, by the end of which I was convinced that I understood the Law completely–but I was wrong. What I had discovered a few years after the fact is that the movie didn't give enough attention to a particularly important aspect of manifestation–taking action. I found out the hard way that, though it was true that imagining what it is we want, feeling as if we already have it, and projecting ourselves into the future–though this was certainly an important part of the creative process–was not enough. I had to learn that in order to manifest what it is we wanted to be, do, or have, we also had to take *massive* action. That since we live in a physical world–which is governed by time and space–we had to go out and interact with our external reality in order to transmute our desires from mere thought-forms into physical, tangible experiences. Now, the tricky part about this, is that we have to act on our ideas by taking "inspired action." Which comes from a vibrational place of "already having it." Rather than taking action which comes from the vibrational place of "trying or wanting to make something happen." For, *trying* to make something happen, or desperately needing it, emits a totally different vibration to that of "it is already done."

Whenever we are *trying* to make something happen we are unknowingly communicating to the Universe that we don't already have it. And that, in order to get what we want, requires a lot of time and effort. Of course, what happens as a result, is that the Universe takes our word for it, and it does in fact become more difficult. To make this creative process a lot easier for you, once again, I'd like you to answer the following questions: "How would you act if you already had what it is you want? How would you conduct yourself if your desires were already fulfilled? How would you feel, how would you walk, what clothes would you wear, and which words would you eliminate from your vocabulary, if you had already achieved your goal?" Your honest answers to these questions will reveal to you exactly which actions you need to take; which perspectives you need to adopt; and what kind of behaviours you need to develop. Now, if you've been working with the Law of Attraction and doing everything right for a long time, yet you don't seem to get results, do not be disheartened, and get discouraged. What you need to understand is that there exists a buffer of time which prevents you from experiencing whatever it is you are visualising until a certain amount of momentum is gathered. And that is actually a good thing!

If you can imagine a world where everything you thought and felt suddenly appeared in front of you in its fully manifested form. Sure, you would be able to materialise a huge sum of money right where you stand in a matter of a second, but what you have to realise is that the same principle would naturally apply to other things that are of a negative nature. Meaning that, if you were to live in such a world, then each time you were to have a fearful, or negative thought, you would have a grand piano dropped on top of your head, or get struck by lightning. For this reason, it is certainly a blessing that, in our Universe, nothing manifests until a certain amount of momentum is gathered, and until all of the cooperative components have been assembled. The fact that you cannot instantaneously manifest a million may seem like a hindrance to your creative abilities, but it's actually a blessing. This buffer of time acts as a protection shield, which allows us to learn the art of manifestation without killing ourselves, and others in the process. So don't be alarmed by this concept of unbiased attraction. Because in our physical world–which is governed by time and space–things will never manifest immediately. The workings of the Law of Attraction are extremely fair and forgiving. We have more than enough time to pick up on our own destructive thoughts, feelings and vibrations, and correct course before they actually show up in our experience. If it were not for this buffer of time between forming a thought and it becoming a thing, if it were not for the existence of this time lag between our thoughts and their full manifestation, then we would've all probably killed ourselves in the early stages of our development, by accidentally thinking a wrong (lethal) thought. Surely you will agree with me that that wouldn't have been a very practical world for us to be born into.

Fortunately, we are born into a world where this "time lag" so to speak gives us an opportunity to redirect our thought-energy away from anything that doesn't serve us and, therefore prevent it from becoming an actual, fully manifested problem that we now have to wrestle with. Meanwhile our emotional guidance system forever indicates where our current thoughts are taking us–to positive or negative outcomes. So if you are in doubt as to whether you should keep thinking whatever it is you are thinking, or step back and readjust your focus, you can check in with your emotions from time to time, just to see how you feel at the present time. So that you can determine–with the highest level of precision–what is in the process of coming to you.

"Logic will get you from A to Z; imagination will take you everywhere."
– Albert Einstein

By acknowledging the immense power of influence which the Law of Attraction has in your life you must be ready, at all times to guard yourself against negativity. For example, when you don't feel particularly well, and someone asks you: "How are you doing today?" tell them with a warm smile on your face that you are doing exceptionally well. Refrain from going off about how much you are struggling, or worrying about something important. Because those words constitute lower vibrations. This does not mean that you are lying; it just means that you are aware that those words do not bring you any closer to your goals, and are not solution-oriented. So what you do instead is you smile and kindly respond: "Yes, I'm doing very well. thank you, though I am having a little bit of trouble with this particular situation, but it is nothing to worry about. I will figure it out." In effect, this doesn't mean that you have to run away from your problems, or keep all of your worries bottled up inside. You just have to ensure that everything you think, say, and do comes from a place of positive expectation, and appreciation. If you are able to pull this off, then the Law of Attraction will have no other choice but to continue lining up other people, circumstances, conditions and events all around you, that will help your desires materialise much sooner.

Don't make the same mistake that I did, which is going around and telling people what you are learning, and what your vision is. You might get so excited about these powerful ideas that you'll naturally want to share it with others. However, I am here to warn you that it is best to keep it to yourself at first. Most people out there are completely fine with where they're at, even if they're living mediocre lives, and squandering their talents/potential. Most people are so utterly comfortable with where they are, that trying something different doesn't even cross their mind. For it becomes too uncomfortable to think about change at that point. So, do not tell anyone your plans, and what you are envisioning yourself doing. For those high energies of happiness, joy and expectation will most likely dissipate when other people start looking at you as if you're a crazy person. Or when they start showering you with reasons as to why you should just be happy with what you have and proceed to lecture you about successful living, which they themselves have no real idea about. If you have not been practising emotional control, and unreactiveness for any respectable amount of time, then those kind of interactions will only weigh you down. Especially when people do not respond the way you want them to respond–with wonder and excitement. If you were to explain to other people some of the things you are learning in this book, chances are they will listen to you, but not without a glazed-over look in their eyes and a confused expression on their face, as if you were communicating in an alien language. Their nonchalant responses and indifference may make you feel disappointed, or annoyed, which will invariably throw you off your high-flying frequency, and retard the progress that you have already made. For that reason, your best move is to keep these powerful ideas to yourself for now, and protect your vibration. Let them do them, and you do you.

"See yourself living in abundance and you will attract it." – Rhonda Byrne

"All that we are is the result of what we have thought." – Buddha

LAW OF INSPIRED ACTION

"By thought, the thing you want is brought to you, by action, you receive it."
– Wallace D. Wattles

The Law of Inspired Action decrees that nothing happens without action, at least in a time-space reality such as the one in which we live. All of us simply must take action in order to get whatever it is that we want and desire, there is no other way around it. You can be the most talented, intelligent, and deserving person in the world, but nothing will materialise in your life unless you take sustained action. You will never receive what you are looking for if you are passively creating plans, visualising, feeling good about your desire, and dreaming about it. In our physical world that is simply not enough. The things that you want in life will never randomly fall out of the sky onto your lap while you are meditating and visualising in your basement. The reality is you have to get out there and fully engage with your world (especially after you've meditated and visualised), or else nothing will happen for you. Anyone who tells you otherwise is probably just trying to sell you something.

Notice how even the word attraction has the word "action" in it, clearly indicating that you will never attract what you want unless you take the corresponding action. No matter how big your goals may be, they still become manageable and reachable if you just break them down into small actionable steps. If one of your goals is to write a book as an example, and you want to get to the end result as quickly as possible, it will naturally make you think about how long it is going to take, and how much material you will need to write, which will likely make you want to give it up before you even start. But, if you decide instead to enjoy the process of writing itself, and just take it as it comes–maybe by committing yourself to writing one page a day–then you will not get overwhelmed, or become frustrated. And by the end of 10-12 months your book will be fully written. This may seem like a long time to reach a single goal, sure. But you have to admit that it is much better to get it done in one year's time, than to never write it and put it out there at all.

The Law of Inspired Action implies that the right, or appropriate action is always preceded by a vision, which means that you will still have to begin with the end result in mind, but without thinking too many steps ahead. You just need to know what you want, and where you are going, and all the right actions will come to you of their own accord. Whenever you impress the image/idea of something that you wish to accomplish upon your subconscious mind, you put yourself into a vibration that will compel you to take the necessary actions, that will help you transmute that image/idea from a thought-form into its tangible/material/corporeal counterpart. In effect, rather than planning ahead of time, and mulling over all of the things which you might have to do in order to get, or become whatever it is that you want. If instead you put your trust in the workings of the Universe, and confidently assume the feeling of your wish already fulfilled, then you will be *inspired* to take the exact actions which will reliably move you in the direction of your dream.

Remember that all thoughts precede action, and actions precede results. In this context, you'll never be able to jump from thoughts directly to results, because action is the medium by which thoughts become things. Therefore, as soon as you become clear as to what it is that you want to be, do, or have, you have to commit to doing something every single day that will move you in the direction of your vision. Of course, it will feel foreign to you in the beginning stages to act in ways that are different to how you usually act. But if you repeat a certain action every day for a month it will eventually become a habit; it will become ingrained in your identity; and it will no longer require motivation, or willpower for its execution. You see, it takes far more energy and effort to initiate a motion than it does to maintain the momentum of that motion. Sometimes even the best plans are doomed for failure due to inability to overcome inertia. So don't fall for the same trap, realise that in order to perpetuate a strong motion and maintain its momentum, you need to have a *burning desire*. Meaning that, you have to want whatever it is you want more than the air you breathe; it has to be life or death; you either get it or you die! Yes, that is an extreme mindset to adopt, but it is highly effective in helping you achieve your goals. Most people fail because they wish for things willy-nilly, and mosey around and wait for motivation, encouragement, or inspiration to come, which hardly ever does. Whereas a burning desire is the fuel, or drive that will enable you to break free from the gravitational pull of your comfort zone, and get your ass into gear! The fact that your goal, or vision is the "unknown" it completely threatens your comfort zone, for your comfort zone is familiar, predictable, certain, and low-risk. And because of this, you will experience fear, as well as tremendous amount of resistance when going after those things that you say you want, but fear doesn't have to stop you.

Please understand that fear will always be there when trying something new; it is a given; it is unavoidable. Never shy away from it because fear truly exists in situations that count! Fear is your friend; it is your personal guide into freedom. If you happen to feel fear as you begin moving towards something you want, that is a direct indication that you are about to make significant progress, and grow; not become incapacitated, and fail. Granted, fear is an unpleasant emotion (which is the reason why most of us would much rather avoid it). But actually fear doesn't have nearly as much of a crippling effect when we develop the courage to blast through it, as it does if we continue stepping back into safety. For example, if you have ever found yourself standing at the top of a 3/5-meter high diving board, then you recognise the amount of fear that the thought of jumping off of it triggers in you. But once you have made the jump and hoped for the best, I am willing to bet that you quickly realised it was actually nowhere near as bad as you initially thought. In fact, it was probably exhilarating, and you immediately felt like jumping off of it again, over and over, until your fear was virtually gone. Now, there are people who have been in the exact same position as you, and were ready to jump off, but never got to enjoy the thrill of that leap of faith because they succumbed to their fears. As a result, whenever you (the fearless diver) see a diving platform you feel thrilled, and become energised; whereas those who stepped back into safety feel petrified, and become paralysed by fear.

Susan Jeffers, author of a phenomenal self-help book "Feel the Fear and Do it Anyway" gives us the best, most straightforward advice when it comes to overcoming our fears, which goes as follows: *"Whenever you are afraid of doing something, just feel the fear and do it anyway."* And that is all there is to it, I couldn't have said it better myself. Whenever you are afraid of doing something, yet you go ahead and do it anyway, you will actually be glad that you did. For what you will quickly discover is that all of the growth and freedom which you were seeking, was on the other side of your fear.

"Fear robs you of your freedom to make the right choices in life that can bridge the gap between where you are and where you want to be. On the other side of fear, lies freedom. If you want to grow, you need to be brave and take risks. If you are not uncomfortable, you are not growing." – Roy T. Bennett

The reason why it feels uncomfortable doing anything new and different is because we are not familiar with it. The fear of the unknown, or foreign environments is ingrained in our DNA. That is why our initial, go-to, knee-jerk response is to mentally project ourself into the future and envision our worst death. However, shifting into a fear-based mindset while getting bombarded with resistance is nothing more than our brain's attempt at keeping us alive; it is not a representation of our ability, or actual dangers that we are about to encounter. The reality is, your brain has the exact map that you need to traverse any new path which you have set for yourself, and lead you to your desired destination as safely and efficiently as possible. But, your brain will not give you the map because it is trying to protect you–by dissuading you from travelling new lands that may be dangerous. Nonetheless, if you dare to step forward anyway and begin traversing this new path, then the mere fact that your brain cannot physically stop you from taking action, it has to fully activate; it has to hand the map (or the instruction manual) over to you and start helping you every step along the way (to help you survive). In other words, when your brain acknowledges that keeping you safe through the use of fear and resistance isn't working, then it'll try to keep you safe by giving you full access to your mental faculties, a heightened state of awareness, and a greater attunement to your surroundings instead.

Those who are successful in life do what they have to do, whether they feel like it or not. They act despite of their fears because they have learnt that there is a direct correlation, or link between actions and results. They understand that fear is an opportunity to grow; rather than a warning sign to cower in their comfort zone. They have become acutely aware of the fact that the more energy and focus that they put into something, then the more they will get out of it. They understand that every action counts; every action is either bringing them closer to their set-goals, or pushes them further away. The difference between the haves and have-nots is that the former group acknowledges the importance of guarding themself against their own counteractions if they are to become successful, and continue to be exceptional at what it is they do. For example, if you set a goal for yourself to read one book a week, and you've decided to read one or two chapters each day. However, on few occasions, rather than reading you ended up watching the television instead, then the act of watching the television was a counteraction. Or if your goal is to get fit and you had decided to workout 3-4 times a week, however on several occasions you were peer pressured into getting drunk at a local bar with your buddies instead, then going out and drinking all night was a counteraction. In effect, on route to achieving your goals and becoming a successful person, you are your worst enemy. You truly are the only one who can stunt your success; not the government; not the environment; not the economy; not the educational system; and not your family, friends, or colleagues.

What can help you to stay on course is becoming familiar with a particular principle which, in economic theory is called "opportunity cost." Opportunity cost refers to something that you have to give up when you choose one alternative over another. In practical terms: whenever you find yourself doing anything that feels even slightly off, you should take a minute to ask yourself: "What am I gaining from this? Where is this going to lead me?" And once you conduct a brief audit of your actions and realise that what you're doing is not leading you any closer to your set-goals, you then need to ask yourself: "What could I be doing instead that would actually lead me to where I want to be?" In effect, as you endeavour to go after all of the things you really want in life, you must be ready, at all times to identify your counteractions and take your progress seriously. Because a predictable and comfortable life isn't worth accepting. Sure, it might be comfortable, but mediocre at best. Most of the time your goals will require you to give up some of those things which you really enjoy, and that can be a total bummer in the beginning, I know. However, all the pain, heartache, and fear which you'll have to experience–when going after some of the things that you *really* want–will be completely forgotten once you reach your goals. For they will become replaced by happiness and satisfaction. Whereas if you stay where you are, and continue to do things as you have always done them, then that gnawing sense of: "Oh God, I wish I could have done *that*," or "I wonder what my life would look like today if I actually did *that*" will pervade your consciousness and eat you up alive.

> *"The definition of insanity is doing the same thing over and over again and expecting different results."* – Albert Einstein

LAW OF PERPETUAL TRANSMUTATION OF ENERGY

"As a man thinketh in his heart, so is he." – James Allen

The Law of Perpetual Transmutation of Energy decrees that energy can neither be created, nor destroyed; it can only move into form, through form, out of form, and back into form again. Hence, energy cannot cease to be, or disappear; it can only move somewhere else, or become something else. For example, we know that water is made up of two hydrogen atoms and one oxygen atom. And those atoms move at a particularly high speed of vibration. Now, water can change into ice if we slow down its rate of vibration, and it can change into steam if we accelerate its rate of vibration. But, the same energy that we know to be water is not being created or destroyed; it is merely moving into different forms such as ice; water; or steam. In effect, water can change its form physically, however, chemically it stays the same. Whether it takes the form of ice, water, or steam, it is still comprised of H2O.

The same principle applies to the energy of our thoughts. That is, if we are harbouring negative thought-energy, then that energy will seek expression through our physical body in a negative form, why? Because thoughts are cosmic energy waves which in their natural state are neither negative nor positive, but will move into whatever form we decide to give them. This is how it works: Thoughts and ideas that are contemplated and reflected upon repeatedly with emotion eventually develop roots in the subconscious. When those thoughts are impressed upon the subconscious (which is the emotional part of the mind), it begins to move the body into a negative, or positive vibration–depending on the nature of the thought which had been impressed. That positive or negative energy within–seeking to express itself–will move the physical body into action without (as within, so without). Which will invariably produce results that are consistent with the thought which perpetuated those actions.

The Law of Perpetual Transmutation of Energy further emphasises the fact that if we truly wish to change the results that we get in our lives (in any area of our life), we have to begin by improving the quality of our thoughts. Thinking is the starting point of all creation. Because Source, Spirit, or Infinite Intelligence *is* energy which thinks. This is how our Universe, and every planet in it, as well as how all of the other forms of life came to be, including ourselves–through the power of focused thought. For some of you, this may sound borderline insane, and so in order to explain this in a way that will be much easier for you to accept and understand, I want you to think about the following. The wristwatch that you wear was once nothing but a thought; an idea in one person's mind. Whoever created the first wristwatch could not have possibly done so without first forming a clear image of it on the screen of his/her mind. Likewise, the clothes that you wear; the car that you drive; the house that you live in; the chair that you sit in; the smartphone that you have; the computer that you have; the Internet which you use to binge-watch funny memes, when you should be studying; the Mona Lisa; the Eiffel Tower; the railroad; the street lamp; and so the cover of this book. Literally everything began as a mere thought in the mind of one individual, at one time, before it ever became an actual thing.

"Your thoughts become things." – Rhonda Byrne

"Everything is created twice, first in the mind and then in reality."
– Robin Sharma

If you are having difficulty working with this Law, then you need to understand that you can't expect the thought-energy you're entertaining to transmute into its equivalent physical form without allowing yourself to get emotionally affected by the idea. You see, the various ideas which you fashion in your conscious mind are like little seedlings, and in order to transmute them into physical form, they first have to be impressed upon your subconscious. The fastest way of turning your ideas over to your subconscious is through repeated reflection/contemplation. This can be easily achieved through regular visualisations and autosuggestions to yourself. In effect, you have to focus your mind on your ideas repeatedly, and continue to feed them your energy, focus, and attention, until you no longer have to–for it has become ingrained in your subconscious. Whenever you focus your thought-energy on a specific idea it enables that idea to develop roots in your subconscious, and the more you visualise your ideal outcome, the more emotionally invested in it you will become. If you are willing to do this, then it won't take long until your vision will begin to transmute from a mere concept into a burning desire. And that will then compel you to take certain actions, which will be essential in transmuting that burning desire into its equivalent physical form.

"The only thing that can grow is the thing you give energy to."
– Ralph Waldo Emerson

Whatever thoughts or ideas that you impress upon your subconscious mind *must* move into physical form; it makes no difference whether it is a positive or negative thought. The subconscious mind must accept whatever thought-energy you impress upon it. The subconscious mind is really the universal, creative mind; it is completely deductive; it does not have the ability to evaluate, and reject ideas. Thus, whichever thought goes into the subconscious it will immediately begin to seek out its manifestation in the most appropriate form available. However, do not be alarmed, because before any thought, or idea can make its way into your subconscious mind, you have the ability to first evaluate that thought, or idea in your conscious mind (part of the mind which has the ability to carefully sift and sort, rationalise, evaluate, accept or reject). This grants you the ability to pick and choose which thoughts, or ideas you are going to allow to pass through to your subconscious mind. And if you had previously allowed some negative ideas to get through that are now causing you problems, then by the same method (rational thinking, and repetition) you have an opportunity to replace them with something better.

That being said though, as soon as a thought passes over to your subconscious mind your whole being begins to vibrate at a level conducive to attracting all of the cooperative components that are in harmony with that particular thought. In basic terms: whatever you plant is exactly what you'll get. As previously mentioned: Law of Attraction doesn't respond to your wishes and mere wants–which originate in your conscious mind–the Law of Attraction always–and only–responds to ideas that are deeply rooted in your subconscious mind, i.e. your most heartfelt desires, or emotionalised thoughts. A simple way of wrapping your head around this is to begin viewing your thoughts as spiritual seeds. In our physical world the physical seeds will always produce after their kind, no matter what. You will never plant a carrot seed and expect a potato to grow because you know that you will always get a particular result based on a particular seed which you plant. Hence, whenever you dwell on thoughts associated with poverty, lack, yearning, or limitation, then what you are doing is transmuting that type of energy into those exact outcomes. Effectively speaking, when you are trying to achieve much better results in your life, yet deep down you are worried, or afraid (offering contradictory vibrations), then you shouldn't be surprised as to why no positive change is taking place.

The Law of Perpetual Transmutation of Energy is completely unbiased; whatever thought-energy that you plant into your subconscious mind, Universe will respond to, and make sure that it grows. It doesn't have the capacity to care about whether what you are planting is good or bad; wanted or unwanted–that is something up to you to decide. Source-Energy loves you unconditionally; it loves you so much that it allows you to experience everything that you could possibly want. So if you plant negative ideas into your subconscious mind, then you will experience them and no one will stop you. Likewise, if you plant positive seeds of happiness, health and prosperity into your subconscious mind, then that will become your experience and no one will stop you. It is your job therefore, to care about which thoughts you will emotionally get involved with and plant into your subconscious. No one can do this for you, but yourself; not even your boss; not your mother; not your kids; not your ill-mannered neighbour; and certainly not God.

"If you can see it in your mind, you can hold it in your hand." – Bob Proctor

LAW OF GENDER

The Law of Gender decrees that all seeds, as well as ideas (an idea is akin to a spiritual seed) have a gestation, or incubation period. For example, a human embryo has a gestation period of around 280 days; a mouse has a gestation period of around 20 days; an elephant has a gestation period of around 650 days. Likewise, a potato has a gestation period of around 60 days; a tomato plant has a gestation period of around 70 days, and so on and so forth. Now when it comes to creative ideas–spiritual seeds–the gestation period refers to the length of time it takes for an idea to move from moment of inception to full manifestation. To this very day nobody can say for sure how long it will take for an idea to come to fruition. We have no clue as to how long it will take to move our ideas from a thought-form into corporeal, physical reality. All that we can do is take into consideration the amount of work that is required to manifest our desire. When we consider the level of difficulty and the amount of work that needs to be done in order to reach our goal, we are able to roughly estimate how long it will take to achieve it. The distance between creating goals and achieving them is the gestation period; it is the gap between where we are now and where we would like to be. Though, we can shorten the amount of time which it takes to achieve our goals by honing our ability to *focus* and *concentrate*.

When we concentrate exclusively on one specific goal at a time, we increase the intensity of our purpose and in turn significantly shorten the span of incubation. In other words, when we supercharge the energy directed to a specific end, we in turn supercharge the growth of that same end. If you are going to experience those things in life that you want the most sooner rather than later, then you must avoid dispersing your creative energy on too many unrelated or unimportant things, which do not positively contribute to your primary objective in life. The fact that an average person tries to accomplish a number of different things at the same time is exactly the reason why it takes them forever to manifest anything worthwhile.

The most common mistake that I see with those who are having a difficult time achieving the things that they really want (and I've been guilty of this myself) is that they don't stick at it long enough. Most people give up on their dreams, and sometimes at a drop of a hat, for their impatience and lack of focus forever extends the transmutation of thought-energy into full manifestation. Whereas those who are not at all concerned with when, or how the things they want are going to come about, and who focus wholeheartedly on one thing at a time, blaze a trail towards their goals in the fastest time possible. If you are going to experience your desires more quickly, then you have to tend to your ideas, your goals, your "seeds," just like a farmer would. You have to care for your vision, nurture it, and continue to move towards it. Just like the physical seed which needs to be in an environment conducive to its growth; your thought-seed needs support from you, and your environment. Just like the physical seed which needs a certain amount of water and sunlight; your thought-seed needs the stimulus of your action and persistence in faith that your idea will eventually bear fruit.

"As you sow, so shall you reap."

The Law of Gender states that we sow in one season and reap in another; we never sow and reap in the same season. Lack of understanding of this truth leads to discouragement when the things we want do not materialise instantaneously. But, we have to acknowledge that they are coming, and that they will arrive only when they–or more importantly, when we–are ready. Since we understand that it takes 70 days for a carrot seed to grow into a carrot, and since we know that a seed for a baby takes around 280 days to grow into a newborn, we do not uproot the carrot after 3 weeks and become frustrated because it isn't ready. And we never become impatient with our partner because after a period of 8 weeks the baby is still nowhere to be found. When it comes to physical seeds we don't have an issue waiting until they fully manifest because we understand exactly how long it will take. However, with regard to spiritual seeds, there are naturally so many variables involved in the equation that no one can know for certain what the gestation period is. And what typically happens is if we miscalculate the process and uproot our ideas prematurely. In other words, because we are not familiar with the Law of Gender most of us are expecting to see the trunk, the branches, and all of the green leaves, long before the idea gets the chance to grow roots. When what we should be doing instead is taking action for the joy of taking action itself, and trusting that the idea is in the process of becoming. James Allen, author of a fantastic little book "As a Man Thinketh" said the following with respect to allowing the Universe to do its work: *Be not impatient in delay. But wait as one who understands. When Spirit rises and commands, the gods are ready to obey."*

In the Bhagavad Gita it states that we have the right to our labour, but not to the fruits of our labour. In this context, the only thing we need to be concerned with is how we choose to focus our energy; not how the world is going to respond. If we focus all of our energy upon giving, providing a service, helping and sharing, then Universe will make certain that we get back everything what we have given out (energetically) a hundredfold. We don't need to worry about the rewards. Now, sometimes what happens is people go out and do everything they can for others. Yet because nobody cares, and nobody responds in like-kind, they become bitter and conclude that the universal Laws are broken. What they had failed to understand, however is that when we provide a useful service, or lend a helping hand to a particular person, it does not follow that specifically that person will give us back what we deserve. The truth is, we may get it back from a completely different person, whom we meet a month later on the train commuting to work, or bump into somebody on the street the next day who will have an amazing opportunity for us. But, if we convince ourselves that nothing is working for us, then we will never even see the opportunity–the commute to work will be mundane, and the bumping on the street will be an annoyance. In effect, we have to be willing to give freely with no ulterior motives. We have to give because we want to. We have to give because it feels good; not because we are anticipating something in return. For whenever we give/do something with a certain agenda behind it, it defeats the whole purpose of the act of giving/doing. In that, giving becomes trading, and doing becomes manipulating.

When we try to do good for other people, then wait for them to respond in like-kind–and because sometimes they don't–we fold our hands and vow to ourself that we will never be nice again, lest we'll be taken advantage of. As a result of this, all of the positive and beneficial rendezvous which would have taken place tomorrow on the street, or a month later on the train, do not happen. Because we have slipped back (for the time being) into lower consciousness where there is no magic, and no opportunity. Your only job therefore is to focus on giving without waiting for anything in return. If you happen to do something good for your friend, it doesn't mean that the Universe will give you back everything you deserve specifically through your friend (but then again, it may). It could be a totally different person, at a completely different time who you will get it back from. Just because you are not getting it back from your friend right there and then, it does not mean that you will never get it back at all. The Infinite Intelligence, Source, or Spirit will determine when, how, and through whom you're going to get back what you deserve. All that you must do is focus on the "labour," and the "fruits" of your labour will take care of themselves at the right time, and at the right place.

LAW OF CAUSE-AND-EFFECT

"You reap what you sow. You get what you earn. You are what you eat. If you give love, you get love. Revenge returns itself upon the avenger." – Mary Browne

The Law of Cause-and-Effect decrees that every cause has its effect, and every effect has its cause. There is no such thing as a "random chance" or "accident" in our Universe; everything happens according to Law. On the surface layer of things it might appear as though certain situations do happen by accident, or chance. However, one who understands this Law knows that this simply is not true. For instance, if you were to throw a pair of dice and cast 3 and 6, that wouldn't have happened by chance, as most people would think. In actuality, the way you held the dice in your palm, the speed at which you threw the dice, the surface which the dice bounced off of, and which corner of the dice hit the table first–those were the determining factors that resulted in you casting 3 and 6; it was not your lucky day, or misfortune.

The Law of Cause-and-Effect perpetuates the idea that everything truly happens for a reason; there are no accidents, because every effect has a direct cause, and like-causes always produce like-effects. With respect to your personal goals in life, I want you to think of your destination as the "effect" and the route to get there as the "cause." If you wish to produce a certain "effect" in your life, then you need to focus your attention upon the "cause," and the "effect" will take care of itself. (You can't control the effect, but you can always control the cause.) The reason why we sometimes have a terrible time achieving our goals, is because we are usually focused on one thing that we cannot control, or do anything about, which is the effect. For example, let us consider an average person who is trying to lose weight. Rather than focusing on what they can control–which is the cause–e.g. taking the right actions; doing what they know they are supposed to be doing. Instead, they are usually focused upon how overweight they are; how they don't have the time to exercise; how painful improving oneself actually is, and so on. And because like-thoughts produce like-effect, the set-goal invariably does become difficult to achieve (for them).

If you are to succeed in pursuit of your life goals, you first need to determine the "effects" that you wish to produce. (These are the goals that you hope to obtain in terms of happiness; health; relationships; finances; material possessions, etc.) And once you do this, you then need to completely redirect your focus upon the "causes" that will be responsible for getting you there. Make no mistake about it, deciding on the effects which you seek is extremely important and, in fact necessary, because your mind is a cybernetic entity which has to have a clear target in sight, if it is to function effectively. However, once you are clear as to exactly what it is that you hope to achieve, you then need to turn all of your attention upon determining the necessary causes, which can be done simply by asking yourself: "What actions do I need to take in order to produce the desired result?" Now, people often find it easy to determine the effects which they seek, but they struggle to determine the causes that will be essential in advancing them in the right direction. Which is understandable, because no one can tell for sure how to get somewhere if they themself had never gone there before. Fortunately, there is a solution.

The most efficient–and reliable–way of pinpointing the exact causes you need to implement in order to achieve your goals, is to look for other people who are already there; who are already where you want to be. You need to find those people and begin to study them; talk to them; seek their advice; listen to them, and do what they tell you to do; ask questions; let them show you the way; and ultimately let them mentor you. This is not a difficult task, especially if you have access to the Internet; you may find these people everywhere. These people already know what the right actions are–with respect to achieving whatever it is that you want. You certainly don't have to figure it all out by yourself. They have already failed for you, and made all of the mistakes for you. They already know what the causes are; they know what is needed to achieve your goal in the quickest time frame possible, and with a fewer mistakes than necessary. By seeking out other people's advice, expertise, and guidance gives you the confidence you need to proceed. By observing other people who are already enjoying the conditions, positions, and circumstances which you yourself desire will act as confirmation that their way of going about it is a "tried-and-true" way; a way which has been proven to work; a way which has been proven to produce the results you seek.

Ultimately, achieving success in any area of your choosing is predictable and can be replicated if you only take the time to pinpoint the right causes which are needed to produce the desired effects. By observing other people who are already successful in areas which you yourself would like to be successful, you get to determine the right actions which you need to take in order to achieve it. In other words, success is replicable, and it is a direct result of certain causes; never chance or luck. If you focus on discovering what those causes are and then implement them as you continue to move towards your own goals in life, then your success is inevitable.

"If you do what other successful people do, you will eventually get the results that other successful people get." – Brian Tracy

LAW OF COMPENSATION

"My belief is firm in a Law of Compensation. The true rewards are ever in proportion to the labour and sacrifices made." – Nicola Tesla

The Law of Compensation decrees that we will always be compensated for our contribution. Our rewards in life will always be in direct proportion to the service we render to others. And if we aspire to increase our compensation we must increase the quality or value of our contribution. If we focus all of our energy on giving as much value as possible, then the rewards will ultimately take care of themselves. Another way of saying this is, if we can fall in love with the idea of being of service to others–to work; to build; to create; to offer value; to share; and to provide a useful product or service–above anything else, then an affluent, joyful, and healthy life is guaranteed. The Law of Compensation represents the idea that if we put little into something we will only get a little bit back; and if we put a lot into something we will get a whole lot back. Moreover, we have to be aware from which place our actions are coming from. Because if we put little into something, but with a lot of effort, or force behind it, we will still only get a little back. And that is because what matters the most is the intention behind it. For instance, if your intention were to leave a £10 tip, but you realise after the fact that you accidentally left £100 and are now grudgingly expecting to get back equivalent to £100, you will still only get back equivalent to £10 because *that* was your intention. Essentially, it isn't about giving the least and wanting to get back as much as possible through effort, or force, e.g. trying to squeeze as much juice as possible from the tiniest little orange. But it is about letting go, and wanting to sincerely give. It is about prioritising the creative, abundant, expansive energy that is only interested in sharing, giving, and uplifting–the kind of energy that has no issue squeezing a hundred most ripe and beautiful oranges if it has to–and allowing *it* to be the driving force behind our actions.

"You can have anything you want in life, as long as you help other people to get what they want." – Zig Ziglar

The Law of Compensation decrees that we cannot reap great fortunes unless we have sown great deeds in advance. Everything that we are reaping today is a measure of what we have sown in the past, and if we wish to reap something more substantial in the future we must sow something as equally substantial in the present. This means that our future success in all areas of our life depends upon what we're doing today. If we wish to get more out of life, then we have to put more into it. We have to contribute substantial time and energy upfront if we are going to be substantially compensated in return. We simply must be willing to do all of the work upfront with the conviction that compensation is coming down the tracks.

Most people's go-to response is to blame conditions and circumstances for the poor quality of results that they are getting in life. What they had fail to understand however, is that they are reaping exactly what they had sown in the past–they have no one else to blame but themselves. The Universe always delivers exactly what we have ordered–no more, and no less. If we desire to reap something greater in the future, then we have to be willing to do more than what is expected of us today. We have to be willing to give freely, and without limitations in mind (within reason of course. Do not start giving away all of your money and belongings). The Law of Compensation will ensure that we get everything that is rightfully ours, but only if we are willing to pay the price. And what is that price? It is the commitment to *more* life; to the advancement of life; to the increase of *all* life. In other words, the Law of Compensation begins to work in our favour when we focus our energy on sincerely wanting to help solve other people's problems. And to deliver our product, or service to the best of our ability, without being too concerned as to how much we are going to get back in return, and when.

"Your income is determined by how many people you serve, and how well you serve them." – Bob Burg

Earl Nightingale, the author of "The Strangest Secret" said it best when he stated: *"The amount of money that you and I earn is always going to be in direct ratio to the need for what we do, our ability to do it, and the difficulty there will be in replacing us."* In order to determine exactly what is coming down the tracks–in terms of compensation–you may begin by auditing the position you hold at your current place of work within a following framework. First of all, how great of a need is there for what it is you do? Secondly, how good are you at what you do? And lastly, how difficult is it to replace you. At this point a lot of people may begin to realise that their so-called "safe, regular 9-to-5 job" is actually not safe at all. Because even if they are really good at what they do, and even if they have held their positions for decades, it's still relatively easy to replace them. Especially if we consider the breakthroughs in technology, robotics, and artificial intelligence that are being achieved today. At the rate at which we are going, before we know it, most of the jobs will no longer require human presence, or assistance.

As of today, we already have self-driving cars that can drive themselves and get people from point A to point B much safer than a human driver can. This implies that the need for drivers–such as taxi; coach; bus; etc.–could potentially be eliminated altogether in the near future. Most stores and outlets today already have touchscreen ordering machines. You do not even have to talk to anyone anymore; all you have to do is place your order, and the machine will spit out your order number, and when your number shows up on the screen, you just walk up to the counter and collect your order. In about a century or two most stores and factory lines could potentially be filled with robots doing the exact same work that humans used to do. And the best part about it (maybe not so much for the worker, but definitely for the employer) is that robots, along with AI can accomplish the same work much better and a lot faster than humans. Moreover, they don't need a break; they don't need a salary; they don't complain; and they rarely mess things up, since they are completely programmed. This also means that there will no longer be a need for human resources, or health and safety departments, as well as smoking shelters, canteens, rest areas, etc. You have to admit that, for any employer, that is a dream come true. But what about you? What will you do? Because if your job can be replaced by a robot, then what does that say about your position? Well, it says that you are disposable. And that a machine–economically speaking–is hell of a lot more valuable than you are.

To offset this dreadful inevitability, and neutralise the competition, you have to acquire new skills and get yourself into a position where it'll become virtually impossible to replace you. You have to begin working with the Law of Compensation by serving more people, and becoming exceptionally good at what it is you do. Because relatively soon being merely good at something won't be enough. Now, even though your current position at work may easily be replaced by a robot–since a robot can do pretty much everything a human being can do–nevertheless, you still have a massive advantage over the machines, because what they certainly can't do–and most likely will never be able to do–is to originate thoughts and ideas; to think creatively, and receive inspiration from Source; to understand what it means to have a soul; and to feel (have empathy).

As AI and technology is becoming more advanced, I feel that it actually presents a perfect opportunity for us humans to finally start using our ability to think. To start using our minds in more creative ways, and serving others emotionally and intellectually, while delegating all the easy, grimy, and boring work to robots and artificial intelligence. That way we can all finally stop squandering our potential, and focus all of our creative energy on pursuing other things which we truly enjoy and are passionate about. Rather than forever dealing with all of the bullshit that comes with a typical brain-numbing, soul-sucking 9-to-5 job, and live a semi-depressed life in the process. If you have been working at a job where you do not have to think for yourself, because your boss is always there to tell you what to do, then it might appear as though starting your own practice or business which sells useful products or services is difficult. But it is actually much simpler than you might think. The golden rule of entrepreneurship is this: find a need, and then fill it. Simple as that. (The bigger the need, the greater the compensation.) The quickest way to find a "need" is to identify a problem, and then come up with a solution. This is not very difficult to do. Just take some time to look around, and you will see what people are complaining about. Listen, and pay attention to what people are asking for. Everyone is looking for solutions to their problems, and people will happily compensate anyone who can come along and help them solve their problem.

Your fortunes in life truly begin with selling your products or services. And if you wish to increase the size of your rewards you need only increase the quality and quantity of your service. You don't have to be a genius to do this. Still, most people will never even consider venturing out on their own, because most people are convinced that entrepreneurship is risky and scary. In reality, a regular job is a lot scarier, and involves far greater risks, because the security of one's position in any company is never in one's control. When we are working for somebody else we are at the complete mercy of the decisions of our employer. When we are working for somebody else–somebody who may not exactly have our best interest at heart–then our income is forever dependent upon the person who doesn't necessarily care what happens to us. Of course employers can be awfully nice, well-meaning and caring individuals, who treat their employees fairly–with respect and understanding. But if the company makes a bad business decision, or a mistake, which they cannot recover from, which results in that company going down the tubes, then we are going down with it. Conversely, working for ourselves, and being our own boss is far more predictable and reliable, for we will always be the ones who are responsible for how much we're going to receive financially. That is, if we need more money, then all we have to do is go out and provide more service. And if we have enough, for the time being, then we are at liberty to take a break any time we choose to relax and smell the roses.

The reason why most people get average results in life is because most people are satisfied with providing an average performance. People usually do just enough to get by, and as a result they *do* get exactly what they need to get by–and no more. Average people are very easy to replace, because average people are easy to find; whereas exceptional people are very difficult to replace, because they are in high demand. In order to become exceptional in any field you have to be committed to excellence; you must have willingness to learn and be ready to adjust your strategies, or business model when necessary; you have to be receptive to new ideas and be ready to exceed the expectations of others. Of course, this isn't always easy, because it requires one to stay sharp as a tack, and be ready to think on one's feet. The main impediment on route to becoming exceptional is the fact that most of us don't want to think; we would rather keep doing the same things, over and over again–things which we totally dislike–without even trying to improve our situation because we have a natural aversion towards making decisions. In most cases, it is because we don't trust ourselves; we don't trust our own judgement; we don't want to fail, or make any mistakes. And as a result, we continue to do as we do, even when we are consciously aware that what we are doing is completely pathetic and totally ineffective.

Most people actually believe that they think all the time, but they really don't. Because mere mental activity does not constitute *actual* thinking. Most people believe that it takes far more effort to originate new and creative ideas, that it takes far more effort to learn something new, and that it takes far more effort to exercise control over one's own financial situation than it does to blindly follow somebody else who is making all of the decisions for them. Because of this, what people will usually do is they will give away their own ability to think to someone else, so that they don't have to think for themself. Most people would much rather be told what to do, and just follow the path which other people (who are willing to take responsibility, and tolerate ambiguity) have laid down before them, instead of charting their own course which has much greater rewards–because it is of their own design. Jim Rohn who was a great motivational speaker, and author of "The Keys to Success" once pointed out the following: *"If you don't design your own life plan, chances are you will fall into someone else's plan."* What a disturbing thought that is. To think that if I don't have a plan for my life, then somebody else will have one *for* me. So much for being a powerful creator of my own reality huh…

"The worst curse to befall anyone is stagnation, a banal existence, quiet desperation that comes out of a need for conformity." – Deepak Chopra

LAW OF RELATIVITY

The Law of Relativity decrees that everything in the Universe is relative. The Law states that nothing is either good or bad; big or small; near or far, until we relate it to something else. The happiest people in the world have a habit of relating their circumstances and conditions to those who are in worse situations, which makes every situation–that may seem grim–look a lot better. Those who understand the Law make it a point to never use the Law to their disadvantage, by comparing themselves to others who seem to be doing better. Needless to say, we will generate nothing but stress, misery, frustration, and envy if we compare ourselves to others who appear to have "more." The truth is everyone has "more" than someone else in one area or the other, and when we compare ourselves to others, we wind up coming from a competitive mindset, where we forget to be grateful for the things which we already have, and become blinded to the fact that our discontent and unhappiness is unreasonably self-imposed. To further emphasise this point, let's take a look at the following thought experiment…

I want you to imagine a man driving in a brand-new sports car, looking at another man sailing a yacht, and he feels resentful of the fact that he's unable to afford something of the sort. A man riding a bicycle behind the man in the sports car floods his own mind with thoughts of injustice and inequality while looking at his beautiful car, because he is convinced that in order to achieve success one has to cheat the system, or become disingenuous. A man walking on the sidewalk feels annoyed, and is frustrated with himself while looking at the man riding a bicycle, for he never had the chance to learn how to ride one. A man in the wheelchair feels hopeless and dejected while looking out of his apartment window at a man walking on the sidewalk, for he wishes that he were also able to walk. Yet the man sailing the yacht has a difficult time forming successful relationships with women, and he feels envious of the man in the wheelchair, because he has a loving partner and a family that sticks by him no matter what. Do you see where I'm going with this? A person working a boring 9-to-5 job (who utterly despises it) actually has more than a person who has a physical ailment which prevents that person from working altogether, or even getting involved in normal, everyday, menial tasks. A person with a physical ailment has more than the child living in an African slum who doesn't have regular access to clean water. Yet still, the child who lives in an African slum has more than a famous celebrity who is blind, because the child can see perfectly clear. We could honestly do this all day. But what I want you to get out from this demonstration is that most of the time we don't realise–and thus appreciate–what we already have, for we get caught up looking at other people, and how well *they* are doing.

Comparing ourselves to others is a hopeless exercise, because everyone is on their own journey; everyone has their own unique problems, as well as personal demons that they are battling with. Nobody's life is perfect, contrary to what social media wants us to believe. What you need to be striving for instead is only ever competing with yourself, and overcoming your own limitations; rather than comparing yourself to other people, and competing with them. It truly doesn't matter how terrible you think your life is, because you are always doing good relative to somebody else–someone who would give an arm and a leg for what you have. Conversely, it doesn't even matter how amazing you think you are at something because chances are great that there is a six-year-old kid somewhere in East Asia who is much faster and better at it than you are anyways. To spare yourself the unnecessary grief you need to stop worrying about how well other people are doing, and concentrate primarily on yourself. Develop gratitude for all that you have in your life, and just play the damn cards you've been dealt. The world is a big place, which means that you'll always find individuals who have "more" than you, and who are much better than you. Therefore, if you're looking for happiness by comparing yourself to others, you will never win! All that will happen is you will tune yourself into a lower frequency, and continue to repel all the good that is coming away from you.

In modern society, people typically use the Law of Relativity to their disadvantage. They may compare their old, beat-up Volkswagen to their neighbour's brand-new Mercedes, and feel as though they aren't doing as well financially. All the while completely overlooking the fact that their neighbour has to now keep up with hefty payments every single month, for a few years probably (hardly an overnight success which they thought it was). Likewise, women will often compare their figure to that of a thin model on social media, and begin to feel shy and insecure, resulting in degradation of their self-image which has a massive impact on their confidence which then bleeds into how they interact socially. In reality, most photos on social media are typically artificially enhanced using photoshop–nobody actually looks like that, and nobody in their right mind expects anyone else to look like that either.

Utilising the Law of Relativity incorrectly manifests in all sorts of problems. As we compare ourselves to other people, we plant seeds of inferiority in our subconscious. Those seeds eventually sprout into all kinds of negative expressions such as chronic stress; depression; lethargy; low self-esteem; low self-confidence–and if taken to the extreme–even suicide. In order to apply the Law of Relativity effectively in our life it would be far more beneficial for us to acknowledge other people's success and achievements, but rather than comparing ourselves to them, become *inspired* by what they have instead. In other words, when you see someone who has something that you want, see it as solid proof that it is possible for you to have it too. No one is made from different cloth; what one person can do–another can do; success is replicable, remember? Whenever you happen to see a person enjoying something that you want, simply observe them, and identify what actions they took to get it. That way it becomes only a matter of time until you can enjoy it also.

However, be aware that it is not always possible to be, or to have exactly what somebody else has since we live in a time-space reality where time is a finite resource. For example, if you are a footballer, do not waste your time comparing yourself to Cristiano Ronaldo. Because you are not being fair to yourself. Ronaldo has been playing and practising football, studying it, and obsessing over it since he was a child. Playing football was all he ever knew. He even had to stop his education so that he could dedicate more of his time to playing the sport. If you would have dedicated the same amount of time to practising and playing the sport, then you would have become at least as good as he is. But if you did not do what Ronaldo did; if you did not obsess over it as much as Ronaldo did; if you haven't put in as many hours into it as Ronaldo did, then do not compare yourself to Cristiano Ronaldo, and beat yourself up for not being as good of a player. Your best move is to compete only with yourself, and to compare yourself today to what you were yesterday. And if you are a better person today than what you were the previous day–even if only by 0.01 percent–then that is a success, celebrate *that*!

Next time you catch yourself undermining your confidence by misusing the Law of Relativity, consciously stop yourself and remind yourself that we all have unique talents and abilities which (if they are fully developed, and nurtured) give us an edge over everybody else. You have to accept that it is impossible for you to be exceptional at *everything*, but nor do you need to be. Sure, one person might be better than you at one thing, but you are far more superior at another. So learn to only focus your energy on the things which you are good at. Because when you do, you will excel at it further than most. And you will not have to compete ever again. Commit from this day forth to using the Law of Relativity to your advantage. Use it to help you advance in your goals; not to undermine your confidence and sabotage your happiness.

LAW OF POLARITY

The Law of Polarity decrees that everything has an opposite; everything that has a top has to have a bottom; everything that has an outside has to have an inside; good and bad; right and wrong; left and right; up and down, etc. The Law of Polarity implies that every bad by default must have something good in it, and if we are willing to search for that good–in all situations–then we'll certainly find it. However, from the lack of awareness of the existence of this Law we tend to misuse it, by dwelling on the negative side of things. Which robs us of any opportunity at acknowledging all of the good that bad experiences bring along with them. Now, if we are to enjoy happy, successful lives, we have to do what other happy and successful people do. Successful people view every situation as necessary for their own development, and that's why they are able to continue to produce phenomenal results. Adopting this kind of attitude gives one access to an unrelenting sense of positive expectation, which will allow one to produce nothing but positive results. In effect, in order to improve the quality of our life experience we have to develop the kind of attitude where we sincerely believe that everything that happens is necessary to achieve whatever it is we are wanting to be, do, or have.

We must develop an understanding that there is a reason for everything that shows up in our experience. We must become aware that the Universe is continually moving us in the direction of our dreams through a process of learning, growing, and adjusting. When something bad happens in your life, instead of becoming reactive to the situation you need to consciously remind yourself that the unpleasant experience at hand is actually a learning experience, that is trying to prepare you for the good that's coming next. That way, rather than being thrown into an emotional turmoil you may begin to see the opportunity for growth which lies within the experience, by asking yourself: "What is good about this situation? What can I learn, or discover about myself from this experience?" These questions will focus your mind on the opportunity which lurks inside every situation, and prevent you from sinking into lower consciousness, where your judgement is clouded and your vision is impaired. Rather than drowning yourself in self-pity when your life seems to be going awry, and shying away from certain unexpected/sudden changes, this approach empowers you to embrace all experiences, and continue to walk the path utterly unfazed. This level, or degree of composure, and poise becomes available to you when you are aware that negative experiences are simply part of the process; that no matter where you are, and what you may be going through, you are exactly where you *need* to be.

"Every adversity, every failure, every heartache carries with it the seed of an equal or greater benefit." – Napoleon Hill

Take some time to study the lives of people whom you know, and use their experiences and ways of going about things as an example for what it means to work in harmony with this Law. For instance, Steve Jobs was forced out of his own company "Apple" in 1985 as a result of a number of disagreements with then-CEO John Sculley. However, rather than accepting defeat, Jobs co-founded a computer company "NeXT," and at the same time created a highly successful computer animation studio "Pixar Animation Studios." In 1997 Apple acquired NeXT, and reinstated Steve Jobs as a CEO. And he began to revolutionise a number of industries with the introduction of iPod, iPhone, iPad, and more. When you hear/read Steve Jobs' success story, the question that you want to be asking yourself is: "Would Steve Jobs have been able to accomplish all of those things if he were never fired from Apple in the first place?" And the answer is probably not. Because in order to become the Steve Jobs who was capable of taking Apple to that next level, he first had to learn some valuable lessons which were not available to him at the particular time and place where he was, prior to his revolutionary innovations.

Likewise, Walt Disney was fired from the newspaper firm "Kansas City Star" in 1919. According to his editor, Walt lacked imagination, and had no good ideas. However, Walt saw his seemingly "bad" situation as an opportunity to try something new, and went on to create many successful cartoon series which most of the world has come to love. Not only that though, he had also built a dozen of theme parks (Disneyland and Disney World) across the world that generate millions of dollars in profit every single day. Now, do you think that the Disney cartoons, theme parks, and resorts would have still existed today if Walt were never fired in 1919? Again, probably not.

J. K. Rowling was also fired from her job at the London Office of "Amnesty International" where she worked as a secretary. But rather than feeling sorry for herself, she instead pursued her dream of becoming a writer. And as we all know, today she is a multi-millionaire author of "Harry Potter;" the most successful book series of all time! Again, do you think that Harry Potter would have existed at all, if Joanne were never fired from her job? The question is rhetorical at this point. You already know the answer. The reality is that these individuals would have been too comfortable and satisfied with their previous positions, that they would have never had the courage to take the initiative, and proactively produce certain changes which were essential in helping them to realise their dreams, and the Universe knows this. That's the reason why sometimes the Universe needs to give us a nudge–however unpleasant it may be–to help navigate us in the right direction. But if we are resisting the nudge–the change–by actively avoiding the feelings of discomfort that change inevitably elicits, then what we are in fact saying is that we are not yet ready to receive what we want, and thereby stalling our progress.

Such success stories portray the Law of Polarity in action, where a person were fired from their job–which by many people would be considered a negative turn of events–yet rather than becoming angry, depressed, or thinking about finding a different job, they viewed those seemingly unfavourable changes as a perfect opportunity to pursue something better. I'm certain that there are countless of similar stories out there in the world, and the comforting fact about them all is that successful people are not much different than you and I; they are regular people just like you and me. The main difference is that those who succeed in life use their minds correctly: they have a goal; a vision; a dream; and they become attuned to thinking on higher frequencies, which enables them to see past the negativity, and in turn accomplish whatever it is they envision.

Now, you should never look at these people with wishful eyes and feel jealousy or envy towards them, and what they have accomplished–thinking that they are lucky, or that they were born under the right star. Rather, you should be looking at them and thinking: "Wow, if they did *that*, that means I can do something great with my life as well." Realise that successful people are not special in some way–a way which is not available to ordinary people. Successful people have merely accepted thoughts which most people would reject–and have rejected–that's why they are ordinary. In other words, when you see those who lead happy, successful and prosperous lives what you are really looking at is nothing more than your own rejected thoughts. Personally, I view this idea in the following way. There exist two versions of yourself which you get to choose to embody, every single day. Version 1 is what you are doing right now, e.g. going about your business; thinking about whatever it is that you are thinking about; having conversations that you are usually having; getting the results that you are usually getting; surviving and getting by; watching other people have their glory, etc. In other words, just living a normal, regular, boring life (this is the "lower-self" version of yourself that doesn't like change, and creative thinking). Version 2 on the other hand, is completely free, happy, excited about life, and is full of vigor and vitality. It loves to meet new and interesting people; it loves to travel; it loves life; it lives in the present moment; it is hypercreative; it provides tons of value to the marketplace, while making a good living from it (this is the "higher-self" version of yourself which wants to continually grow, and is always receptive to new ideas). These are the 2 versions of yourself which you get to choose to live out in your everyday life and my hope for you is that you choose the latter version. That you begin to act in ways and think thoughts which are conducive to you living as the second version of yourself.

Also, remember what had been said previously: Source knows exactly what you want, and what needs to be done, in order for you to get to where you want to be. Well… if you have consciously, or unconsciously been asking for more freedom; you have been asking for something new, different, and better, then maybe you getting fired from your job was the Source's way of putting you on the right track by getting rid of the biggest obstacle in your life, which was holding you back the most from getting/becoming what you *really* wanted. This is the reason why you need to put your trust in the workings of the Universe and know that whatever happens in your life is for your own good. Of course, in the beginning stages of practicing these ideas we are more prone to losing our faith. For if we have not yet achieved a respectable degree of self-mastery when something bad/unexpected happens in our life, our emotions become hijacked, and we indulge ourself in fear, and negative thinking. Which ultimately prevents us from seeing what Source is trying to reveal to us. This is why it is absolutely essential that we not merely under-stand, but also practice this material, because it is a matter of living a life that we truly want to live, or having to settle for a life which somebody else had designed for us. Which, in most cases, isn't very rewarding.

Moreover, appearances can be downright deceptive. Something that at first appears to be a misfortunate, often turns out to be a blessing in disguise. I'll go so far as to say that many of the "bad things" that happen in our life only happen to send us spinning in a different direction from what we have been doing previously. Because what we've been doing up until that point in time was not at all moving us towards our goals. It goes without saying that human beings tend to cling on to routines, and patterns, even when they had become destructive and ineffective. Precisely for this reason, sometimes the only way to force us to change direction is an emergency, or a "pattern inter-rupt." And this emergency might come directly from Source in a form of los-ing our job; losing all of our money, or belongings; having to move out of the country; our partner leaving us; having our house burglarised; crashing our car–whatever–some kind of a catastrophe that'll finally prompt us to say and mean it: "That's it! I've had enough of *this* shit! Let's just go over *there*."

Lastly, most people don't know that failure is actually a big part of suc-cess; that without failure it is difficult to experience success. None of us have learnt to walk the first time our feet touched the ground; all of us fell flat on our faces, time and again, but we kept getting up until we have mastered the art of walking. In effect, we have miserably failed our way to success. Failure and success are opposite ends of the same continuum. And in order to trav-erse the distance which exists between the two ends we simply must be will-ing to experience failure on our way to success. If we actively avoid making mistakes and having failures, what we're actually doing is avoiding success. Think back to the example of Thomas Edison… it is a commonly known fact that Edison had failed thousands of times on route to creating the filament for the incandescent light bulb. Yet his attitude was not at all reflective of the unfavourable results which he was experiencing. After his eventual success an interviewer asked him: "How did it feel to fail a thousand times? Edison replied: "I didn't fail a thousand times. The light bulb was an invention with a thousand steps." In effect, he saw each failure as a success. By successfully ruling out thousands of ways which did not work, eventually led to a way which *did* work. Negative circumstances truly exist to help us create positive circumstances we seek. We do not have to accept failure, or defeat. Because no circumstance, or living condition is final, unless *we* say they are; unless *we* accept them to be so. But when we understand the Law of Polarity and begin to observe the Law, then defeat no longer becomes a viable option.

"All power is from within and therefore under our control." – Robert Collier

"Success is going from failure to failure without a loss of enthusiasm."
– Winston Churchill

LAW OF RHYTHM

"What you were yesterday, you've paid for that. What you are today, you decide what." – Bob Proctor

The Law of Rhythm states that everything in the Universe is in a continuous state of rhythm or cyclical motion, from the cycles of the seasons to the beating of our hearts. The Law of Rhythm reveals that the energy in the Universe is akin to a pendulum; when it swings to the left, it will also swing to the right an equal amount. Every season, every cycle, every "swing" is essential in establishing an equilibrium in all facets of life. The key to mastering this Law is allowing oneself to flow seamlessly with these cycles of life; rather than resisting them. By recognising that everything in the Universe has a rhythm, we can begin to learn to adapt to these rhythms, and find perfect balance in our lives.

The Law of Rhythm reveals that–whether we like it or not–we will inevitably have to experience our fair share of good times and bad times, and our responsibility as conscious beings is to stay emotionally centred in the midst of these cycles. To achieve an emotional equilibrium we have to remind ourselves that when we are going through difficult times, the good times are on the horizon. But, in order to be the beneficiaries of those good times we have to ensure that we do not get affected by the negative circumstances and conditions that the Law of Rhythm invariably brings. Because if we are not careful enough, and we allow ourselves to get absorbed by a negative "swing," it might spread like wildfire and permeate other areas of our life. For example, if the pendulum of your professional life is swinging in a negative direction, and you happen to react to it emotionally, then that will perpetuate a negative thought-cycle, which will not only prevent you from knowing when the swing is coming back in the positive direction, but it will also begin to damage other "swings" that are happily swinging in the right direction.

For this reason alone we must learn to compartmentalise different areas of our life. Otherwise we run the risk of spreading the contagion until it pervades everything that we do, everything that we are, and everything that we touch. We have to become aware of the fact that everything in life naturally ebbs and flows. And if we only allow the Universe to do what it has to without posing any resistance, then any undesirable situation which we find ourselves in is inevitably going to change for the better. Ultimately, the Law of Rhythm will always be in effect, there is absolutely nothing we can do about that. What we can do however, is realise that our thoughts are just as cyclical as the seasons. The only difference is that we–self-conscious beings–have the power to change the season of our thoughts at will. We can jump from doom and gloom straight to optimism and enthusiasm, simply by paying attention to the maxim: "*This too shall pass.*" And what this really means is that we do not have to go along with the negative "swings" of life. We have the choice to stay centred, and just watch them go by without getting swept along. Remember: your present circumstances and conditions are never the final outcome–a few things might go against you today but many good things will go your way tomorrow. When you understand the Law of Rhythm you begin to focus your mind correctly, and cease dwelling on the negative side of things (or swings), for you are aware that the negative conditions and circumstances are not here to stay; thereby positioning yourself for a happy and successful life, no matter which cycle you might find yourself in.

"These laws are eternal, which means that they are forever. These laws are universal, which means that they are everywhere. They exist whether you know it or not, and they are always working whether you are aware of it or not." – Abraham Hicks

In summary: You can pretty well tell how each of these Laws intertwine, and play off of one another. And how it is difficult to talk about any one particular Law without mentioning the others. That being said, some of you who are familiar with the Laws of the Universe might be wondering why did I not include the Law of Mentalism, as it is arguably the most important Law of them all. The reason why I didn't include it here is because the workings of the Law of Mentalism form the basis of this entire book. By now, you understand that the Universe is mental; that thinking is the starting point in all creation; that thinking is the most powerful function of which human beings are capable of; that everything is created twice–first in the mind, and then in physical reality; and that every mind–without exception–can develop greatness.

Understand that you're a powerful and creative being not because somebody tells you that you are, or because you feel and believe that you are. But because the Universe is structured in such a way that you and I cannot be anything other than that. You really *are* the creator of your own reality; you really *can* live the life you have envisioned for yourself; you really *do* have the power to lead a happy, successful and fulfilling life. You have all the power there is at your disposal; you have Source-Energy backing you up. Source-Energy wants you to have everything you want, sometimes even more so than you do. You just have to quit resisting, and allow the Universe to do its job in bringing everything that you have been asking for. Get out of your own way, and remind yourself that you did not come into this physical world in order to bang your head around; to look for things and people to fix; to struggle; to suffer; and reluctantly make your way to your coffin. But rather, you came here in order to have an awesome adventure, and to give birth to as many desires as humanly possible on which the Universe continues to thrive and expand, and which future generations benefit from.

In closing, one easy way of grasping the mysteries of the Universe is by taking a look at our own physical body and understanding how it functions. For instance, we don't have to beat our own heart, grow our hair, and create new cells in our body; our body does all of those things automatically, and it will continue to do so even without our conscious awareness of it. Our physical body could be likened to a micro-universe. Which is to say that what we have in our body is similar in many respects to what we have "out there" in the Universe. The trillions of cells in our physical body are all self-managing, self-directing, and self-organising; our body has everything figured out. And it is the same with the Universe at large; everything is figured out, and taken care of. There are certain Laws in place which manage everything, and none of us have the power to manipulate this structure. And it doesn't even matter whether we understand the workings of the Universe or not, or whether we live in harmony with the Laws or not, because they are always working. Everyone and everything is subject to these powerful Laws.

The Universe is flawless, and extremely fair. There isn't a single person alive who has the power to inhibit your creations, or sell you the short end of the stick. The universal Laws cannot be manipulated, or changed by any human. The only person who has any real power to impede your progress is yourself. So stop trying so hard. Life was never meant to be a struggle. Who sold you on that idea? Stop resisting, and allow the creative, loving, healing energy of Source to flow freely through you, and let it manage your life into perfect order. You don't have to beat your heart through the use of willpower. You don't have to concentrate to make sure that your blood is travelling through your veins. And you don't have to remind yourself to breathe. The universal power does all of these things for you. In effect, your life can be effortless (and so it should be) when you train yourself to move with the tide, which admittedly can sometimes be rough. But, by gaining a greater awareness you can nonetheless find joy in the process. Never forget that the only thing that is ever lined up for yourself and others is well-being. And in order to become the beneficiary of that well-being, you need to allow your cork to float freely, which this entire book is practically about. All things considered, everyone and everything in the Universe is subject to these powerful Laws. No one can escape their effects. And one who understands them–who abides by them–begins to live masterfully.

"With all you are getting, get understanding." – Solomon

PART 2

IDENTIFYING WHAT'S HOLDING YOU BACK FROM
BECOMING YOUR BEST–POWERFUL AND CREATIVE–
VERSION OF YOURSELF

Mainstream Society

"I am sure it must be true that people opt out of the mainstream society because they feel that there are going to be no rewards for them if they stay." – Mary Douglas

This particular epiphany on your journey to mastering yourself is going to be the most rewarding one, albeit most unpleasant. Because it will force you to accept that most of your habits, opinions, and beliefs did not come from a place of alignment with your most heartfelt desires, and true intentions. But rather, your conditioning (a person's conditioning consists of a multitude of habits, beliefs, perspectives and attitude) had been formed exclusively by the outside world, i.e. by other people. What is even more unsettling to come to terms with is the fact that when an individual (particularly one in a position of power or authority) understands how people tend to think, feel, and react, it becomes relatively easy for that individual to manipulate other people into unconscious behaviour, uncreative thinking, and low-vibrational states, such as fear, or anxiety. Which, in turn produces a consumer culture which has a weak sense of identity; that is never happy with itself, and with what it has; and that has been conditioned to continually need something *more* in order to (finally) be happy, and feel content.

In this chapter we are going to explore some of the human drives, and other influences (which we dearly cling on to, and unwittingly support), that pervade our physical world; that negatively influence us, and have us living in complete reaction; that undermine our sense of self-worth, sense of identity, self-esteem, and confidence. The submission and surrender to these influences is what separates us from our personal power, genius, and creativity. The world in which we live does not encourage the masses to live abundantly, let alone become self-empowered individuals who are at ease with themselves; who are accepting of themselves as they are; and who have the ability to generate positive emotions from within themselves without continuously relying upon external factors in order to be happy and feel amazing. What is to follow is recognition of what those influences are, and through becoming conscious of how your energy is being sapped, and perceptions hijacked you may begin to take steps towards setting yourself free from all of the burdens which have been imposed on you and your fellow men, primarily under the guise of "safetyism" and "equality."

The politicians; the lobbyists; the think tanks; the media; the entertainment industry; the NGOs (non-governmental organisations such as the World Economic Forum, Council on Foreign Relations, or Open Society Foundations, just to name a few), and the mainstream everything are acutely aware of how the human psyche works. They know exactly how to manipulate people and which buttons to push to elicit certain responses. They understand the mental processes and social patterns of the public. While our success, happiness, and fulfilment in life is not something that they have in mind. Instead, they want us to believe in scarcity, deficit, and limitation. They want us to feel as though there is never enough goodness to go around for everyone. They do everything in their power to hold us in low-conscious states that are guaranteed to produce either fear; guilt; shame; jealousy; greed; or ill-will. They are leading us astray, and away from our godly nature by distracting us with all kinds of nonsense, and by making sure that we are in a constant competition with each other so that we never unite and potentially rebel. They want us to feel isolated from the rest of the world and are forever trying to corner us into a position in which we are only ever concerned with the "petty little me" who needs protection from everyone, and everything. They put forth a great effort to try and prevent us from becoming all that we are capable of becoming, and are keeping our minds preoccupied with too many unimportant and irrelevant things in order to make certain that we don't ever find the time, or the space to become independent, self-sufficient, confident, self-aware, spiritually awake, and ultimately realise our own worth and limitless potential.

The major factor which plays the biggest role in determining the quality of life that you and I are going to enjoy (or not), and the kind of persons we are going to become–which I'd like to address here first–is our conditioning. These revelations–that I'll be sharing with you in a moment–would not have been possible for me if it were not for Owen Cook. Owen is an amazing public speaker, and a phenomenal teacher in the sphere of social dynamics. Owen taught me in the period of six years just about everything there is to know about social dynamics and social conditioning. I would not have been able to become the person that I am today if it were not for this brilliant man. If after reading this chapter you are still at a loss for answers, and would like to go deeper on the topic of social conditioning, as well as what it takes to become the best version of yourself, I strongly recommend for you to check out Owen's work at www.elevatesociallife.com. And you may also find his material on YouTube. Owen is constantly putting out invaluable content on this platform for free. So even if you don't wind up working with Owen directly, and learning from him in person, you still have access to enough practical information on how to straighten yourself out (with respect to your conditioning) openly available online.

One of the major ideas that I've learnt from Owen–which gave me a solid ground for understanding the complexities and mysteries of why humans behave as they behave–is that we are always trying to save time and energy. This is a general rule of life, and biology. And it is very important to grasp if we truly wish to understand why people do what they do, and why our personal life looks the way that it does. The fact that one of the natural human instincts is to conserve time and energy is precisely the reason why we don't want to think more than we have to, i.e. we don't want to spend more energy than necessary. And so, the idea of following someone else who is willing to make decisions actually sounds enticing. It is a temptation that most people have trouble resisting, and inevitably give into, because it completely absolves them of the responsibility of having to think for themselves. But, the problem with that is if we do not use our own mind and exercise our "thinking muscle," then we'll eventually lose our own ability to think. (If you don't use it, you'll lose it.) And how are we ever to have any hope of living a happy, creative, and abundant life of our own design when all our mental, creative tools are lying dormant within ourself, gathering dust?

"An idle mind is the devil's workshop." – Napoleon Hill

You may already know that if you manage to get yourself into good physical shape, but somewhere down the road you stop going to the gym and exercising, you will eventually lose the muscle that you've gained, and you will not stay as fit as you previously were. When astronauts spend prolonged periods of time in space, their bones become brittle when they come back safely to Earth. They lose density; they become weak. Why is that? Because if bones can conserve energy by being weak in space (since there is no gravity), then they won't stay strong if they don't have to–there is no point. Likewise, kids who are born into rich families–who spoil them, and give them everything– will typically grow up to be mentally weak individuals. Why? Because those kids never had to make decisions–they never had to think for themselves–

while everything was given to them easily, and handed to them on a silver platter. They didn't have any experiences which would give them any depth to their character. They never had to deal with any real problems, or adversity. And because of this, that ability, or that "muscle" responsible for making decisions, thinking creatively, and coming up with solutions was never exercised. Consequently, those mental faculties became weak; they became idle. Which ultimately results in the type of personality for whom the smallest inconvenience becomes the end of the world, and a tantrum ensues.

The problem that we have, especially today, is that we very much enjoy being told what to do, and what to think. Because we do not want to *have to* think. The human brain is inherently "lazy;" it forever tries to conserve time and energy. So why should we have to think, when someone else can do our thinking for us? It only makes sense right? That's why watching television is the most popular hobby in the world, since it doesn't require thinking. It encourages passivity, and exertion of no effort while being rewarded with tons of new and constant stimulation. Not to say that anything is wrong with that *per se*, but if we continue to indulge ourselves in not having to think for too long, eventually it does become problematic. Because when we are not exercising our ability to think, when we are not living our own life and being the stars of our own movies, then watching television becomes highly addictive. To such an extent that even when there isn't anything particularly enjoyable on to watch, we will nonetheless sit there–purely out of habit–and incessantly channel-surf until we can find something that'll give us a hit of dopamine. Which does not usually take long to find, when there are hundreds of different channels out there to choose from.

It's okay to use the television sometimes and get stimulation from it, but don't make the error of allowing the television, and the entertainment industry to use *you*. Like any other human, I enjoy watching movies from time to time. I love the show business (though not so much anymore). I love the fact that I can take a break from thinking once in a while, relax, and get stimulated by the TV, or even a video game for that matter. But there has to be a balance between living our own lives, and those through which we vicariously live. The reason why this is so vitally important to address is because people nowadays (especially kids) can't even function properly without some kind of a device at hand that they can use as a tool to escape reality. Not to mention the amount of time which we spend on social media these days, At this point, the attention span of an average human being is even less than that of a goldfish. People are rapidly forgetting how to properly communicate with one another, how to have meaningful relationships with each other, how to have genuine fun, how to think creatively, and how to use their own imagination. I believe it is because human beings have lived in the modern society for only about a hundred years. And since technology is evolving so rapidly, almost by the day, we simply don't have the time to gracefully adapt to such radical changes in how we live, in such a short period of time. As a result of that, what ends up happening is we become overstimulated by all of this innovation, that most other normal, regular, everyday activities become awfully boring, tedious, and too mentally taxing to engage in by comparison.

Rather than using technology for the enhancement of our lives, instead, it is evident that we are actually being used by it. The fact that we have been trained since we were little kids to live our lives strictly through our physical senses, all of this stimulation becomes extremely pleasing, and addictive to a partially developed mind. As we continue to get exposed to more and more stimulation, we begin to feel as though thinking is laborious; that thinking is hard, and downright ineffective. The rationale of a modern human is: "Why should I have to think and exert mental energy when I have the choice to lay back, relax, and have so much more fun by watching my favourite TV show, or playing my favourite video game?" However, if we take a pause, and take an objective look at what we are doing, is it actually fun? Well, yes, for a little while it is a lot of fun! But if we continue doing it, it eventually becomes a habit and we start to forget what real life even is. We get to a point where we don't even know how to present ourself anymore. How to amuse, and make ourself laugh anymore. Or how to genuinely listen to other people, and have meaningful conversations without constantly fidgeting, and feeling the need to check our phones every two minutes.

In order to become a generally happy individual who is confident, who is unreactive, who is original and creative, who knows how to have a good time, who generates their own good emotions from within, and who accomplishes great things in life, you have to reclaim your ability to think and take full responsibility for the quality of your life. You have to develop your mental faculties, and become *internally fulfilled*. And yes, in the beginning stages, thinking for yourself will probably be tough. But as you practise it more, and push through that initial, uncomfortable stage, then it becomes only a matter of time until creative thinking is completely natural for you. Because it is an ability with which you were born, and no one can take that away from you. To reclaim your personal power you have to be willing to leave your comfort zone behind; to let go of the need for predictability; to let go of the desire to fit in; to reduce the need for stimulation from the external world as a primary source of positive emotions; and to stop waiting for other people to tell you what to do and how to think. If you are constantly looking for others to tell you how to think, and you are listening to them talking about how some things can't be done, then you doom yourself because the majority of people don't actually know what the hell they are talking about. They are not necessarily thinking, but they will always give you their opinion. Henry Ford emphasised this beautifully when he said: "*2 percent of people in the world think, 3 percent _think_ that they think, and 95 percent would rather _die_ than think.*"

Now, being presented with such a statement I can already picture some of you protesting: "What are you talking about? Every person thinks! People think all of the time, and so do I." But if this is something that you honestly believe, then what you are really doing is mistaking mere "mental activity" for actual thinking. But that is not thinking. I can assure you that if people were actually thinking, they would never be doing what you see majority of them doing. When you decide to become the "2 percent," one thing becomes a certainty, you absolutely will achieve, and become everything that you desire. Thinking is the most powerful function of which a human being is capable of, because everything starts in the form of a thought. The fact that we have the ability to originate new, creative thoughts and ideas means that we have the power to dictate our own life experience. When you begin to actually use your mind, when you begin to use your brain, and when you begin to think creatively, you will realise–to your surprise–that you like it so much more than being told how to think. As you continue to practise thinking for yourself it will eventually become a habit; it will become easy. And you'll be amazed at the quality of life which you are capable of living–which you were always capable of living, and enjoying, you just previously didn't know how.

GROUPTHINK & SOCIAL CONDITIONING

"Groupthink is a psychological phenomenon that occurs within a group of people in which the desire for harmony or conformity in the group results in an irrational or dysfunctional decision-making outcome."

Let's begin with a premise that all humans are very much attached to something that is called "groupthink," and understandably so. Groupthink is fantastic. It is a perfect way for humans to conserve time, energy, and effort, by learning from the experiences of others, instead of always having to experience everything first-hand. Although it is my intention to poke holes in, and find fault with groupthink, groupthink is not necessarily a bad thing overall. For the most part, it is actually useful, and practical. For example, you have probably learnt from other people exactly what would happen if you were to put your hand onto a hot stove; if you were to jump off a tall building; or if you were to run into busy traffic. Because somebody else had already done that, or already found the answer to, we now collectively know what's going to happen. Therefore, if you are sitting in a room when a thought of sticking your fingers into an electrical socket flashes across your curious mind, you do not act on that impulse. Because thanks to groupthink, you already know what the outcome of said action will be, and you keep away from the socket.

Groupthink can be extremely important in that sense. However, groupthink can also become a hindrance, and a handicap in other areas of our life, because groupthink is not always right. And that is why it is essential that, if need be, we can still think for ourself because we cannot completely rely upon–and trust–groupthink all of the time. There will undoubtedly be instances where groupthink tells us something that sounds a tad bit off, and when it happens, we have to be willing to reexamine that idea, and find out for ourselves whether what is being said indeed is accurate; rather than accepting it blindly, and just going along with it. For example, groupthink leads us to believe that money and opportunities are scarce. That if we're planning to start our own business and earn a bunch of money we have to be incredibly smart and possess a strong business acumen. It leads us to believe that we'll never be successful in life without a proper formal education, and a half-dozen degrees under our belt. It leads us to believe that we have to look a certain way (like the super-rich guy from the magazine, with a chiseled jaw, and glistening abs), in order to be attractive to beautiful women. Or that we need to retire and completely stop working at the age of 65 (on average), and just take it easy. Of course, this is all a bunch of crap; it is simply not true. If you will only do a little bit of research, some observing, and experimenting, you will quickly discover that–actually–there's an abundance of money and opportunities in the world. There is enough money in the world for everyone to become rich and financially independent. There truly is no such thing as shortage of resources.

Likewise, you will discover that there are hundreds of successful business owners–all around the world–who are not particularly bright, who haven't even gone past the 3rd grade, and some of whom have never even set foot inside of a school in the first place. Yet are consistently making millions. You will discover that a degree, and a formal education will get you a job at the bank, while self-education, discipline, and massive action will bring you enough money to buy the bank. You will discover that when it comes to attracting beautiful women into your life your looks play a very small part; it is not a big factor. What women are actually looking for–and are attracted to–is a man's behaviour, and attitude. (Though in most cases, women are not consciously aware of this.) Women are looking at the way in which the man carries himself; how poised and unreactive he is; how confident he is in his own abilities; how socially savvy and intelligent he is; how much of a leader he is; how driven he is; and most importantly, how care-free and fun to be around he is. It is never about money, and looks–that's just a bonus. (And if a woman is attracted to you strictly because of your money, or looks, then she's not someone who you would want to invite into your life anyway). You will also discover that retiring is not exactly a bright idea. Because the moment you retire–and cease striving towards something worthwhile–is the moment you start dying. It has been scientifically proven that when a person retires, and develops a belief that there is nothing else for them to do, that person's mental–and even physical health–begins to deteriorate from the lack of ambition, purpose, and activity. Getting old should never be associated with becoming weak and useless. On the contrary, getting old the "right way" should mean becoming wiser, while preparing to leave behind big enough evidence to let the world know that you were here, long after you are gone.

The fact that groupthink is actually right about a great number of things it gives off an illusion that groupthink is right about everything, but groupthink is not right about *everything*. However, because the human brain is inherently lazy (it is always trying to save time and energy), we have no problem giving away our thinking to somebody else completely–merely hoping that they know what they are talking about, and that they can do things better than we can. The trouble is that when we are plugged into groupthink, it becomes difficult to entertain the possibility that it could be wrong, especially when millions of other people are plugged into it also. It becomes difficult to accept that all of those people could potentially be wrong because the way we think about it is: "Well, if everybody else is doing it, then it must be true, and it must be correct. Who am I to question all of those people? There must be a very good reason for why things are the way they are. And even though I may not know what that reason actually is, I simply trust that other people do, and I tag along." This is known as the "herd-mentality." It explains that humans have a strong desire to fit in, and be like everyone else in order to be accepted in the "group." Mainly for the purpose of avoiding ridicule and ostracisation. Although acceptance isn't necessarily a bad thing in and of itself, still in most cases, it costs us more than we would like to admit when getting acceptance comes from a wrong frame of mind–a fear-based approach.

For example, let's take our standard, "the norm" modern diet and think about what it is that the majority of people are typically consuming. McDonald's; fried chips; burgers; pizzas; chocolate; ice cream; sodas; energy drinks, etc. Essentially foods that are full of calories, sugars, and high-fructose corn syrup which increases the risk of obesity, diabetes, heart disease, and cancer. (Not exactly a wise decision is it? Yet one that is considered by the masses to be completely normal.) Now, you probably know that eating a carrot, or an apple is much healthier, since these foods are full of nutrients, and vitamins. But, if you were to walk down the street eating a carrot, people would think that you are crazy. They would literally think that there is something wrong with you. On the other hand, if you were to walk down the street munching on a bag of crisps, while guzzling down an energy drink, not a single person would bat an eyelid because that behaviour is considered to be normal. With this in mind, if there is something that you want to be, do, and have, do not look at what other people are thinking, and doing. But simply step out and act on your ideas. Have your first-hand experience and find out for yourself what can or can't be done. Don't ask your neighbour for advice on what you should do, because chances are your neighbour doesn't know. He is not necessarily *thinking*. But he will be more than happy to tell you a cautionary tale about a co-worker who, once upon a time had failed miserably while trying to accomplish the exact same thing, so you should not even attempt it either, because it doesn't work–you'd be wasting your time.

If you wish to get better results in your life, and become a person who is above the "average," you need to quit thinking (or I should say not thinking at all) like the average person. You need to begin trusting your own judgement and condition yourself to learn from your own experience. You need to disconnect from groupthink, and become an avid learner. You need to start reading great books; going to educational seminars; meeting new and interesting people; thinking outside the box and engaging in lateral thinking once in a while; exercising regularly; eating better quality foods; meditating; and developing a better self-image. Moreover, you need to engage in new activities, and expand your horizons; set new goals for yourself, and push beyond your comfort zone; search for people who are already where you want to be, and study them–do what they do. In other words, to live an exceptional life you have to be willing to do what average people will never do, and are actively avoid doing, and that's why they are average. Begin by looking at the world through your own set of eyes, and your own experience. Don't believe something just because other people believe it. If you don't know the answer to something which is important to you, do not ask other people what they think about it, instead, go out and find out for yourself. Once you truly start thinking for yourself, you will quickly realise how much you enjoy it–it becomes addictive. It feels amazing, and liberating not having to rely on other people, and look to them for directions in life. Because nobody in the world knows what gets your juices flowing better than you.

The fact that groupthink pervades every facet of our life, exercising control of our own mind, and using our creative, mental faculties is never going to be particularly easy in the beginning. However, using our own mind does become easier when we decide to let go of groupthink one incremental step at a time. In other words, do not be reckless and go all out crazy; completely rejecting groupthink and quitting your job, moving out into the wilderness, and walking around naked just to make a point. Rather, just start with something small. Focus on improving things that are in your immediate control, such as watching less television, especially news. Focus on reducing the time you spend complaining with your friends. Get rid of all the junk food which keeps you unconscious, and makes you feel fatigued. Get rid of all the drugs and alcohol that are damaging your brain, and destroying your health. That way you give yourself the highest chance at succeeding in reclaiming your creative mind. You have to do this–there is no other way around it. The current standards of living for the average person in the world today could be described as "surviving" and "getting by." And when you are in a surviving mode, you are more prone to be aggressive, irritable, tired, greedy, and selfish. All the while life keeps on bringing you more of the same, because you are a sloppy thinker. But, when you pull yourself out of groupthink, when you take back control of your marvellous mind, and begin to live in harmony with the Laws of the Universe, then your life can be described as "thriving." When you thrive, you are more powerful, you are more generous, you are more positive, you are more solution-oriented, you are more resourceful, you are more grounded in your energy, you are less reactive, you are more reliable, you are more likeable, you are happier, and you are more creative.

Unfortunately, the current state of consciousness in the mainstream is such that people would rather *avoid* thinking. Because they are not aware of the benefits to thinking for themselves. They don't see that there is a need, or purpose for it. Consequently, the world has become accustomed to living in complete reaction to others. But, if you are to set yourself apart and become a person who is above the average, "surviving" human; who will not settle for mediocrity; who transcends their own limitations; and who lives life the way they truly want to live, then you must *proactively* pull yourself out of group-think by finding a good enough reason, or big enough goal that is worth sacrificing your comfort (of being mentally lazy) for. And although discovering that particular reason is something that is beyond the scope of this book, because this is something that needs to be done by you personally–you have to look inward and do some soul-searching to find out what it is that *you* want to get out of your life. Nevertheless, the principles that lie herein still apply: before you can accurately determine what it is that *you* want, and get ahead of the masses, you have to stop relying on other people's opinions, and continue using them as examples for what's considered "normal," or "realistic." Because if you don't, then you will continue to make decisions that are hampered by groupthink, and you are going to fall short every single time.

"Social conditioning is the sociological process of training individuals in a society to respond in a manner generally approved by the society in general, and by peer groups within that society."

What is another trap that all of us inevitably fall into? It is conforming to the norms which the society around us establishes. This is known as *social conditioning*. Social conditioning is the process by which the masses are trained to think, feel, and behave in ways that are generally approved by the societies in which they live. But the strange thing about us humans is that even when those norms become outdated, completely false, or no longer align with the present world, we nonetheless continue conforming to them without reevaluating our ways of going about things. The reason for this is that in the process of growing up we are being led, forced, and influenced to adapt to these norms with such intensity, over a prolonged period of time, that we eventually reach a point where we start to believe in them, and we say: "Look, everybody else is doing it, so it must be true. Everybody else has been doing it for decades now, so it must be right." The problem is that when those norms become accepted in the mainstream–then even if the evidence on the outside suggest that the norms are outdated–we will still protect and defend our position because it has become a part of our identity; it has become part of who we are. Meaning that, to question social conditioning at that point would involve questioning ourselves, and every decision that we've made in our life; something that most people don't have the courage to do, out of fear of discovering that they were wrong for the past 10/20/30/40/50 years. And we all know how much people don't like to admit that they were/are wrong.

"Conformity is the jailer of freedom and the enemy of growth."
– John F. Kennedy

Social conditioning is a foolproof method of indoctrinating, and herding the masses into adopting–and adhering to–certain beliefs, behaviours, customs, and ideologies in order to preserve social stability. It's major goal is to make sure that you are not much different from the person beside of you; to make every human being think and feel the same way. So that they become much more predictable, and a lot easier to control. Over time, the pressure to adapt to these norms becomes so intense that in the end it ensures–and practically guarantees–that no one ever steps outside of those norms and does anything crazy. Of course what social conditioning means by crazy is to become independent, self-empowered, internally fulfilled, and realise that we don't actually need most of the crap that social conditioning tells us we do.

The truth is, every human being is inherently different. That is the way nature intended it. It is a blessing. Imagine how boring it would be if every person on the planet was exactly the same–everyone looked the same; everyone spoke the same; and everyone wanted the same things–that would be horrible! Why do you think that so many people in the world who adapt to these social norms become either unhappy; unhealthy; unfulfilled; shy; insecure; frustrated; pissed off; dissatisfied; angry; sad; depressed; and even suicidal? Because the spiritual side of our personality naturally resists our desire to conform. But the social pressure is so great that most people cave in, and then end up suffering as a result. I have yet to meet an individual who is plugged into groupthink, who also lives a happy, successful, fulfilling life. It does not happen. One either thinks for him/herself, and walks his/her own path, or one allows the society to do one's thinking for him/her, and follows a beaten path. The happiest people on the planet know that no matter how hard they try to be like everyone else–in an attempt to avoid ridicule, and receive total acceptance from the group–they will never be able to accomplish such a feat. They understand that every person is unique; every person has their own unique intentions; and every person lives a unique life experience. They have become aware that the harder they try to conform, or to become a copy of someone else, the more they depress the spirit within them. And the more they deny the very essence of who they are, the worse they feel. That's the reason why most successful people in the world truly don't give a damn what anyone thinks of them. Because they have realised that in order to become all that they are capable of becoming, they had to dismantle that weak part of their personality which *needs* approval.

The most effective approach for conditioning the mind is *repetition*; repetition of various ideas and messages. Although these messages can be obvious and direct; for example when people tell you to stop doing *this*, or quit doing *that*. (Which are easily detectable, and thus, easier to reject if we don't agree with them.) These ideas and messages can also be subtle, and barely noticeable. (Which are more difficult to detect, and therefore examine, before accepting them.) For instance, if you happen to see a commercial on the television where beautiful women are chasing after a guy who's using a particular cologne, the subtle suggestion therein is that you are not good enough to attract a beautiful woman into your life unless you buy the cologne. Bizarre? Of course! But since people don't exercise their own ability to think very often, all the while leaving their minds completely open–and therefore amenable to suggestion–it works like a charm. Because even though you might not believe that the cologne is the magic formula to becoming irresistible to the opposite sex, but by seeing the same commercial (and other similar commercials) over and over again you will eventually begin formulating wrong ideas as as to what constitutes actual value–or in this case–as to what women find attractive in men (in the end driving you to buy their products).

As the result of the incessant barrage of these kind of messages–when it comes to determining the value of individuals–the world has become utterly obsessed with the superficial layer of things. This has become extremely detrimental to our well-being, because the most popular methods which are being utilised in attempts to increase one's value–methods that are being promoted by social conditioning–are extremely unhealthy. For example, models get involved in extreme diets to try and look as skinny as possible; girls paint themselves with cosmetics that have toxic chemicals in them on the daily basis; men take pills, and use steroids in order to look as big as humanly possible; and of course, lip fillers, and plastic surgery. Which by now have become as common as bowel movements. It has become apparent that the social conditioning doesn't really care whether the society is moving towards degeneracy. Sometimes it seems as if that is, in fact the goal, since it continues to encourage materialism and blind consumerism. And it continues to incentivise people to want to purchase things which they don't actually need. It promises to them that all of the solutions to their problems lie within certain products, or ways of going about things. Which, by the way, if you haven't yet noticed, it fails to deliver on that promise every single time. And that is because time-less, traditional human values that nourish the soul, such as honesty; integri-ty; authenticity; family; life purpose; work ethic, etc., have become replaced by empty, superficial values that come from consumer culture, such as cloth-ing brands; car models; the housing; the salary; and ultimately aesthetics. In effect, even if you manage to completely live up to society's standards, and become the most beautiful, richest person on the planet–who lives in a man-sion, owns a dozen luxury cars, a superyacht, and wears nothing but Gucci and Louis Vuitton clothes–without any of the traditional values you will still feel like something is missing; that you are not valuable enough as you are.

Personally, I couldn't tell you how many times I've been tricked by so-cial conditioning into believing that certain products would make me happy, and feel better about myself. And I know that you have experienced this too. Because everyone is affected by it. If you believe you are above social condi-tioning think again. The fact that you were once a baby who were surround-ed by humans, by default means that you have been affected by it, and if not completely, then certainly to a degree. Social conditioning comes into effect immediately after we are born, there is no escaping it. And because our abil-ity to reason only begins to develop several years after we are born (we are unable to rationalise, and reject other people's suggestions for as long as the first seven years of our life), is precisely the reason why we are left with no other choice but to accept all of the ideas that are being fed to us from social conditioning. However, as we begin to mature, and fully develop our mental faculties–usually by the age of twenty-one–at that point, we absolutely have the power to change our old conditioning and replace it with something bet-ter. How? The same way our old conditioning was formed–through constant and spaced repetition. What has to be different this time around, however, is we have to ensure that the ideas which we now choose to repeat to ourselves are nothing less than positive, and empowering–that the ideas are not influ-enced by consumer culture.

Social conditioning is all around us. It mainly comes from our parents; relatives; friends; teachers; movies; religion; pop culture; mainstream media; music, and all the rest of it. And so you see, you might think that the majori-ty of your thoughts are your own–thoughts that are generated, and brought about by you–when chances are great that those thoughts are actually com-ing from someone else through social conditioning. Social conditioning tells us a lot of different things, and of course not all of it is negative and counter-productive–a lot of it is actually very good. For instance, it gives us community values. It encourages us to put aside our differences and respect one another. It encourages us to find partners, to mate, and reproduce. It prevents us from lying, stealing, and killing each other, etc. However, there are also a lot of beliefs–which do not serve us–which have been fed to us through social conditioning; beliefs that are disempowering and downright misleading. This is why it is essential that–as adults–we take the time to reexamine our most cherished beliefs, to find out whether those beliefs still hold true, in order to avoid living out the rest of our lives as babies stuck in adult bodies.

Those beliefs may go back as far as how our personalities were formed when we were little kids. As adults we may be absolutely convinced that our personalities were consciously formed by our own choice, and after long periods of careful, analytical thought. When in actuality, we might have merely been boxed into those personalities as we were growing up, and we did not even know it. For example, you might believe that your shyness, timidness, and lack of expressiveness is just part of who you really are. When the truth is, that is not who you are at all. You may have merely picked up a negative suggestion from someone else (probably in a position of power, or authority) who yelled at you, and convinced you that it is not okay to be loud; that it is not okay to express yourself openly and state your opinion, because you are dumb, or because no one cares. And what happened is you got emotionally involved in that person's negative idea, and since that day, you have accepted it as fact, then carried that negative belief along with you right into your adulthood. Social conditioning can be a terrible thing in that respect. And to become somebody who transcends it–somebody who's no longer affected by it–you have to start looking more to yourself when making certain decisions in life, instead of looking to other people to tell you what to do, and how to think. Essentially, you have to learn to trust yourself more. You have to learn to rely on yourself more. You have to be willing to assess different situations from your own point of view, and look at the world through your own set of eyes. Once you stop letting others control your thinking, you place yourself in a position where you're able to originate new, creative ideas, and come up with proper solutions that benefit you and the people you care about.

Now why is unplugging from groupthink and transcending social conditioning so important? Because you might think that *you* are the one who is making all of the decisions in your life, when actually your decision-making process is being influenced by social conditioning, and by the people around you. In effect, if you are unaware as to what outside influences are interfering in your life, then you may never be able to build a life that you truly want to live. And what's the biggest influence that drives your decision-making process in your day-to-day life? Other people. Other people who have no idea what your personal preferences are; other people who have no idea what is best for you; and frankly, social conditioning does not care about what you want. All that social conditioning cares about is maintaining "social norms" and preserving stability. The principal objective of social conditioning is to ensure that nobody ever comes out of the pack, and makes waves. It encourages everyone to think like everyone else; to be predictable. Social conditioning might seem like a positive thing–and for the most part, it is. Social conditioning is the reason why we don't live in anarchy, and utter chaos. However, when the societal pressure is applied to those who don't think (which is the majority of people in any given society), that pressure can be exploited for the advancement of any kind of agenda, or regime, that certain individuals in positions of power and authority are so desperate to usher in. The fact that there are so many people who no longer know how to think, who are attached to social conditioning–and are now dependent on it–means that even without thinking about what it is that they're doing, they will go along with whatever the "herd" is doing, to avoid getting kicked out from the "group." The pressure of social conditioning can be so intense that even if a rationally thinking person disagrees with what social conditioning is leading them to believe, that person will feel the impulse to keep their mouth shut, and continue to toe the line. Because they understand that doing otherwise runs the risk of a "pitchfork-wielding mob" (the socially conditioned masses) coming after them to burn them at the stake for trying to be different and disobeying the rules. (A recent example of this mass behaviour in its full glory was displayed during the whole mask-wearing malarky in 2020.)

Think about what happened in Germany in the 1930s as an extreme example. After Germany was left in ruins following the first World War–with their people starving, and their economy decimated–social conditioning led Germans to believe that Jewish people were responsible for Germany's defeat, and for them being poor. Not only that, it led them to believe that Germans were the superior race; that Jewish people were the scum of the earth. As the result of that conditioning, ordinary people became perpetrators of all kinds of atrocities that were carried out against Jewish people. Your friendly doctors, police officers, mechanics, and nurses became hostile to their Jewish neighbours. They excluded them from their circles of friends. They banned them from their stores. They teased them, and humiliated them. They pulled the triggers. They escorted them to gas chambers, and locked the doors. Nobody felt any shame, or guilt whatsoever for supporting a sociopath with a plan to wipe out Jewish people from the face of the earth. While others who didn't agree with what the regime was doing, said nothing, for fear of being alienated from the group, and facing persecution themself. And we all know what the result of that type of conditioning was–the Holocaust. (Obviously, there was a lot more to it than that, but I think you get the point.)

Make no mistake about it, the "unthinking masses" are the most dangerous species on planet Earth, because when in large groups, they are easily motivated to behave in irrational and destructive ways. When people get together, and a few start acting foolish, the rest of the crowd sees that, and one by one they begin to follow suit, until a peaceful rally turns into a riot, or until a calm, organised escape turns into a stampede, when few begin to panic, and sprint for their lives. For example, recall what happened back in 2020 in the aftermath of George Floyd's death (an African-American who was killed by the police officer during an arrest in Minneapolis, Minnesota). It is indeed unfortunate what happened to George and many people were rightfully upset about that. However, the incident yet again revived the global movement of "Black Lives Matter" into action–sparking protests against racism and police brutality around the world. But most of the protests rapidly blew up into something else. Because when people began conglomerating in large groups, some individuals saw an opportunity to take the advantage of the unrest, and began attacking police officers, and looting. African-Americans began attacking "white" people, who had nothing to do with the death of George Floyd. Why did those innocent people have to suffer, and assume responsibility for something that they had nothing to do with? Well, they shouldn't have. But the masses are not thinking! An average person's life is so bland, and meaningless that when he/she sees a chance to engage in an outrage, he/she gaily jumps on the opportunity. I believe the reason for this is that by reprimanding somebody else who has become a social pariah makes people feel better about their own failures and inadequacies by comparison. Which gives them an excuse to not have to improve themself, and continue to tell themselves a lie as to how they are doing better than that person. Thereby feeling (falsely) justified for assuming a moral high ground while kicking them in the head.

I personally know a few individuals who were not emotionally impacted by what had happened (they did not care about it in any way). Nevertheless they've decided to jump on the band-wagon and join a particular protest here in the U.K., in order to take photos and post them on social media to get attention ("Hey, look at me, I stand for something important. I'm part of the group, please love me."); to use the opportunity to make it about themselves and proclaim to the world that they are not racist, in hopes of getting a pat on the back from other protestors, and their friends on Facebook. (Pathetic.) Sure, there were some peaceful protests. But for the most part, people were out of control–they had finally woken up! They finally had an excuse to grab a pitchfork and wreak havoc, in order to forget about their own problems; to escape their boring lives for a while. And as the "pitchfork-wielding mob" picked up momentum, they began destroying small businesses, rioting and looting. It was not about George anymore. The George Floyd's death simply gave people an excuse to act like a bunch of fools. And by the end of it, there were tons of broken pieces left for innocent people to pick up. But the worst part of it is that dozens of people, who unfortunately got caught in the midst of it all had actually lost their lives. All thanks to the unthinking masses.

Unplugging from groupthink and transcending social conditioning isn't only important and beneficial for you in your personal life. But it is also beneficial for the people around you, and here is why: I've read a particular story about a murder case which took place many years ago where a number of people had watched the whole ordeal unfold and not a single person did anything to thwart it. In 1964, New York City, a twenty-eight-year-old woman, Catherine Genovese was stabbed to death outside of the apartment complex in which she lived, around 3:00 a.m. Without getting into too much detail all you need to know is that following her day's work Catherine arrived outside of the apartment building, and parked her car. When she began walking towards the apartment Winston Mosley–who was following her–ran up to her, grabbed her, and stabbed her twice in the back with a hunting knife. Catherine screamed something to the effect of: "Oh my God, he stabbed me! Help me!" Several people heard the screams, and rushed to their windows. When one of the men conjured up enough courage, he eventually yelled: "Let that girl go!" and that's when Mosley jumped back into his car and drove away. But, after ten minutes or so Mosley actually returned to the scene and found Catherine lying on the floor–unable to enter the building. At which point he proceeded to rape her and stab her some more, until he had had enough. Finally, about an hour later one of Catherine's neighbours found her bleeding out on the floor, and called the police (the call was made at 4:00 a.m.). Unfortunately though, it was too late, and Catherine died in the ambulance on the way to the hospital.

Now, the strange thing about this particular incident is that a number of people saw what was happening, yet nobody did anything to help her. The reason for this is that people were waiting for other people to do something; to make a decision about what to do. And as a result, in the end, nobody did anything. When the witnesses were interviewed the following day as to why they didn't call the police, or try to help, some said that they thought someone else had already called the police, and that that was the reason why they didn't bother. Others have stated that they thought someone else was probably already running to her rescue. Some said that since they saw everybody else watching out of their windows and doing nothing, they felt uncomfortable to try to do something about it themselves. So they also stood there and watched. It has been reported that there were at least 49 witnesses, and all of those people let a young woman die because they were all waiting for somebody else to do something, or to think of something–tragic indeed. When the killer was later apprehended, and asked by the police how he dared to come back after ten minutes, and continue his assault in front of so many witnesses, he calmly replied: "I knew they wouldn't do anything, people never do." And Mosely was a hardcore criminal, who had committed enough crimes to know that his hypothesis was right.

This is an absolutely real phenomenon, in social psychology it is called the "bystander effect." It explains that the greater the number of bystanders and onlookers becomes, the lesser become the chances of someone stepping forward and actually helping a person. When people see other people walking by–not paying attention, and not offering help–they instinctively feel the urge to do what everybody else is doing (standing and staring or indifferently walking by). There are numerous reasons for why we do this. Some of us believe that others know better than us (in terms of how to save a person) so we just keep out of the way. Some of us feel uncomfortable with the idea of helping while everybody else is watching. Some of us do not want to be the ones to make the decision to help for fear of failing or making matters worse. And others would rather avoid getting involved in other people's predicaments for fear of getting hurt themselves. But I know for a fact that if there were at least one individual who was unplugged from groupthink; who was able to make decisions, and lead others, he would have called the police (regardless of whether the police had already been contacted or not), he would have grabbed a baseball bat, or a broom, he would have asked one or two of his neighbours to come along and they would have been able to scare off the psychopath, and escort the young woman to safety.

This phenomenon also occurred in my hometown of Russia a few years ago where a person drowned because nobody helped him. To give you a little bit of a context: we have two small separate towns that are divided by a lake (approximately 400 meters wide) which connects each town from shore to shore. In order to cross this lake we have a long, solid bridge (made out of concrete) set in place for people to safely cross over. Sometimes in the summer, people–teenagers in particular–endeavour to swim across the lake from one shore to the other without having to use the bridge, purely for fun, and a sense of accomplishment. I, myself had swum across the lake at least a dozen times in the span of fourteen years that I have lived there. Well, that one particular summer, and at that particular time a twenty-year-old boy had decided to swim from one shore to the next. Less than halfway through his journey however, something went wrong, and he began to swim back–splashing around and calling for help. After a few minutes of fighting for his life he finally drowned; he didn't make it back to the shore. Again, a number of people who were crossing the bridge witnessed the whole ordeal unfold. Yet not one of them even attempted to jump into the water and rush to the lad's aid. Instead, some stood perfectly still, assuming that someone else was going to do something about it. Some thought that he was just messing around. Others didn't have enough confidence in themselves to save a person. However, all of the rationalisations aside, my guess is that most of the people present thought that if they did try to help but it turned out to be extremely difficult, then they would have felt guilty for letting him drown. And nobody wanted to take on that kind of responsibility on themselves. Consequently, and unfortunately, the young lad drowned, when he could have still been alive today if there were at least one person present who was not looking at anyone else and just did what he knew was right. Now, if you don't think that this is an accurate representation of how most humans behave, especially in larger groups, then I'd encourage you to take the time to look at some of the social experiments that have been conducted over the years and you'll see just how rare an independently thinking person who is not stifled and constrained by the social pressure around him/her actually is.

I'm almost certain that similar incidents happen all over the world on a regular basis, where people are not thinking; they have no idea what to do; they freeze up; they aren't sure of themselves; they don't want to assume responsibility, and as a consequence, people are getting seriously hurt, and dying in front of their eyes when they could have been saved. Imagine yourself being on the other side of the equation. Wouldn't you wish for just one person to be there for you? Someone who were capable of thinking for themself; someone who weren't looking at other people to tell them what to do; someone who were able to lead others; someone who had enough confidence in themself to come along and help you? I'm sure that the answer is a resounding, and emphatic yes! And the question we want to ask ourself is: "How do I go about becoming *that* person?" Which leads us to the next topic on cultivating core confidence.

SITUATIONAL CONFIDENCE VS. CORE CONFIDENCE

"A man cannot be comfortable without his own approval." – Mark Twain

Social conditioning leads us to believe that we don't have much value unless we possess certain things, or hold a certain position. It convinces us that the only time we have permission to feel confident, and accepting of ourselves is when certain conditions are met. For instance, it is socially acceptable to feel confident when we have a certain status, or hold a certain position; when we have authority; when we talk, or look a certain way; or when we're part of a particular class or group. Otherwise we don't have value, and thus shouldn't be confident–because it is not possible to have inherent value and feel confident (just cause), without a "surface-level" reason. But isn't it strange that we already have all of the confidence we need within ourself. We all know what confidence is, and how it feels. Yet, we only allow ourselves to feel confident when our environment gives us permission; rather than feeling good about ourself most of the time, and in any environment?

As a thought experiment, imagine you've had a new haircut, or bought a new jacket. As you begin walking down the street you are probably feeling very confident about yourself. And when another person glances at you, you immediately assume that they like the way you look. Which makes you feel even more confident. This would be an example of a situation where because of what you are wearing, and because of how you look, is what permits you to feel confident. Now imagine you've organised a big party at your house–it is your house; it is your party; you are the host; and everyone is having a blast. Well, if people are enjoying themselves, and they really like the party–they even come up to you and tell you how much of a great party you have organised–again, that situation will invariably permit you to feel very confident about yourself. Now imagine yourself as a CEO of your own company, where you are very good at what you do; all of your employees speak to you with respect; and nothing gets done without your supervision or permission.

How important, and how confident would you feel in that situation? Pretty great right? There is no question about it. Within the context of these few examples, you would feel like the most important, and the most valuable person on the planet. However, the question we want to ask ourselves is: "Why can't we experience the same level of confidence, and feel valuable when we are not in those particular situations, and when we haven't met certain conditions? Because if emotions are generated from within ourselves, then why would we not permit ourselves to feel confident most of the time?" And the answer is because we've been conditioned to base our confidence on the external world of situations and conditions; rather than the core, inherent value within ourself.

As individuals who are on a journey to self-mastery we must cultivate core confidence by shifting our criteria for what constitutes value from "situational confidence" to our *core value*. Essentially, it's a belief that we *are* important; that we *are* persons of great value; and that we have value inherently, no matter what. You may not believe that you have value inherently, but that is only a perception issue. Because if you manage to get yourself into a car accident as an example, people will rush to help you. If you go missing– no matter what kind of a person you are–people will look for you. Or when a child gets lost, it does not matter which family the child comes from, the child is still important enough for people to spend a ton of resources in order to find the child. Likewise, if you are an evil person, and you have been put in jail for the rest of your life, people will still slay other living beings (animals) to feed you, and treat you with dignity (of course there are exceptions in some cases, and in some facilities). In effect, the life of a human being is priceless! You need to accept that you have value inherently, regardless of your conditions, position, or status. Because you are a creative being who is full of potential; who is an expression of a creative, intelligent power. Furthermore, the fact that your ancestors had survived for thousands of years up until the point you were born is inherently valuable. Meaning, if you are short, if you are a redhead, if your skin is light, dark, or pale, or if your personality is aggressive or meek, realise the fact that those genes and traits still exist to this day, means that those genes and personality traits were extremely valuable, and were fit for one particular purpose or another within certain communities and under certain circumstances. Now, we might not know exactly what those purposes may have been, but the fact still remains–the value *is* there. Other genes and personality traits (which we may not even know of) that were not so valuable, were eventually weeded out of existence; they didn't survive, and thus reproduce. Which, in effect, stands to reason that if you are alive today, you *are* valuable.

One of the most important lessons that I've learnt from Owen Cook is that when it comes to feeling confident, our brain plays a significant part in determining how confident we should feel, and when. He explains that the reason why our brain does this is because it is trying to help keep us out of trouble. In practice: whenever we enter a new situation, or environment our brain begins to look at that environment–and all the details about it–in order to determine how confident we should feel in that particular environment, or situation. Our brain begins to scan our surroundings, and analyse different things, such as how well we fit in that environment; how much authority we have in that environment; how many friends, and other people we might know are in the environment; how much we know about what's going on in that environment, etc. And after it makes a calculation as to where we stand in that environment, it proceeds to give us access to a certain amount of confidence that will be conducive to our *survival* in that environment.

Let me explain. One good way of understanding our emotions and why we sometimes impulsively feel whatever it is that we feel, is to take a look at evolutionary history. Evolutionary history tells us that we have only lived in modern society for approximately the past 100 years. A thousand years ago we lived in Dark Ages and before that–10-20 thousand years ago–we lived in tribes. This is how far back we sometimes have to go in order to understand ourself better. Because that's when all of our conditioning were taking place, for a very long time. Now, imagine yourself living in a tribe and you happen to discover a different tribe–in which you don't know anyone. Since you are a social butterfly who is confident that the world is a friendly place, you decide to walk straight into that tribe without feeling fear–assuming that everyone is your friend. As you come up to a random person in that tribe, feeling confident and gregarious–attempting to initiate a conversation–that person will most likely pick up a rock and bash you across the head with it to death. Why? Because thousands of years ago that was the go-to response. If you didn't know someone–who is not a member of your tribe; who is a foreigner–then that "someone" would immediately be considered as a threat to you and your tribe. The fact that there were no police or any kind of laws set in place, countless of people got beaten to death without any consequences. As a result of this, even to this day, we still have this *healthy* emotion of fear which prevents us from casually entering unfamiliar territory, or foreign environments, and getting ourselves killed. That is why when we enter a new environment our brain reflexively lowers our confidence, and in some cases raises our adrenaline, and it does it to help us. It has to do it in order to prevent us from going into environments in which we don't have authority, status, or recognition, and do something stupid. Like domineering over others; being loud and obnoxious; projecting our voice; or taking up a lot of space, i.e. acting like we own the place, which is bound to piss some people off.

Humans who didn't have this healthy fear of foreign environments got themselves killed, which means that they didn't have babies. And since they didn't have babies hardly anyone evolved that characteristic. In other words, the fearless gene did not spread, and did not continue to exist. On the other hand, humans who did have a natural fear of foreign environments, managed to keep themselves out of trouble, and raise kids. That is why our personalities have this device, where, if we feel confident, we become open–our voice opens up, our body loosens up, and we become relaxed–allowing us to easily meet new people, be charismatic, and feel at ease. But when we enter an environment where we feel as though we don't have authority, or recognition we begin to shut down, and it becomes a lot more difficult to express ourself freely–to be our true, unapologetic selves, and be friendly. The good news about this emotional device that we have evolved is that it's no longer relevant–sometimes it is important–but we should no longer feel fear when we are talking to a stranger on the street, or on the phone, or asking a person who we like out on a date, or applying for a new position at work, or entering a new environment where we don't know anyone, and still be able to interact with people there openly, and carry ourselves confidently. Nowadays we have order, we have police–there are certain laws in place which have to be observed. In the modern world, human beings are much more tolerant of one another, and are less threatened by each other. Even if somebody secretly wishes to do you harm, chances are they wouldn't dare to pick up a rock and bash you across the head with it. Because now there are consequences. The worst-case scenario is if a person–who is stuck in low consciousness–is threatened by your presence, they might verbally attack you and abuse you, or simply wouldn't want to be your friend, because they envy your peace of mind, and freedom of expression. Maybe some wouldn't want to work with you, while others may simply ignore you. But no one is going to die (it is extremely rare that that would happen). The problem is that our brain reacts to these mild-type responses as though we *are* going to die. And so it still tries to shut us down so that we don't draw too much attention to ourself and potentially make enemies.

But why am I telling you all of this? Why is this so important for you to recognise in yourself? If this is a survival instinct which preserves life, how could it possibly be bad? Why do we need to scrutinise it? Because the irony about this survival mechanism is that while it does a great job at getting us out of trouble–by making us more agreeable, and submissive to prevent conflict–it also makes us meek, passive, insecure, and downright ineffective. It affects our body language, our entire thought process, and it stifles our voice which significantly reduces our freedom of expression, and we become shy, timid, and less resourceful. In effect, the qualities which are keeping you safe are the same qualities which are holding you back in your personal life–your career; relationships; money earning opportunities; social skills; leadership abilities, and so on. The reason for this is that when you are not conveying yourself confidently, other people tend to respond accordingly. And so what happens is you don't get the job; the girl that you like rejects your advances; your friends and your kids don't listen to you, and don't take you seriously; your jokes are not landing; you don't get the loan; you don't get the refund, and so on. Why? Because *people feel what you feel*. If you do not feel confident about whatever it is that you're doing, or saying, then other people will feel that "uncertain" energy coming from you, and they will feel uncertain about you, or whatever it is that you are doing in return. When you enter any environment, or interaction with energy that is "protective," rather than "expansive," people naturally reject your ideas, advances, or whatever it is that you are trying to present to them, or convince them of. Because inhibition, shyness, and nervousness are clear signs of ineptitude, and ultimately untrustworthiness. And the best way that I know of how to go about overriding this mechanism is by letting go of self-concern.

I strongly believe that the reason why people feel insecure, and unsure of themselves is because they are focusing all of their attention on themself. They have become accustomed to worrying about how they look, how they sound, what other people are thinking about them, etc. In effect, people have trouble having authentic, powerful conversations, because their interactions are hampered by self-concern; they're spending all of their mental capital on micromanaging other people's perceptions of them; rather than being active participants. In order to get past this we need to build a habit of shifting our focus away from ourself onto other people. In other words, we have to forget about ourself, get out of our own head, and start focusing more on how we can give other people what it is *they* want, and how we can make *them* feel good. Rather than wasting our mental capital on finding the right things to say, and trying to come across a certain way, instead, we must learn to trust that we do not actually need to try so hard to get other people to like us; that we don't need to be thinking all the time–especially when we are smack dab in the middle of a social interaction.

Once we learn how to let go of self-concern we naturally become more *present to the moment*. (We will discuss the idea of presence in more detail in the last chapter.) The amazing thing about presence is that it's contagious; it transmits onto other people. When we're present to the moment it helps other people to become present too, i.e. to get out of their own head, and forget about their frustrations, judgements, and fears. For instance, when a person is trying to put you down verbally, and even physically, while you stay centred, and fully present, you can actually help that person to become relaxed and present to the moment as well. When ill-intentioned people see that you are not reacting to them, they begin to feel ridiculous for trying to put you down in the first place. In most cases, they will say that they were joking, or even apologise when they realise that their attempt at trying to get a reaction out of you was unsuccessful. The fact that nobody wants to look weak, and pathetic for trying to bite off more than they thought they could chew, is the exact reason why most people would rather laugh it off (nervously) and continue a normal, civilised interaction with you. Practicing meditation regularly is truly the most efficient route to becoming more confident within yourself. Merely sitting down (or lying down if you prefer), quieting your mind, and breathing for 10-30 minutes brings you to a place of total presence. And if you continue practicing meditation regularly you will soon realise that you feel better sitting still and doing nothing (breathing and feeling the aliveness in your own body), than you do throughout your stimulus-filled days.

When I first began practicing meditation I have had a particular experience which I will never forget. On one occasion, me and my friends had decided to go out and have some fun. We played bowling, we played snooker, we watched a movie in a cinema (American Sniper), and we played arcades. We enjoyed ourselves completely–it was awesome. The following morning, I did my meditation session, and I actually felt just as good as I did the previous day in mere 20 minutes of sitting in silence without spending a penny or exerting any energy. And this was a pivotal moment on my journey, because I realised that when we quiet our mind and let go of the resistance–when we stop thinking and become relaxed–we become so present to the moment that happiness–and other similar states of consciousness–come to surface involuntarily. Throughout the years of practicing meditation every single day led me to a realisation that happiness is not out there somewhere, but it resides inside of me, and it can be brought up to surface on demand. (More on this in the last chapter.) When you start meditating regularly what you will find is that happiness does not come from stimulation; it comes from fulfilment, or being content. You become a person to whom stimulation becomes meaningless without internal fulfilment. Which is a great position to be in because stimulation comes and goes, leaving you with the same empty feeling time and again. Whereas internal fulfilment stays with you indefinitely, because it is based on something which does not fluctuate; something over which you have immediate control. And what you'll also find is that when other people yell at you, mock you, laugh at you, or tell you that you aren't any good, you will no longer be affected by it. Or when other people try to mess with your emotions in an attempt to make you feel as rotten as they do, you'll no longer react to them. For meditation conditions one to be centred, and the ability to draw one's desired emotional state from within is a by-product of that.

When it comes to dealing with other people, what you have to be aware of is that in the sphere of social dynamics (specifically in every social interaction), there exists something which has been termed by Owen Cook as "the Law of State Transference." (In psychology, this phenomenon is described as emotional contagion.) The Law of State Transference, Owen explains, is the idea that whatever emotional state we are in, other people are going to feel it off of us, and they will begin to feel the same way. The implications of this is that if you feel uncertain–pertaining to you as an individual, your ability, or something that you're doing–then other people won't feel certain about it either. Conversely, if you feel good and confident about yourself, or what it is you are doing, then other people will feel good and confident about you–as well as themselves–when they are around you. This has become a possibility ever since human beings have evolved something that is called "mirror neurons." They are a group of neurons that are located inside of the brain for the purpose of allowing us to feel whatever other people around us are feeling. It gives us an ability to intuitively know–and feel–with pinpoint accuracy as to which emotional state another human being is in, even without them having to communicate it. As far as I understand, we have evolved this mechanism in order to better circumvent a harsh environment from which we came, tens of thousands of years ago, in order to avoid getting ourselves killed by being oblivious to various dangers that were constantly present all around us.

If you can imagine yourself–tens of thousands of years ago–living deep in the jungle, and you're having a face-to-face conversation with your friend.

And as luck would have it, and before you know it, a tiger appears behind you. In that instance, it wouldn't matter if you didn't see or hear the tiger approaching. Because you would instantly recognise the sheer terror on your friend's face–who sees what's going on behind you–and you'd become terrified yourself. Essentially, without you having to think, or communicate (because there is no time for that), your nervous system would instantly make you alert, pump you with adrenaline, and prompt you to run away, without having to look back, or question what it is your friend is afraid of. But, imagine what would have happened if you were looking at your friend running away in fear–and rather than following his lead–instead you stood there and tried to figure out what might be troubling him. The predator would've had more than enough time to pounce on you and tear you to pieces. And so you see, if our ancestors were to survive such harsh environments, it meant that every fraction of a second had to be accounted for. And that is precisely why they had advanced to mimic other humans instantaneously. In other words, those who were smart enough to survive developed eyes on the back of their head, by evolving mirror neurons, and evolving them well.

The problem, however, is that in today's world, people get crazy, afraid, and upset about all kinds of small, insignificant, and irrational stuff–their reactions and emotions can't be trusted. In our modern society you can–for the most part–forget about mirroring other people since most of us don't have to be afraid of predators anymore. Nowadays people are afraid to speak up; to start their own business; to say no; to ask a person they like out on a date; to try something different; to go against the current, and so on. In other words, these days people sweat all kinds of small stuff that won't kill them, and you are still mirroring them! Now, I am not suggesting you stop mirroring other people completely, and become oblivious to your environment. Rather, you need to become so perspicacious that you can recognise when it is a genuine reason for you to react (for example, when someone commands you to turn around, move to the side or duck down in order to avoid danger), and when it is merely a projection of someone else's fears and limitations (for example, when someone tries to convince you that starting your own business is impossible, or that you need to be quiet in a public area, because there are other people around who might be listening in and judging).

One great way to practise being less reactive in the comfort of your own home is by watching movies and imagining yourself being on the set of each convincing scene. More specifically, next time you decide to watch a movie, wait until you come across a strong emotional scene which involves sorrow, deep sadness, extreme hatred, anger, or danger. But rather than emotionally reacting to that scene and experiencing the emotions which the scene is supposed to elicit from you, instead, pause for a moment and tell yourself: "This is just a movie." And then imagine the actors involved in that scene laughing and breaking character in-between takes. As you become a lot better at keeping your reactions in check, you may then take your practise out into the real world. That is, when you find yourself in a situation where someone is yelling at you, trying to dissuade you, to pressure you, to instil fear into you, or make you feel a certain way, rather than immediately reacting to that person you can stop, and tell yourself: "Oh, this is only a projection of this person's own fears and limitations. It doesn't say anything about me as an individual," and continue on your merry way. Or if you care to take your practise up a notch, you can stay and try to lift them out of lower consciousness through the power of your presence.

Ultimately, knowing that you have inherent value while also having the ability to draw your emotional state from within yourself is what will allow you to walk through life with absolute ease. Because when you trust in your faculties, and become present to the moment, everyone else around you may be going crazy (running around out of control), or freezing up (not knowing what to do), whereas you will stay centred, and you won't get affected by all the chaos and uncertainty that is going on around you, which will allow you to think more clearly, and act rationally. Feeling confident about yourself regardless of your conditions and circumstances gives you the space you need to think of a next, proper move, or solution, from a non-reactive place which has power behind it. If we relate this back to the examples I gave previously, now you would be that person who takes charge, and comes up with a plan. You would not hesitate taking matters into your own hands, and asking few of your neighbours to come along with you to help the woman who's getting assaulted on the street. When you feel sure of yourself, and you know what you're doing, other people feel that assuredness emanating off of you, which makes them feel sure of themselves by extension; thereby drastically increasing the chances of them following your lead. For when you feel self-assured, and confident–through the Law of State Transference–others feel completely safe and secure in your presence. Even when it comes to getting involved in highly risky/dangerous situations, such as fending off an armed criminal, or swimming out into the unknown.

Now, if becoming that person were so easy, the world would have been a much better place. However, the amount of social conditioning that we are subjected to on a regular basis, letting go of self-concern, and becoming present to the moment is still not enough to develop core confidence. In order to become that person who can navigate the world with absolute ease; who can think clearly amidst the chaos and uncertainty; who is able to lead and influence others, we also have to learn to accept ourself as we are right now–no matter where we are and what we have–and become *deeply secure with ourself* by reconditioning our mind to perceive ourself, as well as other people from a different lens. Which ultimately requires a shift/change in our mental paradigm. And that is what we are going to turn our attention to next.

COMPARISON VS. SELF-ACCEPTANCE

From the time we're little kids we are conditioned to go through our lives in a constant competition with each other; to be better than our neighbours–to keep up with the Joneses as they say–and compare ourselves to other people to ensure that we are doing at least as well as they are financially; physically; socially; or otherwise in order to avoid being perceived as inferior or incompetent in the eyes of others. As a result of our conditioning, most of us grow up feeling insecure, and perpetually fearful as to where we stand physically; socially; romantically; financially, etc., in comparison to other people–we are never happy with ourself as we are. And this is a big problem when it comes to being secure with ourselves for when we're continuously comparing ourselves to others–trying to determine our own worth, value, and how able and competent we are–we simply cannot win. For when we base our self-esteem, our happiness, our sense of value, and our success on surpassing (being better than) other people, we tend to generate nothing but jealousy, hatred, envy, and discontent. Because–as we had previously discussed–there is always going to be someone who has more, and who does certain things a lot better. Looking for a sense of value, or sense of identity (of someone who is competent, or intelligent) by comparing ourselves to others, is a hopeless approach, and we have to get over it. In order to reclaim our sense of security, and self-esteem, we have to stop looking to other people as a source of validation. And instead become deeply secure with ourselves by changing/shifting our mental paradigm from comparing ourself to others, to accepting ourself as we already are.

The surest way to move from comparison to self-acceptance is to realise and internalise the fact that nobody cares about what you do, and no one is judging you. The reason why nobody cares as much as you think is because most people are stuck in their own head–they are too busy judging *themself*! That is the truth. Most people are so absorbed in their own little world, worrying about how they look, and where they stand–whether socially; ethnically; financially; or geographically–that they don't even have the time, or mental bandwidth left to judge *you*. If you think that people are watching your every move, and judging you based upon what you do, or how you live, it is nothing more than a reflection of you judging yourself. Recognise that most people are so concerned with themselves–worrying about what other people think of them–that all they ever see in you is the general energy which you bring into the interaction. In other words, if you feel insecure about a pimple on your face–or whatever else which might be bothering you–and you begin fixating on it while interacting with someone, thinking to yourself: "Oh God, I hope they don't notice it, I'm so disgusting," then they *will* notice the pimple and feel disgusted in return, or maybe even judge you in some way. Because that's the kind of energy you're putting out (your energy is screaming at them: "Hey! I am disgusting, and I am judging myself. Please judge me as well."). However, if you can get out of your own head, forget about yourself, as well as the damn pimple on your face, and instead shift your focus onto the other party, then they will feel a nice, non-judgemental, positive energy emanating off of you, and no one will even notice whatever it is that you are secretly insecure about.

Or imagine your neighbour purchases a much better–and more expensive–car than yours as an example. Rather than feeling inferior, by assuming that he's judging you, and the car that *you* drive: "Look at this fool, still driving that old heap of crap, what a loser!" Instead, a much more accurate assumption of his thought process would be something to the effect of: "I see my neighbour looking at my new car, I hope he likes it. I think it looks great, and it costs a lot of money, so he ought to be impressed." Do you see what I mean? Rather than making everything about you, make it about them. And when you do, you can look at your neighbour arriving in his new car, genuinely smile and say: "Oh wow, I like your car" (assuming that you genuinely do), without gasping, or drooling, acting weird, or jealous about it, i.e. reacting to him. That's it, that's all it takes, just a simple, positive comment: "Nice car." Then immediately get back to your own business, and continue living your own awesome life. Your neighbour will appreciate that a lot! He might act unfazed, or nonchalant: "Oh yes it's nothing special, but thanks," though deep down inside he will feel very good about himself, about his interaction with you, and about you as a person. Because you weren't jealous, or bitter, you didn't act weird, you didn't try to point out what is wrong with the car, or that he paid too much for it (or too little), and so on.

Whenever you look at other people and think that they are judging you, understand that every other person who is looking at you is probably thinking the exact same thing (that you are judging them). This is another reason why becoming secure with oneself is so vitally important. Because when you stop taking yourself too seriously. When you get out of your own head, and become more care-free. When you let go of self-concern, and focus on giving and helping other people instead. People will admire your non-judgemental energy, your freedom, and lack of inhibition, which will help them get out of their own head too, and make them want to be around you more often. The fact that your presence makes other people feel really good about themselves by default makes you more likable, more valuable, and more interesting. The implications of this are massive! Especially if you are somebody who is having difficulty letting go of deep-rooted insecurities. Because by conditioning yourself to focus on other people will be all you ever need to fall in love with yourself, and dissolve all your insecurities into oblivion. It is really *that* simple.

The comparison paradigm is enormously beneficial for those who have products and services to sell. Because as we get conditioned to live our lives in a constant competition with each other–constantly comparing ourselves to one another–what ends up happening is we begin to feel as though we need to work longer hours (at a job that we don't like), so that we can earn more money in order to buy things (which we don't actually need), so that we can impress those who don't even care. For the sake of your own well-being and all that you love you have to get out of that paradigm. It is based on pure insecurity, and it moulds you into a person around whom it is not particularly pleasant to be around. In the dating world the disadvantages of the comparison paradigm are most evident. We all know *that* guy who's stuck in a comparison paradigm, who feels the need to flash his luxury car, or watch, brag about his accomplishments and the size of his house because he believes that that's what constitutes value, and that women will become attracted to that. But what he fails to understand–every single time–is that women can smell insecurity from a mile away, and they do not reward it. People in general do not enjoy being around others who are insecure, because it reminds them of their own insecurities, and the interaction becomes a pitiful drag. And what's worse is interacting with insecure people who are trying to cover up their insecurities by the material things they have. The energy of the interaction becomes one of trying to force things to happen, trying to prove something, or hide something, and that is not a very pleasant experience either. People instinctively feel a strong distaste, and aversion towards inauthenticity and incongruence. It makes us feel icky, and sullied when we sense that the person we are talking to is trying to gain our trust and confidence by being dishonest. It makes us want to get away from them as quickly as possible.

As far as your money is concerned you have to understand that no matter how much money you earn, there's always going to be someone else who earns more. Hence, you can afford to stop competing with others financially immediately. To illustrate this point Owen Cook asks us to conduct a following thought experiment: Let us suppose that you are earning $100,000 a year, and you decide to move into a new and better neighbourhood. What you will quickly discover is that now you are surrounded by people who are earning $500,000 a year. Now, imagine if you start earning $1,000,000 a year, and decide to move into a different neighbourhood–yet again. Once again, you will quickly discover that you are now surrounded by individuals who are earning $10,000,000 a year. Well, what if you eventually catch up, and start earning $10,000,000 a year? Then you'll be around circles of people who are earning $50,000,000 a year. Okay, now let us suppose that somehow you manage to blow blast everybody and get yourself into a position where you are earning $100,000,000 a year. Do you really think that now you would finally feel secure with yourself earning so much money? Well, unless you fix the inner issue–your mental paradigm–you still wouldn't. Because when you are earning $100,000,000 a year you have to now compare yourself to people who are called "old money." They are the upper-class families who are in possession of enormous inherited wealth which has been accumulated through multiple generations. If you are trying to compete with "old money" as someone who is earning $100,000,000 a year, you will only get mocked. Because your earnings are considered to be loose change by comparison. So where does it end? If you are coming from a comparison paradigm then what you're really saying is that you don't deserve to be happy, and you will never be "enough" as you already are, unless you *are* the "old money." How brutally absurd?!

The comparison paradigm is the most prevalent when it comes to physical appearance. Typically, men who are short torture themselves about their height, and would literally give an arm for to be 6 feet tall. Yet there are other men who *are* 6 feet who feel insecure about not being 6'2" since all of their friends are 6'2"." Conversely, there are men who are 6'3"-6'5" who complain that they are too tall, who would much rather lose a few inches, because it is awkward for them to move around, and interact with people–having to lean forward all the time, and contour their body to adapt to others. Same principle applies to women–especially physically attractive women. On one level a beautiful woman is the most secure person on the planet, because she knows that no matter what happens–just by virtue of her being the beautiful, physically attractive woman–she will still be taken care of to a respectable degree. But on another level a beautiful woman is the most insecure, because her entire identity is based on her looks (which are going to deteriorate). And so, a beautiful woman is still comparing herself to other beautiful women. Women do this to themselves all the time. One might look at another and feel insecure about herself because the other woman has a nicer, more well-shaped backside. While the "better bum" looks at another and feels insecure because the other has more natural hair. The "natural hair" looks at another and feels insecure because the other has nicer breasts. And the "nicer breasts" looks at another and feels insecure because the other is tall, and slim. While the "tall and slim" envies her admirer in return, because she feels insecure about being too lanky and skinny. And she would much rather be small and petite–like her. We can honestly do this all day… it truly never ends. If you're stuck in a comparison paradigm you'll never be enough as you are and be grateful for what you have. Because no matter where you are in life, and no matter what you have, you will always find those who have it better than you. And those who have it better than you will always find others who have it better than them. People who compare themselves to others–seeking approval, acceptance, and sense of value–completely mess themselves up in some cases. Men go overboard with using steroids to a point that they become a walking storage unit; whereas women go overboard with cosmetics, and plastic surgery to a point that it becomes an eyesore. In most extreme cases, some even commit suicide when they realise that they can never succeed in living up to society's superficial standards. But who gets to decide on what these standards are anyway? And whoever is in that position why are we even listening to them? What the hell do they know? These "standards" are forever in flux; they are never an accurate representation of any person's value.

Deriving your sense of value from material possessions, or by comparing yourself to others is a wrong approach to happiness–a hopeless pursuit. Truly, security is an inside job. And it begins with the acceptance of the fact that nobody is judging how well (or not so well) you're doing–everyone has enough on their plate as it is. Regardless of appearances, everyone is on their *own* journey–everyone experiences fear; everyone feels scared from time to time; everyone has doubts; and everyone has their own problems to solve. If you think that you're unhappy or unsuccessful because somebody else is doing better than you–and you are using it as an excuse to torture, and further sabotage yourself–then what you need is not a bigger house, a faster car, or a billion dollars, what you need is a change in your paradigm. If you are serious about becoming deeply secure with yourself, the comparison paradigm has to go. And good place to start is to practice meditation regularly, because after you come out of an amazing 20-minute meditation session you cease to be a *consumer* (when you are in that clear headspace). The way that you feel about yourself after a good meditation session is phenomenal. The last thing that's on your mind is to get a new haircut, to go shopping, or to take a selfie and post it on social media in order to feel good about yourself. If you take a look at yourself in a mirror after an amazing meditation session, you will realise that you actually like the way that you are, and the way you look–your face becomes relaxed and your eyes begin to emit a pleasing energy of youth and vitality, which immediately makes you attractive a thousandfold.

You may think that people are looking at you and judging you based on your appearance, when in reality people are so busy judging themselves that all they ever see in you is the general energy you are putting out. (Of course, it doesn't mean that you shouldn't dress well, eat well and take care of yourself; you should absolutely do all of those things. However, you must do all of those things for *you*, and don't be paranoid about it to a point that it takes you out of the present moment and shoves you back into your head. Make it a point to take care of yourself to the best of your ability and leave it at that.) Understand that it doesn't matter what you look like, as long as you have a warm, positive, alive, "present in the moment" look in your eyes, other people will feel drawn towards you, and what you will notice is that people will often begin commenting on how beautiful, and awesome you are. Conversely, it doesn't matter how physically attractive you may be, if you get stuck in your head, your appearance will be overlooked. If you're feeling insecure, if you're judging yourself, and others, then what you are projecting is a heavy, constricted, and dense energy that is unattractive, and repulsive–the kind of energy that no person in their right mind feels drawn towards. In effect, the key is *prioritisation*. That is, you have to make sure to work on your inner-self first, before relying on your outer appearance to make you attractive.

Lastly, in order to become deeply secure with ourself we have to learn to accept that we have great potential, by letting go of what Owen Cook calls "icon-level thinking." Owen explains that the society in which we live tends to present certain figures who had accomplished great things in life in such a way that it makes other people think: "Wow, that's incredible, I could never do *that*," leaving out a crucial detail that when anyone achieves greatness, or accomplishes amazing things in life–things that seem impossible to ordinary people like you and me–those things are usually accomplished in teams, and not by any one individual. However, because of this limited presentation of facts the thought of accomplishing something similar ourselves doesn't even occur to us. Yet, the truth is that when anyone accomplishes anything in life, it usually comes about as the result of a series of different happenings; rather than a stroke of genius or luck. Usually other people are involved in the process. Usually other people make a massive contribution to the cause. Usually there are a number of different negotiations, as well as a lot of trial and error that takes place. But we do not get to see any of that. We do not get to see the whole process; all we get to witness is the end result and one person responsible for it. What winds up happening is great figures like George Washington, Winston Churchill, Nelson Mandela, Michael Jackson, Michael Jordan, Mahatma Gandhi, Muhammad Ali, or Bruce Lee, just to name a few, become what are commonly known as *icons*. Of course, most of us have massive respect for these individuals, and the title is well-deserved.

However, the problem with the icon-level thinking is that when we engage in it, we no longer believe that we too can make an impact; we no longer believe that we too can make a difference and become great ourself. When we observe other people's achievements we immediately assume that if we wish to make an impact, and achieve something great ourselves, we have to be some kind of a genius who has all of the answers, who's extremely talented and intelligent, who knows exactly what needs to be done and when, and who doesn't require help from anybody. And that couldn't be more further from the truth. We don't actually need to have all of the answers and, in fact, when trying to do something which hasn't been done before, it is impossible to have all of the right answers upfront. All we have to work with at the start of anything is a general plan, a rough idea of how to go about reaching our goal, and a certain amount of focus and determination so that we do not give up at the first sign of a challenge or obstacle, while continuing to traverse the path, and be ready to correct course as many times as necessary until we get there. (Relate this back to the example of Thomas Edison.)

Steve Jobs once said: "*You cannot connect the dots looking forward; you can only connect them looking backwards.*" I believe what Jobs essentially meant by that statement is that nobody knows precisely how to reach a goal until they actually reach it. And only when they reach the goal, they can look back and pinpoint exactly what worked, and discard everything that didn't. Which, in turn, makes it seem (for those who are on the outside looking in) as though the whole journey was planned out all along. But of course, that is rarely the case. Now, that being said, you do not have to be a superhuman who knows exactly what to do in order to achieve whatever it is that you desire. You only have to decide what it is you want, take your first step in the direction of it, and trust that the path will be revealed to you one step at the time. Abraham Hicks had told us on numerous occasions: "*If this time-space reality has the wherewithal to stimulate a desire within you, then this time-space reality has the wherewithal to bring it about into your physical reality.*" In other words, a desire is the manifestation of power. If you can see yourself being, doing, or having something you want in your mind's eye, it is solid proof that there *is* a way of getting it done. And all you have to do is hold your vision firmly in your mind, and trust that the right ideas, right impulses, and right people–for the attainment of your desire–will appear as you move steadily towards it.

"You don't need confidence to succeed, you need a sense of relentless determination combined with an expectation of a positive result." – David Snyder

The fact is, we are all working with the same power, and we are all essentially the same. Individuals who've achieved greatness have not been endowed with some special powers which we haven't got. The primary difference between persons of great stature and those who sit on the sidelines is that people of excellence have learnt how to channel (whether consciously, or unconsciously) their inherent, creative power through them, and direct this power towards specific ends. And also be ready–and willing–to work in harmony with others. Whereas the rest of us–the "normies"–have been conditioned to squander our creative power on devising various ways to make other people like us, as well as believing that greatness requires no help from anybody. So when we try to accomplish something by ourselves, and fail, we assume that we are not special; that genius and greatness is not meant for us; that we are destined to lead a life of quiet desperation. But understand this: we're all cut from the same cloth. And we all have the ability to weave ourself into something spectacular. However, even though we may be the same, since we use our minds differently, we become different. We adopt different perspectives; beliefs; behaviours; values; habits, and so on. In other words, you absolutely can do anything another person can do. But, if you don't have similar habits, beliefs, and perspectives which *that* person has, and you are not being proactive about it either–meaning that you're not even trying to build similar habits, take similar actions, develop similar attitudes and thinking patterns–then you might be cut from the same cloth, sure, but you are not being woven into something great. Well, then how do we know which perspectives, beliefs, and habits we must build in order to bridge this gap between where we are and where we want to go? *Mentorship.* We've already touched on this earlier, but this invaluable aspect cannot be overlooked. Find a person who is doing exactly what you want to do with your life, and get them to mentor you; buy the books; take the courses; attend the seminars; reach out to them directly; do anything to get on their radar and take the advice!

In conclusion: in order to shift your mental paradigm from comparison to self-acceptance, first of all, you have to realise that no one is judging you. Nobody is looking at you and forever thinking about you. Because everyone is obsessed with themself. Truly, no one cares about you, or anything you do as much as you think they do. Next, you must accept that comparing yourself to other people is a losing strategy. That if you're competing with others, you'll never win. Because there's always going to be another person who has "more." And lastly, never forget that all "men" are created equal; that we are all made from the same cloth. What one can do, another can do. Begin to diffuse the icon-level thinking by accepting that those who are viewed as icons are mere mortals who simply did certain things, and have developed certain habits and perspectives which we did not. But, it doesn't mean that we can't. In most cases, we simply *won't.* There is a massive difference.

MAINSTREAM NARRATIVE & RELATIONSHIPS

"Mainstream narrative is simply a given story that we are all educated to accept as reality. Our ego, our self-identity, and our conditioning are formed by the mainstream narrative; by a story which we have been educated to accept as fact through systematic repetition of a given message, particularly through the mainstream media."

The underlying premise of the mainstream narrative is what leads us to believe that there will be *completion* when we achieve certain things in our lives and check them off on our "to do list" so to speak. However, it never bothers to tell us that just because we've achieved those things, it doesn't necessarily mean they are guaranteed to stay with us indefinitely. Society conditions us to want to strive for completion, when there is no such thing as completion. The world in which we live is forever moving fast, things are always changing, and so do people. We can't expect to get somewhere and stay there, and keep things as they are for evermore, because life is full of variables and un-predictability. Social conditioning needs us to believe in the idea that we will be complete in order to incentivise us to go on *their* plan. It tells us that if we can secure a good education, then happiness is guaranteed. If we can secure a job, then happiness is guaranteed. If we can secure a marriage, then happi-ness is guaranteed. But in reality–and from your own personal experience–is that ever the case? Hardly so. Educated people that have degrees coming out of their backside still experience difficulty finding work; people who've been working at a particular company for many years, still get laid off; marriages which start out hot and passionate eventually end up in a train wreck. For in order to attain–and retain–any good thing requires constant work and ability to adapt to change. In our ever-expanding Universe there is no such thing as inertia. (As an aside, our planet is spinning on its axis at approximately 1,000 mph, while it revolves in orbit around the sun at approximately 66,000 mph. And while this is going on, our solar system is orbiting around the centre of the galaxy at approximately 540,000 mph, and the Milky Way galaxy is mov-ing through the Universe at approximately 1,300,000 mph. This gives you an idea as to what is happening "out there" right this second while you are sit-ting/lying motionless reading these lines.) In effect, if you are not progress-ing, and moving forward into growth, then by default, you are being left be-hind–you are moving backwards into disintegration and decay.

When people buy into the idea of wanting to be complete what ends up happening is they will secure an education but still be out of work. They will secure a job until an economic recession hits, or their employer makes a bad business decision. They will secure a marriage and turn into couch potatoes, become overweight, or cheat on their significant other until the marriage in-evitably ends in shambles. That is what a life of someone who believes in the mainstream narrative–who strives for completion–generally looks like. You see, the need–or the desire–for completion comes from a lower state of con-sciousness. It comes out of fear of having to think, and having to make deci-sions. Chances are, your comfort zone right now is doing things as you are told by someone else; rather than thinking for yourself. Because by doing so, you unconsciously believe that you cannot make a mistake, and that nothing can go wrong. If you haven't yet developed a sense of self-trust, then you are more inclined to believe that other people simply know better than you. Be-sides, the way you unconsciously think about this is: "Look, everyone else is doing the same thing, so how could having a good education be bad advice? How could securing a job be bad advice? How could forming a relationship and building a family be bad advice?" It is only natural to assume that we all need this kind of completion (and as soon as possible) in a world that is full of ambiguity and uncertainty (in other words, we instinctually *crave* stability in a world that is confusing as it is. And completion promises to relieve us of at least the fraction of that confusion). Consequently, from a lack of self-trust we begin to blindly follow along for fear of "missing out," or making wrong decisions in life. And by doing so, it is not uncommon that we sooner or later find ourself sharing a life with a wrong person; raising children when we ourselves are still children (undeveloped, lost, and confused); or committing ourselves entirely to unfulfilling work.

If you honestly wish to experience happiness in your marriage or career your new comfort zone needs to become ambiguity and uncertainty. In other words, you have to become comfortable with not knowing what might happen tomorrow; that the way things are right now in your life can take a turn at any given moment, and you must be ready to adjust. You need to develop a sense of self-trust, where you know that no matter what happens in your life, you'll figure it out. Because in life, almost nothing is going to go exactly as we initially plan. And nothing is going to stay the way it is for very long. Ergo, you simply must pay attention, and be aware of what is happening in your everyday life, and learn to adapt to change. You have to make certain that you are always progressing and growing–no matter how incrementally so–in the direction of everything you want to be, do, and have. Otherwise, if you refuse to take responsibility for your life, and buy into the mainstream narrative, then you'll continue to think that your relationship is supposed to be hot and passionate just because you're in one. Or that your career is supposed to take off just because you have a degree. Of course, you can still do all of those things, such as getting a good education; securing a job; or marrying the person you love. All of that is praiseworthy. However, make certain that you do it for the right reasons, and at the right time. Whatever you do, you have to do it because you choose to, and because you sincerely want to. Never do anything for fear of being incomplete or "missing out," because decision-making that is under the influence of a lower state of consciousness never ends well. The evidence to support this claim are too overwhelming to suggest otherwise. (Take a look around you and see how "well" most people are doing.) So, you have to discover what makes you happy; not what your government, teachers, parents, or friends think you should do to get happy, because they are not *you*. No one knows exactly what you want, and need in order to be happy, *but* you. There isn't only one way to live a good, happy, fulfilling life, contrary to what the mainstream narrative would like you to believe. The kind of life that is widely accepted as the "norm" all around the globe is to go through school and get good grades. Then get into a good college, or university and get your degree/s. Then secure a safe job, and get a mortgage on a property. Then find a partner and marry her/him. Then have your kids and cats and dogs, and proceed to teach/program your kids to do precisely what you've done your entire life. And that kind of a life is universally accepted to be a "complete" and happy life. For some, such a life experience is absolutely fine. Some people genuinely love and enjoy that kind of existence. Though it is, however, not for everyone.

Knowing what I know about your spiritual nature, if you are following the mainstream narrative, my prediction is that you secretly despise your existence. Because the mainstream narrative is not designed to make you happy; it is designed to preserve social stability. The uncomfortable truth is that most people do not live lives which they genuinely love and enjoy. The social pressure to conform and follow along the beaten path is so great: ("What are you doing? Most people your age are already married." "What's wrong with you? Most people your age already have children, and are already settled down." "Why would you even attempt to build your own business? Just find a good job like everybody else." "Are you seriously thinking about investing? What the hell? We have a mountain of bills to pay, we cannot afford to take risks."), that most of us inevitably cave in to that pressure and forget about our dreams, goals and personal preferences. Most people will accept a life that is not at all in alignment with their personal preferences and values, but a life that is approved by the society, and then they wonder why they are secretly resentful and semi-depressed.

Now, this subject is extremely complex, involving a million different elements which, I, myself haven't even yet entirely understood. And besides, I wouldn't want to bombard you with too much information all at once, and give you a headache. That being said, in this section (with respect to completion) I'd like to focus exclusively on relationships between men and women. Humans don't naturally understand what it means to have a successful relationship (it is something that we have to learn), and from our lack of understanding we get ourselves into all kinds of relationships, for all of the wrong reasons. And what invariably follows is us helplessly trying to manage those relationships while hurting and emotionally scarring one another in the process. My goal here is to offer you a fresh, well-rounded perspective on how the opposite sexes (both men and women) approach relationships, and what they are trying to get out of them. And as we get into this, I want you to bear in mind that although the ideas presented in the following pages will be centred around relationships between straight males and females, regardless of what your sexual orientation may be, you will still learn something of value about yourself and other people which will be of great benefit to you in your personal life also, so don't be discouraged.

Finding a woman you enjoy spending time with–and wanting to secure a relationship with–is never about getting it done, and assuming completion. What finding the right woman, and establishing a partnership with her truly is about, is creating your own personal universe first–which you absolutely love–into which you can then bring your new partner. You want to think of your life–and your own personal world–as an exciting adventure, or a roller coaster ride. And a woman comes to join you on that ride, but she is not *the* ride. A successful and long-lasting relationship needs to be built on the basis that before you even enter a new relationship you have to have an ecosystem of positive emotions around yourself already established (that includes having good friends; hobbies; passions; goals; and things that you love to do), so that the woman you're with doesn't become the centre of your universe, and therefore in control of your emotions. You want to put yourself in a position where your woman is still a valuable–and very important–part of your ecosystem, but never the epicentre of it, i.e. the sole driving force behind everything that you do, and how you feel. It is not your woman's responsibility to care about how you feel. If she truly loves you for who you are, then she will do everything that pleases you naturally, because women are naturally subservient. Women honestly enjoy supporting, and catering to men–especially those who have their shit together–so you don't need to worry about any of that. You don't need to try and coerce your woman to conform to your own standards and preferences in order to have a relationship you both enjoy. All that you must do is handle your own life, and manage your own affairs first, and only then look to bring a woman into your life who will naturally adapt to you, and follow your lead. Number-one reason why most relationships do not work is because one, or both parties come into them as wounded, undeveloped, insecure, and mistreated puppies who then proceed to leech off one another energetically/emotionally until one or the other finally snaps.

Understand that your woman is not with you in order to help you cope with loneliness; to deal with your drama and insecurities; to fix you and heal your childhood traumas (although she can still do those things if she chooses to, but it should never be expected of her)–that is *your* job. She is in your life in order to help you grow, and to support the vision which you have (for the two of you), without you holding her as a prisoner–continually needing her attention, approval, and reassurance, without which you are not able to function. In order to curtail the statistical probability that your relationship will end in a train wreck, you have to stop looking to women you are with as the primary source of good emotions–the source of your happiness. Although it sounds counterintuitive, everything you do should be done for *you* first and foremost–you should always be the one who is at the centre of your personal universe; not your woman. (And that is not to remotely suggest you should neglect your woman.) Because if you concentrate all of your focus and attention onto your woman–constantly orbiting around her, suffocating her with your "love," trying to please her, or pressuring her to conform to you–*before* you have developed a strong sense of "self," and have established an honest, solid, loving relationship with yourself, then why should your woman conform, love, and follow you in return? Sure, some women may do this out of pity, or for other selfish reasons, but is that something to be proud of? I think not. Instead, why not work on yourself and become the best version of yourself first, before deciding to share a life with another human being? If you do not fully love, and trust yourself, then you can't expect someone else to love, and trust you in return. If you don't know where you are going in life, then you can't expect someone else to follow you. If you haven't yet developed a strong sense of "self;" if you don't know who you are, and what your values are; if you do not have personal boundaries, and a clear sense of direction in life, then you cannot expect your partner to behave a certain way, when you yourself are not even able to clearly define what that "certain way" is.

Now, I am fully aware that men who decide to embark on a journey to self-improvement and self-development usually become the best versions of themselves–that they are satisfied with–around the age of 40, and sometimes even 50. However, this does not mean that you should abstain from relationships altogether until you are completely and utterly content with your progress; it doesn't mean that at all. As long as you are on some kind of a journey to mastery, then that is good enough. And it doesn't matter whether you are at the beginning, middle, or end of your journey either. As long as you're striving towards *something*, then those potent energies of ambition, passion, and purpose–which your drive produces–still generate the exact same effect where your partner feels genuine affection towards you. In turn exponentially increasing the chances of that relationship turning out to be successful.

All in all, the prerequisite for establishing a loving, honest, and successful relationship with a woman–as I hope you already gather–demands that you put yourself first, and manage your own affairs. And what this means is that if you are planning to get a certain education, then do it for you! If you are planning to secure a certain position at a certain company, then do it for you! If you are planning to frequent the gym and work on your fitness, then do it for you! If you are planning to purchase a home where you would like to start a family someday, then do it for you! And so on and so forth. Avoid doing things for other people (unless you sincerely want to, without expecting anything in return), because that's a perfect recipe for disaster. If you do something specifically for someone else with an expectant attitude, you unconsciously make them feel obliged to respond in like-kind. You put them in an uncomfortable position where they feel an unnatural need to reciprocate, when you might not actually deserve it, or when the feeling is not mutual. In most cases, however, people simply won't do it. Because nobody appreciates those who make them want to do things which they don't genuinely feel like doing, but are being guilt-driven into. And if they do, do it, then chances are they will do it grudgingly or half-heartedly–far from the outcome that you'd expect, and would want to succeed in achieving.

Let me give you an example of this. On one particular Christmas, one of my neighbours had decided to post a Christmas card through my letterbox, wishing me a Merry Christmas. After receiving the card, I felt the strongest urge to write one in return. Because it felt like a logical, appropriate, and socially expected thing to do. However, that particular Christmas I was not at all in a "Christmas Spirit" if you will. I was too busy working, and focusing on things that were more important to me than being "jolly." So in the end, I never sent one back, since I did not have the energy within me to pretend as though everything was great and merry, when it clearly wasn't. But it didn't mean that I disliked my neighbour, or that I did not appreciate the gesture; I simply wasn't motivated enough to do *that* which my neighbour was expecting from me. Besides, I never did ask to be sent a card to begin with, so why should I have to care about what my neighbour is doing, and then expecting from me? It is like putting a piece of candy into somebody else's coat pocket, and then demanding that they dance for your amusement, because you did something nice for them. It is not genuine; it is coercive and dishonest. Anyhow, a couple of days later (before the New Year's Eve) I did see my neighbour, and as I was about to wish him a Happy New Year, and all of the glory that awaited him, he violently cut me off and began shouting at me, warning me that if I were to be loud with my friends on New Year's Eve again (in my own house)–because that's what we have done in the past–he would call the police. And that he finally had enough. Now, the truth of the matter is that if I had forced myself to write and send that meaningless (because it wouldn't be coming from the heart) Christmas card back to him, my prediction is that he would have never said anything of sorts. And so you see, because he had decided to execute a particular action, and coated it in expectation–and since I did not meet the expectation–he got totally pissed! And whose problem is that? Certainly isn't mine. For my neighbour's (a fully grown adult's) actions and emotions are not *my* responsibility, but his.

In effect, you will only hurt yourself when you do things to please others and expect something from them in return, be it a certain reaction; emotion; action, or whatever. No matter what you do, you have to do it because you *want to*; it has to come from the heart. That way, if it doesn't pan out the way you wanted it to; if your partner leaves you; if someone does not like, or appreciate the gesture; or if someone does not respond in a certain way, then it is not the end of the world. You haven't lost anything, or been mistreated in any way. Because you did what you yourself *wanted* to do–you did it, you felt good when you were doing it, and you weren't concerned about the outcome–is precisely why you haven't felt any negative emotion about the outcome. Because the outcome was irrelevant. Ultimately, your personal action, and what you choose to do with your life should never be attached to another's reaction, or approval of it. What you do should never be coming from a place of need, or expectation. Everything you do should always come from a sincere place of wanting to give and share, while allowing the person on the receiving end to do with it what he or she wills. For us men, this principle is especially important to abide by if we are to enjoy happy, successful, and intimate relationships with our female counterparts.

A vitally important aspect of a female psyche which we as men need to understand, is that women are predominantly emotional creatures. A woman's mind, and thought process always follows the emotions that she feels at any given time. This means that if your woman had decided to react in a certain way, then rest assured that no amount of logical persuasion, or explanation is going to change her mind, unless you change the way she feels in that moment. In other words, whenever you say to your woman things such as: "I did this for you! How can you be so ungrateful?" or "You can't leave me, look at everything that I've done for you!" or "You can't go *there*, or do *that*, I have sacrificed everything for you!" it never works. For example, a woman's decision to leave the relationship is rarely logically and rationally based, but 99 percent of the time is emotionally influenced. Which is to say that you could give your woman the entire world, but if she doesn't feel–for whatever reason–emotions of love and respect towards you any longer, then everything that you've ever done for her is practically non-existent at that point–it doesn't matter to her. The fact is, when it comes to enjoying harmonious relationships, rather than doing the one and only thing that works, which is developing and embodying characteristics of a man whom women can reliably love and respect, men tend to secure relationships with women by all kinds of other means, which do not work. Usually by promising to give away half of their assets to a woman who agrees to devote a certain amount of her time to them. In effect, most men unknowingly buy a woman's time and attention by guaranteeing her safety and security for the rest of her life, even if a marriage happens to end. This promise acts as a safety net, or incentive for that woman to enter a partnership with a person whom she doesn't feel is actually deserving of her. (Of course, this is not everybody's marriage. I hope you don't misunderstand what I am trying to convey here. Not all humans think and act the same way. There are simply too many variables, and elements of randomness at play to suggest that this is what every marriage is all about.)

As a result, men who actively avoid going through the trouble of bettering themselves still get rewarded with women's time and attention. Because most women will be ready to settle (for less desirable men) for financial, obligatory, guilt-driven, or age-related reasons. And this is the reason why this strategy is still actively being used by men, all around the world–because it works! (Well… kind of.) It serves a biological need of their counterparts for safety and security, which humans will always have. However, this strategy is fragile, and it is not sustainable, because it is not based on true love and affection. Women that are in these type of relationships–who can be completely honest with themselves–will admit that they secretly resent their partners. Because deep down they know–and feel disgusted by the fact–that their men were only able to secure their commitment by catering to their need for safety and security through the use of money, provisions, contracts, and material possessions (which practically any man in the world can easily achieve). Rather than with authenticity; charm; charisma; leadership; strong boundaries; personal values; life philosophy; and genuine connection (aspects and qualities which are difficult to develop, and which money can't buy). Unsurprisingly, that is where most of the nagging and bickering comes from. And men who are in these relationships believe that it is normal; that it is part of every relationship. However, what men in these type of circumstances need to understand, is that this can only ever be true when we strive for completion. In effect, it doesn't *have* to be that way!

When you choose to enter into a new relationship without some kind of a purpose in life–and assuming completion–that is a massive attraction killer. Sooner or later your woman will feel that sense of "no direction" in your relationship so strongly that she will begin to bicker, and complain about the most trivial things in the world. And if it happens in your personal relationship, my advice is that you do not shy away from it, because that's actually a blessing in disguise. What women are doing–on an unconscious level (women are usually not aware they are doing this)–is they are trying to emotionally shake us up and get on our nerves, in hopes that we'll finally take responsibility for the quality of our relationship and make things happen. The issue with this is that most of us don't ever recognise the tension and disharmony within our relationships for what it actually is–a major call to action. But rather, most men tend to think that women are acting irrationally, and creating drama for no other reason than that they are crazy bitches who simply can't be happy with what they already have. However, what we–as men–have to realise and come to terms with, is the fact that a woman will have absolutely no need to bicker, nag, and complain to a man who is fully present with her; who is unreactive; who is confident in his own abilities; who has his shit together; who has a strong sense of identity (whose self-image is not weak and fragile); and who knows where he is going in life.

Women are extremely attuned to all of the subtle energies around them, which makes them excellent (although sometimes irritating and intolerable) partners on our journey to becoming men of grand stature, and great valour. Women are truly here to help us become better men. They can help us identify–and quickly detect–where we are screwing up; where we are being little wusses; where we are not doing our best; or when we have stopped growing mentally/intellectually/spiritually. The problem is that the woman's way of helping her man comes across as nagging and belittling, by shrieking and offering unsolicited advice. Which makes us gentlemen feel stupid, and emasculated; thereby impulsively rejecting the suggestion. (I recommend that you read "Men are From Mars, Women are From Venus" by John Gray. When it comes to understanding–and then resolving–the struggles in communication between the sexes, this book is a godsend.) Rather than interpreting a woman's nagging, poking, and provoking as a call to become a stronger, and better man, men (understandably so) wind up arguing, fighting back, resenting their partner, and ultimately ending the relationship. But if you are to derive as much value as possible from your relationships, you have to understand that a woman who is nagging you, and pissing you off, is most likely a good woman, who wants you to be a winner. Otherwise, if she didn't care about you becoming a better man, then she wouldn't be with you. And so, she will continue to throw little digs and jabs at you, however subtle (or not so subtle), in an attempt to wake you up, because she sees potential in you that you yourself aren't realising. A good woman doesn't actually enjoy hassling you; constantly complaining and nagging. She hates it as much as you do. But she *has* to do it. Because she still loves you, and she wants you to do well. Now, there are cases where a woman is just a negative troll who loves to see you at your lowest point, because she is a negative person. So it will take your own level of awareness to determine whether you're being nagged, purely for the sake of being nagged, or whether you're being genuinely cared for–that your partner wants you to do well–even if sometimes, it may *seem* as though your partner hates your f**king guts!

"Women don't want to win; they want a winner."

Let us now look at the difference between love and co-dependence, and how most people typically fail to distinguish the difference between the two. The society in which we live convinces men that in order to attract a woman, we have to incessantly pander to her; treat her "nice," and be a gentleman (as in never disagreeing with her, or saying anything which may upset her, even if it means going against our personal beliefs, and values); constantly shower her with compliments; buy her flowers; send her cute love letters; write her poems, etc. Social conditioning makes men believe that this is what it takes to attract a woman, and make her fall in love. And with the help of the entertainment industry–the love songs and the romantic movies–we end up forming wrong ideas about love, and what it means to be "in love." If you look at those who have completely bought-in to society's idea of romance, what do you typically see? They get divorced multiple times. They become completely heartbroken; jaded; paranoid; angry; depressed; or suicidal. They wind up in jail, or dead. None of this is a result of love. Real, true love could never do this to anyone, but wanting to be complete, and being dependent on another person for one's own happiness (being obsessed with, or attached to another person) does. Love is something that comes from you. It emanates from you, and envelopes the people around you; it is not something that you get from others. (Of course, other people can give you love, just like you are giving it to them. But, if you want to actually experience love, then it has to start with you.) Co-dependence, on the other hand, is expecting another person to love you, when you haven't learnt how to love yourself–hoping that your partner can fill that void. And when both parties in the relationship are coming from the same frame of mind, it turns into what we call a "toxic relationship."

Realise that you will never *make* a woman fall in love with you by doing certain things *for* her, or by promising her a bunch of stuff–telling her what you think she wants to hear. A woman is either attracted to you, or she isn't. However, a woman does not become attracted to you by the brands of clothing you wear; the things you have; the things you do; the things you say; the way you look; the amount of money you make; or the people you know. The real trigger for attraction–and arousal–in a woman is your *behaviour*, the demand for your attention, and your *perceived value* to her survival and reproduction. Now, this subject is extremely complex, involving a hundred of different elements, all of which we simply do not have time, or space to discuss here. I highly recommend therefore that you pick up Rollo Tomassi's trilogy of "The Rational Male," and learn exactly what it means to be a man of value who enjoys successful relationships with women. For now, however, what I will tell you is the following: When a woman says that she wants to be treated like a princess; that she wants her man to be a gentleman; that she wants her man to write her love letters, send her flowers, take her out on romantic dinners, etc., she is visualising a man whom she's attracted to and whom she respects–someone who is ambitious, who loves himself and the life he leads–let's call him "Brad." She is not visualising a random guy who just happens to like her. She is not visualising a man who is lonely, insecure, who doesn't have real goals in life, who doesn't think much of himself, who is overly nice and shy, and who has a little crush on her. But not for the reasons you think.

The reason why she is visualising "Brad" is because Brad loves his life! Which lets her know that she'll get a lot of good emotions by being around this man. The fact that he doesn't need anything from her–he doesn't beg for her love, he is not dependent on her, he is not pressuring her to approve of him, or laugh at his stupid jokes–makes her feel at ease. Brad is a better option because he is not trying to suck good emotions off of her for him to feel good; Brad has learnt how to generate good emotions from within himself. (Brad has become the source of good emotions, like the sun which shines on you regardless of what you do for it. Instead of a black hole, which continuously sucks good emotions off of other people). Brad knows how to lead; he is not expecting the women he dates to lead the conversation or to determine the direction of their relationship. **Brad is on his path and purpose in life; he** knows precisely what he wants, and where he is going, which absolves the women he dates of the responsibility of having to think, but simply lay back and enjoy the ride. Moreover, the fact that Brad has many other women constantly vying for his attention, and wanting to date him, when he does make a choice to date any one particular woman out of many, his choosing makes that woman feel special. And from that position, if Brad now chooses to send her flowers, write her poems, and take her out on romantic dinners, she will actually appreciate it. And it'll make her feel even more attracted to him. Because she knows that her man is a winner, who is doing these things proactively–because he wants to–not because he doesn't know how else to *get* her.

Conversely, if she chooses to date a different man–let's call him "Tim"– who does not have similar qualities, and for whom she is the only option he has, she will feel nothing of the sort. Because Tim is doing all of those things (which she says she wants) only because he *wants* something from her. And she feels repulsed by that. Since Tim does not have other options with women, it makes her feel as though Tim is not being genuine and authentic when he tries to convince her that he loves her; that they have a real, unique connection; that she is the "one;" that she is his soulmate. In other words, how could Tim possibly know that she's the one, and that she is the perfect match for him, when she is the only one? She can sense that Tim wants her for all of the wrong reasons and it does not in any way, shape or form makes her feel special. Tim says that it is true love, that they have a special connection, and that he is prepared to do anything for her, but deep down she knows that it's just co-dependence doing the talking. She recognises that Tim is acting out of scarcity; rather than abundance. Which distorts his perception, and clouds his judgement. By adhering to the mainstream narrative Tim is unknowingly exhibiting extremely "low-value" behaviours (displaying unattractive qualities) around the women he dates. Thereby dramatically lowering his chances at being considered a viable sexual prospect. And although a woman might still like Tim as a person, or as a friend, but she'll never view him as a sexual, intimate partner. Which results in Tim getting tossed into something that is commonly known as the "friend zone" over and over again.

Now, what happens when a man (who does not understand how attraction really works) tries to follow a woman's advice and buys into her idea of romance *before* he has worked on himself, and *before* he has built a life that he loves? He attempts to show her how much he "loves" her, by stalking her at her place of work; by blowing up her mobile phone with calls and messages; by writing her love letters; by sending flowers to her home address; by buying her expensive gifts, and so on. Until the woman gets extremely creeped out and what does she do? You guessed it right... she calls the police and the lover boy gets prosecuted for sexual harassment. (Obviously I am overexaggerating here, but I hope you get the point.) When we talk about attracting a mate into your life what it boils down to is the following: If you do not have things in your life which bring you joy; if you do not have a good relationship with yourself; and if you do not have other options with women as you happen to get a crush on one particular woman–whom you would like to get to know and start a relationship with–then the way you are coming across to her from that point is not much different to that of a homeless person yanking your sleeve, and asking you for money. It is irritating, and annoying. Because if you are insecure, needy, not confident, and you don't have other options with women, then when you do finally meet a woman who happens to agree to come out on a date with you. What you typically do is you put all of your eggs in one basket, and you put her on a pedestal (which comes across as needy and desperate; not as a mutual exchange of value). And you mess it up–it doesn't go anywhere.

When men who lack the understanding of the basic principles of attraction experience rejection (the "I like you as a friend" bombshell), they usually blame themself, or the women, by saying things like: "She didn't like me because I'm ugly." "She didn't like me because I'm not a millionaire." "She didn't like me because I'm not 6'5"." "She's just a stuck-up bitch." "She is a gold digger." "She is too superficial for me; she only cares about the surface-level things." Whatever. (But consider this: when a woman rejects Brad's advances, he does not take it personally because he lives in abundance. For Brad rejection does not exist; there is only a lack of chemistry. He understands that not every woman is going to like him, and vice versa. And that's okay–there is plenty of more fish in the sea. Whereas when a woman rejects Tim's advances, he continues to pursue her because he lives in scarcity. Since Tim is under the spell of social conditioning, social conditioning leads him to believe that when a woman doesn't love him in return, he must love her even more. Social conditioning convinces him that the woman he is pursuing *is* his soulmate who just doesn't know it yet, and his duty as a man is to chase after her until she does. Which is typically going to creep that woman out. And when she finally gets annoyed and tells Tim to go away–rather than rethinking his strategy, and questioning the mainstream narrative–he assumes that something is wrong with her; that she's the problem.) In truth, the reason why she may not like you is that you don't even like yourself, so why should she?

In order to avoid mistaking co-dependence for love you have to fall in love with yourself. (It doesn't mean to become a narcissist; rather, it is about developing a healthy respect, and appreciation for yourself.) Loving yourself is about having a strong sense of purpose in life, personal boundaries, and a set of values which you will not compromise for anybody. You have to have things in your life that bring you joy, other than your women. So that if any one woman rejects your advances, or your current partner decides to end the relationship, it won't affect you in a negative/destructive way. As you fall in love with yourself, you will naturally want what is best for other people, as much as you do for yourself. Which means that if ending the relationship, or leaving the interaction makes the other person feel better, then so be it. True love will understand. Because true love knows that it doesn't diminish when the person on the receiving end chooses not to (or no longer) reciprocate. In other words, unlike a co-dependent relationship, when you're in a loving relationship with a woman who (for whatever reason) ceases loving you in return, you don't throw a tantrum, verbally abuse her, try to convince her that she's making a mistake, try to buy back her love, and confess your "love" for her some more while she's pulling away, or beat her and end up in a jail cell. That's not what love does; only co-dependence, or unhealthy attachment can do such things.

When you make a woman into your purpose, you are setting your relationship up for failure. Because your purpose in life cannot be your woman; your main purpose *must* be your mission in life. No woman wants to be the reason why you get up in the morning and live your life. (Logically, women will say that they want to be the main purpose, but emotionally they do not respond to it.) When you have some kind of a purpose in life–something that you're *striving* towards–it creates a masculine polarity (a magnet of sorts) between yourself and the women you're with. Whereby the women become attracted to you naturally and indefinitely. And they will want to stick around you, and experience your world by their own conscious choice; never out of pity, obligation, or necessity. If you think that I'm pulling your leg here, then ask any woman you know what she would rather. Would she rather wake up in the morning at a sound of her man (who is certain in what he wants, and what he is doing) telling her–with a purposeful, fully present look in his eyes–"Morning beautiful. Today we are doing *this*. Then, we are going *here*. It is going to be amazing! Tomorrow we have *this* plan. And our future looks like *this*."? Or: "Morning precious. So what are we doing today? Where are we going tomorrow? What do you need me to wear? Please make the decision and tell me what to do. I just want to do everything to keep you happy, because you are my reason for living. If I were to make you mad, and drive you away, then I don't know what I would do without you."? I can guarantee you that the answer isn't going to be the latter. Now, you may think that choosing to love your woman more than anything else in the world does not necessarily follow that you'll become co-dependent and needy, but in reality it is almost a certainty, and here is the reason why…

Between male and female communion there is at play something which is called "sexual polarity," and when there is no sexual polarity in a relationship, there is no attraction. Even though every single person has both masculine and feminine energies within them, nonetheless biologically men are inherently more masculine; whereas women are more feminine, and they both complement each other. You can imagine a masculine essence as a solid, focused, purposeful, very serious, controlled rock. And the feminine as a wild, dramatic, very emotional, and out of control wave. And these energies need one another in order to achieve a perfect balance. Otherwise, by themselves alone, the rock is too boring, too serious, and cold. Whereas the wave is too wild, and out of control, so much so that it will eventually crash and destroy itself. Opposite sexes should absolutely complement each other and bring into the relationship something that the other half simply doesn't have. Which then allows us to experience life in its fullness vicariously through our partners. If we go back to the previous example, the feminine (which is typically going to be a woman) wants to be reassured and led. The feminine is the one who wants to be told where it is going, and what it is wearing; not the other way around. The feminine essence is soft, yielding, submissive, and serving. Whereas the masculine (which is typically going to be a man) wants to lead, decide, build, conquer, resolve. And when these "roles" in a relationship become mixed-up, then it is only a matter of time until frustration and dissatisfaction rear their ugly heads.

Essentially, the feminine essence brings into the relationship fun; relaxation; playfulness; mischief; wildness; patience; emotional support; inspiration, and more. While the masculine essence brings with it a clear direction; a strong purpose; stability; predictability; protection; clarity; focus; strength–both physical and mental–determination, and more. And thus, when there is no balance in a relationship–when there is too much of any one essence present–then too much on a feminine side steers the relationship to destruction. Because there is no accountability, or grounding force present to control, and guide the "wave." Conversely, when there is too much on a masculine side, then the relationship becomes all about moving and building, but never arriving and smelling the roses. The relationship becomes dull, bland, and ultimately lifeless when there isn't any space for laughter, playfulness and appreciation of the present moment, regardless of how much the masculine has built, and is yet to build. In effect, there is no playful energy present to tickle the "rock" out of its state of somber, and bring it into the spirit of life.

The trouble that we find ourselves in today is the fact that relationships are becoming increasingly depolarised, as men are becoming more feminine and women are becoming more masculine. This invariably results in masculine men getting into relationships with masculine women, only to soon discover that they repel one another. Likewise, feminine women will try to settle down with feminine men and to their disappointment inevitably discover that being with their partner is not much different than being with a woman. Which also repels them from one another. This is one of the biggest reasons why relationships hardly ever work out anymore. The fact that most people are completely unaware of this vitally important dynamic between the sexes, they get into relationships with those who do not complement their own essences, and become frustrated. Now, I am no authority on this subject, so I'm going to end it here. However, David Deida talks about this in great detail in his writings. So I highly recommend that you pick up a copy of "The Way of the Superior Man," and begin to study that book. When it comes to enjoying harmonious, intimate relationships with your female counterparts "The Way of the Superior Man" is your Bible! (But don't get alarmed as it is only a 200-page book.)

To help you understand women a little bit better, in terms of how they view relationships with men, I want you to imagine women as travellers and men as individual islands (Owen Cook's concept). When dating, what women are essentially doing is they are visiting, exploring, and experiencing different islands in order to discover which island they would enjoy to inhabit the most. (In this context, a man's island is a metaphor for a man's belief system; life philosophy; values; ideals; personal boundaries; alliances; hobbies; goals; personal preferences; character traits–such as decisiveness; leadership; emotional control; intelligence; sense of humour, etc.) For example, by interacting with Tim, and by experiencing Tim's personality–through the way in which he is behaving–it sub-communicates to a woman that Tim's Island is not that great. Because if Tim is falling head over heels for her without even knowing much about her, it indicates that Tim is probably doing this to every other woman as well. A woman can sense that Tim is inviting her to live on his island without posing any questions or having any standards whatso-ever. Which does not make her feel special, or secure. What it conveys to her instead, is that everyone can easily visit Tim's Island. Because if Tim is prac-tically begging for her to come and live on his island by offering her gifts and paying for expensive dinners without any kind of filter to see whether she is worthy of his time and resources, then it probably means that Tim's Island is awfully easy to get into, and is now populated by a bunch of idiots who are making a mess out of it, and taking advantage of him, i.e. destroying the is-land, and doing whatever the hell they please.

Conversely, Brad's Island is very difficult to get into; everyone wants to come and visit Brad's Island. However, Brad isn't going to accept every sin-gle person who wants to live on his island. Because Brad's Island is sacred, and beautiful–Brad has strong values, standards, boundaries, a clear sense of direction for his island, and a grand vision of prosperity and opulence for its inhabitants. Therefore, if somebody wishes to live on Brad's Island, they first have to be qualified, and then they have to be on their best behaviour if they wish to stay. That is the way in which Brad sub-communicates his personali-ty to the women he dates, and they appreciate that. Even through a brief and subtle interaction, a woman can tell that Brad's Island is secure, fun, and full of adventures. Just by seeing the way Brad carries himself lets her know that on Brad's Island she will be free to mingle with other decent, well-meaning people and make new friends. She appreciates the fact that she can be free to explore the endless possibilities for her own development and advancement, and become a much better woman herself. Whereas on Tim's Island, she will be bored out of her mind because Tim doesn't know how to do anything else but gaze into her eyes, trying to explain for the millionth time how beautiful he thinks she is (because the mainstream narrative told him that is what she wants him to do).

A woman knows that on Brad's Island she will be taken care of, because Brad is resourceful, he has his emotions under control, he is ambitious, pro-active, and driven (complete opposite of apathetic), he is mentally sharp, and focused. She knows that she will never go hungry, or feel uncomfortable, be-cause Brad is capable of providing her with food, furs, and shelter. Whereas Tim lives under a tree, because he has no ambition. Tim is barely capable of bringing her a stinky little rat on a stick here and there. Which results in his woman needing to take on the masculine role in the relationship and becom-ing the "provider," at a cost of her feminine essence becoming dampened. So why would any woman choose to do that, when she can choose a much better island to live on? On Brad's Island she can be her full, feminine self, and relax into her womanhood. She can be care-free and feel safe because Brad is a great provider. Brad also has a lot of good, trust-worthy friends, as well as other alliances. Which means that if Brad's Island gets invaded by a group of pirates, Brad and his friends will meet the aggressors head-on. And will do everything in their power to defend and preserve their community. Whereas on Tim's Island she lives in a perpetual state of fear, anxiety, and insecurity, because Tim is not resourceful, he is not a leader or a good influencer. Moreover, the fact that Tim had sacrificed most of his friendships just to be with his woman, he no longer has many friends to call upon. Which means that if a group of pirates happen to invade Tim's Island, then there won't be much he could do to prevent his woman from getting raped and then auctioned off as a sex slave for the remainder of her life.

Obviously we do not live in a world where we have to constantly navigate a dangerous environment in order to survive anymore. Today, women can provide for themselves. And they can also defend themselves. But, make no mistake about it, the fact that we had evolved from an extremely harsh environment in which we lived for millions of years, women are still evolutionary wired to respond–emotionally–to the exact same qualities in men today which were essential for their own, as well as their offspring's survival back then. With all of that being said, this does not mean that you should abstain from relationships until you develop "Brad's" qualities and become the "ultimate man." Frankly, that is not a very practical, or realistic goal for most men. Understand that as long as you are comfortable with yourself, and you have some kind of value to offer, in today's world it still creates the same effect. And so, to become a man of high-value what you can do from this moment on–no matter where you are, or what you have–is to get your emotions under control, and decide what you want to get out of life. When you achieve emotional control, you become valuable, and attractive to women by default. Because controlling emotions, or putting them to the side, while thinking rationally (especially when it comes to crunch time) is something that feminine women cannot easily achieve. Additionally, if you can provide women with a sense of security, emotional stability, and a clear direction in life, then you will be considered a man of high-value and the women you date will respect you, and graciously reward you for it.

In closing, you have to actively avoid the temptation of seeking completion. Because there is really no such thing. As a biological entity, the fact that you can't help but want to save time and energy, each and every chance you get, the idea of being compete sounds immensely attractive. But, if you truly wish to become exceptional in all endeavours of your life, and rise above the average, "coping and surviving" norm, you have to fall in love with the idea of *never* being complete. You have to condition your brain to enjoy learning, growing, adjusting, adapting, and forever expanding. More than you do being comfortable, and content. Gaining an understanding of all the subtle (as well as not so subtle) ways in which you are being manipulated into a certain personality and lifestyle by the society's influences around you provides you with the biggest chance at successfully dodging, deflecting, and evading all of those things which make up a life of mediocrity and quiet desperation.

As for your personal relationships. Remember that, when you strive for completion you invariably place yourself into a co-dependent mode, and the chances of you building a successful, and harmonious relationship from that point forth become practically zero. The conditioning which wants you to be complete is the same conditioning which only cares about preserving social stability, at all costs. Even at the expense of complete disharmony, and chaos in your personal relationships behind closed doors. You have to stop looking for completion, and dragging other people into relationships with you–using them as means to that end. Understand that love is about wanting the very best for the ones we love. Thus, if a relationship with you is the best possible outcome for the loved one, then you should pursue it. But of course, in most cases, it is not the best outcome for the ones you love. The truth is most of us are much better off learning to love ourself, handling our own emotions, and developing ourself first, before taking on that kind of a challenge, i.e. building a relationship which will be the best, and the most valuable thing in the world for the ones we love. Lastly, never forget that women are your friend, regardless of how irritating, and annoying their reactions may sometimes be. You have to accept that it was never your woman's job to make you feel content, and happy with being a loser, or underachiever. Her "job" in a relationship is to get on your nerves, and rattle your cage when she sees that you are sinking into completion and co-dependence. But on the other hand, treat you like a king, and feed you metaphorical fruit when you are on top of your responsibilities. And so, rather than blaming your women for pointing out the obvious (that you need to do better), be the bigger man and simply make the choice to say "no" to completion, and become a man of *massive* action!

"The only way a relationship will last is if you see it as a place that you go to give, and not a place that you go to take." – Tony Robbins

MAINSTREAM MEDIA

"All propaganda has to be popular, and has to accommodate itself to the comprehension of the least intelligent of those whom it seeks to reach." – Adolf Hitler

"When you think of the long and gloomy history of man, you will find more hideous crimes have been committed in the name of obedience than have ever been committed in the name of rebellion." – Charles Percy Snow

The term "mainstream media" refers to the collective of various mass media firms and organisations that are mostly responsible for shaping public opinion on a variety of different subjects. Most of the information that we are exposed to through television, newspapers, social media, and public schools is influenced by a handful of industries which were created by a certain group, or "class" of people whose main goal it was–and still is–to control the minds (perceptions and attitudes) of the general public. Why is that? I have come to understand that individuals in the positions of power always knew that the human mind, and human "will" were extremely powerful tools. They knew that people had the ability to achieve–and become–anything that they truly desired, but only if they knew how to use their minds properly, and exercise their creative abilities. They knew that if people were to be properly educated; if they were to became self-aware, independent, more conscious and empowered; if they knew how powerful they really were, how to think critically and make rational choices, then most of the major corporations, organisations, governmental institutions and their policies would no longer be needed, as far as "helping" to manage people's affairs (infiltrating their lives and leaving them with less power as a result of each and every "solution"). Thus becoming virtually ignored, and ultimately dissolved.

In other words, the human mind was seen as the greatest threat to institutions, corporations, and the system (the Matrix) as a whole. That is precisely the reason why they had to resort to dumbing people down, and keeping them ignorant in any which way they possibly knew how, in an attempt to preserve the then-current power dynamics which are still rolling to this day. However, rather than using blatant force and violence in order to strip away the power from the people, it was recognised early on that it was going to be necessary to control people's minds instead–manipulating their perceptions of reality. (Because if you get to control what people think, you get to dictate how they feel. Which, in turn dictates how you want them to behave. Simple math.) They knew that it was no longer possible to control people by force in our evolved, "democratic" world any longer, since people no longer tolerated dictatorship and tyranny–they can now smell it from a mile away. Today, everybody knows exactly what it means to be free–physically–i.e. not being locked up in a cage, or slaving away while getting whipped. But, even to this day, most people still do not know what it means to be truly free spiritually, mentally, and emotionally. Because of this, those who are "in charge" of our world are able to control the masses in different–more subtle–ways without any suspicions. Which allows them to lay back, and watch billions of people unknowingly build their own prisons. And willingly march themselves right into the slaughterhouse under a false assumption that they are marching for freedom and democracy.

By using information as the means of controlling how people think and feel, how they perceive the world, the things they value in life, their attitude towards one another, and their behaviour, one is able to lead them in the direction which one wants them to go, with minimal effort. From the time we are born we get conditioned to live in an extremely limited way. And a person's conditioning is a parameter past which they are simply not able to see. Because of this, right up until the day we die, we never get the opportunity to realise how powerful we truly are, and what being alive is really all about. A person can live in total ignorance their entire life without ever noticing, or realising that they're being misguided, and steered away from the truth. For most people are convinced that their conditioning *is* the truth. And the only truth there is. In reality, it is nothing more than a mental program which had been installed into their mind by someone else who had a certain–and I dare to say Satanic and fascistic–agenda for them, their kids and their fellow men. Vernon Howard, an American teacher, and philosopher said: "*You cannot escape from a prison if you don't know you are in one.*" Well, if we take some time to look at just how most people live their lives, and how they behave, I think it's accurate to say that we're *all* in one (a mental prison), in varying degrees. However, the good news is that once you recognise that you *are* in one, you can then begin to pull yourself out of it. You have all the power you need to do so. You have absolute control over your mental and spiritual freedom because your thoughts, and deep-rooted beliefs (which can always be changed at will) *are* the keys to this prison door. You can make the choice to step out of it at once and completely change your life merely by changing your mind. No one has the power to hold you captive indefinitely, and keep you where you do not wish to be–especially with respect to your level of consciousness and awareness–because in a mental and spiritual prison there are no guards.

Noam Chomsky, an American author, linguist, philosopher, and political activist has come to believe that the mainstream media is dominated by individuals who adhere to an elitist ideology. Elitism is the belief, or attitude that individuals who form an elite (a select group of people with an intrinsic quality such as high intellect; wealth; special skills; and experience) are more likely to be constructive to society as a whole, and thus deserve influence, or authority greater than that of anybody else. This gives you a rough idea as to how these individuals view themselves, and how they view the general public. And what they are essentially saying is that you and I are useless and incompetent creatures who are incapable of living a proper life (whatever that means to them), and that we need to be told what to do for our own and everyone else's sake.

"The masses are the bewildered herd, and one of the major functions of the media is to put this herd in its proper place as passive spectators and not active participants in the organisation of a society." – Walter Lippmann

In his little book "Media Control" Noam Chomsky gave us a sneak peek into how these individuals think about the general public: *"This elitist ideology is built on the notion that the mass of the public is just too stupid to be able to understand things. If people try to participate in managing their own affairs, they are just going to cause trouble. Therefore, it'd be immoral and improper to permit them to do this. The 'bewildered herd' needs to be tamed, and it should not be allowed to rage, trample, and destroy things."* Now, being presented with this kind of reasoning we have to ask ourself whether the controlling of the "bewildered herd" is done in order to help societies to prosper, and lead them towards a better quality of life, or to maintain those institutional structures which favour the Elites, who are not at all interested in helping societies to flourish, and who would much rather see the "herd" indefinitely remain where it is, in order to keep the current system and power dynamics going? Personally, I would rather err on the "better be safe than sorry" side when it comes to putting my trust in people whom I have never met, who do not give a damn about what happens to me, and who do not particularly have an excellent track record at telling the truth.

This is exactly the reason why we need to have a more critical approach towards everything we see and hear from those in power, and look at everything that we are being told by the mainstream media with a healthy dose of scepticism. I suggest that you never passively accept what you hear but scrutinise the information which you are getting–give it some careful thought before accepting it as fact. Realise that just because a lot of other people are listening to–and are in agreement with–something that's being said, it does not necessarily mean that it is the truth, and that it is right. Why? Because, as we have already discussed, the majority of people do not think! Most have been programmed and trained to be passive and mentally lazy; to take all authority seriously without asking any questions; to comply without any resistance; and to blindly follow all of the rules. In effect, most people have completely forgotten the meaning of the term "critical thinking." Which, in the more recent years resulted in the entire planet being scared shitless of a virus that is so dangerous, that a simple cloth mask can deter it. Meanwhile, the individuals who told their people that masks should be worn at all times–even if the person is alone in their car–those same individuals have been caught, multiple times, laughing at how ridiculous the whole thing was before going live on air. In some of the other footage, we can even see them scrambling to find a mask, quickly slap it onto their face before a broadcast began, only to then take it off just as promptly, and start mingling freely with other people in the room after the broadcast was finished. (Yes, very dangerous virus indeed.)

"Some institutions have no moral justification... they are just there in order to preserve certain structures of power and domination." – Noam Chomsky

A great source of information, and ideas pertaining to how different institutions and industries manipulate the human mind–and beyond–is a YouTube channel called "Academy of Ideas." I highly recommend that you check it out. It will definitely get you thinking in a more realistic way as to how our world actually works. Essentially, when it comes to all the different dynamics that are at play between ordinary citizens and their "masters," the Academy of Ideas propagates the idea that for the sake of our own, as well as other people's well-being we must develop a more sceptical approach towards authority figures, and in some cases be willing to resist their orders altogether if we think that such authority is corrupt, unjust, or harmful to us, or the society as a whole. In other words, rather than reflexively obeying the orders without asking any questions, for fear of being ostracised, we have to develop guts and speak our truth, even if the truth may cause an uproar. Because if we do not, the consequences may be more disastrous than we can understand. Now, I can foresee that by even considering such advice one may feel some form of resistance. One may feel that individuals who reject authority are dangerous, and are an enormous threat to society (in some, extreme cases, yes). However for the most part, anti-authoritarians are crucial protectors of a flourishing society. Because those who challenge power, the status quo, the rules and regulations, who refuse to cooperate and blindly follow orders, are usually the ones who inspire other people to envision a better future for themself, and to bring about changes that are beneficial not only for the instigator in question, but for the society as a whole.

For example, in the year 1955, on December 1st, Rosa Parks (an African-American woman) refused to give up her seat to a white passenger, and navigate herself to the back of the public bus. Even though her actions resulted in her immediate arrest–for her course of action was in direct violation of the city's racial segregation laws at the time–nevertheless her anti-authoritarian actions inspired a great number of people to get behind her cause (a significant percentage of whom were not even African-American), resulting in the creation of the "Montgomery bus boycott"–a nonviolent civil rights protest, during which a great number of African-American citizens of Montgomery, Alabama refused to ride city buses. Considering the fact that the majority of people who were regularly using the public transport in Montgomery were African-Americans, it caused a huge disruption of the economy in said city. To the extent that only one year later the Supreme Court had decided to rule the segregation on public buses unconstitutional. And that's not to say that it was easy. Though this example is still solid proof that the power is with the people. That sometimes, it takes just one person–who is willing to go against the status quo–to ignite something so strong within the hearts of others, that it inspires them to strive for something better. To realise their own worth. To feel entitled to–and deserving of–more freedom. And to not feel afraid in the act of opposing the law, and questioning the powers that be in the process of claiming what's rightfully theirs. Of course as if that wasn't good enough already, Rosa Parks' anti-authoritarian actions ultimately instigated a chain of other events, which, in the end, led to all racial discrimination, and segregation being banned in the United States entirely.

It is a matter of course that without brave and self-esteemed individuals like Rosa Parks living among us, it is highly unlikely that we'd be living in a world as we know it today. Because a citizenry that has become passive, and totally distracted, which is being governed by an authority that's drunk with power, that is immune to prosecution, that is domineering and controlling at heart, is an excellent formula for the oppression, and enslavement of said citizenry. And we all know that power corrupts, especially those who are spiritually ignorant–who have big egos, or god complexes. Look at North Korea as an example. North Koreans are extremely oppressed not only with regard to harsh, uncalled for, and disproportionate punishments for trivial "crimes" such as watching a Hollywood movie; questioning the country's regime, or merely implying that it is unfair, but also with regard to information; education; Internet; travel; electricity; nutritious food; and contact with the outside world, because of extreme government restrictions. Yet, most Koreans living in North Korea have become accustomed to living in such conditions to the point that it has become the "norm." And they continue to toe the line without a fight because they simply don't know any better; they are being kept in total ignorance. The North Korean authorities control so much of what their people are permitted to see, hear, and do, that they have no other choice but to believe the narrative which they are being fed through the constant use of propaganda, and other methods of social engineering.

As far as I understand, the North Korean government brainwashes their people to believe that their leader (currently Kim Jong Un) is an actual God. That the rest of the world–outside of North Korea–is dangerous, and is forever plotting against North Korea (therefore, nobody is allowed to leave the country unless the government gives the green light. And if one leaves without permission, one will be automatically considered an enemy of the state). That North Korean people should feel privileged, and grateful to be living in a country that is practically a paradise in comparison to the rest of the world. (By seeing horrible images of kids dying from famine in Somalia, then their own struggles pale in comparison.) Those are the facts we hear from people who were born in North Korea, and who've managed to escape. As the years go by, more people are waking up to the fact that they are living a lie, and as the number of people escaping the country rises, other people are waking up as well, and are being inspired to do the same. North Koreans are extremely isolated from the rest of the world. The general public knows nothing except the propaganda which they are continuously being exposed to. In effect, they have unwittingly allowed themselves to be ruled by an authoritarian regime which was "advertised" to them under the guise of safety and security.

When people like you and I (who've never set foot in North Korea) hear about such things, we naturally think to ourselves: "How can someone be so cruel? Why would someone take pleasure in the suffering of others? Who in their right mind would allow this to go on?" It is difficult to believe that any seemingly "normal" human being is capable of doing such things to tens of millions of (their own) people. Especially in a country which proclaims to be democratic. However, we must understand that the human mind–when used incorrectly–actually loves to be in control, and such a feeling of control overrides any sliver of empathy, or sympathy left in that person. When any person–whose mind is partially developed or unformed, and who is unaware of the universal truths of life–finds him/herself in a position of power, then the outcome of that is as tragic as handing a brainless monkey a loaded machine gun, teaching it how to pull the trigger, and then letting it loose in a nursery school. For this reason, those who are courageous enough to defy, and reject authority shouldn't be ostracised, or feared; they should be hailed, or at least heard. For they are the ones who sound the alarm, and awaken the slumbering masses to the presence of a corrupt, and unjust authority. Now, when we observe some of the things that go on in countries like North Korea (or China), we typically think: "So what? It does not affect me, and it does not apply to me, because I live in a free country–I live in a democracy. So why should I care?" (Be it the United States, Australia, or the United Kingdom). However, that kind of rationale comes from a lack of awareness that the democracy as we know it–even in said Countries–is actually staged, mainly with the help of the mainstream media that work as propaganda machines.

Consider this: more than 90 percent of all the Western media is regulated, and controlled by a conglomerate of only a few corporations (BlackRock and Vanguard are the two biggest investment firms that control an immense number of shares in some of the largest companies in the world. These firms practically own the entire world. On the surface, it may seem as though different major brands, and companies–Pepsi or Coca-Cola; Pfizer or Moderna; Apple or Microsoft; CBS or CNN, etc.–are independent, and are in competition with one another. However, in reality they're all answering and pandering to the same group of people). In effect, all of the major media outlets are reading off the same script. Because they are all practically "owned" by the same people. This is why we will never see anything which undermines the government, the intelligent agencies, the military-industrial complex, the Big Tech, or the Big Pharma in the mainstream media (because they're all in bed with each other), unless it is convenient, or absolutely necessary to support a particular narrative which is being pushed at the time. When something significant happens, which we as people of a particular country ought to know–yet, it is something that the Elites would much rather that we don't–the media outlets may air, or write about it once or twice (relaying half of the truth, if we are lucky). But then they'll give all of their airtime and attention to how a celebrity got involved in a scandal, or how a meteor is heading towards the Earth, in an attempt to quickly divert our attention.

Regrettably, the mainstream media is no longer an independent watchdog who were supposed to be observing and reporting on everything that's happening in the world without exception–that's not the case anymore. Real journalism is virtually dead. There are still a few great independent journalists out there, who are not afraid to speak the truth, and who are doing their best to bring to the public the "real news," as well as accurate, unbiased information, even though sometimes it costs them their freedom as in the case of Julian Assange, and in other cases even their lives. Julian Assange is the founder of "WikiLeaks." It is a non-profit media organisation, launched in 2006 for the purpose of collecting secret government documents, leaks, and other forms of classified information from anonymous sources. Assange was effectively doing God's work by providing the people with a safe and secure platform where they had the opportunity to freely share information–which certain governments and organisations tried to keep secret–without the fear of being prosecuted. As of September 2023, Assange is in the process of being handed a hefty 175-year sentence to be served in prison for clearly bogus charges of sexual assault and rape. Bogus because they have already tried to lock him away for espionage, which didn't work. Then, for stolen property, which didn't work. And now, *this*. By doing honest reporting, Julien is being treated appallingly for exercising his right of free speech and press freedom. The publication of all kinds of information–exposing numerous war crimes of the American government in Iraq and Afghanistan–made them absolutely furious! And for that reason, they're trying to make an example out of Julian by ruining his life–to send a warning message to other journalists, and anyone else who is thinking about opposing the Establishment.

Essentially, democracy means freedom; freedom of thought; freedom of the press; freedom of choice; freedom of speech, etc. Democracy implies that power is with the people, but is it? Because if that is the case, then why those who have something to say–something which goes against the current mainstream narrative in "free," democratic countries such as the United States, or the United Kingdom–get censored, silenced, de-platformed or demonetised? Why do innocent people get treated like terrorists, get arrested and beaten to the ground by the police officers for peacefully protesting? Aren't they entitled to their own humble opinion? Likewise, why some of Jan van Helsing's books which present a different way of looking at the world, and challenge people's current perceptions of reality have been demonised, and banned in Europe? Shouldn't people be the ones to decide what they are going to read, and what they're going to accept as the truth and believe? And why is it that any informational video–circling around the Internet–which contradicts the narrative–narrative that is being regurgitated at any particular time, with respect to a particular issue–gets censored, hidden, or deleted from social media platforms altogether to never be seen again? Why is there such a great effort being made to control the information that is being shared between the people? For, if those in positions of power are honest, and trustworthy individuals who truly care about their people, who have no reason to lie and always speak the truth, then why are they so concerned with opposing opinions, questions, and accusations for certain things which they have done, or planning on doing? And the answer is that in practice, the so-called "democracy" is not exactly what it appears to be on paper.

What we–as the people–need to become aware of is that every time we cast a vote for the next president, or prime minister of our choice, our choice doesn't actually matter. Because the president, and those in government are ruled by a higher power anyway. In effect, presidents do not have as much power as we think they do. A president can be likened to a high school principal who doesn't own the educational system, or the school, but who simply reinforces what is already in place within that system, with only a little bit of room for some rearrangements and improvements here and there, that do not actually affect the fundamental structure, and the general plan for its future. Why do you think that before anyone becomes a president promises all kinds of improvements and solutions to a number of different problems. Yet by the time their presidential term comes to an end, only a small fraction of what was promised had been delivered, almost every single time?

Of course, there are a lot of complicated reasons for this (other than the fact that one person is incapable of fixing the *whole* country in a span of only a few years), but one of those reasons is that whenever a president–who may have a lot of great ideas, and solutions to major problems–gets elected, they are then invariably contacted by a certain group of people (some believe that it is the "Deep State," i.e. extremely powerful bureaucrats, bankers, heads of the military-industrial complex, and intelligence agencies. While other people believe that it is the "Shadow Government," or the Illuminati. Though it doesn't matter who they are, or what we call them. What *is* important is the dynamic that's at play, regardless of who we think they are), who then proceed to explain how things actually work, and elaborate on exactly what the president can and cannot do. I assume the goal is to encourage and incentivise the president to "play ball," and continue to pursue the interests of those people, without even thinking of deviating from the set objectives, presumably for fear of one's reputation being dismantled. (The assassinations of Lincoln and JFK come to mind? Or a more recent, less grave example of Donald Trump's demonisation and decimation of character?)

Now look, I completely understand that at first glance this might sound like a plot for a sci-fi movie, and I've had trouble comprehending this at first myself. And the reason being is that I had no way of knowing whether these claims were true or not for a fact. Because I was never a president, or a politician. That being said though, at this point I do treat these claims as a matter of fact because the existence of this higher power has been confirmed publicly and openly by a reliable and exceedingly knowledgeable source–Vladimir Putin–a Russian president who regularly meets, and has conversations with other presidents and individuals who have access to inside information. Certainly he knows how the world in which we live actually works, and what is really going on behind the political curtain. In terms of understanding who these individuals are, Putin describes them as men with briefcases, wearing dark suits. And the point that he was trying to make is that, if you live in the United States, then it doesn't matter whether your president is from a republican or democratic party, because the same thing happens to all administrations. In effect, presidents come and go, but the politics stay the same. Why is that? Because the only choice that people have is *who* gets to lead them. People themselves are never really involved in making any decisions, or applying any changes. They merely spectate and hope that their president will deliver the changes that people want. But of course, those changes never arrive because the president is not working *for* the people, and even if the president were to have a sudden change of heart, he still wouldn't have enough power to do anything about it. The bureaucracy in Western civilisation at this point in history is too strong/complex to be messed with by any one individual.

This is where the illusion of democracy comes from. It comes from a belief that we are free because we have the right to choose who is going to be in charge of our country–as well as our future–completely unaware of the fact that there are others who elect themselves, who are already in charge of our future, whom average people like you and I will never hear about, and who are making all of the major decisions–on a global scale–for all of us (not only reserved for, and restricted to the U.S.) behind the scenes. And the president is just a frontman, a clueless (although not always) pawn who is being used as a decoy. So that the advancement of their global agenda goes undetected, and uninterrupted. Particularly, when their policies, and objectives upset the general public, rather than drawing attention onto themselves and assuming responsibility, the president is there to take all the blame. And then become replaced by another as a beacon of hope from the previous disaster. Having said that, Joe Biden, or Boris Johnson are not Illuminati masterminds with a grand plan to take over the world. These guys don't even know what day it is sometimes. They can't even manage themselves, let alone an entire country. Rather, they are merely in place to give the public the illusion of democracy–a perception that it is alive and well–and that people still have the freedom to choose any individual they deem suitable for determining and shaping their future. When in reality, somebody else *is*–in fact–in charge.

The ultimate role of the mainstream media is to make sure that the public believes only that which those in positions of power, and authority want them to believe. And so far, it has worked wonders. Because when we watch a well-groomed, eloquent person on the television telling us something with confidence and conviction, while millions of other people are listening to it, we immediately assume that it must be the truth and we don't bother asking questions. In effect, you may think that you live in a democracy, and believe that you are free. You might believe that you are having your own thoughts, making your own decisions, and coming to your own conclusions. When in fact, your perception of reality–which includes your thoughts, opinions, and beliefs–is actually being shaped by the mainstream media (but only if you're consumed by it). You see, the only way that people can be manipulated and controlled, is when they are not aware that they are being manipulated and controlled. For what other reason do you think that a lot of ideas and discussions today are being censored left and right other than that they aim to dispel the manipulations, and scare-tactics that are being deployed on ordinary citizens, and that they aim to thwart the advancement of the Globalist Elites' agenda (research Agenda 21 and Agenda 30)? Unfortunately, in the current climate the state of affairs is such that those who know exactly what is going on behind the scenes and who are trying to expose the plans that the "Elites" have in store for us all, get viciously discredited by the media, and then berated by the public who still have blind faith in the media. Of course, in such circumstances it becomes tremendously difficult for those individuals to relay their side of the story. Which ultimately results in the mass of the public willingly continuing to march to their own enslavement, while mocking and laughing at those who are trying to warn them along the way.

Again, you have to understand that controlling the information is how the Elites censor and control what the mass of the public thinks and believes. In effect, those who are consumed by the media will only believe what those in power want them to believe, and nothing else. Relying on the mainstream media alone to deliver the "truth," as well as accurate reporting can become dangerous on so many levels, because those in charge of the narrative do not have our best interest at heart. The best thing you can do is to turn the damn thing off. Get over your mental laziness, and seek out reporting from other sources, e.g. your fellow men, and women who actually care about your future, and who understand you. And stop listening to the Globalist Elites, and politicians who only care about profit, and control, with whom you have absolutely nothing in common. And who could never relate to the troubles and tribulations that you are going through in your day-to-day life, because they do not live in the same reality as you do. All of the rules that apply to you do not apply to them. All of the restrictions that you live under do not exist for them. All of the suffering that is caused by their wars, and policies does not affect them. They are not subject to the same laws which have the power to lock you away in prison for the rest of your life. They are above the system in which you live. They are above the rules of the game. So why would they ever choose to give their power away, and play fair with us "peasants"?

"There is a plot in this country to enslave every man, woman, and child. Before I leave this high and noble office, I intend to expose the plot." – John F. Kennedy (7 days before his assassination)

The mainstream media is tailored to–and specifically designed for–the individuals who are most likely to consume it and who are less likely to question what it is that they are seeing. It is designed for those who live entirely within the system, who are dependent on it, and who are easily influenced. In effect, it is designed for the majority. More specifically, it is designed for those who live predominantly in lower states of consciousness. And it is designed for those who no longer know how to think. Statistics show that the average person, anywhere in the world today consumes approximately four hours of TV programming a day, every day. And it has also been discovered that the human mind moves into a hypnotic, trancelike state within a few seconds of watching TV, where they become most susceptible to suggestions, for many hours each day. Now, that may be fine in an ideal world, but in the world in which we live, what kind of information are we typically susceptible to on a regular basis? Fear; death; terrorists; immigrants; poverty; disease; war; famine; the Russians, and so on. And if we look beneath the surface layer, what does it all suggest? It suggests that we follow. Conform. Be afraid. Compete. Obey. Buy. Consume. Stay asleep. Don't think. Submit to authority. In other words, most of the information in the mainstream is telling us that the world is scary; that we should be afraid; that people from other countries are our enemy; that life is random; that we need to buy *this* and we need to look like *that*; that happiness is over *there*; that we need to be doing what everybody else is doing; that we are never enough; that we don't have any power; that we don't have any value unless_____. (Fill in the blank.) And through continuous exposure to these suggestions what winds up happening is our thoughts, words, and actions begin to align with whatever it is we are seeing and hearing. Resulting in us forming certain beliefs and opinions about a variety of different subjects that are not necessarily accurate, or true. While the illusion of freedom comes from a belief that all of the thoughts, words, and actions which we express are of our own making–and of our own conscious choice–when in reality they are not. And so, in effect what we do is we begin to express, and defend somebody else's beliefs–somebody else's agenda.

If you are not familiar with basic psychology, if you do not understand how the human mind works, and if you are unaware of what influences you, then you can never suspect that you are being boxed into certain beliefs, and perceptions of reality. The fact that you have been trained from the very beginning of your life to only pay attention to the physical–to the surface layer of things–is the exact reason why you do not see, or recognise what is going on beneath the surface, which is where all the influencing and programming takes place. What this means is that until someone grips you by your throat, lifts you off the ground, and physically forces you to think, behave, and feel a certain way–until something that *obvious* happens–then you will still feel as though you are in complete control of yourself; that all is well with regard to your freedom; and that nobody is trying to manipulate your emotions, opinions, and perceptions of reality. **But** I am here to remind you that your freedom can be easily snatched away from you–right from up under your nose– if you are not conscious enough. And that everything is probably not okay if you are consumed by your television, particularly the mainstream media.

Do you think it's a coincidence that big players like Rolex; Versace; Ferrari; Lamborghini, etc., the yacht/helicopter/private jet dealers, and the like are never advertising their products on television? Do you think that's an accident? Of course not. It comes back around to the fact that the media is not tailored for *everybody*, because if it were, the advertisements which you get to see on television would be of a whole different calibre. The aforementioned luxury brands, and services know that people who can afford their products are not sitting in front of their televisions all day, or endlessly surfing the Internet. Successful people (those who think for themselves) are too busy living their lives; studying; reading books; travelling; exercising; spending time with their families; running their businesses; going out and attending different events; engaging in hobbies; pursuing their passions; constantly learning and discovering new things, etc. In other words, successful people lead their own lives, they think for themselves, they know exactly what they want, and they know where they are going in life. If someone can afford those types of products, or services, which I have previously mentioned, then we would be right to assume that that *someone* is probably their own boss; that that *someone* thinks for themself. Moreover, that *someone* is probably making all of the major decisions in life, and they have people working for *them*. That *someone* had already been through enough adversity, so much so, that they have developed a powerful belief in themself, and in their own abilities. That *someone* knows who they are as a person, and they know their own worth. And for those very reasons they are not easily influenced by fear or flashy images telling them what they need to buy, how they need to think, and what they need to believe. But this is not how an average person lives and thinks, is it? That is why average people will never see a Bugatti, or a Rolex watch being advertised on television. Because television is not tailored to a type of person who can afford it. The television is designed for financially poor people who have nothing going on in their life, and who don't want to think. That is precisely the reason why all that you'll ever see on the television is how to get a loan; apply for life insurance; buy cheap holiday tickets; and whatever money you have left you can get guilt-tripped, and shamed into giving it away to a charity, where only a fraction of your donations will go to the actual cause, while the rest of your money will probably go into somebody else's pocket.

It is evident that the mainstream media is designed to dumb down the masses, and to deter them from trying to step up in life–to keep them ignorant, anxious, and afraid. And the reason it works so well is because masses tend to respond to it well. We are to blame for this also, because it seems as though that's what we actually want. You can imagine when the mainstream media was in its infancy–delivering the kind of news which it did–if people looked at it and decided not to consume it–maybe because it was unproductive, negative and unimportant–then the mainstream media would have had to change their approach and bring to the public something that would be of more interest to them. But, since people responded to it favourably, and they have continued to respond to it positively ever since, then if the mainstream media were now to grow a conscience and decide to report positive news instead, it would no longer work, because people don't resonate with that kind of information anymore. At this point, most people don't want to see somebody else winning, or enjoying life, while the rest of the world is suffering. After decades of looking at how "messed up" our world is, most people are no longer able to see that a good life is possible; that the world is not as terrible as one might think; and that there is still–and in fact, always were–hope for humanity. Because of this, if the hypothetical change which we are talking about here were to take place, what would happen is people would either chastise the mainstream media, or they wouldn't consume it any longer. Consequently, the ratings would be low. And what is the main thing that the media cares about? Ratings. Or in other words–profit. That's the reason why we cannot rely on the mainstream media to "change" and bring us the good news, since we are so deep at this point that it probably never will. We only have to stop listening to everything that is wrong with the world, and begin to acknowledge that there is an abundance of beauty and prosperity in it.

"So long as the people do not care to exercise their freedom, those who wish to tyrannize will do so; for tyrants are active and ardent and will devote themselves in the name of any number of Gods, religious or otherwise, to put shackles upon sleeping men." – Voltaire

If we take a minute to slow down, hop off the hamster wheel for just a moment, and take a good look at what is happening in the world, we can't deny the fact that someone or something is constantly trying to divide us through religion; politics; race; class; etc., which are all man-made concepts, designed to separate us from one another. Yet the truth is we are all *one*. We are all expressions of the same creative power–Source, Spirit, Infinite Intelligence, living consciousness (whatever you wish to call it)–having our own unique experiences inside separate physical bodies, or from our own individual points of awareness. But we are not *actually* separated from one another. That's just a misconception; it is an illusion. The physical reality in which we live only gives off the impression that this may be the case. All the while the governments, the religions, the mainstream media, the educational system, and all the rest of it only amplify that illusion. The biggest threat to those in power is a united, collective mind, and "will" of the people. That is why it is always going to be in their best interest to continue to undermine, and suppress the truth that we're all one; that there is absolutely no good reason for us to fear one another; and that comparing ourselves to, and competing with each other is a distraction–a waste of creative energy.

In order for the very small number of people to effectively impose their will and agenda upon billions of people requires billions to be divided, and then manipulated to enslave each other (divide and conquer). Since the more people come together, and the more they believe in something that is different from that which those in power want them to believe, the more difficult to manipulate and control they become. And so, a great place to start regaining at least some of the control, is by acknowledging that there is much more goodness going around the world. More than all of the wrong, the bad, and immoral. We as average people just don't get to see much of the "good stuff" because everything that is wrong with the world is being systematically targeted, and then broadcasted straight into our brains, as we soak it all up and consequently degrade our own chances at building a life that we would otherwise enjoy. In other words, how could we possibly live in higher states of consciousness–where all that we are interested in is thriving, giving, and uplifting–when all that we ever see, and hear about is how people are stealing, lying, killing one another, and how the planet is being destroyed?

All throughout the day we are exposed to all kinds of information that's coming at us from all angles: the drugs; the climate; the terrorists; the immigrants; the famine; the explosions; the accidents; the innocent people dying; the deadly virus; the disease; the homicide, and so forth. And what we ultimately get out from all of it is that the world is on fire! That the world is a scary and unsafe place. That life of a human being is fragile, and may be taken away at a moment's notice. And that, essentially, we're still not at a stage of social evolution where we can think beyond our survival, and start *creating*. Although I'm not suggesting that all of the terrible things that are being reported on are not real, or that they don't happen–some do. But it is only a small portion of what is real. And to be the one who can circumnavigate the life's challenges without being pulled into certain ways of thinking and perceiving by the powers that be, you have to raise your level of awareness and come into your own power. You have to learn to make distinctions between which information is true, and which is false; which information helps you to grow, and which does not. You have to stop distracting yourself with Netflix, social media, and television, while your freedoms are gradually–and silently–being taken away from you. The fact of the matter is the mainstream media will continue to lie to you and shamelessly feed you absolute garbage, and if you're not careful enough, you are going to end up exactly where they want you to be–powerless, poor, and afraid.

Never forget that those who are in charge of our world have to advance their agenda one small step at a time so that we as ordinary people don't become alarmed and alert to the fact that we are getting screwed, by getting hit immediately with something big and obvious. Those in power know that the "big and obvious" (the end result) will inevitably come as long as they continue to tiptoe towards it while diverting our attention onto things that don't matter. And when it does come, it will be too late for people to do anything about it. Because so much would have taken place at that point already, that reverting back to the way things previously were would simply no longer be a viable option. For this reason, and for the sake of the well-being of future generations, you have to think carefully about what the current narrative in the media is trying to convince you of. Rather than unwittingly going along with their agenda by reacting emotionally to what you are seeing, you have to stop yourself and filter that information through the rational part of your mind before drawing any final conclusions. Because if you do not, the conclusions will be drawn for you. And rest assured, those conclusions will be all in favour of snatching away every last piece of freedom which you and your children might still have, until you won't be able to blink (for your own safety) anymore without your governments permission.

"The truth will set you free. But first, it will piss you off." – Gloria Steinem

In closing, I would like to leave you with the following thought: it may feel daunting, and demotivating to know that our world is in the hands of sociopaths who take pleasure in the suffering of people, and who will continue to do everything in their power to make sure that we (the people) have as little freedom, influence and power as humanly possible. But the good news is the power of the people cannot be taken away; it can only be given, whether that be willingly or through manipulation. Fortunately, year after year, more and more people in the world are beginning to wake up and realise that we supposed to thrive; that we do not have to try so hard to survive anymore; and that there actually *is* something special about us "average" humans after all. More and more people are realising that we do have the power to design our own lives, to create our own reality, and live happily ever after even if we *do* live in a world that is not perfect, and *is* run by psychopaths who don't want to see us coming into our own power. More and more people today are realising that as long as we are no longer willing to be controlled by fear–and refuse to believe anything which even slightly implies that the world is going to Satan–then there is no way that we can fail in building successful, joyful, and fulfilling lives for ourselves and others.

　　Truth is, we do not have to fight against anyone, or anything. We don't have to scream, shove, and rage against any of the elements that are devised to hold us back. We simply have to focus on that which is good, and on how we would like things to be. Because when we are focused in that way, everything else which does not fit into that picture of reality falls away, and fades into the background. If one believes in the goodness of the world, then that's all one is ever going to get. Because whenever one is focused in a constructive, positive way, one gains access to higher states of consciousness, such as joy; love; compassion; freedom; empowerment, etc. And those higher vibrations are exponentially more powerful than all the other, lower states of consciousness, such as fear; hate; anger; jealousy; greed; helplessness; deprivation; depression; poverty, and so on. In effect, as you raise your consciousness you begin to draw in all of the knowledge and power there is, whereby nothing can possibly check the forward movements which you are initiating. The world is not going to Satan, because there isn't one there. The world was always–and only–ever going to Source, or God if you will. The planet Earth and its residents are only destined for growth and expansion–more life, love, freedom, success and creativity. It is only up to us as a collective to decide to which degree we allow ourselves to live the fullness of that expansion now, without getting sidetracked by listening to "Nancy Stories" as to how it's only a matter of time until the world ends, as we get shamed and guilt-tripped into giving away our freedoms in order to "save it." If I were you I wouldn't worry about any of that. Because God, or Source, has everything figured out. Everything is in perfect working order. And *it* will decide when it is time for the world to end; not me, not you, and not our politicians.

MONEY

"A salary is the bribe that they offer you to forget your dreams."

Shifting gears now, let's talk about money. Money is an extremely important subject (for obvious reasons), which public schools and societies do not teach us about. And those who have the most of it, understand something that average people do not. Today, an average person's financial situation could be described as mediocre at best. As a direct result of poor conditioning, majority of people in the world have developed one too many fallacies about money which is why they are endlessly struggling, barely making ends meet, living paycheck-to-paycheck, and are completely enslaved by their jobs. However, the good news is that, today we live in an information-rich Age. Today, there is an absolute abundance of information out there–with respect to how financial freedom can be achieved–that is freely available to everybody. This means that average people like you and I can now too achieve financial independence, and become as wealthy as we please, if we take the time to look for that information, and execute what we have learnt. There is no longer an excuse for anyone to continue to live in poverty, because all of the resources, opportunities, markets, money, and means by which one is able to accumulate riches are there. In today's world, opportunities for growth, and success are truly endless. It's about time that the rest of the world begins to catch up, starts thinking beyond mere survival, and begins to thrive!

My primary goal in writing this section is to debunk some of the common scarcity-based mindsets that are prevalent in modern society, which are preventing the afflicted individuals from becoming financially independent. The most common conviction about money that a lot of people tend to have (particularly the religious types), is that being rich is ungodly, unspiritual, or immoral. That all wealthy people are selfish, corrupt, and dishonest, because money is the root of all evil. But money is not the root of all evil. Not even a fraction of it. All forms of evil come from *ignorance*; it has nothing to do with money. Money is just an idea. Money is a symbol of appreciation; a gesture of goodwill and compassion embedded in a receipt–a piece of paper. It is only the destructive impulses which money has the power to sometimes evoke that are evil, i.e. greed; power; control, etc., the kind of impulses that can only come from ignorance. Money in and of itself is not evil, as the mainstream everything would have you believe. Money is neutral. Money only becomes whatever *you* make of it. The way in which money is utilised–be it productively, or destructively–depends on the person who is handling it. This ultimately implies that money does not corrupt; money only amplifies who we are as individuals. Which is to say that if you are a selfish narcissist, then the more money you have, the more obnoxious and intolerable you will become. Whereas if you're a good, honest and loving individual, then the more money you have, the more effective you will become with your good intentions.

All in all, money is not evil, far from it. If this is something that you believe in, then that belief is exactly what is holding you back from living your best life, and becoming the best version of yourself that you know you could be. Money is important, because if you're ever going to develop yourself fully–physically, intellectually, emotionally and spiritually–then you must have certain experiences, and other things to use in order to facilitate that growth. And the world in which we live requires that in order to gain access to those things, and experiences we have to have money to buy them with.

Similarly, money is not the source of happiness either. There are people in the world who are incredibly rich, who have absolutely everything a person could possibly ask for–and yet–are living a miserable existence. Maybe because their ecosystem of positive emotions is poorly established. Or they might be lacking in the spiritual department. Maybe their close relationships are non-existent, and they feel lonely. Maybe they don't know how to socialise and form circles of good friends. Or maybe their health is in a dire condition because of poor lifestyle choices. Conversely, there are those who are by no means rich, but who are still living joyful lives regardless, and are incredibly happy. And by looking at such contrasting examples, implies that money and happiness have nothing to do with each another. That, in effect, having money does not guarantee happiness. Of course, one could use money to buy experiences that would make one feel happy for a while. But that buzz would eventually wear off. And one would soon find oneself feeling exactly the way one felt before the experience, and nothing would change.

One may rationalise to oneself all day long as to how money is the least important thing in their life, but one has to understand this: the biggest "sin" –in living, period–is to be poor. Poverty is abnormal. Because abundance (in all areas of life) is our birthright. Refusing to believe this, or turning the other cheek, telling yourself lies as to how you do not need much, and how you already have enough–in a world that is full of abundance, possibilities, and opportunities–only depresses your spirit, because deep down you know you are capable of so much more! If you do not have much money, and you can barely help yourself, then you cannot help and be of any real value to others. You can still manage to be of some value to the people around you, sure. But the value which you bring to the table will always be limited to your physical presence at any given time. Conversely, if you have a surplus–when you have more than enough–you are able to create more; share more; give more; contribute towards great causes; heal more; build more; travel more; and ultimately reach more people.

Another common reason why most people never seem to earn the kind of money that they really want, is because of the belief that to earn a lot of it, one has to be very smart, and have a very good formal education. Otherwise forget it. Yet, earning a lot of money, and becoming financially independent has nothing to do with formal education. The evidence of this are all around us. There are educated people in the world who are exceptionally smart, who are not earning very much at all. Either because they do not have confidence in themselves; because they are unaware as to how to earn more; or because they believe that poverty is what pleases God. Concurrently, there are other people in the world who are not particularly bright, who have never set foot inside of a school, but who are earning millions, doing what they absolutely love. And by studying those people's lives we become aware that earning a lot of money was never about having a good formal education; it was always about wanting to be of service to others. It is about working with the Law of Compensation. People who have created multiple sources of income–where money flows into their bank accounts even while they are asleep–manage to get themselves into such positions because they understand that riches come from serving a lot of people, solving their problems, and making their lives more enjoyable. Successful people understand that as long as they are bringing value to the market, the market will reward them for it, and no one is going to care about how many degrees, or certificates they have or don't have, because the results speak for themself. (Refer back to chapter 4 on the Law of Compensation.)

The problem with public schools is that their attitude, and methods of learning in classrooms is completely contrary to what it takes to be successful in the real world: Do as you are told; don't make mistakes; don't ask for help from your classmates; and learn the (one) right answer. Yet, in life there are numerous answers to any one given problem. We do not have to do everything by ourself. We should certainly have a team, and work together towards achieving our goals. And we should make as many mistakes, and correct course as many times as necessary. Because a mistake is not really a mistake (it is not a sign of failure), it is just a lesson to learn as to what not to do next time. And so, we go to school excited to learn about life, and about ourselves, but eventually the spirit of learning completely evaporates as we get told to sit down, to shut up and listen. It seems as though nobody even cares about what we are interested in. We are merely told all we need to know for the upcoming test (the knowledge of which will have no practical usefulness in the real world), and what the right answers are. Then all we have to do is learn the right answers, memorise them, repeat them back to the teacher, sit back down, and begin our preparations for the next test which practically no student cares about.

Public schools do not teach prosperity. What they teach instead is how to secure a job by developing a certain skill, and then work your ass off making millions for your employer, while they pay you in peanuts (in contrast to the amount they are earning through your hard work) for your cooperation. The way of earning money which the system encourages us to follow always has a ceiling to the amount which can be earned. Because we are trading our precious time for money. And as we all know, there are only so many hours in a day. This puts us into a position where if we wish to earn more money, our only answer is to work overtime, while forever striving for a better position within the company. But from your own experience, has that ever made you rich, or happier? I highly doubt it. All that happens is you earn just a little extra money for you to spend, or save, until you are forced to work overtime again and again, having barely any free time left to yourself as a result. Our conditioning convinces us that we go to work to earn money, but that's not true. As Bob Proctor once said, we go to work for *satisfaction*, while money is a by-product; a direct consequence of our work well done. If we look at successful artists–painters; singers; entertainers; athletes, and so on–they are not working hard at all. They might be putting a lot of hours into their craft, of course, but if we were to ask them how they feel about their work, 9 times out of 10 they'd say that what they do does not feel like work. Because they *love* what they do.

We may think it's unfair for a professional football player to earn ridiculous amounts of money for running around the field, kicking a ball, while a highly skilled doctor (especially a surgeon) gets paid only a fraction of that, while completely sacrificing him/herself in the process, having to constantly undergo all of the stresses and headaches that are associated with that kind of a job. Unfortunately, that is the way of the system. Why? Of course there are numerous reasons for this, one of which is that people want to be entertained almost more than anything else. But the main reason, I think, is that if you pay millions to a professional football player every single year he'll keep coming back and continue playing the game, because he loves what he does. Whereas if you pay a million to a surgeon (which wouldn't be unreasonable, considering the immense value they bring to the table) in their first year of practice, they might quickly realise how much they hate their job and decide to quit, and immediately retire. In other words, nobody becomes a doctor, a dentist, or a lawyer because they love it. (With only the rarest of the rare exceptions.) People get into those positions usually because they've been sold on the idea that that is where all the money is. The system needs doctors and lawyers, so they are not going to be let off the hook so easily. The system is designed in such a way that it will hold someone like a doctor in check by paying them more than the average person, so that it makes them feel good about their own financial position relative to others. While also making sure that they don't get too little either, lest they decide to do something else entirely. And that kind of a financial situation ensures that the doctor will continue to show up every single day and keep doing the work, even if he/she despises that work.

Why else do you think education is compulsory, other than to produce workers who will be reliable to keep the system running? Agan, the system needs lawyers; scientists; nurses; medical doctors; engineers; technicians; accountants; architects; electricians; bankers, etc. But don't get me wrong, I still think that for some people formal education can be great. But it isn't for everybody. Only for those who can truly find happiness and satisfaction in that which it offers. And who are not at all disturbed by the fact that they won't have to think, and make decisions ever again while assuming a certain position at work. Traditional education seems to end as soon as we learn how to count, read, and write. All that happens after the fact is we're asked to merely read what had already been written by someone else, remember what we have read, and then repeat it back word for word. There truly is no room for creativity, intellectual curiosity, and critical thinking in our educational system. If public schools taught students how to think, create wealth, properly deal and interact with their fellow humans, then we would not need to question their effectiveness. But it is evident that the quality of life which awaits most people–after they put themselves through this "sausage machine" and come out at the other end of it–is far from ideal. Because of this, we need to look into the whole thing and try to figure out where we are going wrong.

"By the time a student graduates they have been bred to be passive; to be directed by others; to take seriously the rewards and punishments of authority; to pretend to care about things that they do not care about; and that one is impotent to change one's dissatisfying situation." - Bruce Levine

How I have come to understand the educational system is that it is sort of a sifting process; a journey if you will–which students must go through–where they are put into two separate piles. From those who are not willing to obey and conform–who are not paying attention (they call it having learning difficulties)–to others who "have what it takes" to follow somebody else's ideas and philosophies without raising questions, or straying away from the consensus as to how things are done in their respective field of expertise.

"The institutional role of the schools for the most part is just to train people for obedience and conformity, and to make them controllable and indoctrinated."
– Noam Chomsky

Noam Chomsky terms the educational system "a system of indoctrination of the young." He propagates the viewpoint that the educational system's role is to train kids to be obedient, and become conformists; to not think; to do as they are told; to stay passive; and to not raise any questions. He points out: the fact that the educational system has an obvious element of stupidity in it, implies that it most likely serves a useful function–a function by which students are filtered out for obedience. Think of it, if one can guarantee a lot of stupidity within the educational system–in a form of mindless assignments, pointless questions, completely irrelevant subjects, and so on–then one can be certain that the only people who will make it through this "filter" are the ones who are willing to do it no matter how dumb it is (because they wish to progress further and move on to the next stage). Even when the "good" students realise that the assignment which they are working on is idiotic, they will complete it anyway, because that's what it takes to get to the next level, or class. Now, practically every classroom has a student (like I was) sitting at the back, who is not going to do it, and who is not going to blindly obey and follow someone else's way of doing things (because he/she clearly sees that their way is moronic). Those people are labelled as having behavioural problems and are usually dismissed. Rather than being praised and rewarded for having a mind of their own, they get shamed–whether overtly or subliminally–into believing that having such a free mind is a curse; that it will get them into trouble; and that they'll never amount to anything. Of course what happens is those people typically end up on the streets selling drugs, or working on factory lines, or cleaning floors–they become nobodies (by the educational system's standards). They become those who do not have any word in society; who do not have any influence, or power in the world (in reality, they do. They only have been conditioned to presume otherwise). Hence, the system does not have to worry about them. Because the immense power of their free, unenslaved mind, had been discredited, and kept at bay through a conviction that because they do not have a degree, or any kind of expertise, nobody cares about what they say, or think–and so they don't.

The forced style of teaching that is prevalent in public schools is a blatant selection technique for obedience. And those who do not comply are left on their own to figure out as to how to make a living. Why? Because the system cannot afford to have someone like me, who is able to think for himself as a medical doctor for instance. What would happen is instead of prescribing a bunch of pills to my patients, without mentioning anything about their lifestyle (regarding physical activity, and nutrition) as I'm encouraged to do,

I would end up treating them in other ways that are more effective, and far more beneficial to them, but not necessarily beneficial to the system. I would wind up questioning the established norms, and disrupting the status quo in the process. The system (the Matrix) simply can't afford to have people like me (especially in great numbers) in such positions. And public schools are a filter which we all have to go through in order to find out who's fit for a particular position, and who isn't. And the one who is "fit" is one who is willing to give up their own ability to think, and put complete trust in the authority. The result of this is people will spend years on their education and get themselves into incredible debt in order to get into and secure a high-paying position, only to eventually realise that it is nothing like they thought it was going to be. However, since they had invested so much into it already, and because they had already sacrificed so much in order to get to where they are, that more often than not people will just turn a blind eye, and continue to do something that they know (or at least feel) is not right.

Of course there are examples of people who have gotten themselves into certain positions and had the courage to abandon them after a realisation that they were not in control, and that there was no room for independent or creative thinking. But, walking away from something that we've been working long and hard for to achieve is extremely difficult. And that is why most people will never do it. It's practically a guarantee that most people will continue to do as they're told, and continue to live an unfulfilled life because the rationale of most people is that at least they are not living on the streets, and anyway are well-off. That is what the educational system does. It tricks one into sacrificing one's happiness and "dreams" for turning into another cog in the wheel which keeps the system running. And the machine spits out a few receipts here and there (a monthly wage) as a form of a band-aid, which mitigates one's frustrations and keeps one's mouth shut.

Stuart Wilde perfectly explained the relationship between the ordinary people and money in one of his "Money Mastery" seminars. Stuart brilliantly observed that the world in which we live simply isn't designed for people to be rich. He pointed out: if we were to divide all of the money in the world among every living person, then everybody would become millionaires. But the system isn't designed to assist people in becoming rich and wealthy. The system is so designed that only a few get to be rich and wealthy while others are kept in ignorance. For the purpose of keeping the system running, while continuing to fill up the pockets of the rich. Imagine if you could go to work for a year and earn a million or three, what would happen is you would gain the power to just retire and enjoy the rest of your life. But that's not how the system works. The plan that the system has in store for the majority is it will spit out just enough money to maintain the equilibrium between the masses running around the streets–protesting; dissenting; tearing the system apart–because they do not have enough, and them cashing in their chips. As in, no longer needing to work because they have enough. In effect, the way that the system works is that it will give a person just enough cash at the end of every month to cover all of their expenses and financial obligations for that particular month, and no more. So that the person will have no other choice but to come back to work in order to earn more, if he or she wishes to avoid ending up sleeping under the bridge the next month.

"Freedom is a nature's gift to all, yet human beings are the only species on this planet that has to pay in order to enjoy it."

Stuart Wilde points our attention to the fact that the world in which we live is owned by approximately a thousand families: they own the governments; the societies; the banking systems; the financial institutions; and all the major corporations. These people decide what interests we will pay, how much rent we will pay, what mortgage terms we will receive, what our monthly car payments will be, and so on and so forth. They decide everything for us. Which ultimately determines the amount of money that the average person working within the system will have. The result of that is the average person becomes limited as to the amount of capital that he or she is able to accumulate. To such a degree that the average person could never compete with the powers that be. And yes those who make these decisions will allow any person to earn money by selling their own products, or services. But not before they *legally* take their (unearned) cut, to make certain that the person doesn't earn too much, lest that person becomes too empowered and gains enough power to take away the control which those who are at the top–so to speak–have. Having said that, if you believe that Jeff Bezos, or Elon Musk are the richest men on the planet, you are sorely mistaken. The richest people on the planet (the likes of Rothschilds, or the royal family of Saudi Arabia) are never even on the list of the richest people in the world; they are in the league of their own.

Stuart Wilde had said on numerous occasions that the world is not designed for the people; it is designed to keep the institutions up; it is designed to support the governments and politicians. While ordinary, working people like you and me are always sent the bill. That is, if the government makes a mistake, we pay for it. If they need funds for a project (which does not benefit the people in any way), we pay for it. If they borrow huge sums of money from another country, and get themselves into massive debt, we pay for it. If they decide to fund unnecessary, and utterly pointless studies for some type of research–spending millions–trying to figure out whether or not a pigeon can fart, we pay for it. (I just made that up, but I think you get the point that Stuart was trying to make.) He explained that societies do not teach us *power*. Rather, they condition us to believe that we are weak; that we have guilt; that we are useless; that we have to follow all of the rules and support everything other than ourselves; and that we supposed to care about things which we do not actually care about. Those who are "in charge" of our world want us to believe that being rich and creative is reserved for a special few–so we, the ordinary folk, shouldn't even waste our time trying to create, or achieve something of substance. And if that conditioning doesn't stick, they want us to believe that if we are doing too well financially, then we are not spiritual, righteous, or good. But the reality is, Source-Energy is absolutely abundant! Source-Energy will eagerly give us anything that we ask for: "Ask, and you shall receive." We have to stop believing this nonsense–it isn't true. We have to stop assuming that God wants us to be poor; that there isn't enough well-being for everyone; and that lacking desire, and being satisfied with the nitty-gritty that we already have is somehow virtuous, righteous, and spiritual.

"Nature is an inexhaustible storehouse of riches." – Wallace D. Wattles

There are truly no limits to what we can be, do, or have. The only problem is that those who run this whole shebang have sold us on the idea that working long and hard will bring us the riches, because they wanted us to work long and hard for *them*. And this belief had been passed down from generation to generation for hundreds of years now. Of course, as we have previously discussed, earning a lot of money has nothing to do with working hard. It is only a matter of being creative, positioning oneself in a niche market, and having something to sell. It is a simple transference of energy–we give people an idea (in the form of solving a problem), and they give us money (a symbol of appreciation). Which we can then use to buy the experiences *we* want. Now, some of you might be wondering: "Well, how did this happen?" While there are many reasons for this I personally love the way Stuart Wilde explains the whole situation when he asks of us to imagine a scenario which took place a very long time ago–a time when churches owned thousands of acres of land, while the common people were dying in starvation, and living in filthy conditions. Sometimes people would come to the church and bang on the door, saying: "What about us? What do we get?" and people who ran the system back in those days were not about to share their wealth with everyone else, so they told them: "You will get yours later. You will get yours in the after-life." And people believed them; they ate it up. They've accepted the idea of "later" because at least they haven't been told "never." But, today we are not so gullible, we don't want a promise for later because there are too many evidence that suggest we are capable of having everything that we want in our current lifetime. We are no longer ashamed asking for more of the good life, because we can see–by other people's example–that all of the resources, and opportunities for that life are available to us, and not only in the afterlife, but also here and now.

"It is your father's pleasure to give you the kingdom." – Jesus Christ

Getting involved in discussions about the modern-day monetary system can be infuriating, and the last thing I want is to leave you demotivated, and discouraged. So here is a positive thought: Although there is a system in place which sets a hard cap on how wealthy you are allowed to become, nevertheless you can still earn enough money to live within the system very comfortably without worrying about much of anything. You can pay your fees, your taxes, your insurances, your bills, buy all of the essentials you need, and still have more than enough left over to live freely, and buy all of the experiences you want for yourself and your family. Do not let the system deter you. You are so much more powerful and creative than the mechanisms which are designed to incapacitate you. You have enough power within yourself to beat the system, and rise above the average norm through the proper use of your mental, creative faculties. Unfortunately, the majority of people don't recognise the immense power of their mind, and their ability to create wealth, because of the belief that those who are wealthy, are only so because they are special; because they are creative; and ultimately, because they are different from us "normal people." Yet the truth is, everyone is creative! Everyone is special and unique in their own, individual way. The problem is that an average person associates creative thinking with something grandiose, such as discovering electricity; writing a best-selling novel; or inventing something outlandish, and ground-breaking. Certainly, such accomplishments are evidence of creative thinking. But, creative thinking is not limited to certain occupations, areas of life, or endeavours; nor is it reserved strictly for the gifted or superintelligent.

David J. Schwartz was an American author who wrote in his book "The Magic of Thinking Big" (which I highly recommend) that we are all creative; that we are all capable of creating something out of nothing. He stressed that the same people who don't think of themselves as being creative do not realise that they do in fact create something here and there. For instance, when a family with an average income devises a plan to send their child to university–that's creative thinking. When a salesperson manages to sell to an impossible customer–that's creative thinking. When an employer makes his or her employees enjoy their work more–that's creative thinking. Similarly, to keep our children occupied constructively, or to prevent a certain disaster, would also be considered practical, everyday creative thinking. Creative thinking is simply about finding new and improved ways of doing anything. But, there is a catch. To do anything, we first must believe that it can be done. Believing that something can be done sets the mind in motion to find ways of getting it done. While the whole of the Universe rallies around that idea and continues to bring everything which moves the believer closer to his or her ideal. It is simply a matter of tuning oneself into the frequency of what one wants, with unwavering faith that one does get what one wants. In effect, believing a solution paves the way to a solution. And what you can do to start developing a belief in yourself is eliminating certain words from your everyday vocabulary, such as: impossible; can't do it; it will not work; not for me; there is no use; I don't know how; I'm not smart enough, and so on, and then watch the genius–which you never knew was there–begin to come out.

Do not allow tradition to paralyse your mind. Because tradition will tell you that the competition is stiff; that the markets are oversaturated; and that building a successful business is next to impossible for the average Joe. Instead, heed what Abraham Hicks had wisely told us: "*It is just as easy to create a castle as it is a button.*" In my opinion, what she meant by this is that the only difference between the difficulty, and the amount of work which needs to be put forth for the completion of these two objects is perception; it is our own belief. It is only natural to assume that creating a castle is far more difficult, and way too complicated than a button because of its obvious size. And because we believe that, it does in fact become more difficult (at least for us). It becomes a self-fulfilling prophecy. Conversely, when we tune ourself into the frequency of our desire (in this example building a castle) with a firm belief that the work is already done, then all of the thoughts, ideas, people, circumstances, and events–necessary for the actualisation of our desire–will flow into our experience so freely and orchestrate around us in such ways that the whole process of getting it done will feel completely effortless from start to finish. In this context, the castle is your own business. And by no means am I suggesting that business is easy–far from it. But I am suggesting that understanding the "rules of the game," coupled with belief in yourself and your creative abilities is the best way of ensuring that the business which you have decided to build grows, and ultimately succeeds.

All in all, if society is not going to teach us better ways of earning money, why won't we look for the advice from people who know what it takes to succeed in the money game? All of the information is out there, and all of the people who have already achieved the results which you may be looking for are easily reachable. Instead of loathing your financial situation, begin to educate yourself about money. Do not spend your time doing what you hate or even slightly dislike (because you are capable of so much more). And quit relying on your employer for your financial destiny. Take full responsibility for your life, and create your own economy. If you truly dislike what you are doing right now, and would much rather prefer to be doing something more fulfilling, if you are serious about improving your money situation, I suggest you research this all-important subject. I suggest that you search for mentors who already are where you wish to be, and who can show you how to earn more money doing what you love, or at the very least something that you're good at. And if you do not have the money to hire a professional mentor or a coach, then for the time being you should get yourself a copy of "Think and Grow Rich" by Napoleon Hill and "The Science of Getting Rich" by Wallace D. Wattles. These two books alone will provide you with a proper perspective on what it means to be rich, and how to properly use your mental faculties to make the riches come to you.

Lastly, if, for whatever reason you have convinced yourself that your money situation is hopeless, then I want you to focus your attention on the following Chinese proverb: "*The best time to plant a tree was twenty years ago. The second-best time is now.*" And what this means is that if you haven't been financially successful up until this point in time–and you wish to have more wealth and success in the future–then the best time to begin taking action is *now*, without wasting your precious time and energy on beating yourself up for not doing it ten, twenty, or forty years ago. Since there is absolutely nothing you can do about that now. What you *can* do is put your mind to work today and begin to look for better, more creative ways of serving others with what you already have, right from where you presently are. In other words, if you are to have any hope of improving your financial situation in the future, then you have to keep your eyes on the higher vision (what you wish to achieve); rather than be ensnared in a lower concern (what you think is preventing you from achieving it). That way you practically ensure that the next ten, twenty, or forty years of your life will be much different than the last.

HEALTH

"To keep the body in good health is a duty... otherwise we shall not be able to keep our mind strong and clear." – Buddha

As we get into the various ideas in this section, the basic premise to keep in mind throughout is that our mind and body are one; they're connected. And because they're connected (both parts of our personality have a direct influence on one another) it becomes imperative to not only exercise our thinking muscle, and be more conscious as to the type of ideas we allow to enter into our minds. But to take care of our physical body also, and be more selective as to the kind/quality of food that we choose to nourish our body with.

The fact is, it doesn't matter how well we're able to take care of our own mind if, simultaneously we are neglecting the physical side of our personality. Because if we are not exercising our physical muscles, and are consuming foods that do not encourage a healthy function of the physical body, then we cannot be clear-minded, fully present in the here and now, be full of energy, vitality, and keep our focus. Expressed differently, we cannot have access to, and operate from high-vibrational states when we are experiencing any kind of physical discomfort: be it a headache; a migraine; a stomach-ache; arthritis; mild symptoms of a common cold; nausea; dizziness; shortness of breath; fatigue; exhaustion; hunger, or any other physical pain. Since a physical discomfort is so immediate, and "real," it does a great job at grabbing our attention and pulling it towards the affected area, leaving us with no other choice but having to deal with the problem until the pain is alleviated.

For the benefit of your overall health you have to begin to monitor your daily food intake: making sure that you are nourishing your body properly. So that your body has everything it needs in order to function appropriately. And as much as I would love to, I cannot give you the exact dietary plan that will be perfect just for you–a plan which will keep you on top of your nutritional needs, and keep your physical body in top condition. Since every person is fundamentally different with respect to what their nutritional, and fitness needs are at any given time, means that you'll have to experiment with different diets and exercising plans for yourself before you can reliably ascertain which program is the right one for you personally. However, there are certain foods, and practices that are universally beneficial, and are appropriate for all people (with only a few rare exceptions). With that in mind, I will provide you with a general overview as to what might be good for you, and what might not, as well as what had personally helped me improve the state of my health–both physical and mental.

Typically, people shy away from learning about health because the discussion about keeping one's physical body in top condition can be too complicated, and overwhelming–involving a million different theories and opinions. But it doesn't have to be. If we only do few things right, everything else will naturally fall into place. Because our body naturally takes care of itself. The physical body is designed to heal itself. The physical body knows exactly what it needs in order to stay healthy. Thus, in most cases, it isn't so much that we need to try harder to improve our health; rather, we just need to get out of the way and provide the physical body with a resistant-free environment that will be conducive to allowing it effectively do what it was naturally designed to do–regenerate. The natural state of a physical body can be described as vital and alive, and when the body detects even a slight deviation from that condition, it begins the process of regeneration back to its natural, optimal state. However, if we continue to disrupt this regeneration process with our bad habits–stressing out; lack of sleep; lack of exercise; lack of relaxation; lack of proper nutrition–it will eventually lead to a development of an illness, disorder, cancer, or disease. We must therefore be vigilant and listen to what it is our body needs, and doesn't need, in order to avoid producing such conditions. For sometimes, these conditions can become fatal, irreversible, or extremely difficult to recover from.

Let us now turn our attention to some of the things that you may be doing (and some of the other things which you absolutely should be doing, but are not doing) that are holding you back, and causing you problems. First of all, let's talk about dairy. It is common knowledge that dairy (cow's milk in particular) is nature's perfect food. But did you know that that statement is only factual if you are a calf? Indeed, cow's milk is specifically designed for calves, not for human beings. Because cow's milk contains certain hormones that are absolutely perfect for the development of a young calf–with respect to its size and weight–but can be detrimental to humans. Majority of humans naturally stop producing significant amounts of lactase (enzyme needed to properly metabolise lactose) as we become more mature, and are able to digest other types of food. For humans (and for most mammals in general) the normal condition is to stop producing the enzymes needed to effectively digest and metabolise milk after we have been weaned. Which in the case of a human being, on average, occurs between the ages of two and five. After that we no longer have the capacity to digest milk–especially on a regular basis–without putting our health at risk. Typically, this will result in cramps, flatulence, bloating, and diarrhoea. And in most cases that would be the end of it. But in other cases, these warning signs may balloon into something more serious. In a sense, it would be much healthier, and safer to obtain the nutrients we need (which we're accustomed to obtaining from dairy milk, such as calcium; potassium; protein; and fats) from some of the other food sources such as vegetables; fruits; beans; whole grains; nuts; and seeds.

Ever since we're little we are taught to believe that in order to be strong and healthy we have to drink a lot of milk on a regular basis. But that statement is only a reflection of the dairy industry's interests, rather than science, or our own interests. Not a lot of people can actually stomach dairy. About 75 percent of the entire world's population is genetically unable to properly digest dairy because majority of people in the world are lactose intolerant. In fact, a number of studies have shown, time ago, that drinking too much milk for those who are lactose intolerant is dangerous, and can even lead to prostate cancer, lung cancer, breast cancer, ovarian cancer, and a myriad of other health problems. Lactose intolerance is a condition which describes individuals who do not possess adequate digestive enzymes called "lactases" to digest the sugar component of cow's milk–called "lactose." Simply put, lactose is the sugar that is found in dairy milk, and our body uses the enzyme called lactase to break down this sugar so that we can absorb it into the body. And so, what winds up happening when those who are lactose intolerant (which is practically most of the world) consume dairy is that the lactose which has not been broken down is left undigested. And it sits in the gut until it eventually gets broken down by bacteria, causing all kinds of discomforts which I have previously mentioned.

The reality is, dairy is not critical for good, optimal health. Anyone who tells you otherwise are either misinformed, or are lying for their own selfish gain. For most of the human history dairy milk played a very small part in people's lives. Milk was nothing more than a survival tool; as opposed to it being deemed the staple of the average person's diet. You can imagine thousands of years ago when the winters made it difficult for the farmers to grow fruits and vegetables, or when people did not have the time, or the means by which to obtain proper food and nutrition, they *had* to turn to milk because it

267

was so readily available. Hence, rather than it being a full-blown necessity, milk was this kind of a safety net; a last resort if you will. Think about this, even though dairy has its downsides, it is nonetheless much better to drink some milk at the cost of suffering cramps and stomach-aches, but keep oneself going. Rather than avoiding it entirely, and potentially starving to death. But, in our modern, capitalistic society, no one is going to starve to death if we choose to avoid dairy products. Because today, we can get our hands on all kinds of other food in a matter of minutes. So the question is, where did the idea that we *need* to drink a lot of milk on the regular basis actually came from? My understanding is during the first World War, the U.S. government had to provide a lot of milk for its soldiers overseas, in order to fight malnutrition and keep soldiers on their feet, as they weren't able to get proper food while in conflict at war. As a result, farmers began breeding more cows, and focusing exclusively on producing as much dairy as humanly possible, while getting rid of all the other crops, and animals. But, when the war ended, the demand had significantly diminished, and the country was left with tons of milk that nobody wanted, or needed. However, instead of going out of business, farmers had to find a way to convince the public that they *had* to drink milk. And that was the beginning of it.

In no time, the dairy producers had an agreement with the government to hold huge "educational" campaigns in public schools which were leading children to believe that in order to be healthy, they had to drink–on average–four glasses of milk every day. But that was not the end of it. The dairy producers then began paying for huge advertising campaigns with celebrity endorsements (Got Milk?) to make the general public believe that it was *essential* for the development and sustainability of a healthy body. And yes, dairy actually has some health benefits. But in the same vein, dairy is not essential either since there are plenty of other foods that contain just as much calcium, potassium, protein, and fat. If you're a person who actually enjoys milk, then there is no need to be upset. For there is plethora of other, and much healthier alternatives out there for you to choose from. For example soy milk; coconut milk; almond milk; rice milk, etc. The point is, we don't need milk in order to be healthy, we merely have been conditioned to think otherwise. Considering that most of the world is lactose intolerant, staying away from dairy products as much as possible is always going to be a wise decision. Because chances are, you can't stomach the stuff. I can guarantee you that when you decide to leave dairy products out of your diet, in a relatively short period of time you will realise that your stomach is much happier, and healthier for it.

How about bread? (White, wheat, or wholemeal bread, there is actually not much of a difference, it still isn't any good.) Since people typically have a difficult time accepting that consuming traditional bread–regularly–is not a good idea they will usually argue for it. Commonly, they will protest: "What are you talking about? Bread is something that our ancestors have consumed for thousands of years, so how could it possibly be bad for us?!" And what I always point out is that the bread which we are eating today is much different from the bread which our ancestors used to consume. Most of the bread on the market today is highly processed and is full of preservatives. Which is precisely the reason why modern bread can sit on a shelf for weeks without decomposing. These preservatives are very unhealthy, and are inflammatory to the gut, and when ingested cause all kinds of problems. Not only that, our modern bread is also genetically modified. The wheat which is being used to make bread today is highly modified. Consider this: Naturally, wheat grows up to about six feet. While the head on the wheat is usually very small. But, what happened approximately half a century ago is farmers began to modify the wheat in an effort to produce bigger yields, and feed more people. That's why the wheat which we have today is a lot shorter, while the head on it is a lot bigger–enabling farmers to produce more wheat. However, at the time of this modification the farmers did not know whether it was still edible or not. But now they are discovering that the gluten in this modified wheat is more or less undigestible.

Gluten is a protein which is highly inflammatory that is found in wheat, which can cause damage to the gut lining. Gluten is particularly harmful for those who have a celiac disease (an autoimmune condition that causes violent reactions towards wheat), a wheat allergy, or gluten intolerance. Most of the time, however, people don't even know that they are sensitive to wheat, or gluten. And what will usually happen is they will continue to experience discomfort in their stomach, or develop certain health complications without knowing the cause, when what they really need to do is put down the bread. Since human intestine cannot break down, or absorb some of the sugars that are found in modern wheat, what happens is these sugars wind up making their way to a large intestine instead, where they begin to get fermented by bacteria–producing fatty acids, and gases that cause all kinds of bowel problems. Since traditional bread does not have a lot of nutrients and is very high glycemic–it drastically raises blood sugar–is the reason why consuming traditional bread on a regular basis is linked to obesity, diabetes, heart disease, cancer, and other inflammatory issues.

Now, I love bread as much as the next person, but we have to be honest here, and we have to face facts before we make the choice to consume traditional bread (regularly). There are of course much healthier alternatives, for example Ezekiel bread. Unlike most regular traditional breads which consist mainly of refined wheat, pulverised whole wheat, and added sugars, Ezekiel bread is made up of grains, legumes, and no added sugars. Ezekiel bread is sprouted and when it undergoes that sprouting process it reduces the phytic acid content, which makes the nutrients more bioavailable. Meaning that it is going to be easier for the body to absorb its nutrients. The sprouting process also reduces the gluten content. So if you are not extremely sensitive to gluten, then Ezekiel bread is a much healthier alternative for you. Another good option is sourdough bread. Sourdough bread is much more nutritious than the regular bread, and it also has a much lower phytate content–thereby increasing mineral absorption–than any other type of bread. Sourdough bread is much easier to digest, and is usually safe for people who are gluten intolerant. Even though sourdough bread is usually made from the same flour as regular, traditional bread, nonetheless its fermentation process improves the nutrient profile to a respectable extent, and therefore is a much healthier alternative. Other than that, avoiding bread in general is always going to be in your best interest, and it will definitely help improve your health. But, if you do enjoy bread, and you have difficulty giving it up–then you don't have to. You just have to ensure that you are not consuming too much of that "low-quality" bread which is modified, is loaded with a bunch of preservatives, as well as other harmful chemicals that you wouldn't want to have in your system on a regular basis.

Of course I have to shine the light on a topic of eating meat, since these days most people do not consider a meal to be an "actual" meal without having a piece of meat of one kind or another on their plate. I am aware that this is a sensitive topic for a lot of people. And I want them to know that the following insights were simply drawn from my personal experience, research, and study. That is, I do not have a certain agenda to push, and I don't have a bias towards one diet or another. In fact, my opinion is neutral. My sole aim here is to raise awareness and show you what has personally worked for me, and helped me to become a lot more clear-minded, focused, and have more energy and vitality. Now, I am not a vegan or a vegetarian. I don't put labels on myself when it comes to my personal food choices. I simply do my best to eat what I feel is good for me (not in terms of how it tastes, but more so, how it makes me feel on an energetic level). And I don't always get it right either, because it's not easy to find good quality, organic, fresh food regularly without fail. Since most of the meat on the general market is low-quality, I have made the decision–a few years ago–to quit eating meat altogether, and then observe what happens. After two years of avoiding meat I had definitely noticed an improvement in my general mood, energy levels, and concentration. Before I have made the decision to stop eating meat, after each meal I always felt the need to lie down for a while, because all of my energy was being utilised on processing the heavy meals that I used to eat. Whereas after the fact, by avoiding meat products, along with dairy, and wheat, each meal began to *give* me energy, instead of sapping it away from me. And even though eventually I did come back around to consuming meat and wheat again, what is different today is that I consume these foods in moderation and I do my best to ensure that the food is free from preservatives, and other harmful chemicals, after which I no longer feel sluggish and confused.

The issue that we have today is that we simply eat way too much meat, to a point where we are almost addicted to it. And we cannot imagine living without it. But in our "industry, trade and commerce" society, buying fresh, organic meat regularly is nearly impossible. Thus, most people who eat meat are probably consuming highly processed meat that is pumped full of chemicals, which give it the illusion of being nutritious and fresh. Processing meat means adding certain chemicals by salting, curing, fermenting, and smoking, which makes the meat taste better. But the harmful chemicals that are being used in the process damage the digestive system. Which in time can lead to strokes, heart disease, and even cancer. What most people don't seem to realise is that the reason why meat tastes so good is *because* it's processed, seasoned, smoked, etc. If you were to try to eat meat which hasn't gone through that process, it would taste like absolute crap! Moreover, the animals that are being raised to be slaughtered for meat are typically raised in terrible conditions, and are crammed together in small, confined spaces–very close to one another–leaving practically no room for any movement whatsoever. It is not uncommon therefore, that the farmers will feed large amounts of antibiotics to their livestock to promote growth and prevent them from developing diseases. But, overuse of certain antibiotics in food-producing animals can lead to them developing drug-resistant bacteria in their stomachs, which can pass on to those who eat meat from the affected animal. What it essentially means is that if your meat isn't tended to properly before you consume it, then you might catch this bacteria (also known as superbugs). And if you're unfortunate enough to develop a sickness from it, it can become extremely difficult to recover from since the bacteria is resistant to drugs and antibiotics.

Another reason farmers need to feed antibiotics to their livestock is because instead of eating grass–as they should–they are being fed grains (typically corn) to gain weight more quickly, and grow faster. Why? Because the faster the animal reaches optimal weight, the sooner it can be sold. And the sooner the farmer can get paid. But because their stomachs are not designed to digest corn (it is designed, and is adapted to eating and digesting grass, or other similar forage), in order to prevent them from having digestive problems and becoming sick farmers *must* feed them antibiotics. Taking all of this into consideration, if you have a difficult time giving up meat then the safest choice of all is going to be consuming grass-fed animal products. Grass-fed animals spend their lives roaming and eating grass in a pasture–as they have evolved to do. Grass-fed animals are not locked up in a stockyard, therefore they have no need for antibiotics. Grass-fed animals can move around freely, and enjoy a healthier, more natural diet. Which results in them having high amounts of omega-3 fatty acids, vitamins, and minerals in their meat.

Keep in mind however, that most of the time the practices which farmers follow are very different to what they say they employ. They might claim that their animals are raised in the pasture, that they eat a healthy diet, and that they are killed in a humane way, when in reality they are not. Farmers are usually overwhelmed with the amount of livestock they have to look after, and the slaughterhouse is similar to an assembly line in a factory setting, where thousands of animals move through the "conveyor belt" every single day. It is simply not possible to adhere to and follow through on every single procedure that is supposed to be in place, since those environments are extremely messy and chaotic, because the demand is so damn high! It is highly disturbing to know what is going on inside of these slaughterhouses. If people were able to see where their meat actually comes from, and how it is being prepared, I believe that most of them would be completely put off eating meat ever again. And of course, the meat industry is acutely aware of this, so they do everything in their power to make certain that all that people get to see is a clean, well-packaged product, alongside all of the nice, colourful adverts where animals are free, happy, and healthy. Meanwhile all of the malpractice–the wailing; the crying; and the suffering–takes place behind closed doors. The reason why this is important to know is because we become what we eat. And if you're eating animal meat which has been through incredible stress, suffering, and pain on the regular basis, then no wonder why you are twitching, are easily annoyed, unfocused, and depressed.

Last but not least, you need to avoid modern food that is foreign to our genes, such as ice cream; chocolate; cake; crisps; cookies; soda (refined sugars), etc., as much as possible. I also recommend you avoid trans fats, found in food such as baked goods; chips; fries; and almost all packaged products–or in other words–avoid anything that does not come from nature, but a lab. Although it is okay to indulge ourself in something sweet and sugary once a week, or preferably even once a month. But since we live in a society where there is an abundance of these products readily available to us (it is incredibly cheap and it tastes really good) we tend to eat way too much of that crap. You know how difficult it is to only take one or two bites out of a chocolate bar and put it down. Or eat a few crisps and leave it at that. What we usually do is we eat the whole bar, and then reach for another one, and to make matters worse, we don't feel like drinking pure, distilled, or mineral water after consuming something sweet, what we actually want is a sweet, sugary soda that is full of chemicals, and which isn't designed to kill dehydration.

Indeed, our bodies need sugar. However, sugar–especially refined sugar–is highly addictive, since sugar activates brain's reward system (similar to drugs) causing it to release dopamine. And if we aren't careful enough eventually we'll begin feeling as though our body is constantly asking for something sweet and sugary, when in reality it's the craving that's' doing the talking. Consuming sweet and sugary products regularly becomes very difficult to stop, leading to all kinds of health problems: obesity; diabetes; high blood pressure; stroke; heart disease, and other diseases. Because this "food" is not actual food. It is specifically designed to taste good, and make one want, and crave more. Our ancestors for example ate nothing but plants, fruits, vegetables, and animals. And once a month–or maybe even once a year–they'd find a honeycomb, a sugarcane, or mix some sort of a concoction and share it between each other. In effect, back then these kind of pleasures were rare. They were considered, I would imagine, as a celebratory kind of thing to enjoy on special occasions; it was not a *lifestyle* like it is today.

The number of toxic agents in our food supply these days is worse than ever. By toxic I mean man-made substances which are foreign to our genes, that disturb the normal, healthy function of the body when ingested. One of the reasons why the majority of food products that are on the market today are full of added sugars is because whenever you take fat, or any other important ingredient out of a product, it tends to taste like shit. But in order to make a product appeal to a wider range of people it still needs to taste good, otherwise people won't buy it. And so, by taking the fat out of a product and marketing it as "low-fat," while adding in sugar where the fat was instead (so that it still tastes relatively good), it incentivises one to buy it also, even if one is a more health-conscious individual. What this means is that if you are working towards becoming healthier, and you vow to yourself to only purchase products with labels such as: "diet" coke; "fat-free" yoghurt; "low-fat" cheese; "sugar-free" biscuits, and so on, and you assume that you're making a wise decision with respect to your health, then think again. For in actuality, these products aren't any better. They still contain a load of other chemicals and ingredients that aren't any good for your health either.

Now, rather than making the topic of eating healthy extremely complicated, before you choose to eat anything you can make it simple, by thinking about it in the following terms: "Will this food give me energy, or leave me drained and exhausted? Will this food make me want to lie down and take a nap, or make me want to get up, and engage with life? Will this food knock me unconscious, or get me focused and present to the moment?" Ultimately, when you are about to put anything in your mouth the question to ask yourself is: "Is this food dead or alive?" In other words, does the food look fresh, ripe, colourful, and full of vitamins and nutrients, or has it been killed, processed, packaged, and preserved? If you are truly serious about your health, then you must make the decision to leave behind all of the food that weighs you down while it sits in your stomach–food which *takes* energy away from you and makes you want to lie down, be lazy, unfocused, and unmotivated. And instead, design a diet around gaining more energy, clarity, and proper nutrients. Which follows that sugars, chemically altered fats, saturated fats, heavily processed, packaged, fried, and preserved foods must be avoided as much as possible. If we are going to enjoy a healthy lifestyle, then this is the price we all must pay, there is just no question about that.

By the way, do not be paranoid about this. None of us are perfect. Even though I know that I shouldn't be eating certain foods, sometimes I still find myself eating something that I *know* is not good for me. Maybe because I am on the move, I am travelling, or it's late at night and I need to eat something. Since an empty, famished stomach is not a happy one, and McDonald's just so happens to be the only place that is open–I will eat McDonald's. Whatever the case may be, I don't beat myself up about it, and you shouldn't either. As long as you continue to build the type of habits and lifestyle that is conducive to eating as healthy as possible, and as long as you don't abuse your body to a pulp, you can rest assured that your immune system will take care of it all, and allow a few mistakes to slip through the crack here and there. So if you happen to fall off, it is not the end of the world. Just pick yourself back up and compensate for the damage 2-5X. In other words, if you want to have a chocolate bar, an ice cream, drink a beer, or smoke a cigarette, then do fifty push-ups first. And if the physical exercise is not a possibility at that particular time and place, jog around the block, or sit down and meditate for fifteen minutes. But still do the push-ups the following day. In effect, we can have our vices, but to avoid them becoming a problem, we just have to *earn* them.

Next, let's turn our attention to physical activity, e.g. exercise. Unfortunately, these days we do not move around much. We have become a sedentary society where most of the time we sit around watching television; playing video games; sitting at office desks; lying around; driving vehicles; operating machinery, etc. And then we wonder why we always have stiff joints; poor posture; low energy levels; why we are always sick and tired; why we easily get injured, and so on. But the answer is simple: lack of physical exercise. We did not evolve for the sedentary lifestyle which the modern society encourages, and is practically built around. Evolutionary history tells us that our ancestors had to walk around for many miles every single day to gather food. They had to climb and sprint once in a while to avoid predator attacks. They had to lift and carry heavy objects and materials to build shelters; rafts; different structures, etc. In other words, they were *using* their bodies regularly. We're not designed–biologically, or structurally–to lounge around all day long, and have everything easily brought to us. This mismatch between how we have evolved (hunter-gatherers) and how we live today (sitting, cruising, and shopping online), i.e. not moving very much, or in other cases, not moving at all for many hours at the time, causes all kinds of health problems.

Physical inactivity is one of the main reasons why we have an epidemic of elderly having to use walking sticks, holding on to their backs while slowly navigating themselves from place to place. And we think that it is normal. When I was little I was absolutely convinced that it would inevitably happen to me too–becoming useless, slow, and full of pain–I believed that that was normal. I was not at all impressed by this inevitable stage of life–getting old. However, as I grew older, I happened to come across a number of individuals who were in their 60s, 70s, 80s, and even 90s who were still perfectly fine, and who were not about to slow down any time soon. They were sharp, they were strong–both mentally, and physically–they were alive and focused, and some even had more energy than most people do in their 40s. How? What I have discovered is that the reason why some were able to enjoy good, optimal health–even at a stage of life when they were supposed to be resting and taking it easy–is because they were ambitious, and totally engaged with life. Because they were striving for something worthwhile–that gave them access to unlimited energy. A great portion of which was then used on taking good care of their physical bodies. In effect, these individuals weren't special; they were not freaks of nature; and they were not the exception to the rule. They simply did what most of us are not willing to do, and actively avoided doing many of the things that most of us habitually do, do.

Society conditions us to believe that as soon as we get "old" we have to retire and slow down, relax, and watch television, while popping all kinds of pills until the day we die. But what social conditioning doesn't tell us is that when we engage in less and fewer activities, we actually begin to condition the body to become weaker. That is, our muscles become weaker; our respiratory system becomes weaker; our immune system becomes weaker; and we become more prone to contracting a disease, or becoming ill. To counter this terrible fate we have to generate the energy–or the will–from within ourself to engage in some form of activity here and there, which isn't difficult to do. You do not have to become the next top bodybuilder; a fitness junky; or an athlete. All that is required is reconditioning yourself to use your body more often; to build a habit of running once in a while; sprinting once in a while; jumping up and down once in a while; lifting, or moving something heavy once in a while; stretching your muscles once in a while, etc. Because by doing so you let the body know that you still need it. You have to let your body know that it has to stay strong, because you would like to keep using it. You must let your body know that you are still engaged with life, lest it becomes atrophied. This can be accomplished in several different ways. For example, rather than ordering your food and have it delivered to your doorstep–walk to the store. Rather than driving to your place of work–ride a bicycle. Rather than hiring a handyman to move some furniture around–do it yourself. Other than that, the best option of them all is always going to be forming a habit of exercising regularly.

Exercising regularly drastically improves your health–physical, mental, and emotional–and it even raises your mood. It increases your energy levels. It helps with relaxation, and the quality of sleep. It releases dopamine, serotonin, and endorphins in your body (these are happy, feel-good hormones), which makes you feel more positive, and optimistic about anything that may be bothering you. It boosts your immune system. It minimises the effects of ageing by promoting the release of testosterone and other growth hormones. It helps to develop and maintain lean muscle mass. It increases your metabolism–which maintains low levels of body fat. It increases bone density, and prevents injuries. As well as reducing the effects of cognitive decline. There are so many benefits to exercising regularly that I cannot even find the right words to describe how incredible it makes me feel after a good workout session. It is something that you must experience for yourself. At the beginning of the book I had said that there is no magic pill to personal transformation, but if there were to be one, then it would be this: You feel depressed because your partner had ended the relationship? Go to the gym. You have lost your job, and along with it your sense of security? Go to the gym. You have lost your self-confidence as the result of a recent failure? Go to the gym. You feel so hopeless that you are losing your will to live? Go to the gym! Since your mind and body are connected, means that if you're having difficulty dealing with a particular problem intellectually or emotionally, through physical exercise you can reinvigorate your faculties and drastically improve your emotional state. To the extent that the problem will no longer feel disastrous and unsolvable. In fact, it will feel like a joke. And if you doubt me, you try it.

Most people avoid exercising because it seems uncomfortable, difficult, and time-consuming. But I can promise you that once you push through that initial resistance enough times, and turn exercising into a new habit, you will eventually rewire your brain to enjoy the activity. And in no time, your personal/intimate/social/professional/family life will begin to improve significantly. And by the way, you are not trying to become the next Ronnie Coleman here, so do not psych yourself out. Exercising as little as 60-90 minutes, 3-5 times a week is enough to condition your body to be strong, and keep on top of your physical health. Avoid telling yourself a lie as to how you do not have any time, or energy to exercise, just because you don't see the negative consequences of physical inactivity right now, at this very moment in time. Realise that eventually the "future you" is going to have to deal with it. The "future you" will still have to face, and deal with all of the choices that you are making, and habits that you are forming today. Do not fall for the trap of believing that you have all of the time in the world, and how you are going to start next week, next month, or next year. But rather, make the decision to start exercising regularly today! Make it a priority, and thank me later.

To get the most out of our healthy habits and practices, we also need to get adequate, good quality sleep. Good quality sleep is extremely important because it helps our immune system to function optimally (our immune system relies upon good quality sleep in order to fight harmful bacteria, and viruses more effectively). It helps wounds heal faster, and it restores sore and damaged muscles. Which is exactly what we need after a good workout session. Sleep is nature's perfect tool for recharging. It is a time for our body to heal itself, and energetically prepare us for the following day. If you're in the habit of waking up moody, exhausted, confused, and unfocused, even when you have slept for a very long time, then what is missing in this equation is the *quality* of your sleep. What I have discovered, and have experienced firsthand is that although sleep *duration* was certainly a big factor with regard to being well-rested and re-energised, there were other factors involved, which greatly affected the quality of our sleep. And if we continue to ignore them–relying solely on the amount of *time* we spend sleeping–then we will continue compensating for our lethargy, fatigue and low energy levels by stimulating ourself–trying to gain energy–throughout the day by other means (particularly coffee and energy drinks). When what we actually need to be doing is arranging our sleeping space in a way that is conducive to the natural process of healing and regenerating.

Considering that we spend one-third of our life (more or less) sleeping, it's imperative that we become aware of, and then implement the things necessary to get the most out of our sleeping time. It is common knowledge that before we go to bed overthinking, drinking coffee or tea, snacking, consuming sugar, or eating large meals, will lower the quality of our sleep, and even keep us up at night. But what is not so common or obvious (at least it wasn't for me) is that our surroundings also affect our sleep quality. As a prelude to this, I want you to become aware of the presence of something called EMFs. They're electromagnetic fields produced by moving electric charges. Everyday electrical devices that we have and use emit certain frequencies, or energies that interfere with the quality of our sleep when they are in the immediate vicinity (even as far as few feet). For instance, if we have a lamp, a TV, or an alarm clock plugged into an electrical socket beside our bed, that device will have an electrical current running through the wires–generating electrical and magnetic fields. Now, we might think that if we turn off the light, or the TV, the energy will disappear, right? Well, no, it actually doesn't. By observing various tests done with EMF meters (meters which pick up different frequencies when they are put close to various devices), it becomes apparent that unless we completely unplug the device from a socket, the energy does not go away. And the current does not stop. Because the voltage stays in the wire, even when the device is switched off. Therefore, before you go to bed you have to make sure to unplug everything which works with electricity, or batteries–that is around your sleeping space. You should also put your mobile phone on "airplane mode" and place it a few feet away from you. If you are willing to try this for a few nights in the row you can then come to your own conclusion as to whether what I am suggesting here has any real significance. In other words, you might not notice any changes whatsoever for the first few nights of rearranging your sleeping space in such a dramatic fashion. However, if you stick with it for an extra night or two, I can guarantee you that your mornings will no longer be groggy, foggy, and confusing.

The second major factor that is important to consider when it comes to enjoying good quality of sleep is something called melatonin (the sleep hormone). Melatonin is created by the pineal gland, and it is triggered by darkness. Darkness is what stimulates melatonin and turns it on. In the context of good quality sleep, this means that if there is any kind of light present in the room while you are sleeping (maybe your computer is running in the background, maybe the daylight from outside is coming in through the curtains, or maybe the TV is switched on), then that will definitely degrade the quality of your sleep, and might even keep you up at night. Through exposure to light–which your retina receives–what happens is it begins to send messages to your brain, letting it know that it's daytime, when it actually isn't. As a result, your brain assumes that you shouldn't be sleeping and it turns off melatonin. This is one of the reason why people who do not sleep well tend to get sick more; they tend to have stiff muscles and experience physical pain more often than others.

People who do not sleep well not only produce less melatonin (a powerful anti-inflammatory, and antioxidant), but they also produce less growth hormones that repair tissue. If you are one of those people who's having difficulty getting adequate sleep, try going to sleep each night after a calm, deliberate wind down. Avoid going to sleep immediately after watching a film (particularly a horror), after a prolonged exposure to blue light–which comes from mobile phones; computers; and other digital devices–or after engaging in something that raises your heart rate, such as watching the news, or worrying about the conference with your ill-tempered boss tomorrow morning. What personally helps me to enjoy better quality of sleep is cutting off all external stimulation and meditating for 20-30 minutes, or reading a good book for 30-60 minutes before going to bed. Whenever I do this, it slows down my heart rate–no matter how hectic my day was–and it stops me from thinking (at least negatively) no matter how stressful I think tomorrow is going to be. Which helps me to relax into my breath and peacefully drift off into slumber on a metaphorical cloud.

Overall, when it comes to improving the quality of your sleep, you have to make sure to keep your room free of electronic devices, especially around your sleeping space. And if that's not an option, then each night before you go to bed, make sure to unplug all of the devices from electrical sockets that are in the room. Or, if you have an "on/off" switch on your electrical outlets, then that would work as well. Moreover, make sure to sleep in a pitch-black, cool, noiseless room. And preferably in the nude. Since removing all of your clothes while you sleep improves blood circulation, while also allowing your skin to breathe. Which is absolutely fantastic for your heart and muscles. (To help facilitate silent and pitch-black sleeping environment I recommend you purchase a good sleeping mask, and noise-cancelling earplugs). Upon awakening, avoid checking your mobile phone right away, and replying to emails and messages. Avoid interacting with other people, watching, or reading the news. Avoid thinking about the problems you've had the day before, or new problems that might be coming your way. In other words, you need to give yourself a chance to start the day on *your* terms, without immediately getting dragged into other people's realities, negative vibrations, and all of the problems that await you. Begin to formulate and adopt an evening/morning routine consisting of positive affirmations, a reminder of your goals and mission in life, and a good 15/30-minute meditation session. That way, you can start and finish your days vibrating on the highest frequencies possible. In effect, gaining an unfair advantage over your competition (whatever that may be).

Now that we know what it takes to improve our physical and emotional health, let's look at how one may go about improving their mental health. One of the fundamental aspects separating humans from all the other creatures on the planet is our intellectual abilities. Since we are multidimensional beings, our mental/intellectual health is just important as the physical. Opportunities for intellectual stimulation are all around us, so there is no good reason, or excuse for us not to exercise our brain and mind. In order to continue enjoying good, optimal mental health, you must exercise your mental faculties. You have to be more open-minded to new experiences and be willing to occasionally learn something new. This can be achieved in a variety of ways. For example, leaning a new language, or a skill; playing a musical instrument; applying for college courses that interest you; playing chess; playing board games; solving puzzles and crosswords; reading, and so forth. The opportunities for learning and strengthening the mind are truly endless.

We absolutely must exercise our brain and mind if we are going to stay mentally sharp, and mentally sane–there is no other way around it. We must use our brain, work it, and build it up, just like a muscle. Because when we stop learning–and thus growing–the brain gradually begins to shrink. (This may also be the reason why elderly people tend to suffer from dementia and memory loss.) You see, the brain has the ability to undergo neuroplasticity: a process by which new synaptic pathways, and connections between neurons inside the brain are created. What this means is that when you do something which you've never done before, and you keep doing it over and over again, what you're doing, first of all, is creating new brain cells. Then, as you repeat the same action, you proceed to give energy to those brain cells. Then, by activating those brain cells, they begin to multiply in greater and greater numbers, until that action; skill; thought pattern, etc., ultimately becomes fixed in your brain. Wherein the action, behaviour or thought pattern becomes *second nature.* In his book "Social Intelligence" Daniel Goleman explains precisely how this process works: *"The first connections made in a neural circuit become strengthened each time the same sequence gets followed, until the pathways become so strong that they are the automatic route–and a new circuit has been put in place."* He continued: *"Because the human brain packs so much circuitry in so little space, it creates continuous pressure to extinguish connections the brain no longer needs, to make space for those it must have."* Essentially, this is how old habits are broken and new ones are formed–through repetition of the same action, or idea until it becomes fixed. While the other circuits (habit/thought patterns) that are not being used eventually dissolve.

If you reflect on your own experience and picture yourself trying to tie up your shoelaces for the very first time, you were probably perplexed by all the intricate manoeuvres, twists and turns that tying up a shoe entailed. But as you continued to do it repeatedly, what you were doing is building cells of recognition in the brain–forming new connections between neurons that are now responsible for performing this particular task with ease. More specifically, through repetition, you activate certain brain cells that are associated with a particular task, action, or thought, and you proceed to give energy to those cells every single time you repeat it. And the more often you repeat it the stronger those connections become, until you build a sufficient number of brain cells that'll allow you to perform the task without any conscious effort. That said, lo and behold, now you can tie up your shoelaces in a matter of seconds without looking at your feet. Likewise, learning to drive a vehicle for the first time certainly–and naturally–felt completely alien to you and extremely awkward. Your hands and legs were all over the place–all the while your focus, and every bit of conscious attention were directed upon million different things that were happening. Whereas today, after so many hours of repetition, and constant learning, your hands and legs do everything reflexively by themselves, leaving your conscious mind free to chat with a person sitting next to you, enjoy the scenery, or daydream while you commute.

With that in mind, the reason why most people never get to experience some of the things that they want to be, do, and have is not because they are dumb, or aren't talented enough. But rather, it is because they haven't put in enough hours into it, and are sabotaging their own success by allowing negative emotions and negative self-talk to hinder the progress they've already made. In other words, from the lack of understanding as to how new habits are built, and unfamiliar territory is traversed, people tend to quit at the first sign of difficulty, or uncertainty, before any significant number of brain cells are given a chance to be built. There is nothing to be lost, only success to be gained if you choose to become more "promotion-oriented" (read the book "Focus" by Heidi Grant Halvorson and Edward Tory Higgins), and begin to eliminate words such as: "I can't; it's too hard; I don't know how; I am not smart enough; I don't want to fail and look stupid" from your thinking and speaking vocabulary. To become something "more" than what you presently are you have to develop self-trust, and make a commitment to overcome one personal challenge, or bad habit in your life. For instance, if you experience anxiety in your social interactions, begin deliberately throwing yourself into random conversations, over and over again. And when you feel the urge to eject from the conversation, force yourself to stay in it for a little while longer. And in the next conversation, a little while longer. What you will notice is that through constant exposure to uncomfortable/unfamiliar situations your anxiety will eventually be replaced with comfort, complete presence, or even excitement. Because the reason why anything feels uncomfortable in the beginning is because it's unfamiliar territory. But once we familiarise ourselves with it–through continuous engagement with it–it eventually becomes "just another day at the office."

Ultimately, we can read and listen, we can be told what to do, we can be guided, we can have all of the information, and know exactly what needs to be done in order to overcome our fears, and challenges. Yet, the reality is, words don't teach; it is only personal experience that teaches. In effect, you may possess all of the knowledge and information regarding the things that need to be done (to solve your problems) all running through your head, but your brain does not want promises; it wants proof. You can tell yourself that you are a confident, talented, smart, creative, and amazing human being by affirming it to yourself until you are blue in the face. But, until you actually take some form of action which affirms that in fact, yes, you *are* creative, you *are* confident, you *are* talented and you *are* amazing, nothing will change. Affirmations and autosuggestions to yourself are not a magic pill or a quick fix. Indeed, those are very powerful tools which will assist you on your journey to self-development. But they will not by themselves bring you to where you want to be–mentally; emotionally; physically, or otherwise. You have to put in the work. You have to take action, and work towards your ideals. Realise that everyone is afraid and everyone experiences fear, especially when trying something new. It is completely natural to feel that way. Fear isn't some malevolent force out to thwart your progress; fear is your best friend. For if you happen to feel fear when you are about to do something, it is just an indication that you're about to grow. When you're only doing the things which do not make you feel uncomfortable, uncertain, or afraid, then you can be sure that you aren't growing. In that, by staying in your comfort zone you are not building new brain cells and forming new neural connections.

You have to accept that when you go after certain things that you want–things which you've never done before–you will most certainly be met with fear (or more specifically, resistance). Because the novelty of the situation is what elicits resistance to it. Expressed differently, because your brain doesn't know how to deal with a new situation yet, because your brain doesn't have the neural connections that are associated with it yet, and because your brain doesn't have any references from your past experiences to fall back onto yet, is the exact reason why you feel uncomfortable. In effect, when we feel fear, we have to accept that uncomfortable feeling of resistance, and still do whatever it is that we want to do anyway. Because resistance is a compass, pointing towards that which is truly important to our growth, and evolution. We have been conditioned to misinterpret resistance as something that is trying to stop us and prevent us from moving forward; when the truth is, resistance is a clear indication that we are moving into new territory, that'll help to expand our brain, and mind further. All things considered, fear (resistance) only exists in situations that count. And so, from this day forth, when you feel fear (resistance) about something, remind yourself that the reason why you feel that way is because what you are about to do is important. And then say to yourself, "I feel resistance about this. Well, then I guess I've got to do it!"

Overall, when it comes to enjoying healthy living you need to relax and play more; find opportunities to laugh more; move your body and engage in physical activities more; read educational books; attend seminars, and learn something new. Likewise, you need to drink more water, and eat more vegetables, greens, fruits, nuts, eggs, beans, and spices. You have to nourish your body with proper nutrition, as well as your mind with proper education. Essentially, you need to make sure that you're getting all of the essentials your body needs such as calcium; potassium; magnesium; proteins; omega-3; vitamin B, C, and D. If you are someone who is suffering from or have been diagnosed as having clinical depression, Alzheimer's, autism, dementia, OCD, ADHD, a disorder, or some type of neurodegenerative/neurological disease, then I strongly recommend that you check out the works of Mark Hyman at www.ultrawellnesscenter.com. Mark Hyman is an American physician, author, public speaker, and an advocate in the field of Functional Medicine. He is also the founder and a medical director of The UltraWellness Center based in Lenox, Massachusetts, United States. Needless to say, Mark is extremely effective at what he does. Mark Hyman's approach to treating his patients is vastly different in contrast to the approach of conventional doctors and physicians. Which is a good thing, because he's not going to prescribe you a load of pills and send you on your merry way. He understands that chemical imbalances in the brain are what causes problems such as Alzheimer's; ADHD; autism; depression, and countless others. And that these chemical imbalances can originate in the gut.

The problem is, conventional doctors, and physicians alike believe that brain is cut off from the gut; that the brain's entry point has an impenetrable wall of sorts. For this reason, when they try to get to the bottom of their patient's health problems, they are not looking where they probably should be. In contrast, Mark Hyman explains how the gut is considered to be the second brain. And why it is the most important part of the immune system. He explains how the gut and the brain are connected, as well as how they communicate with each other. If you have been diagnosed as having clinical depression, autism, OCD, ADHD, or dementia, the traditional doctor or physician will prescribe you a bunch of pills, that will do nothing but alleviate the *symptoms* of your problems for a short while, without targeting and working on fixing the actual *cause*. Most physicians, and doctors are not aware of this connection between the gut and the brain, hence they are forever looking for solutions in all of the wrong places. The fact that the mainstream medicine does not believe that problems in the brain could ever originate in the gut, is exactly the reason why patients will keep coming back to the doctor's office, again and again, with the exact same problems, without ever actually fixing the *cause*–which lies in the gut. That being said, if conventional medicine is not working out for you, you need to try a different approach, and work on fixing your gut. And if you are unable to visit The UltraWellness Center directly, I suggest you pick up a copy of Mark Hyman's book "The UltraMind Solution" and discover exactly what is causing you problems. The book will assist you in creating a personalised plan on how to go about healing yourself from the comfort of your own home by implementing–and then following through on–a few relatively minor dietary and lifestyle changes.

"It is health that is real wealth and not pieces of gold and silver."
– Mahatma Gandhi

SUMMARY

Now that you are aware of all the things that might be holding you back, and are preventing you from living the life that you truly love and deserve, it is worth highlighting some of the important points to take away with you before we move on to the final epiphany:

- On your journey to self-mastery you will be forced to transcend social conditioning. In that, you will have to recondition your mind: discard beliefs that do not serve you, and adopt new ones that help you grow, and move you in the direction of your highest good. Transcending social conditioning is about choosing to trust yourself more. It is about no longer allowing other people to think for you, and tell you what to do, as well as what you should believe in, what is popular, what is possible, and what you can, or cannot do. Ultimately, it is about thinking for yourself. We are bombarded with so many standards in modern society pertaining to what it takes to be successful in life, none of which are under our volitional control, and if we choose to listen to it, we drastically lower the chances at achieving the success *we* seek. We are conditioned to believe that money and opportunities are limited. That if we are to become successful in life we have to be extremely lucky; that we have to have rich parents; that we have to be special and exceptionally smart; or that we have to cheat the system in order to get ahead in life. But, if you make the decision to start looking at life through your own set of eyes, you will inevitably realise that none of that is true. Because you will come across countless examples of ordinary individuals, just like you–who came from nothing–who had achieved everything that they said they would. And if you ask them as to how they managed to beat the odds and take complete control of their lives, they will tell you that all they had to do was proactively, and meticulously make certain changes in their mindsets and perspective, and take action. That, in effect, not even a fraction of their success was attributed to luck. Understand that social conditioning doesn't want you to be extraordinary; it wants you to be just another crab in the bucket. So, it'll do everything in its power to keep you where you are, and be satisfied with that. For the most part, transcending social conditioning suggests that you stop believing everything you hear, or see on television just because a confident, well-groomed persona wearing a suit and tie told you so. That you do not take advice from someone who isn't where you want to be, i.e. never take financial advice from someone who is broke. And that, if you find yourself getting dragged back down into abyss by the other crabs around you, quickly remind yourself that we live in the most abundant times ever, and through sheer force of will, escape the gravitational pull of social conditioning. In time, you'll come to know that getting ahead in life has little to do with luck, high IQ, connections, or cheating the system. But everything to do with self-accountability and self-education backed up by *massive* action!

- Most people believe that to be confident, and feel incredible they have to have the best clothes; the best cars; the best girls; the best abs; be the funniest person in the room; have the most money; or have some special talent which other people approve of. Yet, this isn't what real confidence is; it is a facade. In today's world, cultivating true, core confidence is extremely important; otherwise if left unchecked, our deepest insecurities will continue to run rampant, and wreak havoc in our personal and intimate relationships. The surest way of building core confidence is by deliberately throwing oneself into difficult situations and learning how to deal with them. In a sense, a deep sense of inner security can only ever be developed as a result of overcoming various challenges, obstacles, and releasing trauma. That is what is going to build the depth of one's character; not a new t-shirt, or plastic surgery. Once you develop self-trust–a complete and utter belief in yourself–then rather than relying on external factors to dictate how good you should feel, you will have the efficacy to boost your own mood up, and make yourself feel at ease at any time, and in any environment. Having core confidence means to accept that you do not need to know everything there is to know, or have a special talent for something in order to get to where you want to be. It means to never sell yourself short, because you know what one person can do, another person can do. Ultimately, it means to know that as long as you are trusting the process–the process of building sufficient number of brain cells, and creating the right neural connections–while moving towards whatever it is you want to achieve, or become, then success is more or less guaranteed.

- Building upon the previous point, you have to do whatever it takes to centre yourself in the present moment. Presence is where your power lies. Presence gives you full access to your creativity, as well as emotional/psychological stability–reducing the unnecessary mental noise. The power of the present moment is truly invaluable. All of the negativity–the pain and the suffering–dissolve in the present moment. It is no secret that we will have our fair share of all kinds of problems, mistakes, failures, and setbacks in life. And if we are too busy dwelling on that, then we will not be in a proper mental state to find solutions, and make the right decisions. In order to be effective in life we have to stay centred amidst the chaos, and be present to whatever life throws onto our path. We have to perceive each and every moment as though we had chosen it and stop resisting whatever is happening in it. In reality, nothing is ever wrong in the present; it is only our thinking that makes it so. Nothing that happens is either good or bad; everything "just is." We have to learn to avoid making snap judgements, because our eyes often deceive us. What seems to be adversity or misfortune could very well be a blessing in disguise. Therefore, you have to train yourself to simply observe what is happening in your everyday life, be present to it and just breathe. Soon enough you will realise that you don't actually have as many problems as you thought you did. When you are not present, what typically happens is you experience ordinary situations, but you turn them into problems, since you're looking at them from a wrong lens. That lens is "ego," or "ignorance." But, when you become present to the moment, you gain access to the powerful perspective of your higher-self–the lens of "understanding." And when you are present to the moment–and therefore under the influence of your higher-self–nothing could possibly go wrong. Because you're no longer in re-action to–and at the complete mercy of–all the different forces outside of yourself that are causing your grief.

- In our modern, technologically advanced society everyone is continually vying for your attention: the mainstream media; the social media;

the marketers; the content creators; the entertainment industry, and so on. And if you aren't careful enough you are going to waste your time consuming products and Internet content which adds no tangible value to your life. Rather than living your life vicariously through sports teams; celebrities; content creators; gossip; TV shows, etc., you need to become your own biggest fan and be the star of your own movie. That is, you must learn to draw your emotional state from within yourself, and become the source of great energy. And when you do, you'll begin to like yourself more, and as a result, you'll be less likely to waste your precious time and energy on consuming pointless crap! Drawing your emotional state from within means that you are no longer relying on others to provide you with positive emotions, validation, and approval for you to feel good about yourself. Drawing emotional state from within yourself means that you are at the cause of your life; not anymore at the effect. And the degree to which you are able to draw your emotional state from within is in no small part determined by the ecosystem of positive emotions around you, which you have built. In effect, when you have things in your life that bring you satisfaction and joy, such as: hobbies; positive friends; self-development; and a strong sense of purpose in life, then this type of structure allows you to know exactly what your personal values are, what your boundaries are, and the direction in which you are going in life. It becomes a sort of filter which dismisses everyone and everything that's out to sap your energy, stress you out unnecessarily, drag you down with negativity, and ultimately steer you away from your path and purpose in life.

- You have to cultivate a more optimistic perspective on life, and addict yourself to positivity. When you are feeling positive you are in a highly resourceful state in which you don't get easily annoyed and bogged down by the various stresses and pressures of life. You become better equipped at coming up with proper solutions to your problems on the spot. You become more calm and collected. You become a winner; not a whiner. You begin to utilise the "Law of State Transference" to your advantage. Whereby people around you no longer feel unsafe and uncertain. Developing a positive mindset is about believing in yourself and having a strong sense of self-efficacy. Whereby regardless of what may be going wrong, you know that you'll find a way to make it right. It is about knowing with absolute certainty that whatever you want to achieve in life, you will eventually achieve. It is about forming a habit of learning from your mistakes, and becoming a better person because of your mistakes. And last but not least, it is about reframing various situations and events to your advantage. For example, it is not win or lose; it is win or learn. A failed relationship is not the evidence of your unworthiness; it is an opportunity to meet new people as the new and improved version of yourself. Being happy for everything you have is not about complacency and inaction; it is about being grateful for how far you have come, while still being eager for all that is coming next.

- No matter who you are or what you have, you need to accept that you have value to offer to the world. You have to become a person of great value who is a giver, not a taker. One who is thriving; rather than coping. Becoming a person of great value means to fill up your own emotional cup, i.e. no longer needing to suck other people's energy with your whining and complaining. It means to never again ask for assistance without contributing something in return. It means to be willing to bring positive energy into your dealings with other people without expecting anything in return. It means to aspire to share, and give; as opposed to boost your self-image, get acceptance, or take, and finally *get yours*. And once you become this type of person, what will happen is when you are negotiating a contract for a better position at work, or thinking about asking a certain person out on a date, you will not hesitate, and you won't doubt yourself. Because you'll know that you are valuable enough to take up other people's time and space. And you'll know that by working with you, or by getting into a relationship with you, other people's lives will become better off. And because you believe that, those high-pressure situations–the force of which would incapacitate most people–will no longer have a damaging effect on you, in turn increasing your chances at getting *exactly* what you want.

- When it comes to personal health, there is no one-size-fits-all method, or solution. Staying on top of your health is something that you need to experiment with yourself to reliably determine what works for you, and what does not. However, it is a matter of course that in our modern sedentary and automated world, where everything is done for us and brought to us with minimal effort, *balance* and *moderation* are the foundations upon which our healthy habits must be built. Which is to say that a McDonald's meal and Coke here and there, compensated by regular exercise, proper breathing, and good quality sleep is not going to kill you. Whereas McDonald's and Coke all day, every day, without any form of healthy compensation almost certainly will. All that can be said with respect to how important your health is, is that you can always buy new clothes, build a new house, and replace just about anything that you have in your life right now; except your physical body. You have to put forth a conscious effort to monitor what goes into it, and begin viewing your body as a sacred temple. And then, do all you can to treat it as such. Because it is the only one you can have in your current physical life experience. For if you aren't conscious enough of your bad habits that are affecting your health, and something were to go south, then no money in the world will have the power to bail you out of your bad decision-making.

- You have to prime your own mind for success and happiness. Life is a self-fulfilling prophecy: what you believe to be true, that is what you are ultimately going to get. Believing in abundance–that opportunities and possibilities are endless–shifts your mind into gear to continuously look for them. Generally, people have one of two attitudes towards life. There are those who believe that good things in life–success, happiness, and opportunities–are abundant; and there are those who believe in scarcity, lack and limitation. If you honestly believe that there is an abundance of great opportunities–abundance of money, potential life partners, friends, and happiness–then you'll never have to experience fear, scarcity, lack and limitation in any of these areas. On the other hand, if you believe in scarcity, lack and limitation, then you are more inclined to be stingy, argumentative, negative, obsessive, or hostile, because all you ever seem to be getting in life is "not very much," which is frustrating. Understand that humans have something that is called RAS (Reticular Activating System) lodged inside of the brain. It is a network of neurons which acts as a filter against all the data that's around us–including smells; colours; images; sounds, and so on. Since there is so much data coming at us at any given time, it becomes impossible to process all of it at once. And what RAS does is it only seeks information that's valuable to us in any one given situation. Expressed differently, RAS filters the world through the parameters that we give it, and our beliefs shape those parameters. Our RAS only looks for data that's most important to us; it only focuses on that which is most active in our vibration. RAS can either look for, and focus upon all of the things we deem valuable to our growth, success, and happiness; or it can focus upon things that are a threat to our survival. In effect, if you believe in scarcity, lack and limitation–and you do not expect much–then that's all you're ever going to experience. Because your RAS will filter out all the ideas, possibilities, and opportunities for growth that are all around you. Even if the things that you want are right in front of you–yet you don't believe that you can find them, or that you don't deserve them–your RAS will not focus on them, and you'll completely miss them. Thus, to increase your chances at living a life that you truly desire means you'll have to embrace a mental paradigm of abundance. Since believing in abundance–and with the aid of your RAS–enjoying an abundant life becomes a self-fulfilling prophecy. Through positive affirmations and suggestions to yourself you can begin to prime your mind for abundance. And in due course you will condition your mind to believe that you are entitled to success and happiness; that you are worthy of it; and that you absolutely deserve it.

For all intents and purposes, superior self-awareness is the key to success on your journey to self-mastery. In order to identify precisely what's preventing you from becoming all that you are capable of becoming, acute awareness of your beliefs, habits, emotions, and patterns of behaviour is essential. You'll know you are on the right track when you start thinking for yourself, without having to look to others to tell you how to think, where to go, or what to do. When you develop a healthy sense of entitlement, a strong sense of reality, and a resolute sense of self-efficacy. When you recognise your own value and become comfortable in your own skin. When you no longer need other people, conditions, circumstances and events to be different in order for you to feel amazing. When you begin to give love from yourself, to yourself, and fill your own emotional cup. When you're no longer paranoid about what to do, and what to say in order to impress others. When you are no longer concerned about where you stand socially, financially, or otherwise in comparison to other people. When you start trusting your own judgement more, and become your own counsellor, and a confidant. When you begin to perceive yourself and others in a more positive, favourable light. And when you start thinking better, bigger, and in more constructive, solution-oriented ways.

On that note, never forget that life is a self-fulfilling prophecy. Which means that you really do become what you think about the most. You must accept that whatever you believe to be true (whatever you expect) will show up in your life experience as a result of your expected belief–it is Law. Never forget that you are the creator of your own life experience. You have no one else to blame but yourself for everything you have, or don't have in your life right now. You are working with an infinite power that creates worlds–that is continuously flowing to and through you all day, every day. You are eternally guided, supported, and protected. And if you're experiencing anything other than what this power is offering to you all day long, only indicates that you are not listening and cooperating with it. But not because you are dumb or unworthy of it. But because the various mechanisms within the mainstream society (which are designed to hijack your perception, and then control where you direct your focus and attention) have got you by the balls.

"He who controls others may be powerful, but he who has mastered himself is mightier still." – Lao Tzu

PART 3

REMEMBERING THAT LIFE WAS SUPPOSED TO BE GOOD

Happiness

"Happiness is a feeling that comes over you when you know that life is good, and you can't help but smile. It's the opposite of sadness. Happiness is a sense of well-being, joy, or contentment. When people are successful, or safe, or lucky, they feel happiness. No one ever complained about feeling too much happiness."

Ahh, here we come to the most elusive subject of all–happiness. But not because it is difficult to find, or hard to achieve, but because we tend to search for happiness in all the wrong places. While completely overlooking that one particular place where it can only ever be found–within ourself. The truth is, everyone has experienced happiness at some point in their life; it's just that not everyone is able to maintain it. Why is that? In order to answer this question, one first needs to understand that all emotions such as: joy (happiness); love; peace; excitement; depression; anger; sadness; grief, and so on and so forth, are unique chemical reactions that are produced within a biological instrument–that is all they really are from a physical standpoint. Whereas the person's belief system–habitual ways of thinking–is what is going to dictate which chemical reactions that person is typically going to produce.

When we were little babies we were happy by default–joy was our natural state of being. We did not need to train ourselves to be positive, or have and possess certain things in order to produce chemical reactions of joy. Because joy was all that we ever knew. For instance, when a baby is first trying to walk but falls down, as long as the faces of baby's parents (or of the people around) are not displaying anger, discontent, disappointment, or shame, then the baby nervously laughs, gets back up, and tries again. Why? Because that baby does not yet have an ego–a sense of identity. A baby doesn't know what's expected of him/her. Hell–a baby doesn't even know what judgment is. Thus, a baby is incapable of producing chemical reactions that are associated with self-consciousness. But, if you–as an adult–manage to trip and fall on your ass in public, you are probably going to produce negative chemical reactions of embarrassment, or shame. Since you have already formed a certain identity, which comes with a set of strong beliefs about yourself, other people, and as to what is expected of you–in terms of ability and competency–you now have a certain self-image to protect. And when this image gets threatened (for instance when its validity comes under scrutiny, or its legitimacy is subject to questioning), you feel a negative emotion.

Most of us have been trained by other humans that feeling good for no apparent reason is abnormal; that it is not possible to feel happy by default. For this very reason everything that human beings do collectively, and individually is fundamentally for the pursuit of happiness. But happiness is not something that has to be pursued; happiness is a natural state for us to be in. One would think that by now developments and improvements in the areas of science; medicine; technology; AI; travel; entertainment; communication; security; business opportunities; living conditions, and so forth, would finally make us happier, but is that actually the case? If anything, we are coming to be more depressed than happy for the simple reason that we keep treating happiness as a destination, at which we can't ever seem to arrive. The problem with this backwards approach is that when we do manage to get somewhere–where we believe happiness resides–we soon inevitably discover that we still feel exactly the same as we did before; that happiness wasn't guaranteed; that maybe we are incapable of being happy; or that we do not deserve to be happy, which can be disheartening and downright depressing.

For instance, imagine feeling miserable with where you presently are financially, but then suddenly winning the lottery. In this case, you would experience genuine happiness for maybe a year. But then find yourself back at your usual happiness set point. (Your "happiness set point"–how good you feel by default–is what determines the quality of life that you'll continue to enjoy; not material possessions, or anything else outside of yourself. At this point it is an absolute fact that those who are unfortunate enough to end up in a wheelchair–or become afflicted by any other life-altering condition–as a result of an accident, in about a year's time they usually go back to their natural happiness set point. In effect, after the initial pain and shock subsides, and that person begins to adapt to their new condition and lifestyle, they invariably go back to being either fun and upbeat–just like before–or grumpy and ornery–just like they always were.) If your happiness set point isn't very high by default, you might win a huge sum of money and feel good about it for a while, but eventually you'll sink right back into your old crappy ways of thinking and feeling. And when this happens, you become even more depressed than you previously were. Because whereas before–when you were poor, feeling like shit–you at least had hope, a vision, an idea that once you get the money you will finally be happy. However, when you manage to get the money you've always wanted–yet you still feel the same way as you did before–it brings you to a sobering realisation that happiness has nothing to do with you being rich. And that "reality check" can tamper with your mind, because there is simply nowhere else to go. It's a dead end. It really doesn't matter how much "stuff" we get, because happiness has nothing to do with any of it! As we come to terms with the fact that going about searching for happiness in this way has never worked, and never will, maybe we should start looking for it elsewhere. And that "elsewhere" is not a destination, and it is not somewhere in the future; rather, it is right here, and it is right now.

Have you ever wondered why children are so adept at expressing joy, or why is it that they are able to experience happiness with much better consistency than a typical adult? I have concluded that it is because–for the most part–children live in the present moment. They are not preoccupied with the troubles of tomorrow, or the aches of yesterday. They are not worried about what other people are thinking of them, or expecting from them. You see, we humans are born in a perfect vibration–totally in tune with Source–eager to experience life. The conditioning, and the process of desensitisation from the well-being that is constantly flowing to and through us, begins to take place immediately *after* we are born. Happiness and well-being are truly our birthright; it is our gift from the Universe above. And when we were children, we intuitively knew that the above statement were true. Until our parents, family members, teachers, and other authority figures–figuratively speaking (and sometimes literally)–beat that knowing, along with that happiness, right out of us. Since a child is incapable of defending himself, by responding to outside pressures and coercions with physical power, emotional unreactiveness, or sound counterarguments, the child instead retracts into his head, and begins to create narratives which, in time become convictions (for example that being present and happy is dangerous and will get one into trouble), that are fundamentally incorrect; that do not represent the true nature of the child, or the life itself. And as if that wasn't bad enough already, when the child experiences enough of these proverbial "slaps" (get your head out of the clouds and be realistic; be more practical; get your head out of the sand and face realty; think before you open your mouth, and do not embarrass me), the child begins to feel safer in his head; rather than the present moment. And he continues to live out the rest of his life predominantly stuck in his head.

Next point: since the day we're born we get conditioned away from our own alignment (source of happiness) by various people around us. The reality of life is that every single one of us is responsible for how we feel. Unfortunately adults who are responsible for our development when we're young usually don't know all there is to know about life. So they do a superb job at convincing us that life is not a walk in the park (though with the right conditioning it absolutely can be) by any stretch of the imagination. And that if we don't do as we are told, we will be punished for it, and their love for us will be withdrawn. The type of ideas that we are typically exposed to on the daily basis are those of powerlessness, scarcity, lack and limitation. And when we are young, we are highly impressionable. As such, we become convinced that whatever we think, say, and do has to please *them*, instead of ourselves. We become convinced that it is our job to ensure that other people are satisfied with our existence. We become convinced that sacrificing our happiness and joy in order to keep other people happy is natural. And whoever refuses to adhere to such (bogus) notions is considered abnormal, and difficult. The truth however, is that every single person alive is responsible for their own happiness–their own alignment with Source. Every single person has access to that universal stream of well-being. Every single person has an emotional guidance system within them, which, in real time, moment-by-moment indicates to them where they are in relationship with that whole, broader "self." Self that is happy, powerful, confident, and worthy. Self that is eager, ambitious, vibrant, and sure. Self that is all-knowing, non-judgemental, and loving. Self is everything that people are looking for, but ironically having such a hard time finding it, for they have been trained by others to look for it outside of themselves. As a result of poor conditioning, most people have failed to understand that everyone's connection to "self" lies in the private of their own consciousness, and that it is only a simple shift in perspective away.

It is not at all necessary–and is in fact, futile–to attempt to control other people, circumstances, conditions and events into *their* alignment, so that we can come into ours. However, since not many people understand this, they believe that the reason why they don't feel good, or the reason why they are unhappy–and more specifically–the reason why they are out of alignment, is because of *you*. It is *your* fault! *You* are being naughty! *You* are being inconsiderate! *You* are not listening! *You* are thinking differently! *You* are not doing as you are told! *You* are being problematic! And so on. In effect, by holding you as their object of attention–rather than paying attention to their own connection with self–it makes it *seem* as though *you* are the problem–the reason for their not feeling good. And, of course, as we have already discussed, that cannot be true. Yet, because of people's ignorance, your parents, teachers, and superiors make you feel the need to follow their rules, and do your best to perceive, think and behave in ways that will keep them happy. Which comes at the expense of you coming out of the present moment, and in the absence of presence you are left alone with the mental chatter about what you should do, and what you should have done; what you need to do, and what you didn't do; how you need to look, and what you need to say. The problem with this is that as you move about, interacting with your outside world primarily from your head (the mental chatter, or the conditioned mind), and you witness billions of people doing the same thing, naturally, and progressively, you start to adopt various beliefs, ideals, and perspectives that are essentially flawed when it comes to one's happiness in life.

All what is required of you in order to get back to your natural state of being, to reclaim your happiness, and begin to live a more joyful life–which is your birthright–is first of all you need to get out of your own head and get back to the present moment. Secondly, you have to develop/adopt a philosophy of life which is in harmony with the philosophy of your higher-self. Or put differently, you have to raise your level of consciousness high enough to begin navigating your world (once again) through the powerful perspective of your higher-self. In a sense, the younger, "invincible" version of yourself, which has been "dead" for some time now, must be revived, brought back to life again, and wholeheartedly embraced. However, this does not mean that you need to become a nuisance again, and run around with pants over your head, and just be irresponsible. What it does mean, is getting in touch with the little kid in you who experiences life in the present, and who has no idea what unhappiness even is, for he intuitively knows that whatever other people think, and however other people feel, is none of his business.

PRESENCE

To lay down the basis for what presence essentially is, I will start off by saying that time as we know it is not actually real. Time does not have any real, meaningful power, or reality, outside of the human mind. Time simply does not exist. Time is just a concept which humans have created in order to function more effectively in this time-space reality. The concept of time is essential in a dimension (or a world) such as the one in which we live. Firstly, we need time because we have to co-create with other human beings who are all at different stages of evolution, locations, and circumstances, so that we can go about our lives co-creating in a more convenient, optimal way. Secondly, since we live in a three-dimensional reality, time becomes a sort of a gauge, which helps us to measure distance, growth, and progress, relative to where we are in any given moment. For example, traveling from point A to B takes time. It takes time to prepare a meal. It takes time to grow a plant. It takes time to learn a skill, etc. (At least perceptually so.) It is understandable therefore why we need time in our physical, material world. In that, you cannot become an expert, or a specialist at something now. You cannot plant a seed and expect a tree to grow now. You cannot arrange a meeting in the "now." In other words, you can't tell your employees and co-workers that you need to have a meeting now, while all the people who must attend are in different locations and circumstances. But that is when "time" comes in handy, so that everyone can gauge exactly when that "now" is going to take place–to adjust and prepare themselves to get to the meeting at the precise moment in time. See how difficult it is to explain the timelessness of nature without mentioning *time*? (And by the way, Eckhart Tolle is your go-to teacher if you wish to learn more about presence. Even though I have studied "presence" for many years now, my knowledge and understanding of it pales in comparison.)

Time is crucial in that sense. Though be that as it may, when you are at point A you are at point A *now*, and when you get to paint B you get to point B *now*, and only now, never in the future. When you are learning a new skill you're an amateur *now*, and while you're working towards becoming a master at it someday in the future–and whenever that future comes–you become a master *now*, never actually *in* the future. The future never arrives *as* the future; it can only arrive as the *now*, as Eckhart Tolle once brilliantly said. Unfortunately, the present moment is not something that can be accurately explained, and then understood (because it is not a concept); it can only be experienced by you *now*. But for the sake of at least trying to put it into a proper perspective for you, I'll say this: One hundred years which you can spend living in this world may seem to you like a very long time. But from the perspective of Source it is just a blink of an eyelid. Because time as we know it, and perceive it does not exist "out there" in the Universe. Rather, everything just *is*. You might think of it as one, eternal, uninterrupted moment, in which everything simply *unfolds*. You may think of it as the "eternal-now." Eckhart Tolle, a spiritual teacher and author of a phenomenal book called "The Power of Now" explains that the present moment is all we ever have; that there is no such thing as time. In his book, Eckhart asks us a powerful question: *"Im-*

agine a world without humans and then ask yourself, would it still have time? Past and the future? Could we still speak about time in any meaningful way? If someone were there to ask, 'What time is it?' The trees, the plants, and the animals would all be perplexed by such a question. They would reply, 'Time? The time is now. What else is there?'" This simple question beautifully illustrates the idea that time–which includes past and the future–only exists in the mind. Or more specifically, past and future–and therefore time–are mere mental projections of the mind, that–at least on planet Earth–can only be achieved by a human being in a form of a conscious/subconscious thought.

Think of it in this way: When a duck is floating along the stream–going about its daily business–while another duck crosses its path, and disrupts its peaceful flow, the ducks may get into a brief scuffle. But after it is all set and done, they'll waggle their wings, go their separate ways, and continue with their usual "duck business" as though nothing had ever happened. A duck (or any other creature in fact) does not possess the ability to feel resentment. Because in order to do so one must have suitable mental faculties, which can only be found resident in a conscious mind–part of the mind which animals do not have. A duck does not think about how horrible the other duck was, and that it needs to be punished, or sued (because it does not have the ability to think, and rationalise). A duck is incapable of consciously constructing an identity of a victim for itself, or invent stories as to how life is unjust and unfair. Even though animals navigate their environment through physical sensory factors (just like humans do), they are not operating with any of the intellectual factors–but rather–by instinct. And by instinct, the duck shakes off the negative energy which was bottled up inside, and it moves into the next moment where there's no longer a problem, and everything is back to "normal." Essentially, the fight that they got themselves into briefly interrupted their experience of the present moment, and vigorously flapping their wings was a perfectly natural way of releasing all of the negative energy which they had accumulated as the result of the quarrel. Thereby allowing themselves to immediately get back to the present moment without any kind of resistance: be it in a form of anger; shame; guilt; regret, or what have you.

In contrast, human beings (by misusing their mind) will sometimes carry within themselves resentments, guilt, shame, grief, anger, hatred, and all kinds of negative energy which originated two months or even twenty years ago, while significantly reducing the quality of their experience today. Most people do not understand that people, circumstances, conditions and events are never the source of their pain and suffering; it is only the lack of presence which breeds resistance to–and non-acceptance of–what-is. The problem that we humans have, particularly nowadays, is that we're forever trapped in the movement of thought. Certainly, if the thoughts which we think are positive and constructive, then that's perfect. But, is that actually the case for most of us? It isn't. Therefore, if thinking positively does not come to you naturally– where you feel like you are fighting an uphill battle trying to stay optimistic and composed, in this often times chaotic and complicated world–then presence becomes the next best solution for you. For, presence allows you to go *beyond* "thought," and instead become a detached, witnessing consciousness (to borrow Eckhart Tolle's terminology), which observes incoming thoughts. Presence allows you to monitor and to examine your thoughts without claiming ownership of them–making them exclusively yours, and identifying with them. If you manage to become present enough, that you get rid of the urge to lay claim to every thought which arises in your mind–but instead watch it go by, and dissolve into nothing–you will quickly realise that your thoughts don't actually have as much power, or importance as you had previously believed. Consequently, most of the "problems" you think you have will magically disappear. Why? Because commonly, many of the thoughts which you think in your day-to-day life are not even yours. They are either mental projections of other people, with whom you happen to resonance (vibrationally) at the time, or they are manifestations of your past conditioning which is still running rampant in your consciousness.

> *"You can always cope with the present moment, but you cannot cope with something that is only a mind projection."* – Eckhart Tolle

If you are experiencing any kind of emotional/psychological hurt right now you need to understand that it's only–and always–the result of some form of non-acceptance on your part: some form of unconscious, or sometimes even conscious resistance to "what-is." The good news, however, is that through regular meditation anyone can condition themself to become more accepting and appreciative of the "now." For meditation conditions us to perceive every single moment as if we ourself had chosen it; thereby becoming more accepting of whatever the present moment contains. And the more consistently we practice meditation, the more we free ourselves from all forms of pain and suffering. How so? Meditating regularly invariably brings about a powerful realisation where we start to feel–and know–that whatever problem we think we have, is never actually a problem in the present moment. The more we practise disidentifying ourselves from our own thoughts–simply by taking a step back and observing them–the more present we become. And the more we practise being present, the stronger the power of our presence becomes. Eckhart Tolle said the following with respect to the importance of becoming more present: *"By becoming more present, that is when you begin to generate an energy field within you, and also around you of such a high vibrational frequency that no pain, suffering, and negativity can enter that field and survive. Just as the darkness cannot survive in the presence of light, all pain and negativity will dissolve effortlessly in the power of your presence."* If you are to experience more happiness and joy in your day-to-day life, it is imperative that you make the present moment the primary focus of your life, because your life is happening now, and always now–in the present moment. You have to be willing to say "yes" to the present moment. You have to surrender to what-is, and say "yes" to life. Allow the present moment to be whatever it happens to be. It is unnecessary–and in fact, futile–putting up resistance to something which already *is*–something which cannot be changed–bringing about pain and suffering as a result. Realise that whenever you do this, not only are you resisting a certain condition, circumstance, or event in the *now*, but you are actually resisting life itself, for your life *is* in the present moment.

As an aside, do not misinterpret presence for something that it isn't, as some people unfortunately do. Presence is never about inaction, and passivity. Being present is never about not caring for anything whatsoever, and discontinuing "thought" altogether. For example, if your bills are due, and you do not have the money to pay them, do not just sit there in a Lotus Position and think to yourself: "Well, I guess I can't pay my rent right now. I fully accept that. So be it." That's not what being present to the moment is about. Of course, you can momentarily mentally project yourself into the future in an attempt to solve an incoming problem, or to set up a plan for something that you want to do in the next few moments from now (that could be minutes, hours, days, or years). And you can also momentarily mentally project yourself into the past, in order to fetch a memory of a particular experience that you've had, and use it to your advantage in the "now," or in the near future. By all means do that. Just do not make the mistake of living your life in the future, or the past, predominantly in your *now*.

> *"Life is now. There was never a time when your life was not now."*
> – Eckhart Tolle

In order to grasp the meaning of the quote above you should ask yourself the following question: "Have I ever experienced, thought, or felt anything outside of the now?" And if you really ponder that question for a moment, you will realise that the answer is no. Because nothing in your life had actually happened in the past; it happened in the "now." And nothing will ever happen in the future; it will also happen in the "now." The past and future are nothing more than mental projections of the mind, that have no real power, or reality of their own. But, when we believe in the reality of "time," we give the past and the future power in the "now." In other words, all forms of psychological/emotional pain and suffering need time in order to exist. Without time, there is no mental projection; only aliveness, awareness, and alertness. Eckhart Tolle succinctly emphasised this point when he stated: *"All forms of uneasiness, anxiety, tension, stress, worry, fear, etc., are all caused by too much future and not enough presence. Whereas guilt, regret, resentment, grief, sadness, bitterness, non-forgiveness, etc., are all caused by too much past and not enough presence."* That is, people *cause* themselves to feel bad, because they are deriving their sense of "self" and what different events, circumstances and conditions mean, by identifying with their own mental projections–that aren't real. And the reason why anyone would ever continue to feel like a victim after a particular experience–which elicited those feelings–was over is because they believe that their past is more powerful than the present. Those who are unfortunate enough to develop such a powerless mindset believe that other people, circumstances, conditions and events are responsible for where they are in life in the present, and for how they feel *now*. Sadly, those who do not understand the importance–and the power–of presence, and who are perceiving various events from their socially conditioned minds (or limited perspectives), those people will continue to experience more of the same, no matter how hard they may try to find more happiness and joy in the future.

Now, when we happen to meet such individuals, we sometimes think: "Why don't they ever succeed in finding happiness? They are trying so hard, surely something will happen for them." Unfortunately not, because trying to control, or trying to improve our life–which includes past and the future–is an impossible task, for they do not exist! On top of that, whatever we resist, persists. Which is another way of saying that what we are giving our attention and energy to, is what we are currently growing. The Universe never gives us what we want; it gives us what we are. Whatever we are thinking and feeling about in the present, is what we are currently attracting more of. And so, if we allow our past, or future (which we cannot do anything about) to dominate–and ultimately control–our thinking, then what kind of a life do you think we are attracting more of? What I have learnt over the past decade of practicing meditation–becoming more present to the moment–is that our life is already whole, complete, and perfect. If we decide to make changes in our life, we must focus on changing our life *situation*; not our "life." You see, we are much bigger than our life situation, but we are not bigger than life itself. It is ludicrous trying to improve our life, for "life" doesn't need improving. Hence, whenever you are trying to make certain improvements in your life, focus on improving your ability to stay present, and begin cultivating a more positive, empowering perspective. You can certainly improve your life situation by expanding your horizons and setting new goals, but you cannot improve your life. Life is primary. Life is your deepest inner being. Life is already whole, complete, and perfect. Life is something which simply *happens*. And within that "happening" you have "situations." Hence, if you think that your life is going to improve when you achieve this thing or the other, know that you are operating under a false premise. For life just *is*. It does not need improvements. But your "situation"–circumstances and conditions–may.

If you are in the process of consciously trying to improve the quality of your life, and you are waiting for a future result to finally feel happy and be fulfilled, in that case, what you're doing is resisting the here and now, which is exactly where your life is–in the "now." But if you aren't willing to accept what already is, you are resisting life itself. And if you resist life itself, then it doesn't matter what goes on in it, and what improvements have been made, it will still never be good enough. In other words, if you're coming from this frame of mind (resisting the present moment; forcing things to happen; *needing* something else/better), then even when you do manage to obtain exactly what you want, the future will still seem more promising. Why? Because by this point, you will have conditioned yourself to overlook, and be dissatisfied with the present moment itself. You have become convinced that a good life lies somewhere in the future–which does not exist. For when it arrives, it still arrives as the present moment; never as the future. Do you see the problem? For example, imagine yourself being unhappy with where you are (the present moment), and you believe that happiness lies in your getting a promotion at work (the future result). Let's say you eventually do manage to get promoted. What will happen is you'll realise that happiness didn't last long, or it was never there in the first place. Because as soon as you get what you want (the future result), you are immediately back to square one–back to the present moment again, which you've conditioned yourself to abhor, and resist. But since you are not aware of this, you think to yourself, "Well, maybe the promotion at work wasn't it. Maybe what I actually needed all along is a new house (or whatever)." And a never-ending cycle continues indefinitely.

The point is, life is the only constant, while everything else within it will come and go. And if you allow your happiness be contingent upon anything other than life itself, happiness will continue to evade you, leaving you with an empty feeling which breeds the *need* for further gratification. This doesn't mean however that you should not take pride in, or allow yourself to feel joy for all of the things that you have achieved in your life. You should certainly appreciate all manner of pleasant and beautiful things in life, and bask in various positive conditions and circumstances that you find yourself in from time to time. However, just don't make the mistake of looking for a sense of identity, or permanency, and fulfilment through any of those always-fleeting and always-changing external things. For there isn't anything external which you could possibly experience that can genuinely satisfy you, and make you happy; except temporarily and superficially. What you have to do instead is become internally fulfilled by becoming present to the moment, and by other means which we have already discussed extensively up to this point.

No one intentionally (consciously) chooses negativity, mental conflict, confusion, hatred, or emotional pain and suffering in their life. These things can only occur when there is not enough presence to dissolve them. In effect, if you allow your conditioned mind to run your life, you run the risk of never experiencing genuine happiness. However, your new and improved life begins the moment you decide to disidentify from your mind, and its conditioned patterns, i.e. the moment you become present. Your life begins to improve the moment you cease deriving your sense of self from your past, or projecting yourself into the future, assuming that future is where happiness is. Realise that you are always in the right place at the right time, with all the power of the Universe at your command. And when you become more present–when you become aware of the abundance and well-being which surrounds you–you will have no choice but to experience that permanent state of happiness which you're looking for, regardless of where you are, because it is your birthright.

HAPPINESS

"Happiness is a choice."

So far we have learnt that happiness comes from within ourself. That when we become present to the moment we're going to experience it naturally. But another useful way of looking at it is that happiness is a state of being, which is a by-product of one's attitude, or life philosophy. If your philosophy of life consists of a bunch of disempowering beliefs, you are setting yourself up to experience very little happiness in life. If you believe that the entire world is conspiring against you; that people cannot be trusted; that people only care about themselves; that you are an unlucky person; that you don't deserve to be happy, and so forth, then you will continue to find evidence of how all of those things are true (thanks to your RAS). Conversely, if your life philosophy is one of empowerment, and you believe that all is well; that everything is always working out for you; that you have infinite potential; that the Universe is conspiring for you to win, and only wants what is best for you–even in the face of an "apparent" misfortune, or setback–then you will continue to see evidence that further validate and reinforce your all-empowering beliefs.

It may appear as if external, material objects, circumstances, conditions and events are the cause of our happiness. However, it is the *meaning* which we assign to those things that makes us happy. It is not the "thing" in question that contains happiness or unhappiness within it; it is our own interpretation of it which determines how we feel about it. For example, if you happen to watch a boxing match, either on television, or in the actual venue, by the end of the match you know that there will be those who are happy with the result and those who are unhappy, every single time. You are aware that by the end of any competitive match/game, not everyone will feel the same way about the result. For if your heart, friends, money, and values lie within the team in the blue corner, then when the blue team wins you become happy; whereas those who have a vested interest in the team in the red corner, become unhappy. Every circumstance, condition and event is neutral–is neither good nor bad–for if it were not, everyone involved would be happy, or unhappy with the end result as a *collective*. Feeling happy or unhappy about any one particular condition, circumstance, or event is tied to our own inner response to it. For instance, imagine yourself trying to fall asleep, when all of a sudden you hear someone outside of your house incessantly honking their horn. Now you are pissed! And as they continue to do so, you finally decide to come outside and give them a piece of your mind. However, as you about to explode on the culprit, a relative of yours jumps out of the car, and yells: "Surprise!" and at that moment your meaning instantly changes. You are no longer angry, because as it turns out, a family member of yours just bought you a new car as a gift for recently passing your driving test. Which means that you no longer have to use public transport to get to work. As a result of your new meaning your emotions instantly shift and you feel happy instead.

Same event, same end result (not being able to get adequate sleep which you so desperately need before you go to work in the morning), just a different meaning.

To further emphasise this point, I want you to visualise yourself going through the following scenario. Let us imagine that you woke up one morning feeling relatively happy, and you receive a call from your employer, informing you about the termination of your contract with the company. As a result of your conversation, your emotional state shifts and you start to worry. Because you interpret this interaction to mean that you will not be able to keep up with all your financial duties the following month. However, while still feeling hopeful, you quickly decide to look for another job. But after two weeks of applying for dozens of jobs to no avail, you become progressively demoralised. Because your new meaning is that you might possibly lose everything you have. As the stress continues to mount you manage to get one of your good friends to agree to lend you enough money to pay off all of your bills for the current month, and also keep you going through the next. Now you feel good again, and you finally relax. Because your new meaning is that you have enough time to get your finances in order, and money is no longer an issue. But, as it turns out (for whatever reason), your good friend–though as much as he would love to–is not able to lend you the money–sorry. Once again your meaning changes, and you are back to feeling like crap, hopeless, and exhausted. Then, as a final desperate attempt (an utter shot in the dark), you decide to apply for a position (for which you have exceptional expertise) at a company for which you have always wanted to work, but have not been successful in previous attempts. As fate would have it, you quickly discover that the company is currently looking for someone to fill a particular role for which you are a perfect match, and you get the job. Moreover, the best part about this is that the job is located overseas (in a country in which you have always wanted to live) and the company had agreed to provide you with accommodation, transportation, and cover all of the expenses for the first two months. In the end, what at first seemed like a complete disaster (losing your job) turned out to be one of the best things that ever happened in your life.

Now, stop for a moment and really think about this. What do you think had caused you to experience all of those negative and positive emotions in the given scenario? Was it all of the different events that took place; or was it your own thoughts? I think you already know the answer to this one. Yes, it was you; you did it. By assigning different meanings to various events. Now imagine how much stress, and emotional pain you could have spared yourself if you knew from the beginning that all is well; that everything is going to work out perfectly fine; and that everything will turn out to be all right no matter what happens. In effect, when your life philosophy is complementary with the Laws of nature, there can be no mistakes, and nothing could possibly go wrong. Why? Because nothing is *final*. A few things may go wrong for you today, or even this year, but as long as you are not accepting defeat, and dwelling on how things are at *this* particular moment in time, and as long as you don't fall victim to lower consciousness, then it will eventually pass and create an "opening" for greater things to come. That is because our Universe, and everything else in it (which includes you) is designed for expansion and growth. If it were not so–and since Source had *billions* of years to get something wrong–don't you think that Source would have made a bunch of mistakes by now, and life as we know it would've gone down the tubes at some point in time? Which of course it hasn't. And here we still are.

Life is absolutely designed for you to win. If you are experiencing anything other than success, it is because you are living in ignorance. But when you know with absolute certainty that what you have working for you is intelligent, creative, and powerful energy–that only ever wants what is best for you–then this understanding alone is enough of a good reason for you to be happy, wherever you may be right now. Knowing that everything is always working out for you–even if at present the entire world around you seems to be falling apart–allows you to stay poised, and emotionally unreactive in the midst of all the chaos and uncertainty. For you understand that the only reason why your current circumstances seem bleak, is that more often than not your physical senses deceive you. You understand that your physical sensory factors–with which you almost exclusively navigate your world–are your lowest mental tools. Tools which are incapable of recognising the immense power, the complexity, and all the processes of this unseen force which permeates your physical world, as well as every aspect of your personal life.

"Wherever you go, there you are."

Happiness is not "out there" somewhere; it is inside of you. It doesn't matter where you go, what you do, and what you have, because you bring yourself (your attitude, beliefs, and perspectives) into every situation anyway. Naturally, happiness is always with you, and wherever you go you either bring it with you, or you leave it at home. For example, if you're generally a positive person and you decide to go on a holiday, you might end up in a cheap hotel with a shabby little bar, and a constantly overcrowded swimming pool. Yet still absolutely enjoy your holiday experience. Because *you* bring joy, happiness, and "the good times" along with you. You are not passively waiting for someone/something outside of yourself to come along and rescue you from boredom; to entertain you, and make you feel good. In other words, you are not expecting the outside world to adapt to you, and revolve around you because you are a special snowflake. Instead, wherever you go, happiness and positivity comes with. Which, in turn ensures that regardless of what you do and where you go, you are still going to have a good time. Conversely, people who are generally negative–who have a difficult time being appreciative, and forgiving–could be travelling to a much better holiday destination, and settle into an amazing, beautiful suite in a five-star hotel, with a magnificent view, luxurious food, be surrounded by good-humoured and pleasant individuals, and still manage to have a miserable time. Maybe because the flight was delayed, and they had to wait an additional two hours at the airport. Or maybe the taxi driver was having a bad day, and without meaning to, came across a bit rude. Maybe they overslept and missed breakfast which was included in the holiday package. Maybe the TV in the hotel room wasn't working properly at that particular time, and they felt bored. Maybe the air conditioner unit in the suite was malfunctioning, and they had trouble sleeping.

The possibilities are endless. Though whatever the case may be, by having a negatively-oriented focus (RAS), at the end of the visit their conclusion is: "This holiday sucks!" In effect, what could have otherwise (easily) been a an amazing holiday experience, wound up being a nightmare, with a typical statement: "I'll never come back here again for as long as I live!" Of course, it has absolutely nothing to do with anyone, or anything outside of their own state of mind, and *meanings*. By embodying negative, dense, judgemental energy wherever they go; by lacking in appreciation; by having a negative perspective, and interpreting things in a pessimistic way; and by focusing on all of the injustices, and every little detail that is going wrong, the holiday experience invariably becomes tainted by their own negativity. And unhappiness therefore is self-imposed.

> *"There is nothing either good or bad but thinking makes it so."*
> – William Shakespeare

The mainstream narrative which we are constantly being incentivised to follow is also a huge handicap when it comes to happiness, as it leads us to believe that when we finish our studies and get our degrees, then happiness is guaranteed. Or when we secure a good job; a partner in marriage; a home in which we can comfortably raise a family, then happiness is guaranteed. The mainstream narrative is the reason why we believe in the notion of "happiness somewhere in the distant future." We become conditioned to think that once we finish school we will be happy; once we get a job we will be happy; once we get into a relationship we will be happy; once we get the house we will be happy. But in actual practice, is that the case for most people? Hardly so. Because if we view happiness as a destination, it becomes a never-ending cycle. For once a person reaches a goal, or arrives at a new destination, new desires, along with new sets of problems inevitably arise from that point on. The reason for this is simple. All of the aforementioned "things" are created, and are achieved for growth reasons; not happiness. Happiness has nothing to do with any of it. And if it so happens that we realise it doesn't work, social conditioning then doubles down on this notion by encouraging us to derive happiness from external stimuli. (Oh, you finished your studies, found a girlfriend and bought a new home, and you still aren't happy? Well what you need to do now is titillate your senses.) In effect, instead of looking inward to find happiness and joy (where it *actually* is), we are incentivised by the society in which we live to hopelessly *chase phantoms* (Owen Cook's terminology).

This typically looks like the following: You have finished your studies; you've bought the house; you've secured the job; and you've locked down the wife. But sooner or later you realise that you don't actually feel any happier (even though you had been promised you would). So what you do from there is buy tickets to go and watch a sporting event, or a new movie (external stimuli) with your friends in order to get a little taste of happiness. Sure, you'll probably have a very good time watching the event, or the movie. But as soon as it's over, it will be only a matter of time until you are back to your usual emotional state (which, at this point is probably boredom and apathy). Because you have stopped striving–and therefore growing–from a belief that you've already arrived where happiness is. This then becomes a vicious cycle of sorts where you are forever "chasing phantoms" by trying to get happier through external stimulation and material possessions. At this point you have to get creative, and proactively pull yourself out of apathy by training your mind to be more positive. You can most certainly boost your happiness baseline (or set point) by meditating regularly; setting new goals and having something to look forward to; watching less television (news in particular); travelling more, and exercising. Raising one's happiness set point is not exactly easy in a world full of stimulation that is constantly vying for our attention, and distracting us with flashy and compelling images. But to drastically increase your chances of success at being happy, you have to learn to generate good emotions from within, and motivate yourself.

Do not make the mistake of waiting around for someone/something to come along and save you. I can assure you no one, and no "thing" is coming. You must take matters into your own hands and evade boredom and apathy by deliberately doing things in your everyday life–which you do regularly–differently. You see, sometimes the reason why we aren't experiencing much happiness in life is that our routine has become bland and repetitive. And to raise our happiness set point, we have to interrupt our monotonous routine every single chance we get. For example, what you could do from this point on, is rather than going to the same restaurant every time you decide to have dinner–because it is familiar to you, and you have gotten to know the staff–try a different place once in a while. Rather than using the same route to and from your place of work, take a detour sometimes. Rather than travelling to the exact same destination with your family for a weekend getaway, try a totally different place. Rather than having your car serviced by someone else, wash it yourself. The opportunities for disrupting your routine and broadening your mind are endless. The point is you have to proactively seek changes and expose yourself to new information and stimulus, in order to re-engage your brain with the world around you, and continue to *live*!

Understand that when you are going through the motions of your daily routine, doing things unconsciously–on autopilot–you are not living; you are merely *existing*. And what has to be done in order to dismantle your current conditioning, which says: "I'll be happy when…" is to rewire your brain to feel good now! Realise that every time we think to ourselves how we will be happy "when," what we are actually doing is building synaptic pathways in our brain that lead us to believe we will be happy as soon as we achieve this or that. However, because those are the type of pathways we've built, what happens is once we *do* achieve this or that, we still think we need more. For the simple fact that those pathways are built on the notions of "future" and "when," which means that we'll never be happy "now." To get around this, we have to build new synaptic pathways by reconditioning ourselves to feel good now, by way of jumping on every opportunity to disrupt our old habit patterns, and also by other means previously discussed. And as we continue to do so our old beliefs and ideas about happiness will eventually disappear, while new synaptic pathways (of feeling good now no matter what) will become dominant.

"It's not what we get in life that makes us happy; it's the people we become that makes us happy."

In light of everything what had been said so far, the last thing I'd want for you is to confuse happiness with feeling positive emotions all of the time, or acting flamboyant, and smiling from ear to ear–making sure that the whole world knows how great your life is. That is not what happiness is. Well, it is, and it isn't. Here is what I mean by this. Happiness means different things to everyone. You will never be able to point at someone and accurately predict their level of happiness. You will never be able to say–and be right–that that person is not happy because she is not expressing herself in a particular way, or because he never smiles. For example, I myself mostly express my happiness purely through my eyes. I may not seem like the happiest person in the world in most settings, when I actually 100 percent damn well feel like I am. But, that is how I express happiness–relaxed, yet totally awake; expressionless and still, yet completely curious and interested–whereas someone else's way of happiness may mean for them to be animated, loud and obnoxious.

That said, do not attempt to replicate or copy anyone else's way of happiness. Stay in your own emotional lane, and align with what feels authentic to you. Instead of looking around–trying to pinpoint what makes other people happy–discover what happiness personally means to you. For instance, I feel the happiest when I am fully present to the moment; when I'm engaged in a fascinating, thought-provoking conversation; when I am completely focused on a task; or when I'm moving towards a certain goal that I have. Personally, I find happiness in presence and engagement. Whereas other people find happiness in peace and relaxation. Some people feel the happiest when they are working with a client, or helping other people. Others feel the happiest when they are alone, and in complete silence. Yet others are the happiest when they are surrounded by friends–partying together in a loud, chaotic environment. It is different for everybody. In a sense, if you are not a very charismatic, expressive, or energetic individual, you are still entitled to happiness. For when you feel happy, it shines through everything that you do, and everything that you are. And even though on paper you may not fit the description of a happy individual, in practice you will still be considered to be one. Because the expression of happiness does not have to be flashy, animated, or over-the-top enthusiastic. Even though the vibration of happiness is on the highest frequency possible, it does not necessarily follow that it can only be expressed–and also perceived–as such. A great example that perfectly illustrates this point is the spinning wheel of a fast-moving car. Since the wheel is moving so fast, it actually seems to be motionless. And if we relate this to the expression of happiness, then the fact that the vibration of happiness is so high (in other words, fast), means that it can also be expressed and perceived as practically being at rest. And so, do not confuse the high vibrational nature of happiness (and your connection to Source) for being frantic, boastful, or out of control; for in reality it is calm, collected, and contented.

There are too many of us who shoot ourself in the foot by assuming that happiness looks a certain way, or requires certain things. What I would recommend you do is if today you are genuinely happy with yourself, and your life in general–regardless of what it might look like to those on the outside–you accept it fully and you say: "Yep, this is who I am and this is what I do. I think it's awesome and I absolutely love it!" Conversely, if you are not happy with yourself, and where your life has brought you, then accept *that* and say: "You know what, I totally suck right now. But that's ok. I'm working on it." In other words, do not try to resist your current situation, hide it, or push against it. If you are happy with your life, then be honest with yourself and others without any regard for how they may perceive you. But if you are not happy with your life, or any one–or more–particular aspect of it, then simply acknowledge that things could be better, come up with a plan as to how you are going to make it better, and then start moving towards your new ideal. As long as you are moving towards your ideal you are already winning, and you are a success. Which means that you are allowed to borrow your happiness from the "future, successful you," and live it today. You do not have to postpone your happiness until you eventually get to where you want to be. You have permission to start enjoying your happiness now, for that is where you are ultimately going to end up. So why wait?

"Whoever is happy will make others happy." – Anne Frank

Unhappiness comes from too much self-involvement, and is in a sense selfish. (What about *me*? What do *I* get? *I* am missing something. *I* need help. *I* don't have what *I* want. *My* problems. *My* deficiencies.) The happiest people on the planet have made it a point to quit looking–in every situation and interaction–for what's in it for *them*, i.e. looking to fulfil their own wants and needs. They understand that to focus exclusively on themselves, is to forfeit (for the time being) their happiness. And what we can learn from these individuals (if we wish to be like them), is that we need to forget about ourselves from time to time, and start thinking about other people. We have to be willing to put our wants and needs to the side, and find out what it is that other people want. However, in order to have any spare mental bandwidth to care for other people, we first have to declutter our mind so that we are no longer bogged down by our own personal problems. Of course there will always be problems in one form or another that require our attention, there is no question about that. But there are only three main areas that–when they are managed properly, and maintained–contribute massively and almost exclusively to our overall satisfaction and fulfilment in life. They are our close relationships; our finances; and our calling or purpose in life.

Close relationships are especially important to us. Having a good social circle means to have a safe haven where each member is free to be their full "wacko," authentic selves, without the slightest fear of being judged. Sharing and laughing with our friends and family naturally relieves us of stress and anxiety, and puts us at ease. It provides us with comfort, and a sense of oneness. Most importantly, our strong relationships become a safe house of sorts which we can always run to for help, reassurance, and support in difficult times; and encouragement, praise, and celebrations in good times. It is no secret that we're social creatures. Socialising and bonding, forming social connections and having good friends, naturally makes us happier. When we don't have friends, or a good social circle, this can have negative effects on our mental, and even physical health. Therefore, a good social circle–a support group of like-minded individuals–is definitely something that everyone should strive towards forming, or joining. For taking risks, facing challenges, trying new things, and going after the things we want in life becomes much easier when we know that we have good people in our life who will always support us, and have our back no matter what. This does not mean however that we are incapable of living a good, happy, and fulfilling life all by ourselves. We certainly are capable. Though be that as it may, having a good social circle does make our life a hell of a lot easier. And because it is easier to handle, it is in turn much easier to enjoy. As a good example, you can think about a flock of geese when they fly long distances in the "V" formation. The reason why they do this, is that it not only helps the group to communicate and coordinate better, but it also reduces energy expenditure. Thanks to the bird in front, the bird behind it–by hovering slightly above–conserves energy, as it gets a free lift off of the back of its friend (and it glides). Which results in not having to push against the resistance of the wind as much as it usually would chugging along by itself. By working together, and frequently shifting positions to prevent draining each other out, each bird in the group benefits, and enjoys a much smoother ride. Similarly, investing in your relationships with other people is always going to be a smart decision. And just like in the case of a flock of birds–with the power of your social group–your life journey will become undeniably smoother.

The influence which money (sense of security) has on our being happy is rather obvious. If we do not have enough to fulfil our *own* needs and solve our *own* problems, we cannot expect to have any mental bandwidth left over to care for the needs of others. For when there are certain places you wish to visit; certain communities you wish to join; certain ventures you wish to partake in; certain opportunities you wish to take–but are not able to afford–you cannot help but think about all of those things, without having your mind be focused exclusively on how you could resolve your money issue. Which, by default makes you less interested in what other people want. When you are going through difficult and uncertain times yourself, what happens is rather than genuinely listening to another person's problems, complaints, and frustrations–with the intent of helping them–instead, it makes you think: "Does this person ever shut up?! I've got enough problems of my own." Obviously money is not *everything* (far from it). But money is still very much important, at least at our current stage of social evolution. Not only is it necessary to be able to provide for our own basic needs, it also helps us to achieve our goals, support our family, get a good education, help those in desperate need, travel the world and have adventures without having to *deny* ourselves anything that piques our interest along the way.

Getting your finances in order shouldn't feel like an intimidating or impossible task, for it is not about becoming the next Warren Buffett. You don't even have to become a millionaire to be considered financially independent. You only need to know how much is enough for *you*, and then begin to work towards finding ways of serving enough people who'll compensate you for your efforts, products, or services–enough that you may live comfortably. If you haven't a clue as to exactly what you could possibly bring to the table, or where to even begin, you have to seek out professional advice. There are plenty of experts out there–with a solid acumen for earning money–who will gladly help you and guide you every step along the way to reaching your financial goals (for a reasonable fee). We truly live in an information-rich age. These days you don't have to try and figure it all out by yourself. There is no longer an excuse not to invest in yourself (your personal development and education) by hiring a coach. If money is one of the areas that you're struggling with, I'd encourage you to make it a priority and get some professional help.

The third and final aspect–which, to great extent lessens self-concern–is having a strong sense of purpose (which we have already covered extensively in chapter 2). When we know where we are going in life, as well as what it is we want, it naturally makes us feel more confident, and happy. Even if we haven't yet achieved our desired goals or mission in life, but are moving towards it–no matter how incrementally so–we still feel confident enough, and optimistic enough that we are not focused upon ourselves so much anymore, and we have more than enough mental bandwidth available to think about other people. Conversely, when we do not have some kind of a purpose in life–when we do not know where we are going, and what we're supposed to be doing with our life–then we are not in the position to be genuinely happy for someone else's success. For, that gnawing sense of "no direction" bleeds into everything that we are, and everything that we do. In other words, if we feel like a failure in certain areas of our life, then seeing somebody else's success and happiness only rubs it in our face and reminds us of our own ineptitude, and incompetence. In such circumstance, what most of us usually do–though not always–is we try to think of ways of undermining their success; rather than support and celebrate with them. It goes without saying that lack of purpose makes your life meaningless. It makes you feel hollow, dissatisfied, and bored at best. Not having a clear sense of direction in life is unconducive to you becoming a person of immense value, virtue, and principle. As a result, it puts you into a "coping" state of mind where your dominant tendency is to take, to snatch away, and to get yours; unlike a "thriving" state of mind (which can come from having a strong sense of purpose in life), where "your cup runneth over," and all you want to do is share and give.

All in all, when our relationships, our finances, and our calling, or purpose in life have been taken care of, we feel happy, and satisfied enough that we naturally think less about ourselves, and we become more interested in helping other people thrive. That said though, if we happen to be in a dreadful situation ourself, and we are in need of help just as much as the next person (in any one of those areas), it does not follow that we are unable to be of great value–help/service–to others. In fact, even though to redirect our focus away from our own problems onto other people (when we ourself are struggling) may seem counterintuitive, it is actually the perfect time to do so. And here is why. If you aren't feeling good about yourself, or your situation, and you decide to donate to charity as an example, or spontaneously help out a random person on the street, you will actually feel good in return. Proactively shifting your focus away from yourself onto others–strangely–creates the same effect as having your life handled. In that, it naturally makes you forget about your own problems, shortcomings, and insecurities (at least for the time being). By helping other people solve their problems makes you realise that you're not as useless as you may have thought, and it gives you the confidence to tackle your own challenges. Furthermore, by seeing other people in much worse situations, typically makes you feel grateful and appreciative for your own. And as a consequence, your energy begins to rise, so much so, that–without even anticipating it–your own situation begins to improve.

"The way you view this world and everything in it is a reflection of your own mental attitude toward yourself."

Let us now look at the importance of forgiveness, and non-attachment. Previously we have learnt that happiness is about presence and acceptance, and now to take it a step further, we have to understand that acceptance embodies the principle of non-attachment, i.e. freedom from trying to control something which is not in our power to control. I believe we can all agree that–no matter who we are, where we are, or what we do–we feel happier when we are free. Life becomes undeniably easier to appreciate, and accept for what it is when we are free financially; free to travel and move about at will; free to choose and make decisions; to think freely and express our opinion without constraint, etc. These forms of freedom–which have virtually been taken care of (for the most part) all around the world–are difficult to overlook. For they are so tangible, and so easily recognisable. However, what is not so obvious– that which has not been taken care of, and has been completely overlooked– is our freedom from attachments. Which is an extremely important principle to abide by if we are to enjoy a long, happy, and joyful life.

A great example that perfectly illustrates the dire consequences of having an attachment to something is the character Sméagol from "The Lord of the Rings" series. As you may already know, Sméagol became so attached to "One Ring" that it began to corrupt him, and even alter his appearance to an extent that he was no longer recognisable. In due course, he became a whole different person–a Gollum. Effectively depicting (although admittedly, in an overexaggerated manner) how detrimental, and unhealthy an attachment (or addiction) to something can become. Sméagol's predicament is an excellent reminder that we have to be careful not to give in to our craving (our ego's desire) for having attachments to things–especially attaching our happiness to things–in order to experience true freedom. That said though, I would not want you to misinterpret non-attachment for not caring at all, or completely losing interest in someone/something. That way you will only find yourself at the other end of the spectrum–apathy and indifference. That's not the goal here. Rather, the goal is to strive for higher places, and to have different jobs; relationships; friends; material possessions; interests; pursuits, etc., and fully enjoy them. But without becoming emotionally attached to them. In order to avoid getting hurt by them. This can be accomplished by developing a higher level of awareness and acceptance of the fact that none of the things which you have in your life (people; circumstances; conditions; possessions, and so on) are guaranteed to stay as they are indefinitely. Of course they might stay for a while, but ultimately none of it is permanent. For life is always moving; it is forever in motion. And if you aren't willing to move along with it, you'll get brushed to the side (and sometimes not so gently) as "life" makes its way through on the chariot of "change."

"The only constant in life is change." – Heraclitus

To know genuine freedom means to give freedom to everything else around us (freedom to move on or change). In other words, we have to be okay with the fact that the time will assuredly come when a person, or "thing" that we love would have to leave us behind, and stop living up to our expectations. Because change is not going to take place only when we think it should (or shouldn't). Change is inevitable for everyone and everything; it is an integral part of life–just like breathing air–for the continuation of life. And if someone/something has to leave from our life in order to produce the necessary change (for our own good, or for the good of others), we have to be willing to accept that. Understandably, change can sometimes be unpleasant in such circumstances where we are utterly in love with someone/something, just to one day discover it is about to be gone forever, and that things will never be the same again. Nevertheless, change is a wonderful thing. For when we feel down; when things aren't going our way; when we are stuck in a rut; when we hate our job; when our family life is in shambles–change is what gives us hope. We may totally dislike wherever we may be in our life, in any particular period, but we nonetheless carry on, we keep our head high, and we continue to plough through it. Because we know that our present results are not final, due to this natural principle of change. And rather than getting bogged down by the negative circumstances and conditions we sometimes find ourselves in–rather than becoming upset for where our life has brought us, and resigning to our fate–we instead envision a better future, and we take action towards our new ideal. Because "change" is what provides us with the possibility of that future. In effect, when our life is not going according to plan, we're never doomed, and subconsciously we *know* this. Because even though change can sometimes be harsh and abrupt when things are going extremely well; it is also very forgiving when everything seems to be going tits up.

Unfortunately, some people will sometimes find themself so depressed that they no longer have faith in "change." That they're no longer able to envision a better future and pull themselves out of that dark pit of despair. The reason for this is that depression is all about contraction, suppression, non-acceptance, and non-forgiveness. It is everything that our higher-self is not–expansion; creation; expression. Depression is on such a low frequency that it can be likened to a haze, spell, or a fog, out of which we cannot see clearly, and think productively. In order to get over this, one first has to realise that there are a ton of legitimate reasons to keep moving forward, and then proceed to get out of that depressed state *one incremental step at a time*. However, when it comes to healing ourselves and working towards leaving depression behind, most of us fail miserably. Because what most people do, is they look at how (apparently) happy and care-free everybody else is, and rather than it becoming a motivating factor (as one would think it would) to want to be in the same emotional space even more so, instead it backfires and makes them feel even more depressed. For the emotional standpoint which they are coming, and perceiving from–at that point–is so far away from what most other, "regular" people are experiencing, that they can no longer easily express, or personify those emotional states. And every time they attempt to embody, or imitate that emotional state of happiness they invariably fail. And every failure only amplifies their feelings of discontent, and it further feeds into their mental stories and "meanings" about how they are unworthy, weak, incompetent, and ultimately powerless. But this is exactly what happens when we go about making ourselves feel better in this way (using other people's emotions as a gauge for what is considered "normal," and then beating ourselves up for not being as "normal" as everyone else).

Now, if you are someone who is suffering from depression, I need you to understand that you will never be able to jump from depression, or despair all the way up to happiness, or even hope for that matter. It is simply too big of a vibrational/emotional jump for you to make at that point. What you have to be doing instead is incrementally–and steadily–moving yourself up the "emotional scale" (see image overleaf) by allowing yourself to experience every emotion necessary along the way, until you eventually bridge the gap between where you are and where you want to be (emotionally).

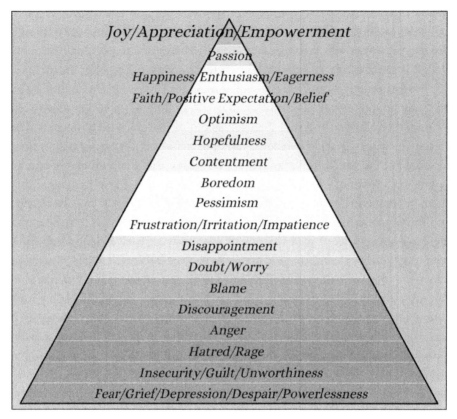

The Emotional Scale. (Abraham Hicks' concept.)

As you can see, the vibrational/emotional gap between depression and hope (let alone happiness or joy) is quite significant. If you are stuck in depression or despair, then any other emotion will almost certainly feel better than what you are feeling right now. Considering that depression comes from suppression of emotion–usually anger–means that you have a free pass to get angry, and vent your heart out, in order to steadily climb up this emotional ladder. Whatever it is you are depressed about, you need to think of that very thing, or person and become enraged–get angry about it! Smash a few plates if you have to. Bring out your hateful feelings to the surface and write your frustrations out on a piece of paper a thousand times until there is no more rage left inside of you. You need to get those suppressed emotions out of your system intelligently, without endangering yourself and others in the process.

It might seem illogical to promote anger and deliberately allow yourself to become enraged when you are trying to get *better*. But the fact that depression rests at the lowest end of the emotional scale, anger becomes a lot more powerful, and it feels much better. (Though if you feel happy, optimistic, or even frustrated, then anger would be a step backwards in the opposite direction.) For whereas depression evokes feelings of powerlessness–it makes the person feel as though they don't have any control over their life–anger gives the person back some of that control (albeit not a lot of it. But just enough to regain their consciousness, and begin to feel their power again). However, it is not at all recommended to call it quits here, and then go about your life as an angry person. (I know a few people who have done exactly that, and I can assure you, it isn't a pretty sight. It's extremely painful to watch, and nobody likes to be around an angry person.) And so, from anger, the next best step in the right direction may be disappointment, or frustration. As you fully experience your feelings of disappointment, or frustration–with respect to whatever it is you feel injustice about–by openly venting it all out (preferably to a non-judgemental person who's willing to listen: usually a therapist), you can eventually make your way up to hopefulness, positive expectation, and even enthusiasm. Then, from that high-vibrational/emotional standpoint you become poised enough to experience happiness. And if you continue to rise in levels of vibration and conscious awareness you will invariably find yourself becoming more joyful, appreciative, and more empowered.

As you can imagine, this is not an impossible task. Although it may not be easy–anyone can do this if they go about it the intelligent way. And the previous illustration will serve you wonderfully, for it provides you with an understanding of which emotion feels better from where you presently are. It gives you an accurate indication as to how far away from that powerful vibrational/emotional state of joy and appreciation (which I assume is what you are shooting for) you *actually* are. Now, on the surface, it might seem as though there are endless causes for what makes people depressed, but there is only one true, primary cause of depression; it is *ignorance*. Whereas the polar opposite of ignorance is *knowledge*. Thus, if you are to rid yourself of depression for good, climbing the emotional ladder when you feel depressed is not going to fix the issue, for the cause (ignorance) might still remain. What you need to do is develop a greater awareness and understanding–in effect–eliminate ignorance, so that you never become depressed in the first place.

For example, if you are depressed because you feel lonely, understand that the reason why you might feel that way is because on a deeper level you are not aware of the fact that we're all connected; that we're all one; and that we can never be alone. While on the surface level you may not know what it means to be an interesting and (energetically) attractive person, whom other people enjoy being around. If you are depressed because the love of your life had left you, and they're never coming back, understand that the reason why you are depressed is because you don't believe that there is an abundance of potential partners out there in the world, with whom you could have a similar–and even stronger–connection. If you are depressed because you had lost somebody close to you, understand that the reason why you are depressed is because you are not aware that there is no such thing as death; that we are eternal beings; and that transitioning from this physical world back to where we came from is an integral part of life. It is completely natural and, in fact beautiful (I am certain that you wouldn't want to be stuck here for all of the eternity with your "idiot" brother, or your "annoying" sister). If you are depressed because somebody mistreated you and made you feel a certain way, understand that the reason why you are depressed is because on the surface level you have become reactive, and you allowed them to control your emotions. While on a deeper level you might not be aware that you are the only one who is in control of the "meanings" which you place on different things that happen in your life. And that, ultimately no one can make you feel a certain way without your consent. If you are depressed because your thoughts are running wild, to such a degree that it is now virtually impossible for you to reach for a single, good-feeling thought, understand that the reason why your brain is "broken" is because you are not aware of the fact that the food which you are consuming on a regular basis is full of harmful chemicals that bring about imbalances in your brain and body. Or it could also be the result of a lack of exercise, good quality sleep, right vitamins, and relaxation (all of which is still caused by ignorance). And so on and so forth.

Conventional medicine doesn't work for most people who are suffering from depression because they are being prescribed a bunch of pills which do nothing but alleviate the symptoms for a short while–without ever treating the actual *cause*–until they invariably have to come back to the doctor's office time and again with the exact same problem. Don't get me wrong though, all forms of healing have their place. However, getting to the root cause of one's health problem and treating the *whole* person is something that conventional medicine is not able (or dare I even say–designed) to do. For the root cause of depression is not anxiety, it is not fear, and it is not worrisome thoughts; it is *ignorance*–which precedes everything else–the cure for which is *knowledge*.

To someone who had never been exposed to such an idea before, it may seem ridiculous to suggest that depression comes from "not knowing." But the fact is, physical body is the manifestation of the mind. Whatever is going on inside a person's mind will ultimately be expressed in the physical body. Look, when an ignorant person (I don't mean that in a contemptuous or disrespectful way) observes or experiences a particular situation, condition, or event which they don't fully understand, that person will interpret the event in a negative way, and they'll begin to either worry or doubt themself. When that negative energy of worry or doubt is passed over to the emotional part of their personality (the subconscious) it turns into an emotion that we know as fear. That fearful energy then has to be expressed through the only medium which it can be expressed–the physical body–and so it manifests on the physical level as anxiety. Since humans are not usually skilled or comfortable with openly expressing their anxious feelings, what they typically do is they suppress them, and the suppression of that negative energy for a prolonged period of time eventually leads to depression. Conversely, if a knowledgeable person (one who has developed a greater awareness) were to observe or experience the exact same situation, circumstance, or event, that person naturally would interpret the situation in a way that wouldn't negatively affect their nervous system. For knowledge leads to understanding (polar opposite of doubt and worry). Understanding leads to an emotional state called faith, or positive expectation. And faith in turn manifests on the physical as perfect health and well-being. Moreover, well-being, unlike its polar opposite (anxiety) can be easily expressed, and it usually is. Since there is no resistance, the energy is able to move freely through the nervous system, which makes the person feel completely at ease. (Bob Proctor's concept.)

This is one of the reasons why self-mastery is so vitally important. For when you do not have control over your own thoughts–and therefore emotions–it is relatively easy for you to get tricked by negative interpretations of reality into a negative vibration, and then into a full-blown depression. But, that is all what negativity is: a trick. Because in the heat of the moment, negative energy always seems to be very real, and is usually justified. But when you come out of it (if you are one of the fortunate ones), you inevitably look back at your actions and you think to yourself: "Damn it, I can't believe I did that!" or "I can't believe I said that! What was I thinking?!" And the truth is, you were not thinking. It wasn't you. The negative energy that was running you was in control of *you*. In effect, when you are in a negative vibration you are not being yourself. Whatever you say, or do from that vibrational standpoint is never aligned with your true character, and personal values. (That's why you sometimes hear people say: "I never knew she had that in her.")

Consider the following incident which took place not long after I began my journey to self-mastery, at the age of twenty-three. Since I was in the beginning stages of my journey, I was still susceptible to low-vibrational energies, so much so that at one point I almost killed myself. In a way, I'm grateful for what happened. For the incident taught me a valuable lesson–to stop attaching my sense of identity, and self-worth to what other people thought of me. The reason I can say I'm glad for what had happened is because I was alone. Nobody else but me was involved in the accident who could have got seriously hurt, and I came out of it with only a few minor scratches, but with an invaluable life lesson. In hindsight, it seems as though the Universe had orchestrated the entire thing specifically to teach me a lesson, which I wasn't able, or willing to learn by myself. Even though–intellectually–I knew about the lesson for quite some time, but evidently had not internalised it. To spare you the boring details, this is what happened: In June, in the summer of 2016 I was driving to work on a completely empty dual-carriage way feeling frustrated and annoyed at the way my life was going at the time. In the midst of thinking about what was bothering me I felt the strongest urge to start pushing on the gas pedal as hard as I could (whether it was to physically express, and release the negative energy which was bottled up inside, or to go faster than my own thoughts in an attempt to outrun them), to a point where I was now going 120 mph. As I came around a bend, I found myself on the edge of the road–awfully close to a metal barrier which separated the oncoming traffic. Immediately, I tried to correct myself by turning away from the barrier, but the back wheels began to pull in the opposite direction (towards the barrier). So now, while trying to correct *that*, the back of the car almost instantly swung around 180 degrees and started flipping sideways across the road. (If you can imagine, I was going 120 mph facing the road. Then, all of a sudden, I was going 120 mph perpendicular to the road–with the passenger side door facing the road ahead–and at that moment, the car started flipping sideways at 120 mph.) I genuinely thought that that was going to be it for me.

I had no idea what was happening while I was getting smashed around in the driver's seat. Though the group of bystanders (who saw the whole ordeal unfold) had told me that I flipped the car–more or less–ten times in total, and that I crashed through a metal barrier while flipping myself onto the oncoming traffic (luckily there were no cars coming towards me at that precise moment in time). By the end of it, the car was an absolute wreck and fortunately, I was fine, with only a few scratches and pieces of glass stuck in my arms. I remember being dizzy as all hell and at the same time extremely alert and awake while getting out of the car (from the mixture of having my brain bounce around in my skull, along with a ton of adrenaline surging through my veins). And those who saw what happened just could not believe how I was still conscious; let alone how I was able to step out of the car, as if nothing had happened. When I realised that I was going to crash, and that there was nothing I could even do about it–since I was going way too fast, and the car was out of control–I just quickly followed my instinct and completely let go of the steering wheel, and curled myself into a ball. It is a good thing I did exactly that, because the metal barrier which I managed to crash myself into had such an impact that it dented the metal frame of the windshield (on the driver's side) deep enough that it would have reached the head of the driver, if one were to be there (and of course my head was practically on the floor). I was extremely lucky because–statistically speaking–the chances of me walking away from such an accident without some kind of an injury were slim to none. Yet there I was, completely fine.

When the ambulance arrived and paramedics saw me standing next to a demolished vehicle, they wasted no time strapping me down onto a stretcher, and immediately rushing me to the hospital. They explained that the reason for such urgency was that they presumed I almost certainly had internal bleeding. But after carrying out some checks, pulling out pieces of glass from my skin, and patching me up, every person there was shocked as to how after all that happened I was still in good enough condition that I was eligible to leave the hospital, and just continue with my day. And that's' what I did. I signed some papers and I left. I walked all the way back home on that beautiful afternoon with fireworks going off in my head (soaking up the epiphany), enjoying the sunlight hitting my face, grateful to live another day.

I typically relay this incident as a cautionary tale to others, for it so perfectly (and gruesomely) illustrates the dangers of allowing oneself to become overrun by suppressed negative energy. Negative energy doesn't care about its consequences, and if you aren't careful enough, it'll make you believe that whatever it is that caused you to feel "bad," actually matters–that it deserves your undivided attention, and serious thought. However, what I quickly realised as I began to spiral out of control at 120 mph–getting smashed around like a helpless ragdoll, without a clue as to what was going to happen every millisecond that went by–is the fact that that which was upsetting me–which I thought was extremely important at the time–was at the bottom of the list of things that mattered. In fact, come to think of it, it wasn't on the list at all.

In effect, I got tricked. When I realised that at any moment my life could take a turn for the worse, all that was going through my mind (that which was *actually* important), were all of the things I wanted to become, and share with the world. The dreams; the goals; the challenges; the projects; and plans that I was still working on. And all I wanted to do was to get out of it alive and to prioritise all of those things all over again. Essentially, my attachment, or my need to receive other people's approval became a distraction (a disease), that made me forget to be grateful for the life which I was already living. Until I realised that what I had to do was *forgive*. After the aforementioned incident, forgiveness was the very lesson I had no choice but to learn, and internalise. And today, I understand full well that in order to completely free ourselves from attachments–whether it means to be attached to something positive or negative–we have to be able–and willing–to forgive the past, and *live our life every single day as though we have been born anew.*

Forgiveness is about letting go; it is about leaving behind any emotional attachments, or negative connotations to something. It means to accept that "something" for what it is–neither good nor bad–and to detach our sense of identity or self-worth from it. It truly doesn't matter what other people think of us; it truly doesn't matter if the people we love would just get up one day and decide to leave from our lives forever; it truly does not matter if we lose everything! (Although we may still become upset, which is completely natural. But ultimately, we have to accept it, and continue to move forward.) The fact is, life *is* about change; life *is* about moving forward. Yesterday's experiences are in the past; there is absolutely nothing we can do about them now. All we can do–which is of any real value to ourself, and others–is to focus on the "here and now." Non-attachment is a perfect remedy for most of our suffering, and most what ails us (attachments to negative/positive experiences; people; ideas; circumstances; and conditions). That is, when we are free from attachments and we happen to find ourself feeling down as a result of a negative/unpleasant experience (be it an interaction, circumstance, condition, or event), we are better equipped to quickly turn our state around. Because we know that negative experiences do not define us; nor do they determine who we are destined to become in the future. Likewise, when we are free from attachments, and we happen to feel phenomenal as a result of a positive experience, we can appreciate it and enjoy every moment of it for as long as it can last, without clasping it and wanting it to stay with us "forever." For we understand that change is inevitable; change is good; change is healthy for our soul; change is what creates space for new experiences to come into our life.

And there is no such thing as a bad experience either; every experience is valuable. Every seemingly "bad" experience has something good in it, and when that "something" is acknowledged–and internalised–it moulds us into a better version of ourself. For example, what happened to me in the afore-mentioned incident was no accident (at least that's what I chose to believe). Universe truly works in mysterious ways in helping us to be, do, and have everything that we desire. The problem is most of us do not understand that everything happens *for* us; rather than *to* us. And that is why if another person were to find themself in my shoes, the incident would have been inter-preted as nothing more than an unfortunate accident–with nothing to learn, and nothing to gain. Whereas I were able to immediately derive a powerful, life-changing lesson from it, and come out of it a much better person.

As we are coming to an end–in order to avoid confusion and misunder-standing–I just want to make a few things clear. Although it is true that hap-piness comes from within ourselves, we nonetheless can't avoid the fact that right now, in this lifetime, we are physical beings, living in a physical world. And our most innate, deepest desire is to become all that we are capable of becoming, and achieve all that we are capable of achieving. As such, seques-tering ourselves in a forest, a temple, or a cave, and meditating all day long is just another way of avoiding the outside world (and missing out on all of the lessons which we need to learn in order to grow), in an attempt to avoid our happy state ever being challenged. That is all well and good, and there is nothing wrong with that *per se*. However, I wouldn't recommend it. Not un-til we still have desire within us, and fire in our belly. We did not come here with one and only goal, or intention of feeling good, and being happy all the time. If that was truly our sole intent, then we would not even come here in the first place. The Source-Energy part of ourself is absolutely happy where it already is; it already has everything it needs. Which follows that if we had made the decision to leave behind our happy, comfortable home to come in-to this complex, sometimes chaotic physical world, surely we knew that a lit-tle bit of suffering and dissatisfaction had some kind of a useful function.

In effect, happiness is overrated. A little bit of unhappiness, or dissatis-faction goes a long way. Because it forces us to find better ways of doing an-ything. It helps us to recognise that we could be, do, or have something *more*. Dissatisfaction is actually a creative state (albeit un unpleasant one), and the quality of our lives become better as a result of our discontent–when utilised properly. For if people were forever happy and satisfied with what they had, then today, if you were to decide to go on a trip with your family to another country as an example, you would have to sail across the sea on a little rickety raft. And by the time you would get to your destination only half of your family would have made it there alive. In other words, if humans were forever satisfied with where they were, then there would be absolutely no need for them to create; to think of something different–something better. I believe it was dissatisfaction that gave us the horseless carriage (automobile). It was dissatisfaction that gave us the incandescent light. It was dissatisfaction that gave us air travel. And it was–for the most part–dissatisfaction that brought us to the state of the world in which we now live. And yes, the world is far from perfect, but that is not the point. Today, a "minimum wage worker" is richer, healthier, and much more comfortable–with plenty of opportunity for success and growth around him/her–than kings and queens were just a few hundred years ago. Because not only do we launch "rockets of desire" when we see something that we want; we are just as strongly giving birth to new desires when we see something that we *don't* want. Precisely for this reason, we shouldn't shy away from experiencing the full range of emotions. For being unhappy, discontent, and dissatisfied is what brings forth those new desires on which the Universe (and our world) continues to thrive and expand.

That being said, I would not want you to misinterpret feeling any negative emotion as something bad; something that has to be avoided at all costs. The state of dissatisfaction only feels "bad" when we do not act on our own ideas and desires, while continuing to hold ourselves in a negative vibration, because we do not believe that we can have it. We do not believe that the solution is already found. We do not believe that all of the things we desire are already complete, and are already ours. And the reason why it feels "bad" is because unexpressed desire–a desire that is not actively being realised; a desire that is not given an open channel for its expression; a desire that hasn't been provided with a medium through which it can come into full manifestation–eventually begins to (figuratively speaking) rot our soul and demoralise our spirit. Still, one may get around this by way of becoming friends with one's emotions, and learning how to leverage–even the lowest of emotions–to one's own advantage. And all the effective ways by which one may do so have been discussed at length throughout the book.

What it all comes down to is the following: Self-mastery is not asking of you to become so happy that you begin to ignore things in your life, and delude yourself with positive self-talk. Meanwhile your career, social life, family life, and your relationships are in disarray. It only asks of you that you accept your current reality for what it actually is–without feeling bad about it, and sinking into a negative vibration–while simultaneously taking steps towards improving it. In this context, self-mastery is never about avoiding the scales just because you aren't willing to admit you have a weight problem. It is about acknowledging that there is a problem, and still being happy, while taking the appropriate steps towards fixing the issue at hand. For example, if one day, you were to discover that your computer has been infected by a vicious virus, you wouldn't want to close your eyes and ignore the problem, in order to preserve your positive emotional state and not do anything about it. Because the situation at hand may not feel particularly good, and getting involved in it might throw you off your high-vibrational horse. The sweet spot of self-mastery is when you can acknowledge that there is a virus, yet stay emotionally unaffected while taking care of it. For you are aware that if you allow yourself to get affected negatively by a particular event, circumstance, or condition, no intelligent action, or solution can come about as a result. In effect, avoiding problems is never the correct answer just because facing the reality of a certain situation may feel unpleasant. You have to become so secure within yourself that you're not afraid to face certain realities (that might be unpleasant and damaging to the ego), and have your state be challenged.

To assist you with this–no matter where you are in life; no matter what you've done wrong; regardless of your shortcomings and insecurities–your new mantra in life is the following: "My life is *already* awesome, *I am* already awesome, and I am enjoying my journey to becoming even *more* awesome!" This is the kind of attitude that will allow you to hold yourself in the highest vibration possible. And it will help you to continue to enjoy your journey regardless of what might be happening in it. This kind of attitude–mixture of self-acceptance and self-improvement–might seem paradoxical. But the paradox can be resolved by realising that accepting yourself doesn't mean to be satisfied with yourself, and forgetting about self-improvement. While simultaneously realising that to improve yourself doesn't mean to hate, or not accept yourself. Coming into this understanding will mean to develop the efficacy to be honest with yourself and others in terms of your progress–in relationship to all that you want to be, do, and have–without ever coming out of your alignment for the fact that you aren't where you wish to be *yet*.

"Everything that everyone wants–be it a material object, financial security, a relationship, condition, or event–they want it because they believe that that is where happiness is. But happiness can be right here and right now if you are in the right vibration." – Abraham Hicks

Epilogue

Even though we are at the end of our literary journey, for yourself it is only the beginning. Reading this book and forgetting about it, without continuing your self-development–by implementing at least some of the ideas you have learnt–is not going to produce the transformation you seek. In that, it simply isn't enough to know how powerful you really are, and be fond of that idea. You also must embody that awareness, if you are to enjoy the quality of life that the path to self-mastery promises to deliver. From the very beginning of the book my goal was to inform you; to inspire you; to motivate you; to raise your awareness; and to ultimately lead you to a realisation of just how powerful you *really* are. But in case I had failed in assisting you with having your own *"Aha!"* moment, and no vibrational/mental/emotional change had taken place, then I want you to consider the following. Every idea presented in this book is positive, constructive, and practical, and will definitely help you to improve the quality of your life. I suggest that before you reject any one of those ideas (maybe because–at present–it seems too far-fetched, or it doesn't make sense), ask yourself if you'd like that idea to be true. And if the answer is yes, then give yourself a chance to see it as true, and begin to look for further evidence of how it could be true. The fact is, if you continue to cling on to your limited perspectives, and continue to disregard new information just because it does not resonate with your current conditioning, I can guarantee you that even if you'd live to be a hundred, you would not live your life for a full, long, and happy hundred years, as one might presume. (For the *duration* of a life does not equal the *quality* of that life.) Instead, you would've only lived one year of your life, repeated a hundred times.

You did not come into this physical life experience to passively observe what's already in place–to be a spectator–and use other people's creations as the basis for what is possible. You did not come here to observe reality; you came here to create reality. And in case you are still unsure as to how exactly you create your own reality, here is a brief recap: Source-Energy, Infinite Intelligence, or Spirit is consciousness which thinks. And you, as a human being also have the ability to think (while no other living creature on the planet is capable of originating new thoughts, or ideas). This one fact alone should prove to you that whatever created you, your Universe, and everything else in it, chose–for whatever reason–to bestow upon you the exact same creative tools which you can utilise to your heart's content.

Bob Proctor explained that human beings live on three planes of understanding: we are spiritual beings; we live in physical bodies; and we have an intellect. Through the use of our intellect we get to direct this spiritual power (power of thought)–which is continuously flowing to and through our consciousness–and shape it into any idea we choose. Then, through physical action we get to bring that idea out of our consciousness and into its full, physical, manifested form. I want you to think of it in the following way: As this power flows into our consciousness we have the creative ability (through the use of imagination, which is one of our intellectual abilities) to begin formulating images/ideas–be they positive or negative–in our mind. Then through the use of our reasoning factor (which is another one of our intellectual abilities), we get to choose which image/idea we would like to take further. And the way we do that is by getting emotionally involved with that image/idea. And as we become emotionally involved with that image/idea, we immediately shift our physical body into a particular vibration that becomes conducive to attracting everything necessary for the realisation of that image/idea.

Now, the problem that most people have with respect to bringing their ideas into tangible, physical reality–and I am guilty of this myself–is that we don't seem to go after the things we want long enough. For, being the physically-oriented beings that we are, we are in the habit of arresting the powers that are working on our behalf by allowing various external factors: our present results; other people; conditions; circumstances; and events to knock us off track. In effect, our problem is that when we form a certain image in our mind of a better result, we immediately begin to look for evidence of that result on the outside. But since we never get to see any immediate change (for the creative process takes time), we get discouraged and we sink into a negative line of thinking. Which inevitably impedes any progress we might have already made. When it comes to our ability to manifest the things we desire, we behave the same way as if we were to plant a seed, and five minutes later dig it back out (assuming that the seed is broken, or that we are doing something wrong), because after this entire time (the whole five minutes) the tree was still nowhere to be seen. That is, we are forever attempting–to no avail– to reap what we sow in the same season we sow it. (Revisit chapter 4 on the Law of Gender.) In other words, because of our ignorance, we do not understand that all of the things we want in life are coming to us on time. And that they will arrive only when they–and more importantly, we–are ready.

The solution to this bad habit of ours comes in the form of developing our "will" (another one of our intellectual abilities). Willpower is what gives us the ability to concentrate and when we concentrate on an idea we are giving that idea more energy, which results in the full manifestation of that idea taking place much sooner. Bob Proctor knew so much about how the mind works in a human personality, that he never failed to amaze me with all the knowledge he had running through his head regarding the subject. Regrettably, Bob Proctor is no longer with us, though his legacy, and his life's work still lives on, and is being continued by a team of very competent individuals who take pride in his teachings at www.proctorgallagherinstitute.com. In reference to the importance of developing our will, Bob Proctor had told us the following: "*'Reason' gives us freedom to choose thoughts and 'will' gives us the ability to lock into an idea and control our vibration. Through the use of our will we are able to stay in a vibration–which we must be in–in order to attract whatever it is that we want to attract–that, which in fact is already here.*" To further clarify, he stated: "*When we choose certain thoughts our brain cells are affected. They begin to vibrate and send off electric waves. When we are <u>concentrating</u> on those thoughts we increase the amplitude of vibration of those cells, and the electric waves become much more potent.*" In effect, what Bob was referring to here is the fact that we can only ever get back what we are sending off–no more, and no less. For every action, there is an equal reaction in the opposite direction. Which means that the more we put into something, the more we will get out of it. And because our focus is usually all over the place explains why most of us hardly ever get the chance to experience the results we seek. For, every time we decide to go after something that we want, but fail (let's say that it doesn't go the way we expected it to), we immediately shift our focus away from where we are going, onto the difficulties and challenges that are now obscuring the path. But, if we wish to manifest anything of substance in our lives, we have to learn to direct all of our creative energy strictly towards that which we want through the proper use of our will (which acts like a laser). And, in the vernacular, be ready to cut through any bullshit which may come between us and our goal.

"I see only the objective, the obstacle must give way." – Napoleon Hill

As an experiment, when you get the opportunity, get a hold of a magnifying glass and place it between the rays of the sun and an inanimate object. Hold that position long enough and you will be able to set the object on fire. How? Because the rays of the sun become much more potent when they are being directed towards a given point. But, if you take the magnifying glass out of the equation, there will be no chance of you starting a fire. For when the energy of the sun is dispersed–when it is not being marshalled towards a specific point–it decreases in its rate of vibration, and by extension–potency. To understand the significance of this experiment I want you to relate it back to your own situation, where the sun is the creative energy that flows through you; the magnifying glass is your intellectual faculty–the will; and the object that you wish to set on fire is your desired goal. In other words, to get what it is you want in life, rather than working with this creative power randomly and haphazardly, what you have to do is begin to hone this power, and lock into your idea regardless of what the evidence in your outside world might suggest. In her book: "The Law of Attraction: The Basics of the Teachings of Abraham" Abraham Hicks talked about this also, she explained: *"When you consider many subjects at the same time, you generally do not move forward strongly toward any one of them, for your focus and power is diffused. Whereas if you are focusing upon that which is most important in any point in time, you move forward more powerfully toward it."* What Abraham was alluding to there is that rather than misusing our creative power by having it shoot all over the place–never focusing it in any one particular direction (or worse, directing it upon something negative)–our job as deliberate creators of our own reality is to choose something that we truly want; feel what it would be like to have it; and then hold ourselves in that vibration while completely ignoring all of the contrary appearances, outside ideas, and opinions that suggest we can't have it.

If, at the present time all of this sounds too far-fetched, or challenging to comprehend, please do not be discouraged. For it's understandable that decades of conditioning cannot be rewritten by reading a single book. However, at the very least, what I'd like you to take away from this entire book is the awareness of the fact that you are a vibrational being, who lives in a vibrational Universe. This is a good place to start. Next, I'd like you to accept the fact that you are an eternal being who inhabits a biological instrument (the physical body), and who utilises this instrument as a perfect channel for creative expression. In effect, you are not your physical body, emotions, name, sexuality, or mind. You are a creative consciousness whose decision it was to come forth into this physical, time-space reality in order to experience–firsthand–the "vividness" and the beauty of its own, and other people's creations. The reason why you don't remember any of this is because as soon as any of us are born, we begin to get programmed (conditioned) by the world around us to pay attention purely to the physical. And what winds up happening is we begin to feel isolated from those higher/spiritual dimensions, to such an extent that we no longer feel connected to the immense power, creativity and abundance of Source. This puts us at a huge disadvantage for we start to believe that what we see, hear, smell, taste, and touch is the only reality (which has any real significance). But that is only an illusion. The truth is, the physical reality in which we live–and navigate through–is no more solid than our thoughts. The fact that the physical world is moving at the speed of light, it gives off the illusion of being solid. And those who are unfortunate enough to find themselves consumed by these illusions tend to forget that Source is only ever interested in expansion, and fuller expression. That Source always stands for growth; never dissolution. Most people are not aware that when things get bad, and out of hand, is not because life is supposed to be hard, or because God is trying to punish them. But because they're making it difficult on themselves by not exercising control of their own mind. Those kind of beliefs are expressions of ignorance. For God's will is always for the increase of life; never for contraction, or diminishment of life. The only things which are ever lined up for you and everybody else (unless you put up resistance to it), are better things, and better ways. Life was never meant to be this enormous struggle. Who sold you on that idea?!

We have been conditioned to believe all sorts of nonsense which is designed to keep us dumbed down, compliant, docile, and afraid. And now it's at a point where everyone is becoming afraid of everything, even their own thoughts and opinions. Nowadays it doesn't matter what you say anymore: you are either a racist, a sexist, or whatever else "ist." And that's exactly how those in various positions of power program the population to silence itself. Just look at all the social justice movements; racial justice movements; feminism, and toxic masculinity; gender politics; identity politics; BLM, LGBTQ+; PC culture; cancel culture, and all the rest of it. None of these things promote love, justice, and unity. Instead, their virtue signalling, and displays of moral superiority and "wokeness," do nothing but divide, segregate, and fuel hate. All that they are doing is expressing ignorance. However, a person of higher awareness understands full well that we are all essentially the same; that we are all made from the same cloth; and that our surface layer differences need to be celebrated, rather than hated and pushed against. All this does is create weak men and women who get offended by just about anything. Rather than promoting empowerment, confidence, being secure with oneself, and having the ability to laugh at oneself (to not take oneself, or one's life too seriously), they instead encourage and promote victimhood as though it was some kind of virtue, which everybody should aspire to. Effectively turning people into little weaklings who feel powerless, and who need protection from all of the conflicting views, beliefs, and opinions that are always out to get them in this big, bad, and scary world of ours.

"Our world is not divided by race, colour, gender, or religion. Our world is divided into wise people and fools. And fools divide themselves by race, colour, or religion."
– Mohamad Safa

I want you to think about what's happening in the world today (particularly in the collective West), and ask yourself: "Is this the kind of world I want my kids to live in?" In other words, is this the kind of future you had envisioned for yourself, where you can't say, or do anything anymore–even in the name of harmless fun–without someone, somewhere becoming offended and shutting you down by taking away your rights? Is this what you were expecting from the educational system, where putting your child through school now comes at a risk of your child "discovering" that he/she was actually born in a wrong body? Because public schools (kindergartens in particular) are now being bombarded with drag queens "performing" for little kids; reading stories that are themed around going through an "identity crisis," and how it is okay to be different; conducting presentations about genitals; teaching them how to "twerk," and only God knows what else. And now, we are at a point where public schools specifically recruit "woke" teachers, who come in and proceed to tell their students that they are neither he nor she, which confuses the hell out of those kids. Then those kids will ask their teacher: "So what am I?" and rather than keeping those kids (who are highly impressionable) out of this madness, they tell them: "Well, whatever you decide to be. Become a cat for all I care. It is literally up to you." **Little** kids (particularly in preschool) should be playing amongst themselves, and learning how to read and write; not questioning their biology (a subject which they do not yet even fully understand), or getting indoctrinated with "new speak"–pronouns and terms–and political agendas.

None of this is progressive, as they would have you. It is absolutely insane. Kids do not even have the mental capacity to comprehend such things. It's completely and utterly irresponsible for us to allow our public schools to do this. Of course, the problem is, if you (as a loving parent) try to intervene and educate your child about their sexuality at home, you have the possibility of social services knocking on your door and taking your kids away from you. Because clearly you are a closed-minded, abusive, and controlling bigot. Seriously, is this what it all comes down to? Tiptoeing through our day-today experience without looking people in the eyes anymore, because we are utterly ashamed to be what we are, and feel sorry for the fact that we have to take up space, have our own opinions, and breathe air? Do we really want to live in such a world where 2+2=5? And if we dare to stick our neck out and assert that actually 2+2=4 we instantly have the police along with the "pitchfork-wielding mob" showing up at our doorstep to go ahead and lock us up in a maximum-security prison, until we're ready to agree and wholeheartedly accept that 2+2 actually does equal 5? Well, I say to hell with that!

A drastic shift in consciousness is what our world needs now more than ever before. For the "leaders" of our world are completely deranged, and are leading all of us in the wrong direction (and at an alarmingly faster pace too as each year goes by). However, the daily practice of self-mastery, along with the philosophy of self-empowerment offer us powerful tools which can easily dissolve those boundaries, limitations, low-vibrational energies, deceptions, divisions, and beyond! Our planet is in dire need of a miracle, before we forget what it means to be free and joyful souls, and unsuspectingly accept this new reality–where isolation, non-creativity, confusion, control, and dependency reign supreme–by our own consent, and acquiescence to it. You, as an individual are the answer (the miracle) to all the changes that the world desperately needs. You don't have to push against anything or resent those who are leading us astray, since one who is connected to Source is more powerful than millions who are not. Your only duty is to keep yourself in a high vibration and lead by example. And there is no better way to do this than to strive to make the world a better place, but not because you hate it; rather, because you know that change is inevitable, and so the change might as well be positive. To not take your life too seriously–making things into a big deal–yet be willing to acknowledge all of the things that are going wrong, and be ready to correct them, without becoming emotionally affected by them. And, to ultimately do your part in assisting other people on their noble mission to create a better world, without resisting the process along the way, by a way of not accepting, or disliking the current state of it.

Lastly, people who live happy, successful lives take their progress seriously. They are aware that people who they associate with must be winners, big thinkers, and go-getters, if they are to succeed at anything. If you look at successful people–no matter how proficient they are at what they do, or how knowledgeable and intelligent they may already be–you'll find that they always have mentors and coaches in their life without whom they wouldn't be where they are today. In order to take your life to the next level you have to understand that the people you surround yourself with are more important to your success and happiness than the talents and abilities you've inherited at birth. In other words, your environment is more important to your success in life than all your talents and abilities combined. Fortunately, it is not necessary to move into a better neighbourhood and join a mastermind group of highly resourceful and efficient individuals (though it is preferred). All that you really need in order to succeed in life is one person who believes in you. Who had already gone through what you are about to go after. Who can put you on the right track, and show you the ropes along the way. And who can take you by the hand and gracefully move you from where you are to where you want to be. That person is a mentor. There are hundreds of professional mentors and coaches out there who have been through whatever it is you're going through right now, and who had achieved whatever it is you're wanting to achieve. Thus, it would be foolish of you not to set aside some time to search for the right mentor who can become your personal guide, and potentially a lifelong friend. One who will not *allow* you to fail. One who will keep you accountable throughout the entire process. And one who will make sure that you are building the right habits, forming proper perspectives, and taking the right actions.

In conclusion: I truly hope that I've inspired you to want to know more, and continue your study. If you have any questions, please do not hesitate to reach out to me at selfmastery_coaching@outlook.com and I'll be more than happy to answer any of your questions, and help to clarify anything you are still uncertain about. Other than that, do not make the mistake of closing this book and sinking back into your usual routine, without trying to improve at least some area of your life. You now know too much. There is no longer an excuse for you to continue to sell yourself short. You now know that you are a lot more resourceful than you previously had thought. You now know that you are more than capable of living the life of your dreams. You now know that you have infinite potential; do not let it go to waste. Do not listen to anyone who tells you how you cannot be, do, or have something, just because they themselves don't believe it to be possible. You now know that you can, and that you will, because you are Godlike! You truly can be, do, and have whatever your heart desires. But don't take my word for it; prove it to yourself. Get out there and put your creative abilities to the test. And if you adhere to the principles laid out in this book, you will most certainly build the life that you've always dreamed of. And if *you* do not yet believe in you, just know that *I* fully believe in you, and I *know* you will do well.

Acknowledgements

It is a matter of course that this book would have been non-existent if it were not for the assistance of a few incredibly wise individuals. My deepest gratitude, appreciation, and thanks therefore goes out to the following wonderful humans who were (and still are) pivotal to my self-development throughout my journey to self-mastery and self-empowerment:

Esther Hicks, for contributing enormously to my personal development and self-discovery, particularly in gaining clarity and a better understanding of my true, human nature, as well as my relationship with Source. The work that you do, and the value that you bring to humanity is absolutely priceless. I will always be grateful for the fact that someone like you lives among us, who brings with her an opportunity for all of us to have direct conversations with Abraham. I can only express immense appreciation and gratitude when your name is mentioned. Thank you for your courage and readiness to share the teachings of Abraham with us, and to remind us of what we had always known to be true about ourself, but unfortunately have forgotten. Thank you for your never-ending love, and passion to uplift the world; for your amazing energy and spirit; for your sense of humour, and reassuring words. You truly are a beautiful soul. If it were not for you, I would still be at a complete loss for answers as to why we humans do what we do and feel what we feel. And for that, I will be forever grateful!

Bob Proctor, for teaching me all there is to know about the workings of the mind, and beyond. In all of the years that I've spent studying faithfully–trying to understand exactly what was causing me to get the results which I was getting in my life–only after a few hours of studying your material, everything immediately fell into place! Words truly cannot express how valuable your teachings have been in my personal life–in all areas of my life. With your guidance, my learning curve was cut by at least a thousand years (and probably even more) in a span of only a few years. For your knowledge base and style of teaching seems to cut right through the fluff, and get straight to the point. Your resolute mission to educate the world, your passion for–and dedication to–your cause, along with your exuberance and firm commitment to helping others get better results in their life is genuinely awe-inspiring. To feel, therefore, anything less than enormous respect, immense gratitude, and appreciation towards you as an individual, and for everything that you have built in your lifetime would truly be a crime. Which, anyone who knows you well enough could never possibly commit. You, my dear friend, will be eternally treasured and loved, and you will be greatly missed!

Eckhart Tolle, for introducing me to the invaluable principles of Eastern Philosophy and helping me recognise how they are still–and always will be–relevant in our day-to-day lives. Through your teachings, and practices (particularly meditation) I've cleansed my mind of so much junk–which I didn't even know was there–it's unbelievable. Your teachings have been particularly powerful in contributing to my spiritual growth and for that I am tremendously grateful! Your ability to explain something as deep and as complex as "presence" in a way that even a four-year-old could understand never ceases to amaze me. You truly are a beautiful human being and an exceptional spirit. Your work is extremely valuable, and is now needed more than ever. Millions of people will attest to that. Your constant passion for the cause, your sense of humour, your lightheartedness, your poise, and your ability to stay present is truly inspiring: something that we should all be striving towards. Because of your ideas and simple (yet powerful) ways of going about raising people's consciousness, I have no doubt that people will continually gravitate towards your teachings. Which makes me fairly confident in the fact that it's only a matter of time until we *do* create a "New Earth," and it's all thanks to you. You are deeply appreciated!

Owen Cook, for helping me understand various intricacies of social and emotional intelligence; social dynamics; personal relationships; self-mastery; self-reliance; self-empowerment, and beyond! Through your guidance I was able to transcend a ton of social conditioning; let go of my insecurities and at long last become comfortable in my own skin. Throughout the whole decade of seriously studying social dynamics you never failed to answer any of the questions I wanted to know the answers to. I am still–to this day–baffled by (in a positive way), and amazed at the way your mind works. You are truly a genius when it comes to understanding deep and complex subjects such as human behaviour, female brain, or social dynamics and be able to relay your findings and ideas in a way that even a person of subpar intelligence would be able to grasp with relative ease. I am extremely grateful for the work that you do, and your commitment to it is truly admirable. Thanks to your teachings I now know exactly what it means to be an effective communicator, an influencer, a leader, and a self-empowered, self-reliant individual. You truly are an exceptional human being, and I do not know where I would be today without your wisdom and guidance. For you have helped me enormously in building up my character on the right/proper foundation, and straightening out my limited, conditioned mind. And for that, I will always be grateful!

A massive thank-you to Vishal Morjaria, along the entire "WOW Book Camp" team, you are truly amazing! Thank you so much for believing in me and my book. A huge thank-you to my "Book Angel" Pauline for always being there for me, and tolerating my "perfectionist" ways. If it wasn't for you, this book would have always remained in my head merely as an idea–a possibility–nothing more. Thank you so much for all your great effort, help, and support in making this book a reality. Vishal, your work is highly appreciated, and I'm truly grateful for the work that you do. With your help, ordinary people like myself can now get the support they need to get their ideas out of their head and onto paper, for the rest of the world to enjoy. I feel blessed to be working with you, you are a star! Thank you so much!

A big thank-you to my mother and grandmother for always being there for me, for always believing in me, encouraging me, and only wanting what is best for me. Thank you for your unconditional love, and constant support. Both of you are a definition of an angel; you are truly beautiful souls. Thanks to you, I absolutely love the life that I have lived. While under your supervision, never for a moment did I think I overstayed my welcome. And I know that I've been a difficult child sometimes, for whom a dash of disdain would have been warranted, and absolutely deserved. But I am extremely thankful to you for never taking your love away, even when I was a complete pain in the ass. I will forever be grateful, and I will always love you no matter what happens!

A huge thanks to all of my friends, both Russian and British for making my life experience a hell of a lot of fun! There was never a dull moment with any of you. I do not remember a single day when we got together and didn't laugh. Through my interactions with you I have become conditioned to never take myself too seriously; to be looser and more carefree, and for that I am extremely grateful! My life would not have been the same without you. And because of you, the type of life which I have lived, I wouldn't trade it for another in a million years. All the things we've been though, and all the experiences we've had are priceless, and will forever stay with me as valued memories. I am extremely grateful for the opportunity to grow up alongside you, I wouldn't want it any other way. You are deeply appreciated!

Above all, I thank my current partner (Ivana) who had been patient with me throughout the whole four years of burying my head in a laptop or computer, relentlessly writing, and working on this project while virtually ignoring the relationship. Thank you very much for your never-ending love, support, and enthusiasm for what I am trying to create, even when it sometimes means that I have to sacrifice other–just as important–aspects of my life. You truly are one of the nicest, most reliable, honest and trust-worthy individuals that I've ever met, and I'm extremely grateful to have you by my side. Thank you for being the beautiful spirit that you are, and thank you for bringing a fresh and new perspective on things into my life. Thank you for always believing in my ability to produce, and always being there for me when I needed you the most. You are eternally loved and appreciated!

A special thank-you to all the following individuals who had contributed in varying degrees to my personal development, whether directly or indirectly: Stuart Wilde, Napoleon Hill, William James, Earl Nightingale, Ralph Smart, Noam Chomsky, Seth Godin, Anthony Robbins, Joseph Campbell, Joseph Murphy, James Allen, Ralph Waldo Emerson, Neville Goddard, Wallace D. Wattles, Dr. Wayne Dyer, Alan Watts, Robert Greene, Jordan Peterson, Jack Canfield, Daniel Goleman, David Schwartz, David Deida, David Icke, Jim Rohn, Rollo Tomassi, Tim Ferriss, Mark Hyman, Steven Pressfield, Andrew Tate, Maxwell Maltz, Genevieve Behrend, Martin Seligman, Shawn Achor, Susan Jeffers, Mark Manson, Brad Blanton, Maximilian Tornow, Julien Blanc, Jeff Allen, and the entire Real Social Dynamics team. Thank you so much, you are all greatly appreciated!

It has been over a decade of constant studying, meeting, coming across, being introduced to, and stumbling upon different individuals who had contributed in one way or another to my self-development, and who had helped to shape me into the person that I am today. That being said, since memory is not the strongest faculty of mine, if I forgot to mention you and give credit where it's due, then please forgive me and make it a point to reach out to me directly at nikita_deangelo@hotmail.com pointing this out. And I will make sure to immediately correct the issue.

Printed in Great Britain
by Amazon

41449591R00199